Muriel James

Cambridge International
AS & A Level Mathematics:

Pure Mathematics 1

Worked Solutions Manual

T0384564

CAMBRIDGE
UNIVERSITY PRESS

Shaftesbury Road, Cambridge CB2 8EA, United Kingdom

One Liberty Plaza, 20th Floor, New York, NY 10006, USA

477 Williamstown Road, Port Melbourne, VIC 3207, Australia

314–321, 3rd Floor, Plot 3, Splendor Forum, Jasola District Centre, New Delhi – 110025, India

103 Penang Road, #05–06/07, Visioncrest Commercial, Singapore 238467

Cambridge University Press & Assessment is a department of the University of Cambridge.

We share the University's mission to contribute to society through the pursuit of education, learning and research at the highest international levels of excellence.

www.cambridge.org
Information on this title: www.cambridge.org/9781108613057

First published 2020

20 19 18 17 16 15 14 13 12 11 10 9 8 7

Printed in Great Britain by Ashford Colour Press Ltd.

A catalogue record for this publication is available from the British Library

ISBN 9781108613057 Paperback with Digital Access

Cambridge University Press & Assessment has no responsibility for the persistence or accuracy of URLs for external or third-party internet websites referred to in this publication, and does not guarantee that any content on such websites is, or will remain, accurate or appropriate. Information regarding prices, travel timetables, and other factual information given in this work is correct at the time of first printing but Cambridge University Press & Assessment does not guarantee the accuracy of such information thereafter.

All worked solutions within this resource have been written by the author. In examinations, the way marks are awarded may be different.

Contents

The items in orange are available on the Elevate edition that accompanies this book.

How to use this book

This book contains worked solutions to the questions in the *Cambridge International AS & A Level Mathematics: Pure Mathematics 1 Coursebook*. Both the book and accompanying Elevate edition include the solutions to the chapter exercises. You will find the solutions to the end-of-chapter review exercises, cross-topic review exercises and practice exam-style paper on the Elevate edition only.

Most of the chapter exercises include questions to help develop your fluency in solving a particular type of problem by practising the procedure several times. Rather than providing worked solutions for all of these questions, we have included a worked solution for one or two of the fluency questions, which can then be used for guidance about the steps required for the related questions. The aim of this is to encourage you to develop as a confident, independent thinker.

Each solution shows you step-by-step how to solve the question. You will be aware that often questions can be solved by multiple different methods. In this book, we provide a single method for each solution. Do not be disheartened if the working in a solution does not match your own working; you may not be wrong but simply using a different method. It is good practice to challenge yourself to think about the methods you are using and whether there may be alternative methods.

All worked solutions in this resource have been written by the author. In examinations, the way marks are awarded may be different.

Additional guidance is included in **Commentary** boxes throughout the book. These boxes often clarify common misconceptions or areas of difficulty.

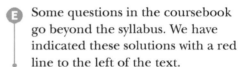 Some questions in the coursebook go beyond the syllabus. We have indicated these solutions with a red line to the left of the text.

1 a $x^2 + 3x - 10 = 0$

$(x + 5)(x - 2) = 0$

$x + 5 = 0$ or $x - 2 = 0$

$x = -5$ or $x = 2$

f $x(10x - 13) = 3$

$10x^2 - 13x = 3$

$10x^2 - 13x - 3 = 0$

$(5x + 1)(2x - 3) = 0$

$5x + 1 = 0$ or $2x - 3 = 0$

$x = -\dfrac{1}{5}$ or $x = \dfrac{3}{2}$

2 c $\dfrac{5x + 1}{4} - \dfrac{2x - 1}{2} = x^2$

Multiply both sides by 4

$5x + 1 - 2(2x - 1) = 4x^2$

Multiplying by 8 will give the same answer.

$4x^2 - x - 3 = 0$

$(4x + 3)(x - 1) = 0$

$4x + 3 = 0$ or $x - 1 = 0$

$x = -\dfrac{3}{4}$ or $x = 1$

f $\dfrac{3}{x + 2} + \dfrac{1}{x - 1} = \dfrac{1}{(x + 1)(x + 2)}$

Multiply both sides by $(x + 1)(x + 2)(x - 1)$

$3(x + 1)(x - 1) + (x + 2)(x + 1) = 1(x - 1)$

$3(x^2 - 1) + x^2 + 3x + 2 = x - 1$

$3x^2 - 3 + x^2 + 3x + 2 = x - 1$

$4x^2 + 2x = 0$

Do **NOT** be tempted to divide both sides by x next.
This will lose the solution $x = 0$.

Factorise

$2x(2x + 1) = 0$

$2x = 0$ or $2x + 1 = 0$

$x = 0$ or $x = -\dfrac{1}{2}$

3 a $\dfrac{3x^2 + x - 10}{x^2 - 7x + 6} = 0$

Multiply both sides by $x^2 - 7x + 6$

$3x^2 + x - 10 = 0$

$(3x - 5)(x + 2) = 0$

$3x - 5 = 0$ or $x + 2 = 0$

$x = \dfrac{5}{3}$ or $x = -2$

Always substitute your answers back into the original equations to make sure that no denominators evaluate to 0.

d $\dfrac{x^2 - 2x - 8}{x^2 + 7x + 10} = 0$

Multiply both sides by $x^2 + 7x + 10$

$x^2 - 2x - 8 = 0$

$(x - 4)(x + 2) = 0$

$(x - 4) = 0$ or $(x + 2) = 0$

$x = 4$ or $x = -2$

If $x = -2$, the denominator becomes

$(-2)^2 + 7(-2) + 10$

Which evaluates to zero so $x = -2$ is **NOT** a solution

The only solution is $x = 4$.

f $\dfrac{2x^2 + 9x - 5}{x^4 + 1} = 0$

Multiply both sides by $x^4 + 1$

$2x^2 + 9x - 5 = 0$

$(2x - 1)(x + 5) = 0$

$2x - 1 = 0$ or $x + 5 = 0$

$x = \dfrac{1}{2}$ or $x = -5$

Check: neither of these solutions, when substituted back into the fraction evaluate to zero so both are valid.

4 c $2^{(x^2-4x+6)} = 8$

Rewrite 8 as 2^3

$2^{(x^2-4x+6)} = 2^3$

Equating powers of 2 gives:

$x^2 - 4x + 6 = 3$
$x^2 - 4x + 3 = 0$
$(x-1)(x-3) = 0$
$x - 1 = 0$ or $x - 3 = 0$
$x = 1$ or $x = 3$

f $(x^2 - 7x + 11)^8 = 1$

Find the eighth root of both sides of the equation.

$[(x^2 - 7x + 11)^8]^{\frac{1}{8}} = [1]^{\frac{1}{8}}$
$x^2 - 7x + 11 = \pm 1$

> Don't forget the two roots here.

$x^2 - 7x + 10 = 0$ or $x^2 - 7x + 12 = 0$
$(x-2)(x-5) = 0$ or $(x-3)(x-4) = 0$
$x = 2$ or $x = 3$ or $x = 4$ or $x = 5$

5 a Using Pythagoras:

$(2x)^2 + (2x+1)^2 = 29^2$
$4x^2 + 4x^2 + 4x + 1 = 841$
$8x^2 + 4x - 840 = 0$

Divide both sides by the common factor of 4:

$2x^2 + x - 210 = 0$ Shown

b $(x-10)(2x+21) = 0$
$x - 10 = 0$ or $2x + 21 = 0$
$x = 10$ or $x = -10.5$

The sides of the triangle are 20 cm, 21 cm and 29 cm.

Check that your answers satisfy the original equation.

$(2(10))^2 + (2(10)+1)^2 = 29^2$
$400 + 441 = 841$
$841 = 841$

> Do not automatically reject negative values for x. In this example $x = -1$ but this gives positive lengths when substituted into the sides of the triangle.

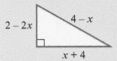

6 Area of a trapezium is $\frac{1}{2}(a+b)h$

$\frac{1}{2}[(x-1) + (x+3)]x = 35.75$

Multiply both sides by 4:

$2[(x-1) + (x+3)]x = 143$
$2[2x+2]x = 143$
$4x^2 + 4x = 143$
$4x^2 + 4x - 143 = 0$
$(2x-11)(2x+13) = 0$
$2x - 11 = 0$ or $2x + 13 = 0$
$x = 5.5$ or $x = -6.5$

Since x is the length of one of the sides of the trapezium, x must be positive.

$x = 5.5$

7 $(x^2 - 11x + 29)^{(6x^2+x-2)} = 1$

Case 1: for any number a we have $a^0 = 1$, so solve $6x^2 + x - 2 = 0$, for some solutions.

$6x^2 + x - 2 = 0$
$(2x-1)(3x+2) = 0$
$x = \frac{1}{2}$ or $x = -\frac{2}{3}$

Case 2: for any number b we have $1^b = 1$, so solve $x^2 - 11x + 29 = 1$ for more solutions.

$x^2 - 11x + 29 = 1$
$x^2 - 11x + 28 = 0$
$(x-4)(x-7) = 0$
$x - 4 = 0$ or $x - 7 = 0$
$x = 4$ or $x = 7$

Case 3: $(-1)^{2b} = 1$ **for any number** b**, so solve** $x^2 - 11x + 29 = -1$ **to see whether the numbers we get lead to** $6x^2 + x - 2$ **being an even number.**

$x^2 - 11x + 29 = -1$

$x^2 - 11x + 30 = 0$

$(x - 6)(x - 5) = 0$

$x - 6 = 0 \text{ or } x - 5 = 0$

$x = 6 \text{ or } x = 5$

Substituting $x = 6$ into $6x^2 + x - 2$

$6(6)^2 + 6 - 2 = 220$

This gives an even number, so $x = 6$ is a solution

Substituting $x = 5$ into $6x^2 + x - 2$

$6(5)^2 + 5 - 2 = 153$

This gives an odd number, so $x = 5$ is **not** a solution

Real number solutions are: $x = -\dfrac{2}{3}$, $\dfrac{1}{2}$, 4, 6 and 7.

1 a $x^2 - 6x = (x - 3)^2 - 3^2$

$= (x - 3)^2 - 9$

 g $x^2 + 7x + 1 = \left(x + \dfrac{7}{2}\right)^2 - \left(\dfrac{7}{2}\right)^2 + 1$

$= \left(x + \dfrac{7}{2}\right)^2 - \dfrac{45}{4}$

2 b $3x^2 - 12x - 1$

Take out a factor of 3 from the first two terms:

$3(x^2 - 4x) - 1$

Complete the square:

$3[(x - 2)^2 - 4] - 1$

$3(x - 2)^2 - 13$

3 c $4 - 3x - x^2$

$4 - (3x + x^2)$

$4 - \left[\left(\dfrac{3}{2} + x\right)^2 - \left(\dfrac{3}{2}\right)^2\right]$

$4 + \left(\dfrac{3}{2}\right)^2 - \left(\dfrac{3}{2} + x\right)^2$

$\dfrac{25}{4} - \left(x + \dfrac{3}{2}\right)^2$

4 b $3 - 12x - 2x^2$

$3 - 2(6x + x^2)$

$3 - 2[(3 + x)^2 - 3^2]$

$3 - 2(3 + x)^2 + 18$

$21 - 2(x + 3)^2$

5 a $9x^2 - 6x - 3$

Using an algebraic method:

$9x^2 - 6x - 3 = (ax + b)^2 + c$

$= a^2x^2 + 2abx + b^2 + c$

$9 = a^2...., \quad -6 = 2ab ...., \quad -3 = b^2 + c ....$

So $a = \pm 3$

If $a = 3$, $-6 = 6b$ so $b = -1$, then:

$-3 = (-1)^2 + c$ so $c = -4$

If $a = -3$, $-6 = -6b$ so $b = 1$

$-3 = 1^2 + c$ so $c = -4$

$9x^2 - 6x - 3 = (3x - 1)^2 - 4 = (-3x + 1)^2 - 4$

6 a $\quad x^2 + 8x - 9 = 0$

$(x + 4)^2 - 16 - 9 = 0$

$(x + 4)^2 = 25$

Square root both sides:

$x + 4 = \pm 5$

$x = -9, \text{ or } x = 1$

7 a $\quad x^2 + 4x - 7 = 0$

$(x + 2)^2 - 4 - 7 = 0$

$(x + 2)^2 = 11$

$x + 2 = \pm\sqrt{11}$

$x = -2 \pm \sqrt{11}$

e $2x^2 + 6x + 3 = 0$

$$2\left[\left(x + \frac{3}{2}\right)^2 - \frac{9}{4}\right] + 3 = 0$$

$$2\left(x + \frac{3}{2}\right)^2 - \frac{9}{2} + 3 = 0$$

$$2\left(x + \frac{3}{2}\right)^2 = \frac{3}{2}$$

$$\left(x + \frac{3}{2}\right)^2 = \frac{3}{4}$$

$$x + \frac{3}{2} = \pm\frac{\sqrt{3}}{2}$$

$$x = -\frac{3}{2} \pm \frac{\sqrt{3}}{2} \text{ or } x = \frac{-3 \pm \sqrt{3}}{2}$$

8 $\dfrac{5}{x+2} + \dfrac{3}{x-4} = 2$

Multiply all terms by $(x+2)(x-4)$:

$5(x-4) + 3(x+2) = 2(x+2)(x-4)$

$5x - 20 + 3x + 6 = 2x^2 - 4x - 16$

$2x^2 - 12x - 2 = 0$ dividing both sides by 2 gives:

$\qquad x^2 - 6x - 1 = 0$

$\qquad (x-3)^2 - 3^2 - 1 = 0$

$\qquad\qquad (x-3)^2 = 10$

$\qquad\qquad\quad x - 3 = \pm\sqrt{10}$

$\qquad\qquad\qquad x = 3 \pm \sqrt{10}$

9 Using Pythagoras:

$\qquad (2x+5)^2 + x^2 = 10^2$

$\qquad 5x^2 + 20x - 75 = 0$

$\qquad\quad x^2 + 4x - 15 = 0$

$\qquad (x+2)^2 - 2^2 - 15 = 0$

$\qquad\qquad\quad (x+2)^2 = 19$

$\qquad\qquad\qquad x + 2 = \pm\sqrt{19}$

$x = \sqrt{19} - 2$ or

$x = -\sqrt{19} - 2$ (reject as a negative value is not valid for the sides of a triangle.)

$x = \sqrt{19} - 2$

10 $(3x^2 + 5x - 7)^4 = 1$

Taking the 4th root of both sides gives:

$3x^2 + 5x - 7 = \pm 1$

Either: $3x^2 + 5x - 7 = 1$

$3x^2 + 5x - 8 = 0$

$$3\left[\left(x + \frac{5}{6}\right)^2 - \frac{25}{36}\right] - 8 = 0$$

$$3\left(x + \frac{5}{6}\right)^2 - \frac{25}{12} - 8 = 0$$

$$3\left(x + \frac{5}{6}\right)^2 = \frac{121}{12}$$

$$\left(x + \frac{5}{6}\right)^2 = \frac{121}{36}$$

$$x + \frac{5}{6} = \pm\sqrt{\left(\frac{121}{36}\right)}$$

$$x + \frac{5}{6} = \frac{11}{6} \text{ or } x + \frac{5}{6} = -\frac{11}{6}$$

$$x = 1 \text{ or } -\frac{8}{3}$$

Or: $3x^2 + 5x - 7 = -1$

$\qquad 3x^2 + 5x - 6 = 0$

$$3\left[\left(x + \frac{5}{6}\right)^2 - \frac{25}{36}\right] - 6 = 0$$

$$3\left(x + \frac{5}{6}\right)^2 - \frac{25}{12} - 6 = 0$$

$$3\left(x + \frac{5}{6}\right)^2 = \frac{97}{12}$$

$$\left(x + \frac{5}{6}\right)^2 = \frac{97}{36}$$

$$x + \frac{5}{6} = \pm\frac{\sqrt{97}}{6}$$

$$x = \frac{1}{6}\left(-5 - \sqrt{97}\right) \text{ or } \frac{1}{6}\left(\sqrt{97} - 5\right)$$

$$x = -\frac{8}{3}, 1, \frac{1}{6}\left(-5 - \sqrt{97}\right), \frac{1}{6}\left(\sqrt{97} - 5\right)$$

11 $y = \left(\sqrt{3}\right)x - \dfrac{49x^2}{9000}$

a The range is the maximum value of x. This is when $y = 0$.

$$\left(\sqrt{3}\right)x - \frac{49x^2}{9000} = 0 \quad\ldots\ldots\ldots [1]$$

$$9000\left(\sqrt{3}\right)x - 49x^2 = 0$$

$$49\left[\left(\frac{9000\sqrt{3}}{98} - x\right)^2 - \left(\frac{9000\sqrt{3}}{98}\right)^2\right] = 0$$

$$\left(\frac{9000\sqrt{3}}{98} - x\right)^2 - \left(\frac{9000\sqrt{3}}{98}\right)^2 = 0$$

$$\left(\frac{9000\sqrt{3}}{98} - x\right)^2 = \left(\frac{9000\sqrt{3}}{98}\right)^2$$

Square root both sides

$$\frac{9000\sqrt{3}}{98} - x = \pm\frac{9000\sqrt{3}}{98}$$

$$x = \frac{9000\sqrt{3}}{49} \text{ or } x = 0 \text{ reject}$$

$$x = \frac{9000\sqrt{3}}{49} \approx 318 \text{ m (3 significant figures)}$$

> Factorising is another possible method to solve Equation [1]
>
> $x\left(9000\sqrt{3} - 49x\right) = 0$
>
> Either $x = 0$, (*reject*) or $9000\sqrt{3} - 49x = 0$
>
> $x = \frac{9000\sqrt{3}}{49} \approx 318$ m (3 significant figures)

b The maximum height reached is the largest value of y.

This occurs when $x = \frac{9000\sqrt{3}}{98}$ since the highest point on the graph is mid-way in the flight. So,

$\frac{9000\sqrt{3}}{49}$ divided by 2 is $\frac{9000\sqrt{3}}{98}$

Substituting into $y = \left(\sqrt{3}\right)x - \frac{49x^2}{9000}$ gives:

$$y = \left(\sqrt{3}\right)\frac{9000\sqrt{3}}{98} - \frac{49}{9000}\left(\frac{9000\sqrt{3}}{98}\right)^2$$

$$y = \frac{27000}{98} - \frac{13500}{98}$$

$$y = 138 \text{ m to 3 significant figures.}$$

> There is another way to approach Question 11, which you will meet in Chapter 8.

EXERCISE 1C

1 a $x^2 - 10x - 3 = 0$.

Using $a = 1$, $b = -10$ and $c = -3$ in the quadratic formula gives:

$$x = \frac{-(-10) \pm \sqrt{(-10)^2 - 4 \times 1 \times (-3)}}{2 \times 1}$$

$$x = \frac{10 + \sqrt{112}}{2} \text{ or } x = \frac{10 - \sqrt{112}}{2}$$

$$x = 10.29 \text{ or } x = -0.29 \text{ (to 3 sf)}$$

2 $x(3x - 2) = 63$

$3x^2 - 2x - 63 = 0$

$$x = \frac{-(-2) \pm \sqrt{(-2)^2 - 4 \times 3 \times (-63)}}{2 \times 3}$$

$$x = \frac{2 + \sqrt{760}}{6} \text{ or } x = \frac{2 - \sqrt{760}}{6}$$

$x = 4.928$ or $x = -4.261$ (reject)

$x = 4.93$ to 3 significant figures.

3 $x(2x - 4) = (x + 1)(5 - x)$

$3x^2 - 8x - 5 = 0$

$$x = \frac{-(-8) \pm \sqrt{(-8)^2 - 4 \times 3 \times (-5)}}{2 \times 3}$$

$$x = \frac{8 + \sqrt{124}}{6} \text{ or } x = \frac{8 - \sqrt{124}}{6}$$

$x = 3.189$ or $x = -0.5226$ (reject)

$x = 3.19$ to 3 significant figures.

4 $\frac{5}{x - 3} + \frac{2}{x + 1} = 1$

Multiplying both sides by $(x - 3)(x + 1)$ gives:

$5(x + 1) + 2(x - 3) = 1(x - 3)(x + 1)$

$x^2 - 9x - 2 = 0$

$$x = \frac{-(-9) \pm \sqrt{(-9)^2 - 4 \times 1 \times (-2)}}{2 \times 1}$$

$$x = \frac{9 + \sqrt{89}}{2} \text{ or } x = \frac{9 - \sqrt{89}}{2}$$

$x = 9.22$ or $x = -0.217$ to 3 significant figures.

5 $ax^2 - bx + c = 0$

$$x = \frac{-(-b) \pm \sqrt{(-b)^2 - 4 \times a \times c}}{2 \times a}$$

$$x = \frac{b \pm \sqrt{b^2 - 4ac}}{2a} \text{ or } \frac{b}{2a} \pm \frac{\sqrt{(b^2 - 4ac)}}{2a}$$

Compare with $x = \frac{-b \pm \sqrt{b^2 - 4ac}}{2a}$ or

$$\frac{-b}{2a} \pm \frac{\sqrt{(b^2 - 4ac)}}{2a}$$

The solutions both increase by $\frac{b}{a}$

1 **b** $x + 4y = 6$ ....[1]

$x^2 + 2xy = 8$ ....[2]

> It is best to avoid fractions (if possible) when using substitution.

$x = 6 - 4y$

Substitute into [2] gives:

$(6 - 4y)^2 + 2(6 - 4y)y = 8$

$8y^2 - 36y + 28 = 0$

Divide by 4

$2y^2 - 9y + 7 = 0$

$(y - 1)(2y - 7) = 0$

$y = 1$ or $y = \frac{7}{2}$

Substitute into [1]

If $y = 1$ then $x = 2$

If $y = \frac{7}{2}$ then $x = -8$

> Always substitute back into the linear equation.

Solutions are $\left(-8, \frac{7}{2}\right)$ and $(2, 1)$

f $4x - 3y = 5$ ....[1]

$x^2 + 3xy = 10$ ....[2]

> Before you start, look for the least complicated method.

Method 1

Make x the subject of [1]

$$x = \frac{5 + 3y}{4}$$

Substitute into [2]

$$\left(\frac{5 + 3y}{4}\right)^2 + 3\left(\frac{5 + 3y}{4}\right)y = 10$$

$$\frac{(5 + 3y)^2}{16} + \frac{3y(5 + 3y)}{4} = 10$$

$$(5 + 3y)^2 + 12y(5 + 3y) = 160$$

$$45y^2 + 90y - 135 = 0$$

$$y^2 + 2y - 3 = 0$$

$$(y + 3)(y - 1) = 0$$

$y = -3$ or 1

Substitute back into [1]

$4x - 3(-3) = 5$ and $4x - 3(1) = 5$

$x = -1$ $x = 2$

Solutions are $(-1, -3)$, $(2, 1)$

The alternative method below is much easier:

Method 2

From [1], multiply $4x - 3y = 5$ by x and then add the new equation to [2]

$4x^2 - 3xy = 5x$

$x^2 + 3xy = 10$

Adding gives $5x^2 = 5x + 10$ or $x^2 - x - 2 = 0$

$(x - 2)(x + 1) = 0$

$x = 2$ or -1

Substituting back into the linear equation [1] gives

$4(2) - 3y = 5$ and $4(-1) - 3y = 5$

$y = 1$ $y = -3$

Solutions are $(-1, -3)$, $(2, 1)$

n $x + 2y = 5$ ....[1]

$x^2 + y^2 = 10$ ....[2]

> A common mistake is to rewrite [2] as $x + y = \sqrt{10}$.

From [1] $x = 5 - 2y$

Substitute for x in [2]

$(5 - 2y)^2 + y^2 = 10$

$5y^2 - 20y + 15 = 0$

$y^2 - 4y + 3 = 0$

$(y - 3)(y - 1) = 0$

$y = 3$ or 1

Substituting back into [1] gives:

$x + 2(3) = 5$ and $x + 2(1) = 5$

$x = -1$ and $x = 3$

Solutions are $(-1, 3)$, $(3, 1)$

2 a Let the numbers be x and y

$x + y = 26$ ....[1]

$xy = 153$ ....[2]

From [1] $x = 26 - y$

Substitute for x into [2]

$(26 - y)y = 153$

$y^2 - 26y + 153 = 0$

$(y - 9)(y - 17) = 0$

$y = 9$ or 17

Substituting into [1] gives:

$x = 17$ or 9

The two numbers are 9 and 17

b [1] remains the same and [2] becomes

$xy = 150$ ....[2]

[2] now becomes:

$(26 - y)y = 150$ which simplifies to:

$y^2 - 26y + 150 = 0$

Solving using the formula gives:

$$y = \frac{-(-26) \pm \sqrt{(-26)^2 - 4 \times 1 \times (150)}}{2 \times 1}$$

$y = 13 - \sqrt{19}$ and $y = 13 + \sqrt{19}$

Leading to the two numbers $13 - \sqrt{19}$ and $13 + \sqrt{19}$

3 Let the lengths of the sides of the rectangle be x and y.

$2x + 2y = 15.8$ ....[1]

$xy = 13.5$ ....[2]

From [1] $x = 7.9 - y$

Substitute for x in [2]

$(7.9 - y)y = 13.5$

$y^2 - 7.9y + 13.5 = 0$

$$y = \frac{-(-7.9) \pm \sqrt{(-7.9)^2 - 4 \times 1 \times (13.5)}}{2 \times 1}$$

$y = \frac{27}{5}$ or $\frac{5}{2}$

Substituting $y = \frac{27}{5}$ into [2] gives $x = \frac{5}{2}$

Substituting $y = \frac{5}{2}$ into [2] gives $x = \frac{27}{5}$

The lengths of the sides of the rectangle are $2\frac{1}{2}$ cm and $5\frac{2}{5}$ cm.

4 Let the sides of the squares be x cm and y cm.

Total perimeter is $4x + 4y = 50$ ....[1]

Total area is $x^2 + y^2 = 93.25$ ....[2]

From [1] $x = \frac{25 - 2y}{2}$

Substitute for x in [2]

$\left(\frac{25 - 2y}{2}\right)^2 + y^2 = 93.25$

$(25 - 2y)^2 + 4y^2 = 373$

$8y^2 - 100y + 252 = 0$

$2y^2 - 25y + 63 = 0$

$$y = \frac{-(-25) \pm \sqrt{(-25)^2 - 4 \times 2 \times (63)}}{2 \times 2}$$

$y = 9$ or $3\frac{1}{2}$

Substitute $y = 9$ into [1] gives $x = 3\frac{1}{2}$

Substituting $y = 3\frac{1}{2}$ into [1] gives $x = 9$

The squares are each of side length $3\frac{1}{2}$ cm and 9 cm

5 Let the two radii be x and y

$2\pi x + 2\pi y = 36\pi$ ....[1]

$\pi x^2 + \pi y^2 = 170\pi$ ....[2]

Simplifying each equation:

$x + y = 18$ ....[1]

$x^2 + y^2 = 170$ ....[2]

From [1] $x = 18 - y$

Substituting for x in [2]

$(18 - y)^2 + y^2 = 170$

$y^2 - 18y + 77 = 0$

$(y - 11)(y - 7) = 0$

$y = 11$ or 7

Substitute $y = 11$ into [1] gives $x = 7$

Substitute $y = 7$ into [1] gives $x = 11$

The radii are 7 cm and 11 cm.

6 $x + y = 20.5$ ....[1]

$5xy = 360$ ....[2]

From [1] $x = 20.5 - y$

Substitute for x into [2]

$5(20.5 - y)y = 360$

$5y^2 - 102.5y + 360 = 0$

$y = \dfrac{-(-102.5) \pm \sqrt{(-102.5)^2 - 4 \times 5 \times (360)}}{2 \times 5}$

$y = 16$ or $\dfrac{9}{2}$

Substituting $y = 16$ into [1] gives $x = 4\frac{1}{2}$

Substituting $y = 4\frac{1}{2}$ into [1] gives $x = 16$

$x = 4\frac{1}{2}$, $y = 16$ or $x = 16$, $y = 4\frac{1}{2}$

7 $h + r = 18$ ....[1]

$\frac{1}{2}(4\pi r^2) + \pi r^2 + 2\pi rh = 205\pi$ ....[2] which simplifies to:

$3r^2 + 2rh - 205 = 0$

From [1] $h = 18 - r$

Substitute for h in [2]

$3r^2 + 2r(18 - r) - 205 = 0$

$r^2 + 36r - 205 = 0$

$(r - 5)(r + 41) = 0$

$r = 5$ or $r = -41$ (reject)

Substituting $r = 5$ into [1] gives $h = 13$

Solution $r = 5$, $h = 13$

8 a $y = 2 - x$ ....[1]

$5x^2 - y^2 = 20$ ....[2]

Substitute for y in [2]

$5x^2 - (2 - x)^2 = 20$

$x^2 + x - 6 = 0$

$(x - 2)(x + 3) = 0$

$x = 2$ or $x = -3$

Substituting $x = 2$ into [1] gives $y = 0$

Substituting $x = -3$ into [1] gives $y = 5$

A is at $(2, 0)$ and B is at $(-3, 5)$ (or vice versa)

b Using Pythagoras $AB = \sqrt{(2 - -3)^2 + (0 - 5)^2}$

$AB = \sqrt{50}$

The length of AB is $5\sqrt{2}$

9 a $2x + 5y = 1$ ....[1]

$x^2 + 5xy - 4y^2 + 10 = 0$ ....[2]

From [1] $x = \dfrac{1 - 5y}{2}$

Substitute for x in [2]

$\left(\dfrac{1 - 5y}{2}\right)^2 + 5\left(\dfrac{1 - 5y}{2}\right)y - 4y^2 + 10 = 0$

$(1 - 5y)^2 + 10(1 - 5y)y - 16y^2 + 40 = 0$

$-41y^2 + 41 = 0$

$-41(y^2 - 1) = 0$

$-41(y - 1)(y + 1) = 0$

$y = 1$ or $y = -1$

Substituting $y = 1$ into [1] gives $x = -2$

Substituting $y = -1$ into [1] gives $x = 3$

A is at $(-2, 1)$ and B is at $(3, -1)$ or vice-versa.

b Midpoint of AB is at $\left[\left(\dfrac{-2+3}{2}\right), \left(\dfrac{1-1}{2}\right)\right]$ or $\left(\dfrac{1}{2}, 0\right)$

11 $7y - x = 25$ ....[1]

$x^2 + y^2 = 25$ ....[2]

From [1] $x = 7y - 25$

Substitute for x in [2]

$(7y - 25)^2 + y^2 = 25$

$y^2 - 7y + 12 = 0$

$(y - 3)(y - 4) = 0$

$y = 3$ or $y = 4$

Substituting $y = 3$ into [1] gives $x = -4$

Substituting $y = 4$ into [1] gives $x = 3$

A is at $(-4, 3)$ and B is at $(3, 4)$ or vice-versa.

Midpoint of AB is at $\left[\left(\dfrac{-4+3}{2}\right), \left(\dfrac{3+4}{2}\right)\right]$ or $\left(-\dfrac{1}{2}, \dfrac{7}{2}\right)$

Gradient of line $AB = \dfrac{3-4}{-4-3}$ or $\dfrac{1}{7}$

Gradient of a line perpendicular to AB is -7

Equation of perpendicular bisector of AB is the line with gradient -7 which passes through the point $\left(-\dfrac{1}{2}, \dfrac{7}{2}\right)$

Using $(y - y_1) = m(x - x_1)$

$\left(y - \dfrac{7}{2}\right) = -7\left(x - -\dfrac{1}{2}\right)$

$2y - 7 = -14\left(x + \dfrac{1}{2}\right)$

$2y - 7 = -14x - 7$

The equation is $7x + y = 0$

12 $y = x + 1$ ....[1]

$x^2 - y = 5$ ....[2]

From [1], substitute for y in [2]

$x^2 - (x + 1) = 5$

$x^2 - x - 6 = 0$

$(x - 3)(x + 2) = 0$

$x = 3$ or $x = -2$

Substituting $x = 3$ into [1] gives $y = 4$

Substituting $x = -2$ into [1] gives $y = -1$

A is at $(-2, -1)$ and B is at $(3, 4)$

As $AP : PB = 4 : 1$

Point P is $\dfrac{4}{5}$ of the way along AB

P is at $\left\{\left[-2 + \dfrac{4}{5}(3 - -2)\right], \left[-1 + \dfrac{4}{5}(4 - -1)\right]\right\}$

P is at $(2, 3)$

14 a Let the parts be x and y.

$x + y = 10$ ....[1]

$x^2 - y^2 = 60$ ....[2]

From [1] $x = 10 - y$

Substitute for x in [2]

$(10 - y)^2 - y^2 = 60$

$-20y = -40$

$y = 2$

Therefore $x = 8$

b $x + y = N$ .... [1]

$x^2 - y^2 = D$ ....[2]

$(N - y)^2 - y^2 = D$

$N^2 - 2Ny = D$

$2Ny = N^2 - D$

$y = \dfrac{N^2}{2N} - \dfrac{D}{2N}$

$y = \dfrac{N}{2} - \dfrac{D}{2N}$

$x = N - \left(\dfrac{N}{2} - \dfrac{D}{2N}\right)$

$x = \dfrac{N}{2} + \dfrac{D}{2N}$

The two parts are $\dfrac{N}{2} + \dfrac{D}{2N}$ and $\dfrac{N}{2} - \dfrac{D}{2N}$

1 a **Method 1 (Substitution)**

$x^4 - 13x^2 + 36 = 0$

Let $y = x^2$ then:

$y^2 - 13y + 36 = 0$

$(y - 4)(y - 9) = 0$

$y = 4$ or $y = 9$

$x^2 = 4$ or $x^2 = 9$

$x = \pm 2$ or $x = \pm 3$

Method 2 (Factorise directly)

$(x^2 - 4)(x^2 - 9) = 0$

$x^2 = 4$ or $x^2 = 9$

$x = \pm 2$ or $x = \pm 3$

l $\dfrac{8}{x^6} + \dfrac{7}{x^3} = 1$

$8 + 7x^3 = x^6$

$x^6 - 7x^3 - 8 = 0$

$(x^3 - 8)(x^3 + 1) = 0$

$x^3 = 8$ or $x^3 = -1$

$x = 2$ or $x = -1$

2 b $\sqrt{x}\left(\sqrt{x} + 1\right) = 6$

$x + \sqrt{x} - 6 = 0$

Let $y = \sqrt{x}$ then:

$y^2 + y - 6 = 0$

$(y + 3)(y - 2) = 0$

$y = -3$ or $y = 2$

$\sqrt{x} = -3$ (no solutions as $\sqrt{x}$ is never negative)

$\sqrt{x} = 2$

$x = 4$

f $3\sqrt{x} + \dfrac{5}{\sqrt{x}} = 16$ multiply both sides by $\sqrt{x}$

$3x - 16\sqrt{x} + 5 = 0$

Let $y = \sqrt{x}$ then:

$3y^2 - 16y + 5 = 0$

$(3y - 1)(y - 5) = 0$

$y = \dfrac{1}{3}$ or $y = 5$

$\sqrt{x} = \dfrac{1}{3}$ or $\sqrt{x} = 5$

$x = \dfrac{1}{9}$ or $x = 25$

3 a $y = 2\sqrt{x}$ ....[1]

$3y = x + 8$ ....[2]

From [1], substitute for y in [2]

$3\left(2\sqrt{x}\right) = x + 8$

$x - 6\sqrt{x} + 8 = 0$

b Let $y = \sqrt{x}$ then:

$y^2 - 6y + 8 = 0$

$(y - 2)(y - 4) = 0$

$y = 2$ or $y = 4$

$\sqrt{x} = 2$ or $\sqrt{x} = 4$

$x = 4$ or $x = 16$

Substituting $x = 4$ into [2] gives $y = 4$

Substituting $x = 16$ into [2] gives $y = 8$

A is at $(4, 4)$ and B is at $(16, 8)$ or vice-versa.

c Using Pythagoras $AB = \sqrt{(16 - 4)^2 + (8 - 4)^2}$

$$AB = 4\sqrt{10}$$

4 $y = ax + b\sqrt{x} + c$

Substituting $x = 0$ and $y = 7$ into $y = ax + b\sqrt{x} + c$ gives:

$c = 7$, so

$y = ax + b\sqrt{x} + 7$

Substituting $x = 1$ and $y = 0$ into $y = ax + b\sqrt{x} + 7$

$a + b = -7$ .... [1]

Substituting $x = \dfrac{49}{4}$ and $y = 0$ into $y = ax + b\sqrt{x} + 7$

$0 = \dfrac{49}{4}a + \dfrac{7}{2}b + 7$ ....[2]

Simplifying [2]

$7a + 2b = -4$ ....[3]

Multiply [1] by 2 and subtract [3]

$-5a = -10$

$a = 2$

Substituting $a = 2$ into [1]

$b = -9$

So, $a = 2$, $b = -9$, $c = 7$

5 $y = a(2^{2x}) + b(2^x) + c$

Substituting $x = 0$ and $y = 90$ into
$y = a(2^{2x}) + b(2^x) + c$
$90 = a(2^0) + b(2^0) + c$
$90 = a + b + c$ ....[1]

Substituting $x = 2$ and $y = 0$ into
$y = a(2^{2x}) + b(2^x) + c$
$0 = a(2^4) + b(2^2) + c$
$0 = 16a + 4b + c$ ....[2]

Subtract [1] from [2] and simplify
$-30 = 5a + b$ ....[3]

Substituting $x = 4$ and $y = 0$ into
$y = a(2^{2x}) + b(2^x) + c$
$0 = a(2^8) + b(2^4) + c$
$0 = 256a + 16b + c$ ....[4]

Subtract [1] from [4] and simplify
$-6 = 17a + b$ ....[5]

Subtract [3] from [5]
$a = 2$

Substituting $a = 2$ into [3] gives $b = -40$

Substituting $a = 2$, $b = -40$ into [1] gives $c = 128$

So, $a = 2$, $b = -40$, $c = 128$

EXERCISE 1F

1 a $y = x^2 - 6x + 8$ is a parabola

Comparing $y = x^2 - 6x + 8$ with $y = ax^2 + bx + c$

The value of $a = 1$ so $a > 0$ which means the parabola is a $\cup$ shape.

The x intercepts are found by substituting $y = 0$ into:
$y = x^2 - 6x + 8$
$0 = x^2 - 6x + 8$
$0 = (x - 2)(x - 4)$
$x = 2$ or $x = 4$

The x intercepts are at $(2, 0)$ and $(4, 0)$.

The y intercept is found by substituting $x = 0$ into
$y = x^2 - 6x + 8$
$y = 8$

The axes crossing points are $(0, 8)$, $(2, 0)$ and $(4, 0)$

The curve has a minimum (or lowest) point which is located at the vertex.

There is a line of symmetry which passes midway between $x = 2$ and $x = 4$, also passes through the vertex.

Its equation is $x = 3$

Substituting $x = 3$ into $y = x^2 - 6x + 8$ gives
$y = 3^2 - 6(3) + 8$
$y = -1$

The vertex (minimum point) is at $(3, -1)$

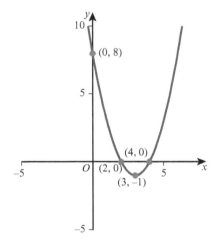

d $y = 12 + x - x^2$ is a parabola

Comparing $y = 12 + x - x^2$ with $y = ax^2 + bx + c$

The value of $a = -1$ so $a < 0$, which means the parabola is an $\cap$ shape.

The x-intercepts are found by substituting $y = 0$ into

$y = 12 + x - x^2$
$0 = 12 + x - x^2$
$0 = (3 + x)(4 - x)$
$x = -3$ or $x = 4$

The x intercepts are at $(-3, 0)$ and $(4, 0)$.

The y-intercept is found by substituting $x = 0$ into:

$y = 12 + x - x^2$
$y = 12$

Axes crossing points are $(0, 12)$, $(-3, 0)$ and $(4, 0)$

The curve has a maximum (or highest) point which is located at the vertex.

There is a line of symmetry which passes midway between $x = -3$ and $x = 4$ and also passes through the vertex.

Its equation is $x = \dfrac{1}{2}$

Substituting $x = \dfrac{1}{2}$ into $y = 12 + x - x^2$ gives

$y = 12 + \dfrac{1}{2} - \left(\dfrac{1}{2}\right)^2$

$y = 12\dfrac{1}{4}$

The vertex (maximum point) is at $\left(\dfrac{1}{2}, 12\dfrac{1}{4}\right)$

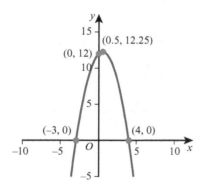

2 a $2x^2 - 8x + 5$
$2(x^2 - 4x) + 5$
$2[(x - 2)^2 - 2^2] + 5$
$[2(x - 2)^2 - 8] + 5$
$2(x - 2)^2 - 3$

b The line of symmetry of the graph passes through the vertex which is at $(2, -3)$.
Line of symmetry is $x = 2$.

3 a $y = 7 + 5x - x^2$
$y = 7 - (x^2 - 5x)$
$y = 7 - \left[\left(x - \dfrac{5}{2}\right)^2 - \dfrac{25}{4}\right]$
$y = \dfrac{53}{4} - \left(x - \dfrac{5}{2}\right)^2$

b Its graph is a $\cap$ shape.
The curve has a **maximum** (or highest) point i.e. a turning point which is located at the vertex $\left(\dfrac{5}{2}, \dfrac{53}{4}\right)$

The maximum point of the curve is at $\left(\dfrac{5}{2}, \dfrac{53}{4}\right)$ or $\left(2\dfrac{1}{2}, 13\dfrac{1}{4}\right)$

5 $x^2 - 7x + 8$

We are asked for the minimum value in this question. There are two methods which you can use:
Method 1 factorisation (if possible)
Method 2 completing the square

$x^2 - 7x + 8$ does not factorise so:
Completing the square gives:
$\left(x - \dfrac{7}{2}\right)^2 - \dfrac{49}{4} + 8$
$\left(x - \dfrac{7}{2}\right)^2 - \dfrac{17}{4}$

Be careful! Here you are asked for the minimum value, not the minimum point.

Minimum value is $-4\dfrac{1}{4}$ [when $x = 3\dfrac{1}{2}$]

7 $y = 4x^2 + 2x + 5$ is a $\cup$ shaped parabola.

Complete the square to find the vertex (minimum point).

$$y = 4\left(x^2 + \frac{1}{2}x\right) + 5$$

$$y = 4\left[\left(x + \frac{1}{4}\right)^2 - \left(\frac{1}{4}\right)^2\right] + 5$$

$$y = \left[4\left(x + \frac{1}{4}\right)^2 - \frac{1}{4}\right] + 5$$

$$y = 4\left(x + \frac{1}{4}\right)^2 + \frac{19}{4}$$

The vertex is at $\left(-\frac{1}{4}, \frac{19}{4}\right)$, which is above the x axis.

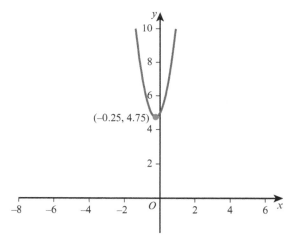

8 **Graph A** has its vertex at (4, 2). The point (6, 6) lies on the curve.

There are no x-intercepts.

There are three forms of a quadratic equation:

1 $y = ax^2 + bx + c$
Any three different coordinate points on the parabola enables three equations to be formed and solved simultaneously. However, this is a long method and can be prone to calculation errors.

2 $y = a(x - d)(x - e)$
To use this form you need to know the location of the x-intercepts (if any).

3 $y = a(x - f)^2 + g$
To use this form, the location of the vertex (f, g) needs to be known, plus one additional point on the parabola.

Using $y = a(x - f)^2 + g$ and substituting $f = 4$, $g = 2$

$$y = a(x - 4)^2 + 2$$

Now substituting $x = 6$, $y = 6$ gives

$$6 = a(6 - 4)^2 + 2$$

$$a = 1$$

So, $y = (x - 4)^2 + 2$

Graph B The vertex is at $(-2, -6)$.

The x intercepts are not clear.

The point (0, 10) lies on the curve.

Using $y = a(x - f)^2 + g$ and substituting $f = -2$, $g = -6$

$$y = a(x - -2)^2 - 6$$

$$y = a(x + 2)^2 - 6$$

Now substituting $x = 0$, $y = 10$ gives

$$10 = a(0 + 2)^2 - 6$$

$$a = 4$$

So, $y = 4(x + 2)^2 - 6$

Graph C There are more than three pieces of information which can be read off the graph.

e.g. the vertex is at (2, 8).

The x intercepts are $x = -2$, $x = 6$.

The point (0, 6) lies on the curve etc.

Using $y = a(x - d)(x - e)$

Substituting $d = -2$, $e = 6$

$$y = a(x + 2)(x - 6)$$

Now substituting $x = 2$, $y = 8$ gives

$$8 = a(2 + 2)(2 - 6)$$

$$a = -\frac{1}{2}$$

So, $y = -\frac{1}{2}(x + 2)(x - 6)$

9 $y = x^2 - 6x + 13$

The graph is a $\cup$ shaped parabola

Completing the square gives:

$y = (x-3)^2 + 4$

The vertex is at $(3, 4)$

$y = x^2 - 6x + 13$ is **A**

$y = -x^2 - 6x - 5$

The graph is an $\cap$ shaped parabola

Completing the square gives:

$y = -(x^2 + 6x) - 5$

$y = -[(x+3)^2 - 9] - 5$

$y = -(x+3)^2 + 4$

The vertex is at $(-3, 4)$

$y = -x^2 - 6x - 5$ is G

> $y = -x^2 - bx - c$ is a reflection of $y = x^2 + bx + c$ in the x-axis, i.e. $f(x) \rightarrow -f(x)$
> $y = x^2 - bx + c$ is a reflection of $y = x^2 + bx + c$ in the y-axis, i.e. $f(x) \rightarrow -f(-x)$
> You will meet this again in Chapter 2.

Graph F is $y = x^2 + 6x + 5$ as it is a reflection of G in the x-axis

Graph D is $y = -x^2 + 6x - 13$ as it is a reflection of A in the x-axis

Graph E is $y = x^2 + 6x + 13$ as it is a reflection of A in the y-axis

Graph B is $y = x^2 - 6x + 5$ as it is reflection of F in the y-axis

Graph C is $y = -x^2 + 6x - 5$ as it is a reflection of G in the y-axis

Graph H is $y = -x^2 - 6x - 13$ as it is a reflection of E in the x-axis

(There are other ways to reach these solutions.)

10 Using $y = a(x - d)(x - e)$

Substituting $x = -2$ and $x = 4$ gives:

$y = a(x - -2)(x - 4)$

Substituting $x = 0$, $y = -24$ gives:

$-24 = a(0 - -2)(0 - 4)$

$a = 3$

Equation is $y = 3(x + 2)(x - 4)$ or
$y = 3x^2 - 6x - 24$

11 We do not know the x-intercepts nor the coordinates of the vertex.

We form three equations by substituting the three given coordinates into

$y = ax^2 + bx + c$ and solve them simultaneously.

Substituting $(-2, -3)$ gives $-3 = a(-2)^2 + b(-2) + c$
or $-3 = 4a - 2b + c$.......[1]

Substituting $(2, 9)$ gives $9 = a(2)^2 + b(2) + c$ or
$9 = 4a + 2b + c$............[2]

Substituting $(6, 5)$ gives $5 = a(6)^2 + b(6) + c$ or
$5 = 36a + 6b + c$..........[3]

[1] $-$ [2] gives $-12 = -4b$ so $b = 3$

[2] $-$ [3] gives $4 = -32a - 4b$

As $b = 3$, $4 = -32a - 12$ so $a = -\dfrac{1}{2}$

Substituting $a = -\dfrac{1}{2}$ and $b = 3$ into [1] gives:

$-3 = -2 - 6 + c$ so $c = 5$

The equation is $y = 5 + 3x - \dfrac{1}{2}x^2$

12 Using $y = a(x - f)^2 + g$

The vertex is at (p, q).

Substituting $f = p$ and $g = q$ gives:
$y = a(x - p)^2 + q$

Expanding gives:

$y = a(x^2 - 2px + p^2) + q$

$y = ax^2 - 2apx + ap^2 + q$ Proved

1 b $(x-3)(x+2) > 0$

Sketch the graph of $y = (x-3)(x+2)$

The graph is a $\cup$ shaped parabola.

The x-intercepts are at $x = -2$ and $x = 3$.

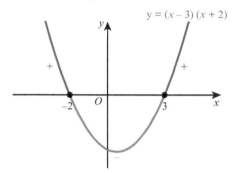

For $(x-3)(x+2) > 0$ we need to find the range of values of x for which the curve is positive (above the x axis).

The solution is $x < -2$ or $x > 3$

f $(1-3x)(2x+1) < 0$

Sketch the graph of $y = (1-3x)(2x+1)$

The sketch is an $\cap$ shaped parabola.

The x-intercepts are at $x = -\dfrac{1}{2}$ and $x = \dfrac{1}{3}$.

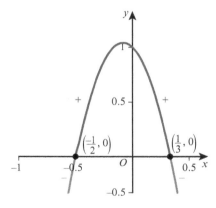

For $(1-3x)(2x+1) < 0$ we need to find the range of values of x for which the curve is negative (below the x axis).

The solution is $x < -\dfrac{1}{2}$ or $x > \dfrac{1}{3}$

2 a $x^2 - 25 \geqslant 0$

Factorising the left-hand side of the inequality:

$(x-5)(x+5) \geqslant 0$

Sketch the graph of $y = (x-5)(x+5)$

The sketch is an $\cup$ shaped parabola.

The x-intercepts are at $x = -5$ and $x = 5$.

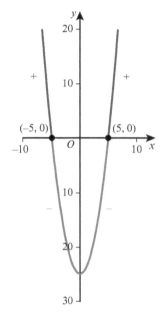

For $x^2 - 25 \geqslant 0$ we need to find the range of values of x for which the curve is either zero or positive (on or above the x-axis).

The solution is $x \leqslant -5$ or $x \geqslant 5$.

e $6x^2 - 23x + 20 < 0$

Factorising the left-hand side of the inequality:

$(3x-4)(2x-5) < 0$

Sketch the graph of $y = (3x-4)(2x-5)$

The sketch is a $\cup$ shaped parabola.

The x-intercepts are at $x = \dfrac{4}{3}$ and $x = \dfrac{5}{2}$.

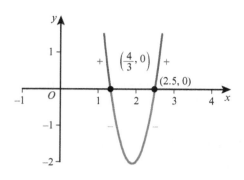

For $6x^2 - 23x + 20 < 0$ we need to find the range of values of x for which the curve is negative (below the x-axis).

The solution is $\dfrac{4}{3} < x < \dfrac{5}{2}$

---

3 b $15x < x^2 + 56$

Rearrange to give:

$x^2 - 15x + 56 > 0$

Factorising the left-hand side of the inequality:

$(x-7)(x-8) > 0$

Sketch the graph of $y = (x-7)(x-8)$

The sketch is a $\cup$ shaped parabola.

The x-intercepts are at $x = 7$ and $x = 8$

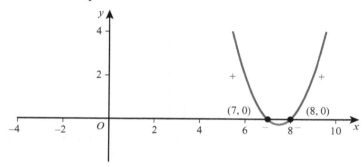

For $x^2 - 15x + 56 > 0$ we need to find the range of values of x for which the curve is positive (above the x-axis).

The solution is $x < 7$ or $x > 8$

g $(x+4)^2 \geqslant 25$

Expand brackets and rearrange:

$x^2 + 8x - 9 \geqslant 0$

Factorising the left-hand side of the inequality:

$(x-1)(x+9) \geqslant 0$

Sketch the graph of $y = (x-1)(x+9)$

The sketch is a $\cup$ shaped parabola.

The x-intercepts are at $x = 1$ and $x = -9$

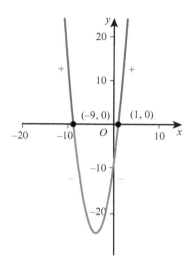

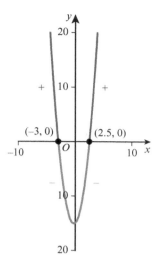

For $x^2 + 8x - 9 \geq 0$, we need to find the range of values of x for which the curve is either zero or positive (on or above the x-axis).

The solution is $x \leq -9$ or $x \geq 1$

4 $\dfrac{5}{2x^2 + x - 15} < 0$

$\dfrac{\text{positive value}}{\text{negative value}} < 0$ (the numerator here is always positive)

Factorising the denominator gives:

$\dfrac{5}{(2x - 5)(x + 3)} < 0$

5 is a positive value, so we need to find values of x

which make $(2x - 5)(x + 3)$ negative i.e. < 0

so, $(2x - 5)(x + 3) < 0$

A sketch of $y = (2x - 5)(x + 3)$, is a $\cup$ shaped parabola.

The x intercepts are at $x = 2.5$ and $x = -3$ (found when solving $2x - 5 = 0$ and $x + 3 = 0$)

We want $(2x - 5)(x + 3) < 0$ so, we need to find the range of values of x for which the curve is negative (below the x-axis).

The solution is $-3 < x < 2.5$

5 b $x^2 + 4x - 21 \leq 0$

Factorising the left-hand side of the inequality:

$(x + 7)(x - 3) \leq 0$

A sketch of $y = (x + 7)(x - 3)$ is a $\cup$ shaped parabola.

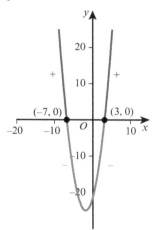

The x-intercepts are at $x = -7$ and $x = 3$

For $x^2 + 4x - 21 \leqslant 0$ we need to find the range of values of x for which the curve is either zero or negative (on or below the x axis)

The solution is $-7 \leqslant x \leqslant 3$

$x^2 - 9x + 8 > 0$

Factorising the left-hand side of the inequality:

$(x - 1)(x - 8) > 0$

The graph of $y = (x - 1)(x - 8)$ is a $\cup$ shaped parabola.

The x-intercepts are at $x = 1$ and $x = 8$

For $x^2 - 9x + 8 > 0$ we need to find the range of values of x for which the curve is positive (above the x-axis).

The solution is $x < 1$ or $x > 8$

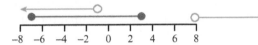

The diagram shows both solutions to be true when $-7 \leqslant x < 1$

6 $2^{x^2 - 3x - 40} > 1$

Since $2^0 = 1$, and $2^{\text{positive number}} > 1$

We need to solve $x^2 - 3x - 40 > 0$

Factorising the left-hand side of the inequality:

$(x + 5)(x - 8) > 0$

The sketch of $y = (x + 5)(x - 8)$ is a $\cup$ shaped parabola.

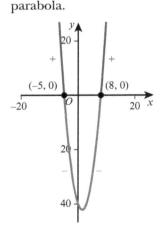

The x-intercepts are at $x = -5$ and $x = 8$

For $x^2 - 3x - 40 > 0$ we need to find the range of values of x for which the curve is positive (above the x axis).

The solution is $x < -5$ or $x > 8$

7 a $\dfrac{x}{x - 1} \geqslant 3$

Rearrange $\dfrac{x}{x - 1} - 3 \geqslant 0$

Write as a single fraction on the left-hand side:

$$\frac{x}{x - 1} - \frac{3(x - 1)}{x - 1} \geqslant 0$$

$$\frac{x - 3(x - 1)}{x - 1} \geqslant 0$$

$$\frac{3 - 2x}{x - 1} \geqslant 0$$

Find the values of x which each make the numerator and the denominator zero.

i.e. $3 - 2x = 0$ so $x = \dfrac{3}{2}$

$x - 1 = 0$ so $x = 1$ (if the denominator of a fraction is zero then its value is undefined)

Use a number line to test numbers around $x = \dfrac{3}{2}$ and $x = 1$

If $x = 0$ then substituting into $\dfrac{3 - 2x}{x - 1}$ becomes $\dfrac{3 - 2(0)}{0 - 1}$ which is negative.

If $x = 1.25$ then substituting into $\dfrac{3 - 2x}{x - 1}$ becomes $\dfrac{3 - 2(1.25)}{1.25 - 1}$ which is positive.

If $x = 2$ then substituting into $\dfrac{3 - 2x}{x - 1}$ becomes $\dfrac{3 - 2(2)}{2 - 1}$ which is negative.

the value of the fraction is undefined at $x = 1$ the value of the fraction is zero at $x = \dfrac{3}{2}$

$\dfrac{x}{x - 1} \geqslant 3$ for values of x which satisfy:

$1 < x \leqslant \dfrac{3}{2}$

b $\dfrac{x(x-1)}{x+1} > x$

Rearrange $\dfrac{x(x-1)}{x+1} - x > 0$

Write as a single fraction on the left-hand side:

$\dfrac{x(x-1)}{x+1} - \dfrac{x(x+1)}{x+1} > 0$

$\dfrac{x(x-1) - x(x+1)}{x+1} > 0$

$\dfrac{x^2 - x - x^2 - x}{x+1} > 0$

$\dfrac{-2x}{x+1} > 0$

Find the values of x which each make the numerator and the denominator zero.

i.e. $-2x = 0$ so $x = 0$

$x + 1 = 0$ so $x = -1$ (if the denominator of a fraction is zero then its value is undefined)

Use a number line to test numbers around $x = 0$ and $x = -1$

If $x = -2$ then substituting into $\dfrac{-2x}{x+1}$

becomes $\dfrac{-2(-2)}{-2+1}$ which is negative.

If $x = -\dfrac{1}{2}$ then substituting into $\dfrac{-2x}{x+1}$

becomes $\dfrac{-2\left(-\dfrac{1}{2}\right)}{-\dfrac{1}{2}+1}$ which is positive.

If $x = 1$ then substituting into $\dfrac{-2x}{x+1}$ becomes $\dfrac{-2(1)}{1+1}$ which is negative.

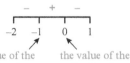

the value of the fraction is undefined at $x = -1$ | the value of the fraction is zero at $x = 0$

$\dfrac{x(x-1)}{x+1} > x$ for values of x which satisfy

$-1 < x < 0$

c $\dfrac{x^2 - 9}{x-1} \geqslant 4$

Rearrange $\dfrac{x^2-9}{x-1} - 4 \geqslant 0$

Write as a single fraction on the left-hand side:

$\dfrac{x^2-9}{x-1} - \dfrac{4(x-1)}{x-1} \geqslant 0$

$\dfrac{x^2 - 9 - 4(x-1)}{x-1} \geqslant 0$

$\dfrac{x^2 - 9 - 4x + 4}{x-1} \geqslant 0$

$\dfrac{x^2 - 4x - 5}{x-1} \geqslant 0$

Find the values of x which each make the numerator and the denominator zero.

i.e. $x^2 - 4x - 5 = 0$

$(x-5)(x+1) = 0$

so $x = 5$ or $x = -1$

$x - 1 = 0$ so $x = 1$ (if the denominator of a fraction is zero then its value is undefined).

Use a number line to test numbers around $x = -1$, $x = 5$ and $x = 1$

If $x = -2$ then $\dfrac{x^2 - 4x - 5}{x-1}$ becomes

$\dfrac{(-2)^2 - 4(-2) - 5}{-2 - 1}$ which is negative

If $x = 0$ then $\dfrac{x^2 - 4x - 5}{x-1}$ becomes

$\dfrac{(0)^2 - 4(0) - 5}{0 - 1}$ which is positive

If $x = 2$ then $\dfrac{x^2 - 4x - 5}{x-1}$ becomes

$\dfrac{(2)^2 - 4(2) - 5}{2 - 1}$ which is negative

If $x = 6$ then $\dfrac{x^2 - 4x - 5}{x-1}$ becomes

$\dfrac{(6)^2 - 4(6) - 5}{6 - 1}$ which is positive

the value of the fraction is zero at $x = -1$ | the value of the fraction is undefined at $x = 1$ | the value of the fraction is zero at $x = 5$

$\dfrac{x^2-9}{x-1} \geqslant 4$ for values of x which satisfy:

$-1 \leqslant x < 1$ or $x \geqslant 5$

d $\quad \dfrac{x^2 - 2x - 15}{x - 2} \geqslant 0$

$\dfrac{(x-5)(x+3)}{x-2} \geqslant 0$

Find the values of x which each make the numerator and the denominator zero.

For the numerator, solve $(x-5)(x+3) = 0$

so $x = 5$ or $x = -3$

For the denominator, solve $x - 2 = 0$

so $x = 2$ (if the denominator of a fraction is zero then its value is undefined)

Use a number line to test numbers around $x = -3$, $x = 2$ and $x = 5$

If $x = -4$ then $\dfrac{(x-5)(x+3)}{x-2}$

becomes $\dfrac{(-4-5)(-4+3)}{-4-2}$ which is negative.

If $x = 0$ then $\dfrac{(x-5)(x+3)}{x-2}$ becomes

$\dfrac{(0-5)(0+3)}{0-2}$ which is positive.

If $x = 3$ then $\dfrac{(x-5)(x+3)}{x-2}$ becomes

$\dfrac{(3-5)(3+3)}{3-2}$ which is negative.

If $x = 6$ then $\dfrac{(x-5)(x+3)}{x-2}$ becomes

$\dfrac{(6-5)(6+3)}{6-2}$ which is positive.

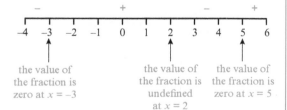

the value of the fraction is zero at $x = -3$

the value of the fraction is undefined at $x = 2$

the value of the fraction is zero at $x = 5$

$\dfrac{x^2 - 2x - 15}{x - 2} \geqslant 0$ for values of x which satisfy:

$-3 \leqslant x < 2$ or $x \geqslant 5$

e $\quad \dfrac{x^2 + 4x - 5}{x^2 - 4} \leqslant 0$

$\dfrac{(x+5)(x-1)}{(x-2)(x+2)} \leqslant 0$

Find the values of x which each make the numerator and the denominator zero.

For the numerator, solve $(x+5)(x-1) = 0$

so $x = -5$ or $x = 1$

For the denominator, solve $(x-2)(x+2) = 0$

so $x = 2$ or $x = -2$ (if the denominator of a fraction is zero then its value is undefined).

Use a number line to test numbers around $x = -5$, $x = -2$, $x = 1$ and $x = 2$

If $x = -6$ then substituting into $\dfrac{(x+5)(x-1)}{(x-2)(x+2)}$

becomes $\dfrac{(-6+5)(-6-1)}{(-6-2)(-6+2)}$ which is positive.

If $x = -3$ then substituting into $\dfrac{(x+5)(x-1)}{(x-2)(x+2)}$

becomes $\dfrac{(-3+5)(-3-1)}{(-3-2)(-3+2)}$ which is negative.

If $x = 0$ then substituting into $\dfrac{(x+5)(x-1)}{(x-2)(x+2)}$

becomes $\dfrac{(0+5)(0-1)}{(0-2)(0+2)}$ which is positive.

If $x = 1.5$ then substituting into $\dfrac{(x+5)(x-1)}{(x-2)(x+2)}$

becomes $\dfrac{(1.5+5)(1.5-1)}{(1.5-2)(1.5+2)}$ which is negative.

If $x = 3$ then substituting into $\dfrac{(x+5)(x-1)}{(x-2)(x+2)}$

becomes $\dfrac{(3+5)(3-1)}{(3-2)(3+2)}$ which is positive.

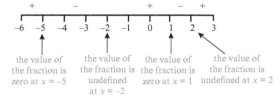

the value of the fraction is zero at $x = -5$

the value of the fraction is undefined at $x = -2$

the value of the fraction is zero at $x = 1$

the value of the fraction is undefined at $x = 2$

$\dfrac{x^2 + 4x - 5}{x^2 - 4} \leqslant 0$ for values of x which satisfy:

$-5 \leqslant x < -2$ or $1 \leqslant x < 2$

f $\dfrac{x-3}{x+4} \geqslant \dfrac{x+2}{x-5}$

Rearrange $\dfrac{x-3}{x+4} - \dfrac{x+2}{x-5} \geqslant 0$

Write as a single fraction on the left-hand side:

$$\dfrac{(x-3)(x-5) - (x+2)(x+4)}{(x+4)(x-5)} \geqslant 0$$

> Be careful with the numerator!

$$\dfrac{x^2 - 8x + 15 - [x^2 + 6x + 8]}{(x+4)(x-5)} \geqslant 0$$

$$\dfrac{x^2 - 8x + 15 - x^2 - 6x - 8}{(x+4)(x-5)} \geqslant 0$$

$$\dfrac{7 - 14x}{(x+4)(x-5)} \geqslant 0$$

$$\dfrac{7(1 - 2x)}{(x+4)(x-5)} \geqslant 0$$

Find the values of x which each make the numerator and the denominator zero.

For the numerator, solve $7(1 - 2x) = 0$

so $x = \dfrac{1}{2}$

For the denominator, solve $(x+4)(x-5) = 0$

so $x = -4$ or $x = 5$ (if the denominator of a fraction is zero then its value is undefined).

Use a number line to test numbers around $x = -4$, $x = \dfrac{1}{2}$ and $x = 5$

If $x = -5$ then $\dfrac{7(1 - 2x)}{(x+4)(x-5)}$ becomes

$\dfrac{7(1 - 2(-5))}{(-5 + 4)(-5 - 5)}$ which is positive.

If $x = 0$ then $\dfrac{7(1 - 2x)}{(x+4)(x-5)}$ becomes

$\dfrac{7(1 - 2(0))}{(0 + 4)(0 - 5)}$ which is negative.

If $x = 1$ then $\dfrac{7(1 - 2x)}{(x+4)(x-5)}$ becomes

$\dfrac{7(1 - 2(1))}{(1 + 4)(1 - 5)}$ which is positive.

If $x = 6$ then $\dfrac{7(1 - 2x)}{(x+4)(x-5)}$ becomes

$\dfrac{7(1 - 2(6))}{(6 + 4)(6 - 5)}$ which is negative.

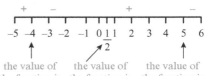

the value of the fraction is undefined at $x = -4$ the value of the fraction is zero at $x = \dfrac{1}{2}$ the value of the fraction is undefined at $x = 5$

$\dfrac{x-3}{x+4} \geqslant \dfrac{x+2}{x-5}$ for values of x which satisfy:

$x < -4$ or $\dfrac{1}{2} \leqslant x < 5$

EXERCISE 1H

1 b $x^2 + 5x - 36 = 0$

$a = 1$, $b = 5$, $c = -36$

Substituting into $b^2 - 4ac$ gives:

$5^2 - 4(1)(-36)$ which is > 0 so there are two distinct real roots.

e $2x^2 - 7x + 8 = 0$

$a = 2$, $b = -7$, $c = 8$

Substituting into $b^2 - 4ac$ gives:

$(-7)^2 - 4(2)(8)$ which is < 0 so there are no real roots.

2 $2 - 5x = \dfrac{4}{x}$

Rearrange and simplify:

$5x^2 - 2x + 4 = 0$

$a = 5$, $b = -2$, $c = 4$

Substituting into $b^2 - 4ac$ gives:

$(-2)^2 - 4(5)(4)$ which is < 0 so there are no real roots.

3 $(x+5)(x-7)=0$ which expanded gives:

$x^2 - 2x - 35 = 0$

So, $b=-2$ and $c=-35$

4 b $4x^2 + 4(k-2)x + k = 0$

So, $a=4$, $b=4(k-2)$, $c=k$

For two equal roots $b^2 - 4ac = 0$

$[4(k-2)]^2 - 4(4)(k) = 0$ which simplified gives:

$16k^2 - 80k + 64 = 0$ or:

$k^2 - 5k + 4 = 0$

$(k-1)(k-4) = 0$

So, $k=1$ or $k=4$

e $(k+1)x^2 + kx - 2k = 0$

$a=k+1$, $b=k$, $c=-2k$

For two equal roots $b^2 - 4ac = 0$

$k^2 - 4(k+1)(-2k) = 0$

$k^2 + 8k(k+1) = 0$

$9k^2 + 8k = 0$

$k(9k+8) = 0$

$k=0$ or $k=-\dfrac{8}{9}$

5 b $2x^2 - 5x = 4 - k$

Rearranging gives: $2x^2 - 5x + (k-4) = 0$

$a=2$, $b=-5$, $c=k-4$

For two distinct roots $b^2 - 4ac > 0$

$(-5)^2 - 4(2)(k-4) > 0$ which simplifies to:

$8k - 57 < 0$

$k < \dfrac{57}{8}$

d $kx^2 + 2(k-1)x + k = 0$

$a=k$, $b=2(k-1)$, $c=k$

For two distinct roots $b^2 - 4ac > 0$

$[2(k-1)]^2 - 4(k)(k) > 0$

$-8k + 4 > 0$

$k < \dfrac{1}{2}$

6 b $3x^2 + 5x + k + 1 = 0$

$a=3$, $b=5$, $c=k+1$

For no real roots $b^2 - 4ac < 0$

$5^2 - 4(3)(k+1) < 0$

$-12k + 13 < 0$

$k > \dfrac{13}{12}$

e $kx^2 + 2kx = 4x - 6$

$kx^2 + (2k-4)x + 6 = 0$

$a=k$, $b=2k-4$, $c=6$

For no real roots $b^2 - 4ac < 0$

$(2k-4)^2 - 4(k)(6) < 0$ which simplifies to:

$4k^2 - 40k + 16 < 0$ or

$k^2 - 10k + 4 < 0$

The sketch of $y = k^2 - 10k + 4$ is a $\cup$ shaped parabola.

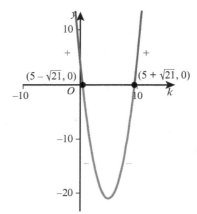

$k^2 - 10k + 4$ does not factorise so to find the k-intercepts we must use the quadratic formula.

$k = \dfrac{-(-10) \pm \sqrt{(-10)^2 - 4 \times 1 \times (4)}}{2 \times 1}$

$k = \dfrac{10 + \sqrt{84}}{2}$ or $k = \dfrac{10 - \sqrt{84}}{2}$ which simplify to give:

$k = 5 + \sqrt{21}$ or $k = 5 - \sqrt{21}$

The k-intercepts are at $k = 5 + \sqrt{21}$ and $k = 5 - \sqrt{21}$

For $k^2 - 10k + 4 < 0$ we need to find the range of values of k for which the curve is negative (below the k axis).

The solution is $5 - \sqrt{21} < k < 5 + \sqrt{21}$

7 $kx^2 + px + 5 = 0$

$a = k, \; b = p, \; c = 5$

For repeated real roots $b^2 - 4ac = 0$

$p^2 - 4(k)(5) = 0$

$k = \dfrac{p^2}{20}$

8 $kx^2 - 5x + 2 = 0$

$a = k, \; b = -5, \; c = 2$

For real roots $b^2 - 4ac \geqslant 0$

$(-5)^2 - 4(k)(2) \geqslant 0$

$k \leqslant \dfrac{25}{8}$

9 $2kx^2 + 5x - k = 0$

$a = 2k, \; b = 5, \; c = -k$

$b^2 - 4ac$ is $5^2 - 4(2k)(-k)$ which simplifies to:

$25 + 8k^2$

$25 + 8k^2 \geqslant 25$ for all values of k i.e. it is always positive

So, $b^2 - 4ac > 0$ which proves that the roots are real and distinct for all real values of k.

10 $x^2 + (k - 2)x - 2k = 0$

$a = 1, \; b = k - 2, \; c = -2k$

$b^2 - 4ac$ is $(k - 2)^2 - 4(1)(-2k)$

which simplifies to $k^2 + 4k + 4$ or $(k + 2)^2$

$(k + 2)^2$ is always $\geqslant 0$

Therefore the roots are real for all values of k.

11 $x^2 + kx + 2 = 0$

$a = 1, \; b = k, \; c = 2$

For real roots $b^2 - 4ac \geqslant 0$

So, $k^2 - 4(1)(2) \geqslant 0$ or $k^2 - 8 \geqslant 0$

Factorising the left-hand side of the inequality gives:

$\left(k - \sqrt{8}\right)\left(k + \sqrt{8}\right) \geqslant 0$

The sketch of $y = \left(k - \sqrt{8}\right)\left(k + \sqrt{8}\right)$ is a $\cup$ shaped parabola.

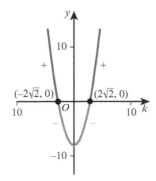

The k-intercepts are $k = 2\sqrt{2}$ and $k = -2\sqrt{2}$

we need to find the range of values of k for which the curve is either zero or positive (on or above the k axis).

The solution is $k \leqslant -2\sqrt{2}$ or $k \geqslant 2\sqrt{2}$

Therefore the equation has real roots if $k \geqslant 2\sqrt{2}$,

the other values of k are $k \leqslant -2\sqrt{2}$.

EXERCISE 1I

1 If $y = kx + 1$ is a tangent to $y = x^2 - 7x + 2$ then there should only be one solution to the equation formed by solving $y = kx + 1$ and $y = x^2 - 7x + 2$ simultaneously.

$x^2 - 7x + 2 = kx + 1$ when rearranged gives:

$x^2 - (7 + k)x + 1 = 0$

$a = 1, \; b = -(7 + k), \; c = 1$

For one repeated real root $b^2 - 4ac = 0$

$[-(7+k)]^2 - 4(1)(1) = 0$

$k^2 + 14k + 45 = 0$

$(k+5)(k+9) = 0$

$k = -5$ or $k = -9$

2 The x-axis has the equation $y = 0$

If $y = 0$ is a tangent to $y = x^2 - (k+3)x + (3k+4)$ then there should only be one solution to the equation formed by solving $y = 0$ and $y = x^2 - (k+3)x + (3k+4)$ simultaneously.

$x^2 - (k+3)x + (3k+4) = 0$

$a = 1$, $b = -(k+3)$, $c = (3k+4)$

For one repeated real root $b^2 - 4ac = 0$

$[-(k+3)]^2 - 4(1)(3k+4) = 0$

$k^2 - 6k - 7 = 0$

$(k+1)(k-7) = 0$

$k = -1$ or $k = 7$

3 If $x + ky = 12$ is a tangent to $y = \dfrac{5}{x-2}$ then there should only be one solution to the equation formed by solving $x + ky = 12$ ....[1]

and $y = \dfrac{5}{x-2}$ ....[2] simultaneously.

From [1] $y = \dfrac{12-x}{k}$ and substituting for y in [2] gives:

$\dfrac{12-x}{k} = \dfrac{5}{x-2}$

Simplifying and rearranging gives:

$x^2 - 14x + (5k+24) = 0$

$a = 1$, $b = -14$, $c = (5k+24)$

For one repeated real root $b^2 - 4ac = 0$

$(-14)^2 - 4(1)(5k+24) = 0$

$k = 5$

4 a If $y = k - 3x$ is a tangent to $0 = x^2 + 2xy - 20$ then there should only be one solution to the equation formed by solving $y = k - 3x$ ......[1] and $x^2 + 2xy - 20 = 0$ .....[2] simultaneously.

Substituting for y in [2] gives:

If $x^2 + 2x(k - 3x) - 20 = 0$

Rearranging this equation gives:

$5x^2 - 2kx + 20 = 0$

$a = 5$, $b = -2k$, $c = 20$

As $b^2 - 4ac = 0$ for one repeated root

$(-2k)^2 - 4(5)(20) = 0$

$k = \pm 10$

b First, substitute $k = -10$ into $y = k - 3x$ giving:

$y = -10 - 3x$

And then as $x^2 + 2xy - 20 = 0$ solving these two equations simultaneously gives:

$x^2 + 2x(-10 - 3x) - 20 = 0$

$-5x^2 - 20x - 20 = 0$

This simplifies to:

$x^2 + 4x + 4 = 0$

$(x+2)^2 = 0$

$x = -2$

Substituting $x = -2$ into $y = -10 - 3x$ gives:

$y = -4$

Second, substitute $k = 10$ into $y = k - 3x$ giving:

$y = 10 - 3x$

And then as $x^2 + 2xy - 20 = 0$ solving these two equations simultaneously gives:

$x^2 + 2x(10 - 3x) - 20 = 0$ and then simplifies to:

$x^2 - 4x + 4 = 0$

$(x-2)^2 = 0$

$x = 2$

Substituting $x = 2$ into $y = 10 - 3x$ gives:

$y = 4$

The coordinates are $(2, 4)$ and $(-2, -4)$

6 $y = 2x - 1$ ....[1]

$y = x^2 + kx + 3$ ....[2]

Substitute for y in [2]

$2x - 1 = x^2 + kx + 3$

Rearrange:

$x^2 + (k-2)x + 4 = 0$

$a = 1$, $b = k - 2$, $c = 4$

For two distinct roots $b^2 - 4ac > 0$

$(k - 2)^2 - 4(1)(4) > 0$

$k^2 - 4k - 12 > 0$

$(k - 6)(k + 2) > 0$

A sketch of $y = (k - 6)(k + 2)$, is a $\cup$ shaped parabola.

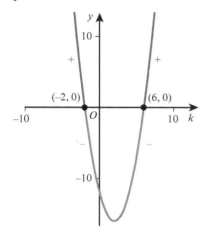

The k–intercepts are at $k = -2$ and $k = 6$

For $k^2 - 4k - 12 > 0$ we need to find the range of values of k for which the curve is positive (above the k-axis).

The solution is $k < -2$ and $k > 6$.

9 $y = mx + 5$ ....[1]

$y = x^2 - x + 6$ ....[2]

Substitute for y in [2]

$mx + 5 = x^2 - x + 6$

Rearrange:

$x^2 - (1 + m)x + 1 = 0$

$a = 1$, $b = -(1 + m)$, $c = 1$

If the straight line does not meet the curve, then there are no real solutions to the equation.

So, $b^2 - 4ac < 0$

$[-(1 + m)]^2 - 4(1)(1) < 0$

$m^2 + 2m - 3 < 0$

$(m - 1)(m + 3) < 0$

A sketch of $y = (m - 1)(m + 3)$ is a $\cup$ shaped parabola.

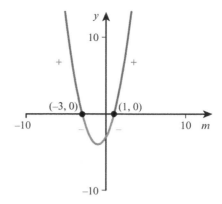

The m-intercepts are at $m = -3$ and $m = 1$

For $m^2 + 2m - 3 < 0$ we need to find the range of values of m for which the curve is negative (below the m-axis).

The solution is $-3 < m < 1$

11 $y = kx + 6$ ....[1]

$x^2 + y^2 - 10x + 8y = 84$ ....[2]

Substitute for y in [2]

$x^2 + (kx + 6)^2 - 10x + 8(kx + 6) = 84$

Simplified and rearranged:

$(1 + k^2)x^2 + (20k - 10)x = 0$

If the straight line is a tangent to the curve, then this equation has one root

so $b^2 - 4ac = 0$

$a = 1 + k^2$, $b = 20k - 10$, $c = 0$

$(20k - 10)^2 - 4(1 + k^2)(0) = 0$

$(20k - 10)^2 = 0$

$k = \dfrac{1}{2}$

12 $y = mx + c$ ....[1]

$y = x^2 - 4x + 4$ ....[2]

If the line is a tangent to the curve then there should be one solution to the equation

$mx + c = x^2 - 4x + 4$

Rearranged:

$x^2 - (4 + m)x + (4 - c) = 0$

$a = 1, \ b = -(4 + m), \ c = (4 - c)$

For one (repeated) root $b^2 - 4ac = 0$

$[-(4 + m)]^2 - 4(1)(4 - c) = 0$

$16 + 8m + m^2 - 16 + 4c = 0$

$m^2 + 8m + 4c = 0$ proved.

13 $y = mx + c$ ....[1]

$ax^2 + by^2 = c$ ....[2]

Substitute for y in [2]

$ax^2 + b(mx + c)^2 = c$

Expanded gives:

$ax^2 + bm^2x^2 + (2bcm)x + bc^2 - c = 0$

$(a + bm^2)x^2 + (2bcm)x + (bc^2 - c) = 0*$

If a line is a tangent to the curve then an equation of the form:

$ax^2 + bx + c = 0$ should have one solution.

i.e. $b^2 - 4ac = 0$

For our equation*

$$(2bcm)^2 - 4(a + bm^2)(bc^2 - c) = 0$$
$$4b^2c^2m^2 - 4abc^2 + 4ac - 4b^2c^2m^2 + 4bm^2c = 0$$
$$-4abc^2 + 4ac + 4bm^2c = 0$$
$$4bm^2c = 4abc^2 - 4ac$$

$m^2 = \dfrac{4abc^2 - 4ac}{4bc}$ dividing each term by $4c$

$m^2 = \dfrac{abc - a}{b}$ Proved

1 c $y = 2x^3 - 1$

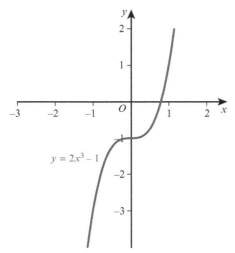

The graph represents a function. As each value of the domain has one value for the range and vice versa, $y = 2x^3 - 1$ is a one-one function.

h $y^2 = 4x$

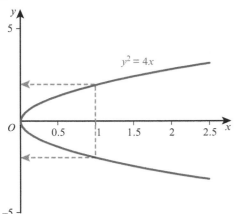

The graph does not represent a function as each input value has two output values.

If we draw all possible vertical lines on a graph, the graph is:

- a function if each line cuts the graph no more than once
- not a function if one line cuts the graph more than once.

2 a

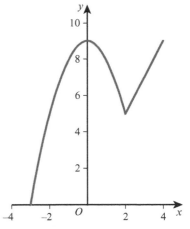

b This is a many-one function.

Only one-one and many-one **relations** are called **functions**. A many-one function has one output value for each input value but each output value can have more than one input value.

3 a

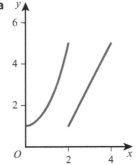

b The graph does not represent a function. It represents a many-many relation because when $x = 2$, there are two possible values for y.

Similarly when $y = 3$ (for example), there are two possible values for x.

> Reminder: the **domain** is the set of **input** values and the **range** is the set of **output** values for a function. Always use **set notation** to describe them.

4 a domain: $x \in \mathbb{R}$ for $-1 \leqslant x \leqslant 5$
range: $f(x) \in \mathbb{R}$ for $-8 \leqslant f(x) \leqslant 8$

b domain: $x \in \mathbb{R}$ for $-3 \leqslant x \leqslant 2$
range: $f(x) \in \mathbb{R}$ for $-7 \leqslant f(x) \leqslant 20$

5 a $f(x) = x + 4$ for $x > 8$ is represented by a continuous linear graph with a positive gradient.

Substituting $x = 8$ into the function gives $f(x) = 12$.

Since the domain is $x > 8$, the range is $f(x) > 12$.

e $f(x) = 2^x$ is represented by an increasing, continuous, exponential graph.

Substituting $x = -5$ gives $f(x) = \dfrac{1}{32}$

Substituting $x = 4$ gives $f(x) = 16$

Solution: $\dfrac{1}{32} \leqslant f(x) \leqslant 16$

> To determine the range of a function, it is often helpful to sketch its graph in the given domain, as Question 6 shows.

---

6 c The graph of $f(x) = 3 - 2x^2$ for $x \leqslant 2$ is a $\cap$ shaped parabola. Its sketch looks like this:

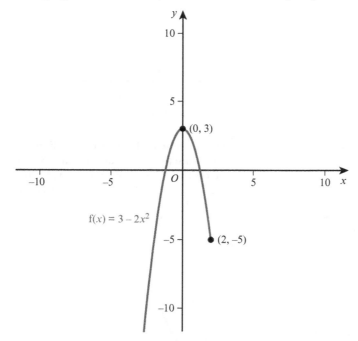

The maximum value is $f(x) = 3$ (when $x = 0$).

There is no minimum value for this domain.

Solution is $f(x) \leqslant 3$.

When finding the range of a linear graph,
e.g. $f(x) = 2x + 1$, $x \in \mathbb{R}$ and $-1 \leqslant x \leqslant 2$, we
only need to substitute $x = -1$ and $x = 2$ into
$f(x) = 2x + 1$.
This gives the range as: $-1 \leqslant f(x) \leqslant 5$.
However, for quadratic graphs, we need to think
about the position of the vertex when we are
finding the range.
e.g. If $f(x) = (x - 1)^2 - 4$, $-3 \leqslant x \leqslant 4$
Substituting $x = -3$ into $f(x) = (x - 1)^2 - 4$ gives
$f(x) = 12$
Substituting $x = 4$ into $f(x) = (x - 1)^2 - 4$ gives
$f(x) = 5$

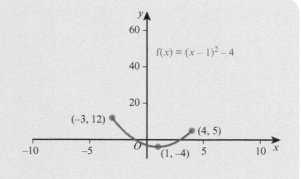

But the range is not $5 \leqslant x \leqslant 12$ because the vertex (lowest point) on the graph is at $(1, -4)$ and so the
minimum value of $f(x)$ is -4.
The range is therefore $-4 \leqslant x \leqslant 12$.

7 **c** The graph of $f : x \mapsto 8 - (x - 5)^2$ for
$4 \leqslant x \leqslant 10$ is an $\cap$ shaped parabola.

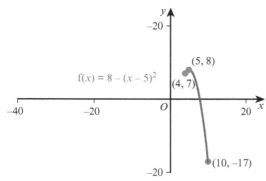

For this domain the maximum value of
$f(x)$ is found by substituting $x = 5$ into
$f(x) = 8 - (x - 5)^2$ (since $x = 5$ is the vertex):
$f(5) = 8 - (5 - 5)^2$
$f(5) = 8$

The minimum value of $f(x)$ is found by
substituting $x = 10$ into $f(x) = 8 - (x - 5)^2$
$f(10) = 8 - (10 - 5)^2$
$f(10) = -17$
Solution is $-17 \leqslant f(x) \leqslant 8$

8 **a** $f(x) = x^2 + 6x - 11$
$f(x) = (x + 3)^2 - 20$

The graph of $f(x) = x^2 + 6x - 11$ is a
$\cup$ shaped parabola.

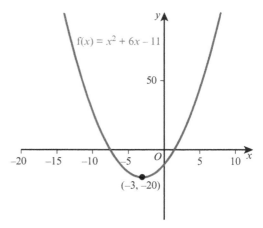

The vertex is at $(-3, -20)$.
The range of the function is $f(x) \geqslant -20$.

Reminder: for a quadratic function of the
form:
$f(x) = ax^2 + bx + c$
the function is a $\cup$ shaped parabola if $a > 0$
and an $\cap$ shaped parabola if $a < 0$.

b $f(x) = 3\left[\left(x - \dfrac{10}{6}\right)^2 - \dfrac{100}{36}\right] + 2$

$f(x) = 3\left(x - \dfrac{10}{6}\right)^2 - \dfrac{100}{12} + 2$

$f(x) = 3\left(x - \dfrac{5}{3}\right)^2 - \dfrac{19}{3}$

The graph of $f(x) = 3\left(x - \dfrac{5}{3}\right)^2 - \dfrac{19}{3}$ is a $\cup$ shaped parabola.

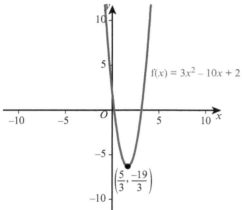

The vertex (minimum point) is at $\left(\dfrac{5}{3}, -\dfrac{19}{3}\right)$

The range of the function is $f(x) \geqslant -6\dfrac{1}{3}$.

9 a $f(x) = 7 - 8x - x^2$
$f(x) = 7 - (x^2 + 8x)$
$f(x) = 7 - [(x+4)^2 - 16]$
$f(x) = 23 - (x+4)^2$
The graph of $f(x) = 23 - (x+4)^2$ is an $\cap$ shaped parabola.

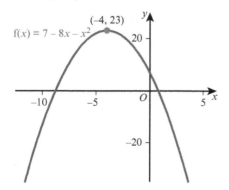

The vertex (maximum point) is at $(-4, 23)$
The range of the function is $f(x) \leqslant 23$.

b $f(x) = 2 - 6x - 3x^2$
$f(x) = 2 - (3x^2 + 6x)$
$f(x) = 2 - 3(x^2 + 2x)$
$f(x) = 2 - 3[(x+1)^2 - 1]$
$f(x) = 5 - 3(x+1)^2$
The graph of $f(x) = 5 - 3(x+1)^2$ is an $\cap$ shaped parabola.
We know this because the coefficient of x^2 is negative.
The vertex (maximum point) is at $(-1, 5)$.
The range of the function is $f(x) \leqslant 5$.

11 $f : x \mapsto x^2 + 6x + k$
$f : x \mapsto (x+3)^2 - 3^2 + k$
$f : x \mapsto (x+3)^2 + (k-9)$
The graph of $f : x \mapsto (x+3)^2 + (k-9)$ is a $\cup$ shaped parabola.
We know this because the coefficient of x^2 is positive.
The vertex (minimum point) is at $(-3, (k-9))$.
The range of the function is $f(x) \geqslant k-9$.

12 $g : x \mapsto 5 - ax - 2x^2$
$g : x \mapsto 5 - (2x^2 + ax)$
$g : x \mapsto 5 - 2\left(x^2 + \dfrac{a}{2}x\right)$
$g : x \mapsto 5 - 2\left[\left(x + \dfrac{a}{4}\right)^2 - \dfrac{a^2}{16}\right]$
$g : x \mapsto 5 - 2\left(x + \dfrac{a}{4}\right)^2 + \dfrac{a^2}{8}$
$g : x \mapsto \left(\dfrac{a^2}{8} + 5\right) - 2\left(x + \dfrac{a}{4}\right)^2$
The graph of $g : x \mapsto \left(\dfrac{a^2}{8} + 5\right) - 2\left(x + \dfrac{a}{4}\right)^2$ is an $\cap$ shaped parabola.
We know this because the coefficient of x^2 in $g : x \mapsto 5 - ax - 2x^2$ is negative.
The vertex (maximum point) is at $\left(-\dfrac{a}{4}, \dfrac{a^2}{8} + 5\right)$.
The range of the function is $g(x) \leqslant \dfrac{a^2}{8} + 5$.

4

13 Given: $f(x) = x^2 - 2x - 3 \ x \in \mathbb{R}$ for $-4 \leqslant f(x) \leqslant 5$
$f(x) = x^2 - 2x - 3$
$f(x) = -4$
Solving $x^2 - 2x - 3 = -4$ gives:
$x^2 - 2x + 1 = 0$
$\quad (x-1)^2 = 0$
$\qquad\qquad x = 1$

The minimum point for this domain is $(1, -4)$.
$f(x) = x^2 - 2x - 3$
$f(x) = 5$
Solving $x^2 - 2x - 3 = 5$ gives:
$x^2 - 2x - 8 = 0$
$(x - 4)(x + 2) = 0$
$x = 4$ or $x = -2$

The maximum points for this domain are $(4, 5)$ and $(-2, 5)$.

A graph of $y = x^2 - 2x - 3$ with these results is shown.

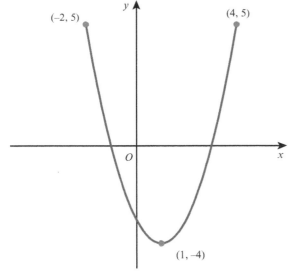

We are required to find the value of a for this graph such that $-a \leqslant x \leqslant a$.

Summarising:
$a = 2$ since $-a \leqslant x \leqslant a$ gives $-2 \leqslant x \leqslant 2$
$[a \neq 4$ since $-4 \leqslant x \leqslant 4$ gives the range $5 \leqslant f(x) \leqslant 21]$
Solution is $a = 2$

14 $f(x) = x^2 + x - 4 \qquad$ for $a \leqslant x \leqslant a + 3$
$\qquad\qquad\qquad\qquad$ so $-2 \leqslant f(x) \leqslant 16$
$f(x) = x^2 + x - 4$
$f(x) = -2$
Solving $x^2 + x - 4 = -2$ gives
$x^2 + x - 2 = 0$
$(x + 2)(x - 1) = 0$
$x = -2$ or $x = 1$

So the minimum points for this domain are at $(-2, -2)$ and $(1, -2)$
$f(x) = x^2 + x - 4$
$f(x) = 16$
Solving $x^2 + x - 4 = 16$ gives
$x^2 + x - 20 = 0$
$(x + 5)(x - 4) = 0$
$x = -5$ or $x = 4$

So the maximum points for this domain are at $(-5, 16)$ and $(4, 16)$.

A graph of $y = x^2 + x - 4$ with these results is shown.

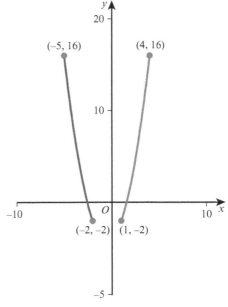

Summarising:
$\quad a \leqslant x \leqslant a + 3$
$\quad 1 \leqslant x \leqslant 4$
$-5 \leqslant x \leqslant -2$
Solution is $a = 1$ or $a = -5$.

15 a $f(x) = 2x^2 - 8x + 5$

$f(x) = 2(x^2 - 4x) + 5$

$f(x) = 2[(x - 2)^2 - 2^2] + 5$

$f(x) = 2(x - 2)^2 - 8 + 5$

$f(x) = 2(x - 2)^2 - 3$

The graph of $f(x) = 2(x - 2)^2 - 3$ is a $\cup$ shaped parabola because the coefficient of x^2 is positive.

The vertex (lowest point) is at $(2, -3)$

b $x = 2$ is a line of symmetry for the graph of $f(x) = 2x^2 - 8x + 5$ $x \in \mathbb{R}$ (without domain restrictions).

So, if $f(x) = 2x^2 - 8x + 5$ and $0 \leqslant x \leqslant k$ then $k = 4$.

c If $k = 4$ then substituting $x = 4$ into

$f(x) = 2x^2 - 8x + 5$

gives $f(4) = 2(4)^2 - 8(4) + 5$

So, $f(4) = 5$ and as the vertex is when $f(2) = -3$, the range is $-3 \leqslant x \leqslant 5$.

16 b $f(x) = x^2 + 2$ is a $\cup$ shaped parabola.

There are no restrictions on the domain so $x \in \mathbb{R}$

$f(x) = x^2 + 2$ has a vertex (lowest point) at $(0, 2)$

Range: $f(x) \in \mathbb{R}$, $f(x) \geqslant 2$.

e $f(x) = \dfrac{1}{x - 2}$

x can take any value except $x = 2$. (If $x = 2$, then $f(x) = \dfrac{1}{2 - 2}$ and this fraction is undefined.)

So, the domain is $x \in \mathbb{R}$, $x \neq 2$

The graph of $f(x) = \dfrac{1}{x - 2}$ is a hyperbola.

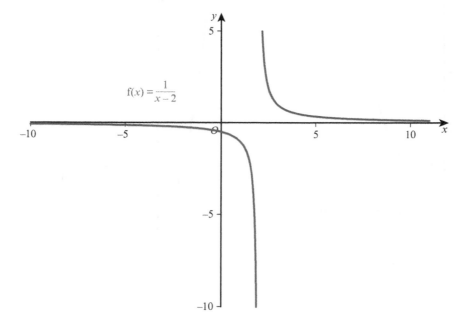

As x becomes very large and positive, then the value of f(x) approaches zero (but never actually equals zero).

As x becomes very large and negative then the value of f(x) approaches zero (but never actually equals zero).

So the range is f(x) $\in \mathbb{R}$, f(x) $\neq 0$

EXERCISE 2B

1 a $fg(6) = f\left(\sqrt{6+3} - 2\right)$

$fg(6) = f(1)$

$= 1^2 + 6$

$= 7$

> There is an equally valid alternative method which is to find the composite function fg(x) first and then substitute $x = 6$. Since the question does not ask you to do this, there is no need to do so.

2 b h : $x \mapsto x + 5$ for $x \in \mathbb{R}$, $x > 0$ (the function 'add 5')

k : $x \mapsto \sqrt{x}$ for $x \in \mathbb{R}$, $x > 0$ (square root x)

So, $x \mapsto \sqrt{x + 5}$ is the function 'first do h, then do k'

i.e. kh

> Remember for two functions, f and g, the composite function fg only exists if the range of g is contained within the domain of f.

3 a f(x) $= ax + b$

Substituting $x = 5$ and f(5) $= 3$ gives:

$3 = 5a + b$ ....[1]

Substituting $x = 3$ and f(3) $= -3$ gives:

$-3 = 3a + b$ ....[2]

Subtracting [2] from [1] gives:

$6 = 2a$ so $a = 3$

Substituting $a = 3$ into [1] gives:

$3 = 15 + b$ so $b = -12$

Solution is $a = 3$ and $b = -12$.

b $ff(x) = f(3x - 12)$

$= 3(3x - 12) - 12$

$= 9x - 48$

$9x - 48 = 4$

$x = 5\dfrac{7}{9}$

4 a $gf(x) = g(2x + 3)$

$= \dfrac{12}{1 - (2x + 3)}$

$= \dfrac{12}{-2 - 2x}$

$= -\dfrac{6}{x + 1}$

b $-\dfrac{6}{x + 1} = 2$

$-6 = 2x + 2$

$x = -4$

7 $hg(x) = h\left(\dfrac{2}{x + 1}\right)$

$= \left(\dfrac{2}{x + 1} + 2\right)^2 - 5$

$= \left(\dfrac{2x + 4}{x + 1}\right)^2 - 5$

$11 = \left(\dfrac{2x + 4}{x + 1}\right)^2 - 5$

$\left(\dfrac{2x + 4}{x + 1}\right)^2 = 16$

$\dfrac{2x + 4}{x + 1} = \pm 4$

$2x + 4 = 4(x + 1)$ or $2x + 4 = -4(x + 1)$

$x = 0$ or $x = -\dfrac{4}{3}$

8 $\text{gf}(x) = \text{g}\left(\dfrac{x+1}{2}\right)$

$$= \dfrac{2\left(\dfrac{x+1}{2}\right) + 3}{\left(\dfrac{x+1}{2}\right) - 1}$$

$$1 = \dfrac{2\left(\dfrac{x+1}{2}\right) + 3}{\left(\dfrac{x+1}{2}\right) - 1}$$

$$\left(\dfrac{x+1}{2}\right) - 1 = 2\left(\dfrac{x+1}{2}\right) + 3$$

Multiplying both sides by 2 gives:

$$(x+1) - 2 = 2(x+1) + 6$$
$$x - 1 = 2x + 2 + 6$$
$$x - 1 = 2x + 8$$
$$x = -9$$

9 $\text{ff}(x) = \text{f}\left(\dfrac{x+1}{2x+5}\right)$

$$= \dfrac{\dfrac{x+1}{2x+5} + 1}{2\left(\dfrac{x+1}{2x+5}\right) + 5}$$

Multiplying numerator and denominator by $(2x+5)$ gives:

$$= \dfrac{x+1+1(2x+5)}{2(x+1) + 5(2x+5)}$$

$$= \dfrac{3x+6}{12x+27}$$

$$= \dfrac{x+2}{4x+9}$$

10 a $\text{fg}(x) = \text{f}(x+1)$
$$= (x+1)^2$$
   Answer is fg

e $x^2 + 2x + 2$ can be rewritten as $x^2 + 2x + 1 + 1$
   or $(x+1)^2 + 1$
   As $\text{fg}(x) = (x+1)^2$ so:
$$\text{gfg}(x) = \text{g}(x+1)^2$$
$$= (x+1)^2 + 1$$
   Answer is gfg

11 $\text{gf}(x) = \text{g}(x^2 - 3x)$
$$= 2(x^2 - 3x) + 5$$
$$2(x^2 - 3x) + 5 = 0$$
$$2x^2 - 6x + 5 = 0$$

This does not factorise. Using the quadratic formula:

$a = 2, b = -6, c = 5$

$$x = \dfrac{--6 \pm \sqrt{(-6)^2 - 4(2)(5)}}{2(2)}$$

$$x = \dfrac{6 \pm \sqrt{-4}}{4}$$

As $b^2 - 4ac < 0$, there are no real solutions to the equation.

12 $\text{fg}(x) = \text{f}\left(\dfrac{2}{x}\right)$

$$= k - 2\left(\dfrac{2}{x}\right)$$

If $x = k - 2\left(\dfrac{2}{x}\right)$ then:

$x^2 = kx - 4$ or $x^2 - kx + 4 = 0$

For two equal roots, $b^2 - 4ac = 0$

$a = 1, b = -k, c = 4$, so:

$$(-k)^2 - 4(1)(4) = 0$$
$$k^2 - 16 = 0$$

So, $k = -4$ and $k = 4$.

14 $\text{ff}(x) = \text{f}\left(\dfrac{x+5}{2x-1}\right)$

$$= \dfrac{\dfrac{x+5}{2x-1} + 5}{2\left(\dfrac{x+5}{2x-1}\right) - 1}$$

Multiplying numerator and denominator by $(2x-1)$ gives:

$$= \dfrac{x+5+5(2x-1)}{2(x+5) - 1(2x-1)}$$

$$= \dfrac{11x}{11}$$

$$= x \qquad \text{Proved}$$

15 a $f(x) = 2x^2 + 4x - 8$

$\qquad = 2(x^2 + 2x) - 8$

$\qquad = 2[(x+1)^2 - 1^2] - 8$

$\qquad = 2(x+1)^2 - 10$

b The graph of $f(x) = 2(x+1)^2 - 10$ is a $\cup$ shaped parabola.

We know this because the coefficient of x^2 in $f(x) = 2x^2 + 4x - 8$ is positive.

Its vertex is at $(-1, -10)$.

A one-one function has one output value for each input value and vice versa.

Values of k for which the function is one-one are $k \geqslant -1$.

The least value of $k = -1$.

16 a $f(x) = x^2 - 2x + 4$

$\qquad x^2 - 2x + 4 \geqslant 7$

$\qquad x^2 - 2x - 3 \geqslant 0$

$\qquad (x-3)(x+1) \geqslant 0$

A graph of $y = (x-3)(x+1)$ is a $\cup$ shaped parabola.

The x-intercepts are at $x = 3$ and $x = -1$.

We want $x^2 - 2x + 4 \geqslant 7$ which is the part of the graph above and on the x-axis.

So, $x \geqslant 3$ or $x \leqslant -1$.

b $x^2 - 2x + 4 = (x-1)^2 - 1^2 + 4$

$\qquad\qquad\qquad = (x-1)^2 + 3$

c The graph of $f(x) = (x-1)^2 + 3$ is a $\cup$ shaped parabola.

The vertex (lowest point) of the graph is at $(1, 3)$.

The range of f is $f(x) \geqslant 3$.

18 a $ff(x) = f\left(\dfrac{2}{x+1}\right)$

$\qquad = \dfrac{2}{\dfrac{2}{x+1} + 1}$

Multiplying numerator and denominator by $(x+1)$:

$\qquad = \dfrac{2(x+1)}{2 + (x+1)}$

$ff(x) = \dfrac{2(x+1)}{x+3}$ $\quad x \in \mathbb{R},\ x \neq -3$

b $\dfrac{2}{x+1} = \dfrac{2(x+1)}{x+3}$

Multiplying both sides by $(x+1)(x+3)$:

$2(x+3) = 2(x+1)(x+1)$

$\quad 2x + 6 = 2(x^2 + 2x + 1)$

Dividing both sides by 2 gives:

$\qquad x + 3 = x^2 + 2x + 1$

$\quad x^2 + x - 2 = 0$ Shown.

c $x^2 + x - 2 = 0$ which when factorised is:

$(x+2)(x-1) = 0$

$x = -2$ or $x = 1$

19 a $\qquad f(x) = x^2 + 4x + 3$ can be written as:

$\qquad f(x) = (x+2)^2 - 2^2 + 3$ or

$\qquad f(x) = (x+2)^2 - 1$

As $\quad PQ(x) = P(x+2)$

$\qquad PQ(x) = (x+2)^2 - 1$

So, $\qquad f(x) = PQ(x)$

$PQ(x)$ exists because the range of Q is contained within the domain of P.

Answer is $PQ(x)$

Domain is $x \in \mathbb{R}$

Range is $f(x) \in \mathbb{R}$, and $f(x) \geqslant -1$

> Always test whether a composite function exists before giving your answer.

b $\qquad f(x) = x^2 + 1$

$\qquad QP(x) = Q(x^2 - 1)$

$\qquad\qquad\quad = (x^2 - 1) + 2$

$\qquad\qquad\quad = x^2 + 1$

So, $\quad f(x) = QP(x)$

Answer is $QP(x)$

Domain is $x \in \mathbb{R}$

Range is $f(x) \in \mathbb{R}$ and $f(x) \geqslant 1$

c $\qquad f(x) = x$

$\qquad RR(x) = R\left(\dfrac{1}{x}\right)$

$\qquad\qquad = \dfrac{1}{\dfrac{1}{x}}$

$\qquad\qquad = x$

So, $f(x) = RR(x)$

Answer is $RR(x)$

Domain is $x \in \mathbb{R}, x \neq 0$

Range is $f(x) \in \mathbb{R}, f(x) \neq 0$

> The **domain** of a composite function is either the same as the domain of the FIRST function or lies inside it.
> The **range** of a composite function is either the same as the range of the SECOND function or lies inside it.

d $f(x) = \dfrac{1}{x^2} + 1$

$$QPR(x) = QP\left(\dfrac{1}{x}\right)$$

$$= Q\left(\dfrac{1}{x^2} - 1\right)$$

$$= \dfrac{1}{x^2} - 1 + 2$$

$$= \dfrac{1}{x^2} + 1$$

So, $f(x) = QPR(x)$

Answer is $QPR(x)$

Domain is $x \in \mathbb{R}, x \neq 0$

Range is $f(x) \in \mathbb{R}, f(x) > 1$

e $f(x) = \dfrac{1}{x+4}$

$$RQQ(x) = RQ(x+2)$$

$$= R(x+2+2)$$

$$= R(x+4)$$

$$= \dfrac{1}{x+4}$$

$f(x) = RQQ(x)$

Answer is $RQQ(x)$

Domain is $x \in \mathbb{R}, x \neq -4$

Range is $f(x) \in \mathbb{R}, f(x) \neq 0$

f $f(x) = x - 2\sqrt{x+1} + 1$

$$PS(x) = P\left(\sqrt{x+1} - 1\right)$$

$$= \left(\sqrt{x+1} - 1\right)^2 - 1$$

$$= x + 1 - 2\sqrt{x+1} + 1 - 1$$

$$= x - 2\sqrt{x+1} + 1$$

So, $f(x) = PS(x)$

Answer is $PS(x)$

Domain is $x \in \mathbb{R}, x \geqslant -1$

Range is $f(x) \in \mathbb{R}, f(x) \geqslant -1$

g $f(x) = x - 1$

$$SP(x) = S(x^2 - 1)$$

$$= \sqrt{x^2 - 1 + 1} - 1$$

$$= \sqrt{x^2} - 1 \quad \left(\text{take the } +\sqrt{}\right)$$

$$= x - 1$$

So, $f(x) = SP(x)$

Answer is $SP(x)$

Domain is $x \in \mathbb{R}, x \geqslant -1$

Range is $f(x) \in \mathbb{R}, f(x) \geqslant -1$

1 **b** $f(x) = x^2 + 3$ for $x \in \mathbb{R}, x \geqslant 0$

$$y = x^2 + 3$$

$$x = y^2 + 3$$

$$y^2 = x - 3$$

$$y = \sqrt{x - 3}$$

$$f^{-1}(x) = \sqrt{x - 3}$$

e $f(x) = \dfrac{x+7}{x+2}$

$$y = \dfrac{x+7}{x+2}$$

$$x = \dfrac{y+7}{y+2}$$

$x(y+2) = y+7$

$xy + 2x = y+7$

$xy - y = 7 - 2x$

$y(x-1) = 7 - 2x$

$y = \dfrac{7-2x}{x-1}$

$f^{-1}(x) = \dfrac{7-2x}{x-1}$

2 a $f: x \mapsto x^2 + 4x \qquad x \in \mathbb{R},\ x \geqslant -2$

$f: x \mapsto (x+2)^2 - 4$

The graph of this function is a $\cup$ shaped parabola.

The vertex (lowest point) of the graph is at $(-2, -4)$.

The range of $f(x)$ is $f(x) \geqslant -4$.

The domain of $f^{-1}(x)$ is the same as the range of $f(x)$.

i.e. $x \geqslant -4$

Range of $f^{-1}(x)$ is the same as the domain of $f(x)$

So the range is $f^{-1}(x) \geqslant -2$.

> - It is not necessary to find the inverse function before stating its domain and range.
>   The domain of $f^{-1}(x)$ is the range of $f(x)$.
>   The range of $f^{-1}(x)$ is the domain of $f(x)$.
> - An inverse function $f^{-1}(x)$ can exist if, and only if, the function $f(x)$ is a one-one mapping.

b $f: x \mapsto x^2 + 4x$

$y = x^2 + 4x$

$x = y^2 + 4y$

Complete the square of the right-hand side:

$x = (y+2)^2 - 4$

$(y+2)^2 = x+4$

$y+2 = \sqrt{x+4}$

$y = -2 + \sqrt{x+4}$

$f^{-1}(x) = -2 + \sqrt{x+4}$

(Take the positive root here as the domain of the inverse is $x \geqslant -4$).

3 a $f: x \mapsto \dfrac{5}{2x+1}$

$y = \dfrac{5}{2x+1}$

$x = \dfrac{5}{2y+1}$

$x(2y+1) = 5$

$2xy + x = 5$

$2xy = 5 - x$

$y = \dfrac{5-x}{2x}$

$f^{-1}(x) = \dfrac{5-x}{2x}$

b The domain of f^{-1} is the same as the range of $f: x.$ i.e. $x \leqslant 1.$

5 a $g: x \mapsto 2x^2 - 8x + 10$

$y = 2x^2 - 8x + 10$

$y = 2(x^2 - 4x) + 10$

$y = 2[(x-2)^2 - 2^2] + 10$

$y = 2(x-2)^2 - 8 + 10$

$y = 2(x-2)^2 + 2$

The graph of $y = 2(x-2)^2 + 2$ is a $\cup$ shaped parabola.

The vertex (lowest point) of the graph is at $(2, 2)$.

The function $g: x \mapsto 2x^2 - 8x + 10$ for $x \in \mathbb{R},\ x \geqslant 3$, is a one-one function for this domain, and therefore it has an inverse.

b $y = 2(x-2)^2 + 2$

$x = 2(y-2)^2 + 2$

$\dfrac{x-2}{2} = (y-2)^2$

$\sqrt{\dfrac{x-2}{2}} = y - 2$ we take the positive root here as the domain of the inverse is $x \geqslant 3$

$y = 2 + \sqrt{\dfrac{x-2}{2}}$

$g^{-1}(x) = 2 + \sqrt{\dfrac{x-2}{2}}$

6 a $f : x \mapsto 2x^2 + 12x - 14$ this can be written as:

$$y = 2(x + 3)^2 - 32$$

The graph for this function is a $\cup$ shaped parabola.

The vertex (lowest point) of the graph is at $(-3, -32)$.

If $f : x \mapsto 2x^2 + 12x - 14$ is a one-one function, then, its inverse $f^{-1}(x)$ should also be a function.

So we have to restrict the domain of $f : x \mapsto 2x^2 + 12x - 14$ $x \in \mathbb{R},\ x \geqslant k$ becomes:

$f : x \mapsto 2x^2 + 12x - 14$ $x \in \mathbb{R},\ x \geqslant -3$

The least value of k is -3

b
$$y = 2x^2 + 12x - 14$$
$$x = 2y^2 + 12y - 14$$
$$x = 2(y^2 + 6y) - 14$$
$$x = 2[(y + 3)^2 - 3^2] - 14$$
$$x = 2(y + 3)^2 - 32$$
$$2(y + 3)^2 = x + 32$$
$$(y + 3)^2 = \frac{x + 32}{2}$$

$y + 3 = \sqrt{\dfrac{x + 32}{2}}$ we take the positive root as the domain of the inverse is $x \geqslant -32$

$$y = -3 + \sqrt{\frac{x + 32}{2}}$$

$$f^{-1}(x) = -3 + \sqrt{\frac{x + 32}{2}}$$

8 a $f(x) = 9 - (x - 3)^2$ for $x \in \mathbb{R}$ for $k \leqslant x \leqslant 7$

The graph of $f(x) = 9 - (x - 3)^2$ $x \in \mathbb{R}$ is an $\cap$ shaped parabola.

We know this because the coefficient of x^2 is negative.

The vertex is at $(3, 9)$. If $f(x) = 9 - (x - 3)^2$ is a one-one function then $k = 3$

b i
$$f(x) = 9 - (x - 3)^2$$
$$y = 9 - (x - 3)^2$$
$$x = 9 - (y - 3)^2$$
$$(y - 3)^2 = 9 - x$$
$$y - 3 = \sqrt{9 - x}$$
$$y = 3 + \sqrt{9 - x}$$

We take the positive root as the domain of the inverse is $x \leqslant 9$.

$$f^{-1}(x) = 3 + \sqrt{9 - x}$$

ii Domain of $f^{-1}(x)$ is the same as the range of $f(x)$ i.e. $x \leqslant 9$

The range is the same as the domain of $f(x)$ i.e. $3 \leqslant f^{-1}(x) \leqslant 7$.

9 a $f(x)$ is the inverse of $f^{-1}(x)$ only if they are both one-one functions.

$$f^{-1}(x) = \frac{5x - 1}{x}\ \ x \in \mathbb{R}\ \text{for}\ 0 < x \leqslant 3$$

$$y = \frac{5x - 1}{x}$$

$$x = \frac{5y - 1}{y}$$

$$xy = 5y - 1$$
$$5y - xy = 1$$
$$y(5 - x) = 1$$

$$y = \frac{1}{5 - x}$$

$$f(x) = \frac{1}{5 - x}$$

For $f(x)$ to exist, it needs to be one-one.

The range of $f^{-1}(x) = \dfrac{5x - 1}{x}$ is $f^{-1}(x) \leqslant \dfrac{14}{3}$

(This comes from substituting the values of the domain i.e. $0 < x \leqslant 3$ into $f^{-1}(x) = \dfrac{5x - 1}{x}$.)

b The domain of $f(x) = \dfrac{1}{5 - x}$ must be $x \leqslant \dfrac{14}{3}$

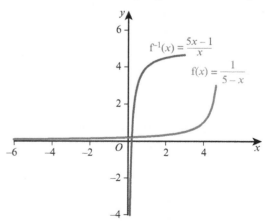

For one-one functions $f^{-1}(x)$ is a reflection of $f(x)$ in the line $y = x$.

10 $f(x) = 3x + a$

$gf(-1) = g(-3 + a)$

$\qquad = b - 5(-3 + a)$

$\qquad = b + 15 - 5a$

$2 = b + 15 - 5a$

$5a - b = 13 \ldots\ldots [1]$

Now find the inverse of $g(x)$

$g(x) = b - 5x$

$y = b - 5x$

$x = b - 5y$

$y = \dfrac{b - x}{5}$

$g^{-1}(x) = \dfrac{b - x}{5}$

$g^{-1}(7) = \dfrac{b - 7}{5}$

$1 = \dfrac{b - 7}{5}$

$b = 12$

Substitute for b in $[1]$ gives:

$5a - 12 = 13$

$a = 5$

Solution $a = 5, b = 12$

11 a $f(x) = 3x - 1$

$y = 3x - 1$

$x = 3y - 1$

$y = \dfrac{x + 1}{3}$

$f^{-1}(x) = \dfrac{x + 1}{3}$

$g(x) = \dfrac{3}{2x - 4}$

$y = \dfrac{3}{2x - 4}$

$x = \dfrac{3}{2y - 4}$

$x(2y - 4) = 3$

$2xy - 4x = 3$

$2xy = 4x + 3$

$y = \dfrac{4x + 3}{2x}$

$g^{-1}(x) = \dfrac{4x + 3}{2x}$

b $\dfrac{x + 1}{3} = \dfrac{4x + 3}{2x}$

$2x(x + 1) = 3(4x + 3)$

$2x^2 + 2x = 12x + 9$

$2x^2 - 10x - 9 = 0$

$a = 2, b = -10, c = -9$

For this equation to have two real roots,

$b^2 - 4ac \geqslant 0$

$b^2 - 4ac = (-10)^2 - 4(2)(-9)$

$\qquad = 172$

$172 \geqslant 0$

The equation has two real roots.

12 a $f : x \mapsto (2x - 1)^3 - 3 \ x \in \mathbb{R}$ for $1 \leqslant x \leqslant 3*$

$y = (2x - 1)^3 - 3$

$x = (2y - 1)^3 - 3$

$(2y - 1)^3 = x + 3$

$2y - 1 = \sqrt[3]{x + 3}$

$y = \dfrac{1 + \sqrt[3]{x + 3}}{2}$

$f^{-1}(x) = \dfrac{1 + \sqrt[3]{x + 3}}{2}$ or $\dfrac{1}{2}\left(1 + \sqrt[3]{x + 3}\right)$

b Domain of $f^{-1}(x)$ is the same as the range of $f(x)$.

Range of $f(x)$ is $-2 \leqslant f(x) \leqslant 122$ (from substituting the values of the domain* into $f(x)$).

Domain of $f(x)$ is $-2 \leqslant x \leqslant 122$

14 a $f(x) = \dfrac{1}{x - 1}$

$y = \dfrac{1}{x - 1}$

$x = \dfrac{1}{y - 1}$

$x(y - 1) = 1$

$xy - x = 1$

$xy = x + 1$

$y = \dfrac{x + 1}{x}$

$f^{-1}(x) = \dfrac{x + 1}{x}$

b $f(x) = f^{-1}(x)$

$\dfrac{1}{x - 1} = \dfrac{x + 1}{x}$

$x = (x + 1)(x - 1)$

$x = x^2 - 1$

$x^2 - x - 1 = 0$ shown

c Solve $x^2 - x - 1 = 0$

Using the quadratic formula

$a = 1, b = -1, c = -1$

$$x = \frac{--1 \pm \sqrt{(-1)^2 - 4(1)(-1)}}{2(1)}$$

$$x = \frac{1 \pm \sqrt{5}}{2}$$

15 a $f(x) = \dfrac{1}{3 - x}$

$$y = \frac{1}{3 - x}$$

$$x = \frac{1}{3 - y}$$

$$x(3 - y) = 1$$

$$3x - xy = 1$$

$$xy = 3x - 1$$

$$y = \frac{3x - 1}{x}$$

$$f^{-1}(x) = \frac{3x - 1}{x}$$

$f(x) \neq f^{-1}(x)$ so, it is not a self-inverse function.

b $f(x) = \dfrac{2x + 1}{x - 2}$

$$y = \frac{2x + 1}{x - 2}$$

$$x = \frac{2y + 1}{y - 2}$$

$$x(y - 2) = 2y + 1$$

$$xy - 2x = 2y + 1$$

$$xy - 2y = 2x + 1$$

$$y(x - 2) = 2x + 1$$

$$y = \frac{2x + 1}{x - 2}$$

$$f^{-1}(x) = \frac{2x + 1}{x - 2}$$

$f(x) = f^{-1}(x)$ so, $f(x)$ is a self-inverse function.

c $f(x) = \dfrac{3x + 5}{4x - 3}$

$$y = \frac{3x + 5}{4x - 3}$$

$$x = \frac{3y + 5}{4y - 3}$$

$$x(4y - 3) = 3y + 5$$

$$4xy - 3x = 3y + 5$$

$$4xy - 3y = 3x + 5$$

$$y(4x - 3) = 3x + 5$$

$$y = \frac{3x + 5}{4x - 3}$$

$$f^{-1}(x) = \frac{3x + 5}{4x - 3}$$

$f(x) = f^{-1}(x)$ so, $f(x)$ is a self-inverse function.

16 a $\quad fg(x) = f(4 - 2x)$

$$fg(x) = 3(4 - 2x) - 5$$

$$fg(x) = 7 - 6x$$

Find $(fg)^{-1}(x)$.

$$y = 7 - 6x$$

$$x = 7 - 6y$$

$$y = \frac{7 - x}{6}$$

$$(fg)^{-1}(x) = \frac{7 - x}{6}$$

b i Find $f^{-1}(x)$

$$y = 3x - 5$$

$$x = 3y - 5$$

$$3y = x + 5$$

$$y = \frac{x + 5}{3}$$

$$f^{-1}(x) = \frac{x + 5}{3}$$

Find $g^{-1}(x)$

$$y = 4 - 2x$$

$$x = 4 - 2y$$

$$2y = 4 - x$$

$$y = \frac{4 - x}{2}$$

$$g^{-1}(x) = \frac{4 - x}{2}$$

$$f^{-1}g^{-1}(x) = f^{-1}\left(\frac{4 - x}{2}\right)$$

$$= \frac{\dfrac{4 - x}{2} + 5}{3}$$

Multiply numerator and denominator by 2:

$$f^{-1}g^{-1}(x) = \frac{4 - x + 10}{6}$$

$$f^{-1}g^{-1}(x) = \frac{14 - x}{6}$$

ii $g^{-1}f^{-1}(x) = g^{-1}\left(\dfrac{x+5}{3}\right)$

$= \dfrac{4 - \left(\dfrac{x+5}{3}\right)}{2}$

Multiply numerator and denominator by 3:

$g^{-1}f^{-1}(x) = \dfrac{12 - (x+5)}{6}$

$g^{-1}f^{-1}(x) = \dfrac{7-x}{6}$

c $(fg)^{-1}(x) = g^{-1}f^{-1}(x)$

This is always true assuming the inverses and composite functions exist and that there are no problems with domains and ranges.

EXERCISE 2D

1 d The function f shown is many-one. The inverse relation would be one-many which is not a function.

For a function f to have an inverse which is also a function f^{-1}, it has to be a one-one function.

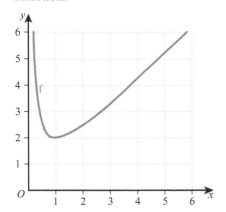

2 $f: x \mapsto 2x - 1$ for $x \in \mathbb{R}$ for $-1 \le x \le 3$

a $y = 2x - 1$
   $x = 2y - 1$
   $y = \dfrac{x+1}{2}$

$f^{-1}(x) = \dfrac{x+1}{2}$

b Substituting $x = -1$ into $f: x \mapsto 2x - 1$ gives -3.

Substituting $x = 3$ into $f: x \mapsto 2x - 1$ gives 5.

The domain of $f^{-1}(x)$ is $-3 \le x \le 5$.

The range is $-1 \le x \le 3$.

c

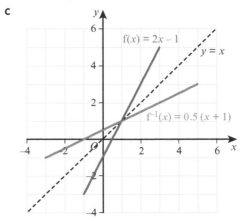

The graphs of $y = f(x)$ and $y = f^{-1}(x)$ are reflections of each other in the line $y = x$.

3 a The range of $f(x) = \dfrac{4}{x+2}$ is $0 < f(x) \le 2$

Since when $x = 0$, $f(x) = 2$ and as x becomes very large and positive, $f(x)$ approaches the value zero.

b $f(x) = \dfrac{4}{x+2}$

$y = \dfrac{4}{x+2}$

$x = \dfrac{4}{y+2}$

$x(y+2) = 4$

$xy + 2x = 4$

$xy = 4 - 2x$

$y = \dfrac{4-2x}{x}$

$f^{-1}(x) = \dfrac{4-2x}{x}$

c The domain of $f^{-1}(x)$ is the range of $f(x)$
i.e. $0 < x \leqslant 2$

The range of $f^{-1}(x)$ is the domain of $f(x)$
i.e. $f^{-1}(x) \geqslant 0$

d

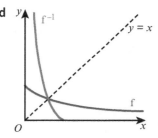

The graphs of $y = f(x)$ and $y = f^{-1}(x)$ are reflections of each other in the line $y = x$.

4 b $f(x) = \dfrac{2x-3}{x-5}$

$y = \dfrac{2x-3}{x-5}$

$x = \dfrac{2y-3}{y-5}$

$x(y-5) = 2y-3$

$xy - 5x = 2y - 3$

$xy - 2y = 5x - 3$

$y(x-2) = 5x - 3$

$y = \dfrac{5x-3}{x-2}$

$f^{-1}(x) = \dfrac{5x-3}{x-2}$

$f(x)$ is a not a self-inverse function. It is not therefore symmetrical about the line $y = x$.

c $f(x) = \dfrac{3x-1}{2x-3}$

$y = \dfrac{3x-1}{2x-3}$

$x = \dfrac{3y-1}{2y-3}$

$x(2y-3) = 3y-1$

$2xy - 3x = 3y - 1$

$2xy - 3y = 3x - 1$

$y(2x-3) = 3x-1$

$y = \dfrac{3x-1}{2x-3}$

$f^{-1}(x) = \dfrac{3x-1}{2x-3}$

$f(x)$ is a self-inverse function. It is therefore symmetrical about the line $y = x$.

5 a $f(x) = \dfrac{x+a}{bx-1}$

$y = \dfrac{x+a}{bx-1}$

$x = \dfrac{y+a}{by-1}$

$bxy - x = y + a$

$bxy - y = x + a$

$y(bx-1) = x + a$

$y = \dfrac{x+a}{bx-1}$

$f^{-1}(x) = \dfrac{x+a}{bx-1}$

As $f^{-1}(x) = f(x)$, the function is self-inverse.
Proved

b $g(x) = \dfrac{ax+b}{cx+d}$

$y = \dfrac{ax+b}{cx+d}$

$x = \dfrac{ay+b}{cy+d}$

$cxy + dx = ay + b$

$cxy - ay = b - dx$

$y(cx - a) = b - dx$

$y = \dfrac{b-dx}{cx-a}$

$f^{-1}(x) = \dfrac{-dx+b}{cx-a}$

Comparing $f^{-1}(x)$ with $f(x)$,
the function is self-inverse if $a = -d$.

EXERCISE 2E

1 b Given $y = 5\sqrt{x}$, $\begin{pmatrix} 0 \\ -2 \end{pmatrix}$ represents a translation 2 units down so we add on -2 to the function. The answer is:

$$y = 5\sqrt{x} - 2$$

e Given $y = \dfrac{2}{x}$, $\begin{pmatrix} -5 \\ 0 \end{pmatrix}$ represents a translation 5 units to the left so we replace x with $x + 5$. The answer is:

$$y = \dfrac{2}{x + 5}$$

h Given $y = 3x^2 - 2$, $\begin{pmatrix} 2 \\ 3 \end{pmatrix}$ represents a translation 3 units up so we add on 3 to the function and 2 units to the right so we replace x with $x - 2$.

$$y = 3(x - 2)^2 - 2 + 3$$

The answer is:

$$y = 3(x - 2)^2 + 1$$

2 b As $y = x^3 + 2x^2 + 1 - \mathbf{5}$ gives:

$$y = x^3 + 2x^2 - 4$$

This represents a translation $\begin{pmatrix} 0 \\ -5 \end{pmatrix}$.

d $y = x + \dfrac{6}{x}$

If we replace the x's by $x - 2$ we get:

$$y = (x - 2) + \dfrac{6}{(x - 2)}$$

Remove the brackets

$$y = x - 2 + \dfrac{6}{x - 2},$$

This represents a translation $\begin{pmatrix} 2 \\ 0 \end{pmatrix}$.

e $y = \sqrt{2x + 5}$

Rewrite both functions:

$y = \sqrt{2[x + 2.5]}$ is translated to $y = \sqrt{2[x + 1.5]}$,

If we replace x by $(x - 1)$ then

$y = \sqrt{2[(x - 1) + 2.5]}$ is translated to $y = \sqrt{2[x + 1.5]}$

This represents a translation $\begin{pmatrix} 1 \\ 0 \end{pmatrix}$.

3 a $y = f(x) - 4$

This is the translation $\begin{pmatrix} 0 \\ -4 \end{pmatrix}$.

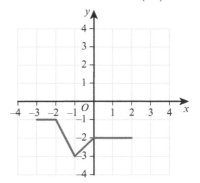

b $y = f(x - 2)$

This is the translation $\begin{pmatrix} 2 \\ 0 \end{pmatrix}$.

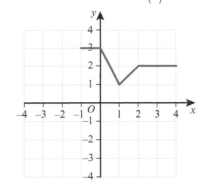

c $y = f(x + 1) - 5$

This is the translation $\begin{pmatrix} -1 \\ -5 \end{pmatrix}$.

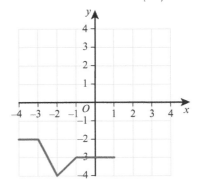

4 a

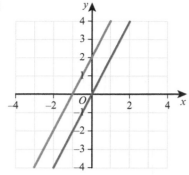

b '2' has been added at the end of the equation $y = 2x$ to give $y = 2x + 2$

The translation which represents this is $\begin{pmatrix} 0 \\ 2 \end{pmatrix}$.

So $a = 2$.

c Alternatively, replacing x by $(x + 1)$ in the equation $y = 2x$ gives $y = 2(x + 1)$ or $y = 2x + 2$

The translation which represents this is $\begin{pmatrix} -1 \\ 0 \end{pmatrix}$.

So $b = -1$.

5 $y = (x + 3)(x - 2)(x - 5)$

A translation of $\begin{pmatrix} 2 \\ 0 \end{pmatrix}$ means replacing all the x's in the above equation with $x - 2$
i.e. $y = (x - 2 + 3)(x - 2 - 2)(x - 2 - 5)$
Solution is $y = (x + 1)(x - 4)(x - 7)$

6 $y = x^2 - 4x + 1$ is translated by the vector $\begin{pmatrix} 1 \\ 2 \end{pmatrix}$.

A translation $\begin{pmatrix} 1 \\ 0 \end{pmatrix}$, means replacing all the x's in the above equation with $x - 1$

i.e. $y = (x - 1)^2 - 4(x - 1) + 1$

A translation $\begin{pmatrix} 0 \\ 2 \end{pmatrix}$ requires adding 2 to the function.

So, a translation by the vector $\begin{pmatrix} 1 \\ 2 \end{pmatrix}$ gives:

$y = (x - 1)^2 - 4(x - 1) + 1 + 2$

Expanding and rearranging gives:

$y = (x - 1)(x - 1) - 4x + 4 + 1 + 2$
$y = x^2 - 2x + 1 - 4x + 4 + 1 + 2$
$y = x^2 - 6x + 8$

7 The graph of $f(x) = ax^2 + bx + c$ is translated by the vector $\begin{pmatrix} 2 \\ -5 \end{pmatrix}$.

A translation by the vector $\begin{pmatrix} 2 \\ -5 \end{pmatrix}$, requires:

- Replacing all the x's in the above equation with $x - 2$

- Adding -5 to the resulting function

(These steps can be performed in either order. See Section 2.8)

$f(x) = a(x - 2)^2 + b(x - 2) + c - 5$

Expanding gives:

$f(x) = a(x^2 - 4x + 4) + bx - 2b + c - 5$
$f(x) = ax^2 - 4ax + 4a + bx - 2b + c - 5$
$f(x) = ax^2 - (4a - b)x + (4a - 2b + c - 5)$
$g(x) = 2x^2 - 11x + 10$

Comparing coefficients of $f(x)$ and $g(x)$:

$a = 2$

$4a - b = 11$

So substituting for a gives:

$8 - b = 11$ so $b = -3$

$4a - 2b + c - 5 = 10$

So substituting for a and b gives:

$8 + 6 + c - 5 = 10$ so $c = 1$

Solutions are $a = 2$, $b = -3$, $c = 1$

1 a $y=-g(x)$ is a reflection of $y=g(x)$ in the x-axis.

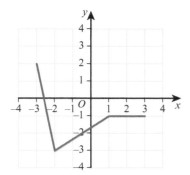

b $y=g(-x)$ is a reflection of $y=g(x)$ in the y-axis.

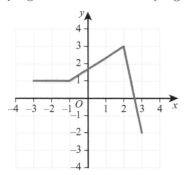

2 a $y=5x^2$ after reflection in the x-axis
i.e. $f(x)=-f(x)$
Multiply the right-hand side by -1
Solution is $y=-5x^2$

b $y=2x^4$ after reflection in the y-axis
i.e. $f(x)=f(-x)$
Replace all x's by $-x$
$y=2(-x)^4$
Solution is $y=2x^4$

c $y=2x^2-3x+1$ after reflection in the y-axis
i.e. $f(x)=f(-x)$
Replace all x's by $-x$
$y=2(-x)^2-3(-x)+1$
Solution is $y=2x^2+3x+1$

d $y=5+2x-3x^2$ after reflection in the x-axis
i.e. $f(x)=-f(x)$
Multiply the right-hand side by -1
$y=-1(5+2x-3x^2)$
Solution is $y=3x^2-2x-5$

3 a Given $y=x^2+7x-3$
Multiplying each term on the right-hand side by -1 gives:
$y=-x^2-7x+3$
The graph of $y=-f(x)$ is a reflection of the graph $y=f(x)$ in the x-axis.
Solution is reflection in the x-axis

b Given $y=x^2-3x+4$
Replacing each x by $-x$ gives:
$y=(-x)^2-3(-x)+4$ or:
$y=x^2+3x+4$
The graph of $y=f(-x)$ is a reflection of the graph $y=f(x)$ in the y-axis.
Solution is reflection in the y-axis

c Given $y=2x-5x^2$
Multiplying each term on the right-hand side by -1 gives:
$y=-2x+5x^2$ or $y=5x^2-2x$
The graph of $y=-f(x)$ is a reflection of the graph $y=f(x)$ in the x-axis.
Solution is reflection in the x-axis

d Given $y=x^3+2x^2-3x+1$
Multiplying each term on the right-hand side by -1 gives:
$y=-1(x^3+2x^2-3x+1)$
$y=-x^3-2x^2+3x-1$
The graph of $y=-f(x)$ is a reflection of the graph $y=f(x)$ in the x-axis.
Solution is reflection in the x-axis

1 a $y = 3f(x)$ is a stretch parallel to the y-axis stretch factor 3.

All y-coordinates for points on the original graph are multiplied by 3.

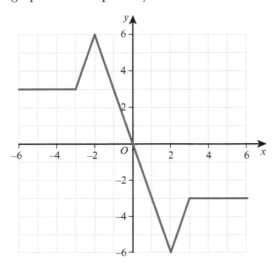

b $y = f(2x)$ is a stretch parallel to the x-axis stretch factor $\frac{1}{2}$.

All x-coordinates for points on the original graph are divided by 2.

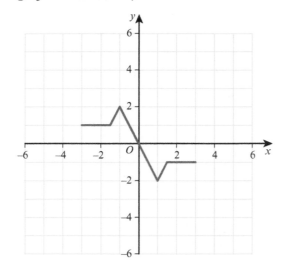

2 a $y = 3x^2$ after a stretch parallel to the y-axis with stretch factor 2.

All y-coordinates for points on the original graph are multiplied by 2.

i.e. $y = 2(3x^2)$

Solution is $y = 6x^2$

b $y = x^3 - 1$ after a stretch parallel to the y-axis with stretch factor 3.

All y-coordinates for points on the original graph are multiplied by 3.

i.e. $y = 3(x^3 - 1)$

Solution is $y = 3x^3 - 3$

c $y = 2^x + 4$ after a stretch parallel to the y-axis with stretch factor $\frac{1}{2}$.

All y-coordinates for points on the original graph are multiplied by $\frac{1}{2}$.

i.e. $y = \frac{1}{2}(2^x + 4)$ which is $2^{-1} \times 2^x + \frac{1}{2}(4)$

Solution is $y = 2^{x-1} + 2$

d $y = 2x^2 - 8x + 10$ after a stretch parallel to the x-axis with stretch factor 2.

All x-coordinates for points on the original graph are multiplied by $\frac{1}{2}$.

Replace all x's by $\frac{1}{2}x$

i.e. $y = 2\left(\frac{1}{2}x\right)^2 - 8\left(\frac{1}{2}x\right) + 10$

Solution is $y = \frac{1}{2}x^2 - 4x + 10$

e $y = 6x^3 - 36x$ after a stretch parallel to the x-axis with stretch factor $\frac{1}{3}$.

All x-coordinates for points on the original graph are multiplied by 3.

Replace all x's by $3x$

$y = 6(3x)^3 - 36(3x)$

Solution is $y = 162x^3 - 108x$

3 a $y = x^2 + 2x - 5$

Replacing x by $2x$ gives:

$y = (2x)^2 + 2(2x) - 5$ which is the same as:

$y = 4x^2 + 4x - 5$

Solution is a stretch parallel to the x-axis with stretch factor $\dfrac{1}{2}$.

b $y = x^2 - 3x + 2$

Multiplying each term in the right-hand side by 3 gives:

$y = 3(x^2 - 3x + 2)$

$y = 3x^2 - 9x + 6$

Solution is a stretch parallel to the y-axis with stretch factor 3.

c $y = 2^x + 1$ onto the graph $y = 2^{x+1} + 2$

Multiplying the right-hand side by 2 gives:

$y = 2(2^x + 1)$

$y = (2)2^x + 2(1)$ simplifying gives

$y = 2^{x+1} + 2$

> Be careful $(2)2^x$ is $2^1 \times 2^x$ or 2^{x+1} NOT 4^x

Solution is a stretch parallel to the y-axis with stretch factor 2.

d $y = \sqrt{x - 6}$

Replacing x by $3x$ gives: $y = \sqrt{3x - 6}$

Solution is a stretch parallel to the x-axis with stretch factor $\dfrac{1}{3}$

EXERCISE 2H

1 a $y = g(x + 2) + 3$ represents:

- one horizontal transformation i.e. translation $\begin{pmatrix} -2 \\ 0 \end{pmatrix}$

- one vertical transformation i.e. translation. $\begin{pmatrix} 0 \\ 3 \end{pmatrix}$

(The order is not important)

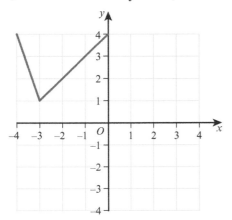

b $y = 2g(x) + 1$ represents two vertical transformations (the order is important):

- a stretch parallel to the y-axis with stretch factor 2 (All y-coordinates for points on the original graph are multiplied by 2.)

followed by

- a vertical translation $\begin{pmatrix} 0 \\ 1 \end{pmatrix}$ (add 1 to the new y-coordinates).

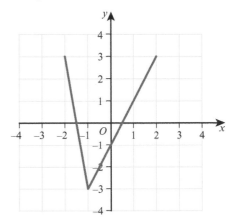

c $y = 2 - g(x)$ or $y = -g(x) + 2$ represents two vertical transformations (the order is important):

- a reflection in the x-axis i.e. $y = -g(x)$
- a translation $\begin{pmatrix} 0 \\ 2 \end{pmatrix}$ (add 2 to the new y-coordinates).

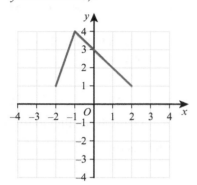

d $y = 2g(-x) + 1$ represents one horizontal transformation and two vertical transformations (their order is important):

- a reflection in the y-axis i.e. $y = g(-x)$
- a vertical stretch parallel to the y-axis with stretch factor 2 (all y-coordinates for points on the original graph are multiplied by 2)
- a vertical translation vector $\begin{pmatrix} 0 \\ 1 \end{pmatrix}$.

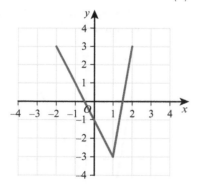

e $y = -2g(x) - 1$ represents three vertical transformations (the order is important):

- a vertical stretch parallel to the y-axis with stretch factor 2 (all y-coordinates

for points on the original graph are multiplied by 2)

- a reflection in the x-axis i.e. $y = -g(x)$
- a vertical translation vector $\begin{pmatrix} 0 \\ -1 \end{pmatrix}$ (add -1 to the new y-coordinates).

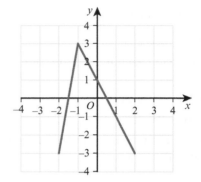

f $y = g(2x) + 3$ represents one horizontal transformation and one vertical transformation (the order is not important):

- a stretch parallel to the x-axis with stretch factor $\frac{1}{2}$ (all x-coordinates for points on the original graph are multiplied by $\frac{1}{2}$)
- a vertical translation vector $\begin{pmatrix} 0 \\ 3 \end{pmatrix}$ (add 3 to the new y-coordinates).

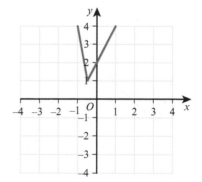

g $y = g(2x - 6)$ represents two horizontal transformations (the order is important):

- a horizontal translation $\begin{pmatrix} 6 \\ 0 \end{pmatrix}$ (replace x with $(x - 6)$)

- a stretch parallel to the x-axis with stretch factor $\frac{1}{2}$ (all x-coordinates for points on the original graph are multiplied by $\frac{1}{2}$).

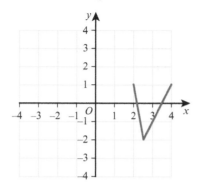

h $y = g(-x + 1)$ represents two horizontal transformations (the order is important):

- a horizontal translation $\begin{pmatrix} -1 \\ 0 \end{pmatrix}$ (replace x with $(x + 1)$.
- a reflection in the y-axis (replace x with $-x$).

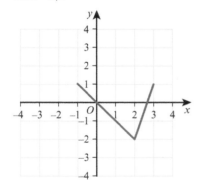

2 a The original graph has had one horizontal transformation and one vertical transformation (the order is not important):

- a reflection in the y-axis ($f(x) = f(-x)$)
- a vertical stretch parallel to the y-axis with stretch factor 2 (all y-coordinates have been multiplied by 2)

Solution is $y = 2f(-x)$

b The original graph has had two vertical transformations (the order is important):

- a reflection in the x-axis ($f(x) = -f(x)$)
- a translation by vector $\begin{pmatrix} 0 \\ 2 \end{pmatrix}$ (add 2 to the new y-coordinates)

Solution $y = -f(x) + 2$

c The original graph has had one horizontal transformation and two vertical transformations (their order is important):

- a translation by vector $\begin{pmatrix} 1 \\ 0 \end{pmatrix}$ (replace x with $x - 1$) i.e. $f(x) = f(x - 1)$
- vertically stretched parallel to the y-axis with stretch factor 2 (all y-coordinates have been multiplied by 2 i.e. $2f(x - 1)$)
- translated by vector $\begin{pmatrix} 0 \\ 1 \end{pmatrix}$ (add 1 to the new y-coordinates).

Solution $y = 2f(x - 1) + 1$

3 Given $y = x^2$

a a stretch in the y-direction with factor 3 gives $y = 3x^2$

followed by a translation by the vector $\begin{pmatrix} 1 \\ 0 \end{pmatrix}$ gives $y = 3(x - 1)^2$

b a translation by the vector $\begin{pmatrix} 1 \\ 0 \end{pmatrix}$ gives $y = (x - 1)^2$

followed by a stretch in the y-direction with factor 3 gives $y = 3(x - 1)^2$

4 Given $y = x^2$

a a stretch in the x-direction with factor 2 gives $y = \left(\frac{1}{2}x\right)^2$ or $y = \frac{1}{4}x^2$ (since x is replaced by $\frac{1}{2}x$)

followed by:

a translation by the vector $\begin{pmatrix} 5 \\ 0 \end{pmatrix}$ gives $y = \frac{1}{4}(x - 5)^2$ (since x is replaced by $x - 5$).

b a translation by the vector $\begin{pmatrix} 5 \\ 0 \end{pmatrix}$ gives

$y = (x - 5)^2$ (since x is replaced by $x - 5$)

followed by:

a stretch in the x-direction with factor 2 gives

$y = \left(\dfrac{1}{2}x - 5\right)^2$ (since x is replaced by $\dfrac{1}{2}x$)

c

5 Given $f(x) = x^2 + 1$

a a translation $\begin{pmatrix} 0 \\ -5 \end{pmatrix}$ gives:

$f(x) = x^2 + 1 - 5$ or $f(x) = x^2 - 4$

followed by:

a stretch parallel to the y-axis with stretch factor 2 gives:

$2f(x) = 2(x^2 - 4)$ or $y = 2x^2 - 8$

b Given $f(x) = x^2 + 1$

a translation $\begin{pmatrix} 2 \\ 0 \end{pmatrix}$ gives:

$f(x) = (x - 2)^2 + 1$ (since x is replaced by $x - 2$)

followed by:

a reflection in the x-axis gives:

$f(x) = -f(x)$ or $y = -[(x - 2)^2 + 1]$

or $y = -x^2 + 4x - 5$

6 a $y = g(x)$

- reflected in the y-axis gives $y = g(-x)$ and then

- stretched with stretch factor 2 parallel to the y-axis gives $y = 2g(-x)$

b $y = f(x)$

- translated by the vector $\begin{pmatrix} 2 \\ -3 \end{pmatrix}$ gives:

  $y = f(x - 2) - 3$ and then

- reflected in the x-axis gives:

  $y = -[f(x - 2) - 3]$ or $y = 3 - f(x - 2)$

7 Given $y = f(x)$

a stretch parallel to the y-axis with stretch factor $\dfrac{1}{2}$ gives $y = \dfrac{1}{2}f(x)$

followed by:

translation $\begin{pmatrix} 0 \\ 3 \end{pmatrix}$ gives $y = \dfrac{1}{2}f(x) + 3$

b reflection in the x-axis gives $y = -f(x)$

followed by:

translation $\begin{pmatrix} 0 \\ 2 \end{pmatrix}$ gives $y = -f(x) + 2$

c translation $\begin{pmatrix} 6 \\ 0 \end{pmatrix}$ gives $y = f(x - 6)$

followed by:

stretch parallel to the x-axis with stretch factor $\dfrac{1}{2}$ gives $y = f(2x - 6)$

d stretch parallel to the y-axis with stretch factor 2 gives $y = 2f(x)$

followed by:

translation $\begin{pmatrix} 0 \\ -8 \end{pmatrix}$ gives $y = 2f(x) - 8$

8 Given $y = x^3$

a translation $\begin{pmatrix} -5 \\ 0 \end{pmatrix}$ gives $y = (x + 5)^3$

followed by:

stretch parallel to the y-axis with stretch factor $\dfrac{1}{2}$ gives $y = \dfrac{1}{2}(x + 5)^3$

b Given $y = x^3$

translation $\begin{pmatrix} -1 \\ 0 \end{pmatrix}$ gives $y = (x + 1)^3$

followed by:

stretch parallel to the y-axis with stretch factor $\dfrac{1}{2}$ gives $y = \dfrac{1}{2}(x + 1)^3$

followed by:

reflection in the x-axis gives $y = -\dfrac{1}{2}(x + 1)^3$

followed by:

translation $\begin{pmatrix} 0 \\ -2 \end{pmatrix}$ gives $y = -\dfrac{1}{2}(x + 1)^3 - 2$

c Given $y = \sqrt[3]{x}$

translation $\begin{pmatrix} 3 \\ 0 \end{pmatrix}$ gives $y = \sqrt[3]{x-3}$

followed by:

stretch parallel to the y-axis with stretch factor 2 gives $y = 2\sqrt[3]{x-3}$

followed by:

reflection in the x-axis gives $y = -2\sqrt[3]{x-3}$

followed by:

translation $\begin{pmatrix} 0 \\ 4 \end{pmatrix}$ gives $y = -2\sqrt[3]{x-3} + 4$

9 Given $f(x) = \sqrt{x}$,

a reflection in x-axis gives $f(x) = -\sqrt{x}$,

followed by:

translation $\begin{pmatrix} 0 \\ 3 \end{pmatrix}$ gives $f(x) = -\sqrt{x} + 3$

followed by:

translation $\begin{pmatrix} 1 \\ 0 \end{pmatrix}$ gives $f(x) = -\sqrt{x-1} + 3$

followed by:

a stretch parallel to the x-axis with stretch

factor 2 gives $f(x) = -\sqrt{\frac{1}{2}x - 1} + 3$

b Given $f(x) = \sqrt{x}$

translation $\begin{pmatrix} 0 \\ 3 \end{pmatrix}$ gives $f(x) = \sqrt{x} + 3$

followed by:

stretch parallel to the x-axis with stretch

factor 2 gives $f(x) = \sqrt{\frac{1}{2}x} + 3$

followed by:

reflection in the x-axis gives $f(x) = -\sqrt{\frac{1}{2}x} - 3$

followed by:

translation $\begin{pmatrix} 1 \\ 0 \end{pmatrix}$ gives $f(x) = -\sqrt{\frac{1}{2}(x-1)} - 3$

10 Given $g(x) = x^2$

a translation $\begin{pmatrix} -4 \\ 0 \end{pmatrix}$ gives $g(x) = (x+4)^2$

followed by:

reflection in the y-axis gives $g(x) = (-x+4)^2$

followed by:

translation $\begin{pmatrix} 0 \\ 2 \end{pmatrix}$ gives $g(x) = (-x+4)^2 + 2$

followed by:

stretch parallel to the y-axis with stretch factor 3 gives:

$g(x) = 3[(-x+4)^2 + 2] = 3(4-x)^2 + 6$

b Given $g(x) = x^2$

stretch parallel to the y-axis with stretch factor 3 gives $g(x) = 3x^2$

followed by:

translation $\begin{pmatrix} 0 \\ 2 \end{pmatrix}$ gives $g(x) = 3x^2 + 2$

followed by:

reflection in y-axis gives:

$g(x) = 3(-x)^2 + 2$ or $g(x) = 3x^2 + 2$

followed by:

translation $\begin{pmatrix} -4 \\ 0 \end{pmatrix}$ gives $g(x) = 3(x+4)^2 + 2$

11 Given $f(x) = \sqrt{x}$

translation $\begin{pmatrix} 2 \\ 0 \end{pmatrix}$ gives $f(x) = \sqrt{x-2}$

followed by:

reflection in y-axis gives $f(x) = \sqrt{-x-2}$

Or

reflection in y-axis gives $f(x) = \sqrt{-x}$

followed by:

translation $\begin{pmatrix} -2 \\ 0 \end{pmatrix}$ gives $f(x) = \sqrt{-(x+2)}$

$f(x) = \sqrt{-x-2}$

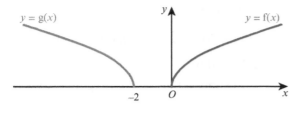

$y = g(x)$ $y = f(x)$

-2 O

12 Given $y = f(x)$ is mapped onto the graph of $y = f(2x + 10)$

translation $\begin{pmatrix} -10 \\ 0 \end{pmatrix}$ gives $y = f(x + 10)$

followed by:

stretch parallel to the x-axis with stretch factor $\frac{1}{2}$ gives $y = f(2x + 10)$

Or

stretch parallel to the x-axis with stretch factor $\frac{1}{2}$ gives $y = f(2x)$

followed by:

translation $\begin{pmatrix} -5 \\ 0 \end{pmatrix}$ gives $y = f(2(x + 5))$ or $y = f(2x + 10)$

Chapter 3
Coordinate geometry

1 a $P(-4, 6)$, $Q(6, 1)$

Using Pythagoras:

$PQ = \sqrt{(6 - -4)^2 + (1 - 6)^2}$

$PQ = \sqrt{10^2 + (-5)^2}$

$PQ = \sqrt{100 + 25}$

$PQ = \sqrt{125}$ or $5\sqrt{5}$

$Q(6, 1)$, $R(2, 9)$

Using Pythagoras:

$QR = \sqrt{(2 - 6)^2 + (9 - 1)^2}$

$QR = \sqrt{(-4)^2 + 8^2}$

$QR = \sqrt{16 + 64}$

$QR = \sqrt{80}$ or $4\sqrt{5}$

$P(-4, 6)$, $R(2, 9)$

$PR = \sqrt{(2 - -4)^2 + (9 - 6)^2}$

$PR = \sqrt{6^2 + 3^2}$

$PR = \sqrt{36 + 9}$

$PR = \sqrt{45}$ or $3\sqrt{5}$

Using Pythagoras, if triangle PQR is right angled:

$\left(3\sqrt{5}\right)^2 + \left(4\sqrt{5}\right)^2$ should equal $\left(5\sqrt{5}\right)^2$

> Choose the longest side to be the hypotenuse when testing for a right-angled triangle.

$45 + 80$ should equal 125

$125 = 125$

Therefore triangle PQR is right angled.

2 $P(1, 6)$, $Q(-2, 1)$

Using Pythagoras:

$PQ = \sqrt{(-2 - 1)^2 + (1 - 6)^2}$

$PQ = \sqrt{(-3)^2 + (-5)^2}$

$PQ = \sqrt{9 + 25}$

$PQ = \sqrt{34}$

$Q(-2, 1)$, $R(3, -2)$

Using Pythagoras:

$QR = \sqrt{(3 - -2)^2 + (-2 - 1)^2}$

$QR = \sqrt{5^2 + (-3)^2}$

$QR = \sqrt{25 + 9}$

$QR = \sqrt{34}$

$P(1, 6)$, $R(3, -2)$

Using Pythagoras:

$PR = \sqrt{(3 - 1)^2 + (-2 - 6)^2}$

$PR = \sqrt{2^2 + (-8)^2}$

$PR = \sqrt{4 + 64}$

$PR = \sqrt{68}$

As $PQ = QR$, the triangle is isosceles and as $\sqrt{68} > \sqrt{34}$, PR is chosen as the hypotenuse.

Using Pythagoras, if triangle PQR is right angled:

$\left(\sqrt{34}\right)^2 + \left(\sqrt{34}\right)^2$ should equal $\left(\sqrt{68}\right)^2$

$34 + 34$ should equal 68

$68 = 68$

Therefore triangle is right angled at angle Q.

Area of a triangle $= \dfrac{1}{2} \times$ base

$\qquad\qquad\qquad \times$ perpendicular height

$\qquad = \dfrac{1}{2}\sqrt{34} \times \sqrt{34}$,

$\qquad = \dfrac{1}{2} \times 34$

$\qquad = 17$ units^2

3 $P(a, -1)$, $Q(-5, a)$

Using Pythagoras:

$PQ = \sqrt{(-5 - a)^2 + (a - -1)^2}$

$PQ = \sqrt{(-5 - a)^2 + (a + 1)^2}$

$PQ = 4\sqrt{5}$

So, $4\sqrt{5} = \sqrt{(-5 - a)^2 + (a + 1)^2}$

Squaring gives:

$80 = (-5 - a)^2 + (a + 1)^2$

$80 = 25 + 10a + a^2 + 1 + 2a + a^2$

$2a^2 + 12a - 54 = 0$

$a^2 + 6a - 27 = 0$

$(a + 9)(a - 3) = 0$

$a = -9$ or $a = 3$

5 Given $P(-6, -5)$ and $Q(a, b)$

Midpoint of a line segment is

$M = \left(\dfrac{x_1 + x_2}{2}, \dfrac{y_1 + y_2}{2} \right)$

$M = \left(\dfrac{-6 + a}{2}, \dfrac{-5 + b}{2} \right)$ which is the same as

$(-2, -3)$

So, $\dfrac{-6 + a}{2} = -2$ and $\dfrac{-5 + b}{2} = -3$

$-6 + a = -4$ and $-5 + b = -6$

Solving each equation gives:

$a = 2$, $b = -1$

> A sketch is always useful when doing coordinate geometry questions. Make sure you label your points and join them in the correct order as stated in the question.

6 a A sketch showing the information given in the question is shown.

Be sure to join the points in the order:
$A \to B \to C \to D \to A$

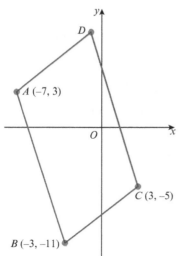

$A(-7, 3)$, $C(3, -5)$

Midpoint of AC is

$= \left(\dfrac{x_1 + x_2}{2}, \dfrac{y_1 + y_2}{2} \right) = \left(\dfrac{-7 + 3}{2}, \dfrac{3 + -5}{2} \right)$ which

is the same as $(-2, -1)$

b Let D have the coordinates (m, n)

Since $ABCD$ is a parallelogram, the midpoint of BD is the same as the midpoint of AC.

Midpoint of $BD = \left(\dfrac{-3 + m}{2}, \dfrac{-11 + n}{2} \right) = (-2, -1)$

Equating the x-coordinates:

$\dfrac{-3 + m}{2} = -2$

$-3 + m = -4$

$m = -1$

Equating the y-coordinates:

$\dfrac{-11 + n}{2} = -1$

$-11 + n = -2$

$n = 9$

D is the point $(-1, 9)$.

c $A(-7, 3)$, $C(3, -5)$.

Using Pythagoras:

$AC = \sqrt{(3 - -7)^2 + (-5 - 3)^2}$

$AC = \sqrt{10^2 + (-8)^2}$

$AC = \sqrt{100 + 64}$

$AC = \sqrt{164}$ or $2\sqrt{41}$

$B(-3, -11)$, $D(-1, 9)$

Using Pythagoras:

$BD = \sqrt{(-1 - -3)^2 + (9 - -11)^2}$

$BD = \sqrt{2^2 + 20^2}$

$BD = \sqrt{4 + 400}$

$BD = \sqrt{404}$ or $2\sqrt{101}$

7

> Be careful! Question 7 does not mention that A, P and B lie on a straight line. If the distance AP equals the distance BP, then P could be anywhere on the perpendicular bisector of AB.

Given $P(k, 2k)$, $A(8, 11)$ and $B(1, 12)$ and the distance AP is equal to the distance BP.

Using Pythagoras:
$$AP = \sqrt{(8-k)^2 + (11-2k)^2}$$
$$BP = \sqrt{(1-k)^2 + (12-2k)^2}$$
$$\sqrt{(8-k)^2 + (11-2k)^2} = \sqrt{(1-k)^2 + (12-2k)^2}$$

Square both sides:
$$(8-k)^2 + (11-2k)^2 = (1-k)^2 + (12-2k)^2$$

Left-hand side gives:
$$64 - 16k + k^2 + 121 - 44k + 4k^2$$
$$= 5k^2 - 60k + 185$$

Right-hand side gives:
$$1 - 2k + k^2 + 144 - 48k + 4k^2$$
$$= 5k^2 - 50k + 145$$
So, $5k^2 - 60k + 185 = 5k^2 - 50k + 145$
$$10k = 40$$
$$k = 4$$

8 $A(-6, 3)$, $B(3, 5)$ and $C(1, -4)$.
Using Pythagoras:
$$AC = \sqrt{(1--6)^2 + (-4-3)^2}$$
$$AC = \sqrt{7^2 + (-7)^2}$$
$$AC = \sqrt{49 + 49}$$
$$AC = \sqrt{98}$$
Using Pythagoras:
$$AB = \sqrt{(3--6)^2 + (5-3)^2}$$
$$AB = \sqrt{9^2 + 2^2}$$
$$AB = \sqrt{81 + 4}$$
$$AB = \sqrt{85}$$
Using Pythagoras:
$$BC = \sqrt{(1-3)^2 + (-4-5)^2}$$
$$BC = \sqrt{(-2)^2 + (-9)^2}$$
$$BC = \sqrt{4 + 81}$$
$$BC = \sqrt{85}$$
$AB = BC$ so triangle ABC is isosceles.

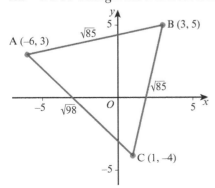

We do not know if this triangle is right angled but we can calculate the area.
Let D be the midpoint of AC.
BD is the perpendicular height of the triangle.

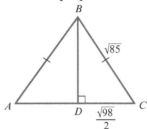

Using Pythagoras to find BD:
$$BD = \sqrt{\left(\sqrt{85}\right)^2 - \left(\frac{\sqrt{98}}{2}\right)^2}$$
$$BD = \sqrt{85 - \frac{98}{4}}$$
$$BD = \sqrt{\frac{121}{2}}$$

Area of triangle $ABC = \frac{1}{2} \times$ base
$$\times \text{ perpendicular height}$$
$$= \frac{1}{2}\left(\sqrt{\frac{121}{2}} \times \sqrt{98}\right)$$
$$= 38.5 \text{ units}^2$$

9 Using Pythagoras:
$$AB = \sqrt{(3--7)^2 + (k-8)^2}$$
$$AB = \sqrt{10^2 + (k-8)^2}$$
$$AB = \sqrt{100 + k^2 - 16k + 64}$$
$$AB = \sqrt{k^2 - 16k + 164}$$
$$BC = \sqrt{(8-3)^2 + (5-k)^2}$$
$$BC = \sqrt{5^2 + (5-k)^2}$$
$$BC = \sqrt{25 + 25 - 10k + k^2}$$
$$BC = \sqrt{k^2 - 10k + 50}$$
As $AB = 2BC$
$$\sqrt{k^2 - 16k + 164} = 2\sqrt{k^2 - 10k + 50}$$
Squaring both sides:
$$k^2 - 16k + 164 = 4(k^2 - 10k + 50)$$
$$k^2 - 16k + 164 = 4k^2 - 40k + 200$$
$$3k^2 - 24k + 36 = 0$$
$$k^2 - 8k + 12 = 0$$
$$(k-6)(k-2) = 0$$

$k = 2$ or $k = 6$

Reject $k = 6$ as this would be a straight line and not a triangle (see sketch).

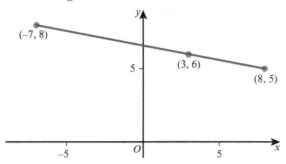

(−7, 8)

5

(3, 6)

(8, 5)

O

−5

5

x

Solution is $k = 2$

10 $x + y = 4$ ....[1]

$y = 8 - \dfrac{5}{x}$ .....[2]

Solving [1] and [2] simultaneously gives points A and B.

From [1] $y = 4 - x$

Substituting for y in [2] gives:

$4 - x = 8 - \dfrac{5}{x}$

$4x - x^2 = 8x - 5$

$x^2 + 4x - 5 = 0$

$(x - 1)(x + 5) = 0$

$x = 1$ or $x = -5$

Substituting $x = 1$ into [1] gives:

$1 + y = 4$ so $y = 3$

Substituting $x = -5$ into [1] gives:

$-5 + y = 4$ so $y = 9$

Points A and B are at: (1, 3) and (−5, 9)

Midpoint of $AB = \left(\dfrac{1 + -5}{2}, \dfrac{3 + 9}{2} \right)$ or (−2, 6)

12

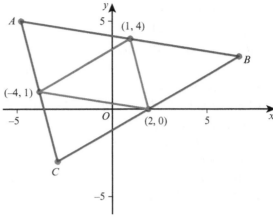

A

5 (1, 4)

B

(−4, 1)

−5

O

(2, 0)

5

x

C

−5

Let A have coordinates (x_1, y_1)

B have coordinates (x_2, y_2)

C have coordinates (x_3, y_3)

Midpoint of $AB = \left(\dfrac{x_1 + x_2}{2}, \dfrac{y_1 + y_2}{2} \right) = (1, 4)$

So, $\dfrac{x_1 + x_2}{2} = 1$ or $x_1 + x_2 = 2$ ....[1]

$\dfrac{y_1 + y_2}{2} = 4$ or $y_1 + y_2 = 8$

Midpoint of $BC = \left(\dfrac{x_2 + x_3}{2}, \dfrac{y_2 + y_3}{2} \right) = (2, 0)$

So, $\dfrac{x_2 + x_3}{2} = 2$ or $x_2 + x_3 = 4$

$\dfrac{y_2 + y_3}{2} = 0$ or $y_2 + y_3 = 0$

Midpoint of $AC = \left(\dfrac{x_1 + x_3}{2}, \dfrac{y_1 + y_3}{2} \right) = (-4, 1)$

So, $\dfrac{x_1 + x_3}{2} = -4$ or $x_1 + x_3 = -8$

$\dfrac{y_1 + y_3}{2} = 1$ or $y_1 + y_3 = 2$

We now have:

$x_1 + x_2 = 2$ .....[1]

$x_2 + x_3 = 4$ .....[2]

$x_1 + x_3 = -8$ ...[3]

Subtracting [2] from [1] gives:

$x_1 - x_3 = -2$ ....[4]

Then adding [4] to [3] gives:

$2x_1 = -10$ so $x_1 = -5$

As $x_1 + x_2 = 2$,

$-5 + x_2 = 2$ so $x_2 = 7$

As $x_1 + x_3 = -8$
$-5 + x_3 = -8$ so $x_3 = -3$
We also have:
$y_1 + y_2 = 8$ ....[5]
$y_2 + y_3 = 0$ ....[6]
$y_1 + y_3 = 2$ ....[7]
Subtracting [6] from [5] gives:
$y_1 - y_3 = 8$ ....[8] then adding [8] to [7] gives:

$2y_1 = 10$ so $y_1 = 5$
As $y_1 + y_2 = 8$
$5 + y_2 = 8$ so $y_2 = 3$
As $y_1 + y_3 = 2$
$5 + y_3 = 2$ so $y_3 = -3$
Solution is A is at$(-5, 5)$, B is at $(7, 3)$, C is at $(-3, -3)$.

EXERCISE 3B

1 a $A(-6, 4)$, $B(4, 6)$ and $C(10, 7)$

Gradient of $AB = \dfrac{y_2 - y_1}{x_2 - x_1}$

$= \dfrac{6 - 4}{4 - -6}$

$= \dfrac{1}{5}$

Gradient of $BC = \dfrac{7 - 6}{10 - 4}$

$= \dfrac{1}{6}$

b Collinear points lie on a straight line. Even though AB and BC share point B they are not collinear because the gradient of AB is not the same as the gradient of BC.

2 The midpoint of $P(-4, 5)$ and $Q(6, 1)$ is:

$M = \left(\dfrac{-4 + 6}{2}, \dfrac{5 + 1}{2} \right)$

$M = (1, 3)$

R has coordinates $(-3, -7)$.

Gradient of $RM = \dfrac{-7 - 3}{-3 - 1}$ or $\dfrac{5}{2}$

Gradient of $PQ = \dfrac{1 - 5}{6 - -4}$ or $-\dfrac{2}{5}$

If the gradients of two perpendicular lines are m_1 and m_2, then $m_1 \times m_2 = -1$.

$\dfrac{5}{2} \times -\dfrac{2}{5} = -1$ therefore RM is perpendicular to PQ.

4 A sketch looks like:

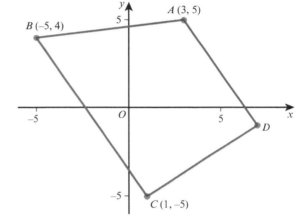

Gradient $BC = \dfrac{-5 - 4}{1 - -5}$ or $-\dfrac{3}{2}$

So, gradient $AD = -\dfrac{3}{2}$

Let D have the coordinates (x, y).

Gradient $AD = \dfrac{y - 5}{x - 3}$

As BC and AD have the same gradient:

$-\dfrac{3}{2} = \dfrac{y - 5}{x - 3}$

So
$-3(x - 3) = 2(y - 5)$
$-3x + 9 = 2y - 10$
$2y + 3x = 19$ ....[1]

As angle $ADC = 90°$, the gradient of $AD \times$ gradient of $CD = -1$

The gradient of CD is $\dfrac{2}{3}$

So $\dfrac{y--5}{x-1}=\dfrac{2}{3}$

$3(y+5)=2(x-1)$

$3y+15=2x-2$

$3y-2x=-17$ ....[2]

Multiplying [1] by 2 gives $4y+6x=38$ ....[3]

Multiplying [2] by 3 gives $9y-6x=-51$ ....[4]

Adding [3] and [4] gives:

$13y=-13$

$y=-1$

Substituting into [1] gives:

$2(-1)+3x=19$

$-2+3x=19$

$x=7$

The coordinates of D are $(7,-1)$

5 If A, B and C are collinear, then the gradients of AB and BC must be equal.

Gradient $AB=\dfrac{5-8}{k-5}$ or $\dfrac{-3}{k-5}$

Gradient $BC=\dfrac{4-5}{-k-k}$ or $\dfrac{-1}{-2k}$

So, $\dfrac{-3}{k-5}=\dfrac{-1}{-2k}$

$-3(-2k)=-1(k-5)$

$6k=-k+5$

$7k=5$

$k=\dfrac{5}{7}$

6 $A(-9,\ 2k-8)$, $B(6,\ k)$ and $C(k,\ 12)$.

If angle ABC is $90°$ then:

Gradient of $AB\times$ Gradient of $BC=-1$

Gradient $AB=\dfrac{k-(2k-8)}{6--9}$ or $\dfrac{-k+8}{15}$

Gradient $BC=\dfrac{12-k}{k-6}$

So, $\dfrac{-k+8}{15}\times\dfrac{12-k}{k-6}=-1$

$\dfrac{(-k+8)(12-k)}{15(k-6)}=-1$

$(-k+8)(12-k)=-15(k-6)$

$-12k+k^2+96-8k=-15k+90$

$k^2-5k+6=0$

$(k-2)(k-3)=0$

$k=2$ or $k=3$

7 Let the coordinates of C be $(x,\ y)$

If angle ABC is $90°$, then AB and BC are perpendicular.

Gradient $AB=\dfrac{6-8}{8-0}$ or $-\dfrac{1}{4}$

The gradient of BC is 4 since for perpendicular lines: $m_1\times m_2=-1$

Gradient $BC=\dfrac{y-6}{x-8}$

$\dfrac{y-6}{x-8}=4$

$y-6=4(x-8)$

$y-6=4x-32$

$y=4x-26$

As C is on the y-axis, $x=0$

So, $y=-26$

$C=(0,-26)$

8 a A, B and C must be collinear.

AB and BC have the same gradient and both lines pass through Point B.

Gradient $AB=\dfrac{8-4}{19-7}$ or $\dfrac{1}{3}$

Gradient $BC=\dfrac{2k-8}{k-19}$

$\dfrac{2k-8}{k-19}=\dfrac{1}{3}$

$3(2k-8)=1(k-19)$

$6k-24=k-19$

$5k=5$

$k=1$

b If angle CAB is $90°$,

Gradient $CA\times$ gradient $AB=-1$

Gradient $CA=\dfrac{2k-4}{k-7}$

Gradient $AB=\dfrac{8-4}{19-7}=\dfrac{1}{3}$

$\dfrac{2k-4}{k-7}\times\dfrac{1}{3}=-1$

$\dfrac{2k-4}{3k-21}=-1$

$2k-4=-1(3k-21)$

$2k-4=-3k+21$

$5k=25$

$k=5$

9 $\frac{x}{a} - \frac{y}{b} = 1,$

At P, $y = 0$ so:

$\frac{x}{a} - \frac{0}{b} = 1$

$\frac{x}{a} = 1$

$x = a$ so P is at $(a, 0)$

At Q, $x = 0$ so:

$\frac{0}{a} - \frac{y}{b} = 1$

$-\frac{y}{b} = 1$

$y = -b$ so Q is at $(0, -b)$

Gradient $PQ = \frac{-b - 0}{0 - a}$ or $\frac{b}{a}$

$\frac{b}{a} = \frac{2}{5}$ so $b = \frac{2a}{5}$

Using Pythagoras:

Length of $PQ = \sqrt{(0 - a)^2 + (-b - 0)^2}$

$= \sqrt{a^2 + b^2}$

Length of $PQ = 2\sqrt{29}$

$\sqrt{a^2 + b^2} = 2\sqrt{29}$

Squaring both sides gives:

$a^2 + b^2 = 116$

Substituting for b gives:

$a^2 + \left(\frac{2a}{5}\right)^2 = 116$

$a^2 + \frac{4a^2}{25} = 116$

$25a^2 + 4a^2 = 2900$

$29a^2 = 2900$

$a^2 = 100$

$a = \pm 10$ but a is positive so $a = 10$

Substituting into $b = \frac{2a}{5}$,

$b = \frac{2(10)}{5}$

Solution $a = 10$, $b = 4$

10 Given $P(a, a - 2)$ and $Q(4 - 3a, -a)$

a Gradient of the line $PQ = \frac{-a - (a - 2)}{4 - 3a - a}$

$= \frac{2 - 2a}{4 - 4a}$

$= \frac{2(1 - a)}{4(1 - a)}$

$= \frac{1}{2}$

b The gradient of a line perpendicular to $PQ = -2$, since for perpendicular lines $m_1 \times m_2 = -1$

c Using Pythagoras:

$PQ = \sqrt{[(4 - 3a) - a]^2 + [-a - (a - 2)]^2}$

$= \sqrt{[4 - 3a - a]^2 + [-a - a + 2]^2}$

$= \sqrt{[4 - 4a]^2 + [-2a + 2]^2}$

$= \sqrt{16 - 32a + 16a^2 + 4a^2 - 8a + 4}$

$= \sqrt{20a^2 - 40a + 20}$

$10\sqrt{5} = \sqrt{20a^2 - 40a + 20}$

Square both sides:

$500 = 20a^2 - 40a + 20$

$20a^2 - 40a - 480 = 0$

$a^2 - 2a - 24 = 0$

$(a - 6)(a + 4) = 0$

$a - 6 = 0$ or $a + 4 = 0$

$a = 6$ or $a = -4$

11

You should know the properties of special quadrilaterals to help you to answer coordinate geometry questions.

a $M = \left(\frac{4 + 8}{2}, \frac{10 + 2}{2}\right)$ or $M = (6, 6)$

b M is the midpoint of AC so:

$M = \left(\frac{a + b}{2}, \frac{1 + c}{2}\right)$

So, $\frac{a + b}{2} = 6$

$a + b = 12 ..... [1]$

and $\frac{1 + c}{2} = 6$

$1 + c = 12$

$c = 11$

As the diagonals of a rhombus intersect at $90°$, gradient of $AC \times$ gradient $BD = -1$

$\frac{c - 1}{b - a} \times \frac{10 - 2}{4 - 8} = -1$ and as $c = 11$,

$\frac{10}{b - a} \times -2 = -1$

(be careful here as only the numerator of the first fraction is multiplied by -2)

$\frac{10(-2)}{b - a} = -1$

$-20 = -1(b - a)$

$-20 = -b + a \dots [2]$

Adding $[1]$ and $[2]$ gives:

$2a = -8$

$a = -4$

Substituting for a in $[1]$ gives:

$-4 + b = 12$

$b = 16$

Solution: $a = -4$, $b = 16$ and $c = 11$

c All four sides of a rhombus are of equal length.

$A = (-4, 1)$ and $B = (8, 2)$

Using Pythagoras:

$AB = \sqrt{(8 - -4)^2 + (2 - 1)^2}$

$AB = \sqrt{144 + 1}$

$AB = \sqrt{145}$

The perimeter of the rhombus is $4\sqrt{145}$.

d The area of the rhombus $= \dfrac{AC \times BD}{2}$

$A = (-4, 1)$, $B = (8, 2)$, $C = (16, 11)$, $D = (4, 10)$

Using Pythagoras:

$AC = \sqrt{(16 - -4)^2 + (11 - 1)^2}$

$AC = \sqrt{400 + 100}$

$AC = \sqrt{500}$

$BD = \sqrt{(4 - 8)^2 + (10 - 2)^2}$

$BD = \sqrt{16 + 64}$

$BD = \sqrt{80}$

$\text{Area} = \dfrac{\sqrt{500} \times \sqrt{80}}{2}$

$\text{Area} = \dfrac{\sqrt{40000}}{2}$

$\text{Area} = 100$

EXERCISE 3C

1 a Line with gradient 2 and passing through the point (4, 9)

Using $y - y_1 = m(x - x_1)$ with $m = 2$, $x_1 = 4$ and $y_1 = 9$:

$y - 9 = 2(x - 4)$

$y - 9 = 2x - 8$

$y = 2x + 1$

2 a Given points on the line (1, 0) and (5, 6)

Gradient $m = \dfrac{y_2 - y_1}{x_2 - x_1} = \dfrac{6 - 0}{5 - 1} = \dfrac{3}{2}$

Using $y - y_1 = m(x - x_1)$ with $m = \dfrac{3}{2}$, $x_1 = 1$ and $y_1 = 0$:

$y - 0 = \dfrac{3}{2}(x - 1)$

$2y = 3x - 3$

3 a $y = 3x - 5$ has gradient 3. Any line parallel to this line has the same gradient i.e. $m = 3$.

The line passes through the point (1, 7).

So $x_1 = 1$ and $y_1 = 7$

Using $y - y_1 = m(x - x_1)$:

$y - 7 = 3(x - 1)$

$y - 7 = 3x - 3$

$y = 3x + 4$

c $y = 2x - 3$ has gradient 2

Using $m_1 \times m_2 = -1$, any line perpendicular to this line has the gradient $m = -\dfrac{1}{2}$

The line passes through the point (6, 1).

So $x_1 = 6$ and $y_1 = 1$

Using $y - y_1 = m(x - x_1)$:

$y - 1 = -\dfrac{1}{2}(x - 6)$

$2y - 2 = -x + 6$

$x + 2y = 8$

4 a (5, 2) and (−3, 6)

Gradient line $= \dfrac{6 - 2}{-3 - 5} = -\dfrac{1}{2}$

Using $m_1 \times m_2 = -1$, gradient of the perpendicular $= 2$

Midpoint of $AB = \left(\dfrac{5 + -3}{2}, \dfrac{2 + 6}{2} \right) = (1, 4)$

∴ the perpendicular bisector is the line with gradient 2 passing through the point (1, 4).

Using $y - y_1 = m(x - x_1)$, $x_1 = 1$, $y_1 = 4$ and $m = 2$:

$y - 4 = 2(x - 1)$
$y - 4 = 2x - 2$
$\quad y = 2x + 2$

5

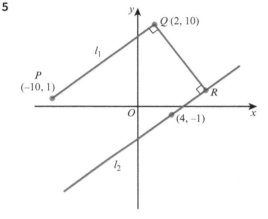

First find the equation of the line which is perpendicular to l_1 and which passes through $Q(2, 10)$.

Gradient of $l_1 = m = \dfrac{10 - 1}{2 - -10} = \dfrac{3}{4}$

The gradient of a line perpendicular to l_1 is $-\dfrac{4}{3}$, since for perpendicular lines $m_1 \times m_2 = -1$

$Q(2, 10)$ lies on this perpendicular line.

So equation of the line using $y - y_1 = m(x - x_1)$:

$y - 10 = -\dfrac{4}{3}(x - 2)$

$3y - 30 = -4(x - 2)$
$3y - 30 = -4x + 8$

$3y + 4x = 38 \ldots\ldots[1]$

Then to find the equation of l_2:

Gradient of $l_2 = \dfrac{3}{4}$

As $(4, -1)$ lies on l_2 using $y - y_1 = m(x - x_1)$:

$y - -1 = \dfrac{3}{4}(x - 4)$

$4(y + 1) = 3(x - 4)$
$4y + 4 = 3x - 12$

$4y - 3x = -16 \ldots\ldots[2]$

Point R is at the intersection of these two lines.

Solving:

$3y + 4x = 38 \ldots\ldots[1]$ and $4y - 3x = -16 \ldots\ldots[2]$

Multiply [1] by 3 and [2] by 4 gives:

$9y + 12x = 114$ and $16y - 12x = -64$

Adding these two equations gives:
$25y = 50$
$\quad y = 2$

Substituting $y = 2$ into [1] gives:
$3(2) + 4x = 38$
$\quad\quad x = 8$

R has coordinates (8, 2).

6 a $P(-4, 2)$ and $Q(5, -4)$.

Gradient of $PQ = \dfrac{-4 - 2}{5 - -4} = -\dfrac{2}{3}$

Gradient of the perpendicular line $= \dfrac{3}{2}$, since for perpendicular lines $m_1 \times m_2 = -1$

Using $y - y_1 = m(x - x_1)$ to find the equation of the line with gradient $\dfrac{3}{2}$ which passes through $P(-4, 2)$:

$y - 2 = \dfrac{3}{2}(x - -4)$

$2y - 4 = 3(x + 4)$
$2y - 4 = 3x + 12$
$\quad 2y = 3x + 16$

b At point R (on the y-axis), $x = 0$

Substituting into $2y = 3x + 16$ gives:
$2y = 16$
$\quad y = 8$
So, R is at (0, 8)

c Angle RPQ is 90°

Area of triangle $PQR = \dfrac{1}{2} \times PR \times PQ$

Using Pythagoras:
$PR = \sqrt{(0 - -4)^2 + (8 - 2)^2}$
$PR = \sqrt{16 + 36}$
$PR = \sqrt{52}$

Using Pythagoras:

$PQ = \sqrt{(5--4)^2 + (-4-2)^2}$

$PQ = \sqrt{81+36}$

$PQ = \sqrt{117}$

Area of triangle $PQR = \frac{1}{2} \times \sqrt{52} \times \sqrt{117}$

$= 39$ units^2

7 a $3x - 2y = 12 \ldots\ldots[1]$

$y = 15 - 2x \ldots\ldots[2]$

Solving [1] and [2] simultaneously gives the coordinates of A.

From equation [2] substitute for y in equation [1]:

$3x - 2(15-2x) = 12$

$3x - 30 + 4x = 12$

$7x = 42$

$x = 6$

Substitute for y in [2]:

$y = 15 - 2(6)$

$y = 3$

The coordinates of A are (6, 3).

b Line l_1 has equation $3x - 2y = 12$

Rearranging gives:

$2y = 3x - 12$

$y = \frac{3}{2}x - 6$

The gradient of l_1 is $\frac{3}{2}$

Let the line through A which is perpendicular to the line l_1 be l_3.

The gradient of l_3 is $-\frac{2}{3}$

l_3 passes through (6, 3)

Using $y - y_1 = m(x - x_1)$:

$y - 3 = -\frac{2}{3}(x-6)$

$y - 3 = -\frac{2}{3}x + 4$

$y = -\frac{2}{3}x + 7$

8 a $A(-10, 5)$, $B(-2, -1)$

Midpoint of $AB = \left(\dfrac{-10+-2}{2}, \dfrac{5+-1}{2}\right)$ or (−6, 2)

Gradient of $AB = \dfrac{-1-5}{-2--10}$ or $-\dfrac{3}{4}$

Gradient of the line perpendicular line to $AB = \frac{4}{3}$ since for perpendicular lines

$m_1 \times m_2 = -1$

Find the equation of the perpendicular bisector PQ using $y - y_1 = m(x - x_1)$:

$y - 2 = \frac{4}{3}(x--6)$

$y - 2 = \frac{4}{3}x + 8$

$y = \frac{4}{3}x + 10$

b Substitute $y = 0$ to find where the bisector intersects the x-axis:

$0 = \frac{4}{3}x + 10$

$\frac{4}{3}x = -10$

$x = -7.5$

P has coordinates (−7.5, 0)

Substitute $x = 0$ to find where the bisector intersects the y-axis:

$y = \frac{4}{3}(0) + 10$

$y = 10$

Q has coordinates (0, 10)

c Using Pythagoras:

$PQ = \sqrt{10^2 + (-7.5)^2}$

$PQ = 12.5$

10 F is at the midpoint of EG and it also lies on FH. To find the coordinates of F, find the equation of FH and solve it simultaneously with the equation of EG:

Equation of EG is $x + 2y = 16 \ldots.[1]$

Gradient of EG is found by rearranging $x + 2y = 16$

$2y = 16 - x$

$y = 8 - \frac{1}{2}x$ or $y = -\frac{1}{2}x + 8$

Gradient of EG is $-\dfrac{1}{2}$

As FH is perpendicular to EG, it has a gradient $= 2$, since for perpendicular lines $m_1 \times m_2 = -1$

$H(5, -7)$ also lies on FH. To find its equation, use $y - y_1 = m(x - x_1)$:

$y - -7 = 2(x - 5)$

$y + 7 = 2x - 10$

$y = 2x - 17$ ....[2]

To solve [1] and [2], substitute for y in [1]:

$x + 2(2x - 17) = 16$

$\qquad x + 4x - 34 = 16$

$\qquad\qquad 5x = 50$

$\qquad\qquad\quad x = 10$

Substitute for x in [2]:

$y = 2(10) - 17$

$y = 3$

F has coordinates $(10, 3)$.

To find the coordinates of E, first find the position of G.

At G, $y = 0$.

Substituting into $x + 2y = 16$ gives $x + 2(0) = 16$

$x = 16$ so G is at $(16, 0)$

As F is the midpoint of EG, the coordinates of E can be found using vectors:

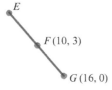

$\overrightarrow{GF} = \begin{pmatrix} -6 \\ 3 \end{pmatrix}$ so $\overrightarrow{FE} = \begin{pmatrix} -6 \\ 3 \end{pmatrix}$

E is at $(4, 6)$.

11 $A(-4, -1)$, $B(8, -9)$ and $C(k, 7)$.

The midpoint (M) of $AB = \left(\dfrac{-4 + 8}{2}, \dfrac{-1 + -9}{2} \right)$

So $M = (2, -5)$

The gradient of $AB = \dfrac{-9 - -1}{8 - -4}$ or $-\dfrac{2}{3}$

MC is perpendicular to AB. So its gradient is $\dfrac{3}{2}$,

since for perpendicular lines: $m_1 \times m_2 = -1$

As M is at $(2, -5)$ and C is at $(k, 7)$, the gradient of MC can also be written as:

$\dfrac{7 - -5}{k - 2}$ or $\dfrac{12}{k - 2}$

So, $\dfrac{12}{k - 2} = \dfrac{3}{2}$

Solving gives:

$24 = 3(k - 2)$

$24 = 3k - 6$

$k = 10$

12

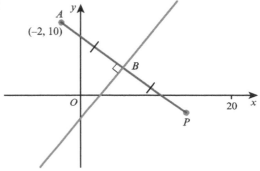

The points $A(-2, 10)$ and P are equidistant from the line $4x - 3y = 12$, and when joined, make a line perpendicular to $4x - 3y = 12$ ....[1]

Find the gradient of the line $4x - 3y = 12$:

$\qquad\qquad 3y = 4x - 12$

$\qquad y = \dfrac{4}{3}x - 4$ so $m = \dfrac{4}{3}$

A line perpendicular to this has a gradient $-\dfrac{3}{4}$, since for perpendicular lines $m_1 \times m_2 = -1$

Using $m = -\dfrac{3}{4}$ and the point $(-2, 10)$ the equation of the perpendicular line is:

$y - 10 = -\dfrac{3}{4}(x - -2)$

$4y - 40 = -3(x + 2)$

$4y - 40 = -3x - 6$

$3x + 4y = 34$ ....[2]

To solve [1] and [2], multiply [1] by 4 and [2] by 3 to give:

$16x - 12y = 48$ ....[3]

$9x + 12y = 102$ ....[4]

Adding [3] and [4]

$25x = 150$

$x = 6$

Substituting into [1] gives:

$4(6) - 3y = 12$

$3y = 12$

$y = 4$

The perpendicular line intersects the line of reflection at (6, 4) call this B (see diagram).

Using vectors $\overrightarrow{AB} = \begin{pmatrix} 8 \\ -6 \end{pmatrix} = \overrightarrow{BP}$

P has coordinates (14, −2).

15 a A sketch is shown. We are asked to find the equation of the third side i.e. AB.

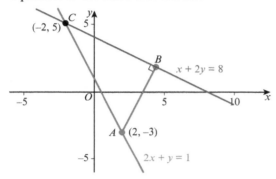

Equation of BC is $x + 2y = 8$

The gradient of BC is found by rearranging this equation i.e.

$2y = -x + 8$

$y = -\dfrac{1}{2}x + 4$

Gradient of BC is $-\dfrac{1}{2}$

As AB is perpendicular to BC, then using $m_1 \times m_2 = -1$:

$-\dfrac{1}{2} \times \text{gradient } AB = -1$

Rearranging, the gradient of AB is 2

The equation of AB is found by using $y - y_1 = m(x - x_1)$ with $m = 2$, $A = (2, -3)$:

$y - -3 = 2(x - 2)$

$y + 3 = 2x - 4$

The equation of the third side is:

$y = 2x - 7$

b Solving $x + 2y = 8$ ....[1]

and $y = 2x - 7$.....[2]

simultaneously gives the coordinates of B.

Using [2] to substitute for y in [1]:

$x + 2(2x - 7) = 8$

$x + 4x - 14 = 8$

$5x = 22$

$x = 4.4$

Substituting this into [2] gives:

$y = 2(4.4) - 7$

$y = 1.8$

B has coordinates (4.4, 1.8)

16 Let the gradients of the lines be $m_1 = -1$ and $m_2 = -3$

So $y = -1x + a$ and $y = -3x + b$

If the difference in the y-intercepts is 5 then:

$a - b = 5$ ......[1]

The difference in the x-intercepts is 7 then:

$a - \dfrac{b}{3} = 7$.....[2]

Solving [1] and [2] gives: $a = 8$, $b = 3$

Hence a pair of possible equations are:

$x + y = 8$ and $3x + y = 3$

There are many solutions to this problem so this solution is not unique.

In the remaining exercises in this chapter, you will need to use the fact that the normal to a circle at any point on its circumference passes through the centre of the circle. So if we know the equation of the circle we can find the equation of both the tangent and the normal at any point on the circumference.

EXERCISE 3D

1 b $2x^2 + 2y^2 = 9$ dividing both sides by 2 gives:

$x^2 + y^2 = \dfrac{9}{2}$

Comparing this with $(x-a)^2 + (y-b)^2 = r^2$, which is the equation of a circle with centre (x, y) and radius r:

$(x-a)^2 + (y-b)^2 = r^2$, $a = 0$, $b = 0$, $r^2 = \dfrac{9}{2}$

$r = \sqrt{\dfrac{9}{2}}$ or $\dfrac{3\sqrt{2}}{2}$

Centre $(0, 0)$ and radius $\dfrac{3\sqrt{2}}{2}$

g $x^2 + y^2 - 8x + 20y + 110 = 0$

Rewrite as:

$x^2 - 8x + y^2 + 20y + 110 = 0$

Complete the squares:

$(x-4)^2 - 4^2 + (y+10)^2 - 10^2 + 110 = 0$

$(x-4)^2 + (y+10)^2 = 6$

Compare with $(x-a)^2 + (y-b)^2 = r^2$

$a = 4 \quad b = -10 \quad r^2 = 6$

Centre $= (4, -10)$ and radius $= \sqrt{6}$.

2 b Centre $(5, -2)$, radius 4

Equation of circle is $(x-a)^2 + (y-b)^2 = r^2$ where $a = 5$, $b = -2$ and $r = 4$.

$(x-5)^2 + (y-(-2))^2 = 4^2$

$(x-5)^2 + (y+2)^2 = 16$

3 As $(x-a)^2 + (y-b)^2 = r^2$

Substituting $a = 2$ and $b = 5$ gives:

$(x-2)^2 + (y-5)^2 = r^2$.....[1]

Now, as the point $(6, 8)$ lies on the circle, substitute $x = 6$, $y = 8$ into [1] to find r.

$(6-2)^2 + (8-5)^2 = r^2$

$16 + 9 = r^2$

$r^2 = 25$

$(x-2)^2 + (y-5)^2 = 25$

4 The centre of the circle, C, is the midpoint of AB.

$C = \left(\dfrac{-6+2}{2}, \dfrac{8+(-4)}{2}\right) = (-2, 2)$

Radius of circle, r, is equal to BC.

Using Pythagoras:

$r = \sqrt{(-2-2)^2 + (2--4)^2} = \sqrt{52}$

Equation of circle is $(x-a)^2 + (y-b)^2 = r^2$

where $a = -2$, $b = 2$ and $r = \sqrt{52}$.

$(x+2)^2 + (y-2)^2 = \left(\sqrt{52}\right)^2$

$(x+2)^2 + (y-2)^2 = 52$

5 The circle $(x-3)^2 + (y+2)^2 = 9$ has centre $(3, -2)$ and radius $\sqrt{9} = 3$

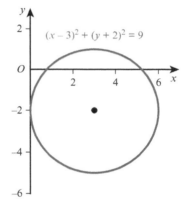

This diagram is a sketch, so the coordinates need not be accurately plotted; however, the y-axis should be a tangent to the circle and the x-intercepts should be approximately in the correct place.

6 If the circle touches the x-axis and its centre is $(6, -5)$, then the radius of the circle is 5 units.

Given $(x-a)^2 + (y-b)^2 = r^2$, substituting $r^2 = 5^2$, $a = 6$ and $y = -5$ gives:

$(x-6)^2 + (y--5)^2 = 25$

$(x-6)^2 + (y+5)^2 = 25$

7 The centre of the circle lies on the perpendicular bisector of PQ.

Midpoint of $PQ = \left(\dfrac{1+7}{2}, \dfrac{-2+1}{2}\right) = \left(4, -\dfrac{1}{2}\right)$

Gradient of $PQ = \dfrac{1--2}{7-1} = \dfrac{1}{2}$

Gradient of perpendicular bisector of $PQ = -2$, since for perpendicular lines: $m_1 \times m_2 = -1$

Equation of perpendicular bisector of PQ is

$$\left(y--\dfrac{1}{2}\right) = -2(x-4)$$

$$y + \dfrac{1}{2} = -2x + 8$$

$$2y + 1 = -4x + 16$$

$$4x + 2y = 15 \text{ shown.}$$

8 If $r = 2\sqrt{2}$ or $\sqrt{8}$ then $r^2 = 8$

Using $(x-a)^2 + (y-b)^2 = r^2$

Substituting $x = 3$, $y = 2$ and $r^2 = 8$ gives:

$(3-a)^2 + (2-b)^2 = 8 \ldots [1]$

Substituting $x = 7$, $y = 2$ and $r^2 = 8$, gives:

$(7-a)^2 + (2-b)^2 = 8 \ldots [2]$

Subtracting $[2]$ from $[1]$ gives:

$(3-a)^2 - (7-a)^2 = 0$ which simplified gives:

$9 - 6a + a^2 - (49 - 14a + a^2) = 0$

$9 - 6a + a^2 - 49 + 14a - a^2 = 0$

$8a - 40 = 0$

$a = 5$

Substituting into $[1]$ gives:

$(3-5)^2 + (2-b)^2 = 8$
$4 + (2-b)^2 = 8$
$(2-b)^2 = 4$
$2 - b = \pm 2$
$b = 0$ or $b = 4$

Substituting $a = 5$, $b = 0$ and $r^2 = 8$ into $(x-a)^2 + (y-b)^2 = r^2$ gives:

$(x-5)^2 + (y-0)^2 = 8$

Or $(x-5)^2 + y^2 = 8$

Substituting $a = 5$, $b = 4$ and $r^2 = 8$ into $(x-a)^2 + (y-b)^2 = r^2$ gives:

$(x-5)^2 + (y-4)^2 = 8$

Solutions are $(x-5)^2 + y^2 = 8$ and $(x-5)^2 + (y-4)^2 = 8$

9 A sketch is shown:

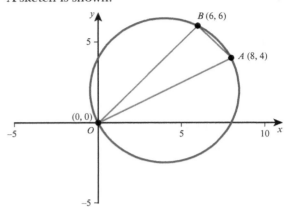

If OA is a diameter of the circle then angle OAB should be $90°$ (angle in a semicircle).

So, OB should be perpendicular to AB.

Gradient of $OB = \dfrac{6-0}{6-0} = 1$

Gradient $AB = \dfrac{6-4}{6-8} = -1$

Gradient $OB \times$ gradient $AB = 1 \times -1$ or -1

So, OA must be the diameter of the circle.

The perpendicular bisectors of OA, AB and OB all pass through the centre of the circle but only two bisectors are needed to locate it.

Midpoint of $AB = \left(\dfrac{6+8}{2}, \dfrac{6+4}{2}\right) = (7, 5)$

Gradient of $AB = -1$

Gradient of perpendicular bisector of $AB = 1$, since for perpendicular lines $m_1 \times m_2 = -1$

Equation of perpendicular bisector of AB is

$$(y-5) = 1(x-7)$$
$$y = x - 2 \ldots\ldots\ldots\ldots [1]$$

Midpoint of $OB = \left(\dfrac{0+6}{2}, \dfrac{0+6}{2}\right) = (3, 3)$

Gradient of $OB = 1$

Gradient of perpendicular bisector of $OB = -1$, since for perpendicular lines $m_1 \times m_2 = -1$

Equation of perpendicular bisector of OB is

$$(y-3) = -1(x-3)$$
$$y = -x + 6 \ldots\ldots\ldots\ldots [2]$$

Solving equations $[1]$ and $[2]$ gives

$$x = 4, \ y = 2$$

Centre of circle $C = (4, 2)$

Using Pythagoras:

Radius $= CO = \sqrt{(4-0)^2 + (2-0)^2} = \sqrt{20}$

Hence, the equation of the circle is

$(x-4)^2 + (y-2)^2 = 20$

11 If $A(6, -6)$ lies on the circle then substituting $x = 6$, $y = -6$ into the circle equation, both sides should balance.

$(x-3)^2 + (y+2)^2 = 25$

$(6-3)^2 + (-6+2)^2 = 25$

$9 + 16 = 25$ this is true

So A does lie on the circle.

The perpendicular to the tangent to the circle at the point $A(6, -6)$, should pass through the centre of the circle $C(3, -2)$.

Gradient $AC = \dfrac{-2 - -6}{3 - 6}$ or $-\dfrac{4}{3}$

Gradient of tangent at A is $\dfrac{3}{4}$ since for perpendicular lines $m_1 \times m_2 = -1$

Using $y - y_1 = m(x - x_1)$, $A(6, -6)$ and $m = \dfrac{3}{4}$

$y - -6 = \dfrac{3}{4}(x - 6)$

$y + 6 = \dfrac{3}{4}(x - 6)$

$y = \dfrac{3}{4}x - \dfrac{21}{2}$

12 The line $2x + 5y = 20$ cuts the x-axis at $A(10, 0)$ (from substituting $y = 0$ into $2x + 5y = 20$),

y-axis at $B(0, 4)$ (from substituting $x = 0$ into $2x + 5y = 20$)

C (the centre of the circle) is at $\left(\dfrac{10+0}{2}, \dfrac{0+4}{2}\right)$ or $(5, 2)$

Radius of the circle is AC (or CB)

Using Pythagoras to find the radius AC gives:

$$AC = \sqrt{(5-10)^2 + (2-0)^2}$$

Radius $AC = \sqrt{29}$

Substituting $C(5, 2)$ and $r^2 = 29$ into $(x-a)^2 + (y-b)^2 = r^2$ gives:

$(x-5)^2 + (y-2)^2 = 29 \ldots\ldots[1]$

If $(0, 0)$ lies on the circle then substituting $x = 0$, $y = 0$ into $[1]$, both sides should balance.

$(0-5)^2 + (0-2)^2 = 29$

$25 + 4 = 29$ this is true

So the circle does pass through $(0, 0)$.

14 A diagram is shown.

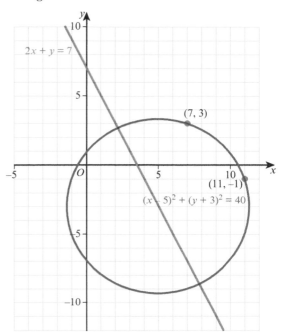

The centre of the circle lies on the perpendicular bisector of $(7, 3)$ and $(11, -1)$.

Midpoint of $(7, 3)$ and

$(11, -1) = \left(\dfrac{7+11}{2}, \dfrac{3+-1}{2}\right)$ or $(9, 1)$

Gradient of the line joining $(7, 3)$ and

$(11, -1) = \dfrac{-1-3}{11-7}$ or -1

The perpendicular bisector has the gradient 1, since for perpendicular lines $m_1 \times m_2 = -1$

Equation of perpendicular bisector, using $y - y_1 = m(x - x_1)$, $m = 1$, and $(9, 1)$ is:

$y - 1 = 1(x - 9)$

$y = x - 8 \ldots\ldots[1]$

Given also that the centre lies on $2x + y = 7 \ldots\ldots[2]$

Solving $[1]$ and $[2]$ gives $x = 5$ and $y = -3$

So, the centre of the circle C is at $(5, -3)$

Find the radius of the circle using Pythagoras and points $C(5, -3)$ and $(7, 3)$ [or $(11, -1)$]:

$r = \sqrt{(7-5)^2 + (3--3)^2}$

$r = \sqrt{4 + 36}$

$r = \sqrt{40}$

The equation of the circle is:

$(x-a)^2 + (y-b)^2 = r^2$ $a = 5$, $b = -3$, $r = \sqrt{40}$

$(x-5)^2 + (y--3)^2 = 40$

$(x-5)^2 + (y+3)^2 = 40$

17

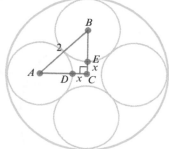

a i The radius of each green circle is 1 unit.

Angle BCA is $90°$, $AB = 2$ units

Let $DC = EC = x$

Using Pythagoras:

$(1+x)^2 + (1+x)^2 = 2^2$

$2(1+x)^2 = 4$

$(1+x)^2 = 2$

$1+x = \pm\sqrt{2}$

$x = \sqrt{2} - 1$ or $x = -\sqrt{2} - 1$ (reject)

Radius of the orange circle is $1 + 1 + x$ or:

$1 + 1 + \sqrt{2} - 1$ or $1 + \sqrt{2}$

b i

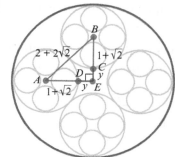

$AB^2 = AE^2 + BE^2$

$\left(2 + 2\sqrt{2}\right)^2 = \left(1 + \sqrt{2} + y\right)^2 + \left(1 + \sqrt{2} + y\right)^2$

$\left(2 + 2\sqrt{2}\right)^2 = 2\left(1 + \sqrt{2} + y\right)^2$

$2 + 2\sqrt{2} = \pm\sqrt{2}\left(1 + \sqrt{2} + y\right)$

Either $\sqrt{2} + 2 = 1 + \sqrt{2} + y$ or

$\sqrt{2} + 2 = -1 - \sqrt{2} - y$

$y = 1$ or $y = -3 - 2\sqrt{2}$ (reject, as the length cannot be negative)

The radius of the blue circle is

$1 + \sqrt{2} + 1 + \sqrt{2} + 1$ or $3 + 2\sqrt{2}$

EXERCISE 3E

1 Substitute $y = x - 3$ into $(x-3)^2 + (y+2)^2 = 20$:

$(x-3)^2 + (x-3+2)^2 = 20$

$(x-3)^2 + (x-1)^2 = 20$.

$2x^2 - 8x + 10 = 20$

$2x^2 - 8x - 10 = 0$

$x^2 - 4x - 5 = 0$

$(x-5)(x+1) = 0$

$x = 5$ or $x = -1$

Substituting $x = 5$ into $y = x - 3$ gives:

$y = 2$

Substituting $x = -1$ into $y = x - 3$ gives:

$y = -4$

The intersection points are at $(5, 2)$ and $(-1, -4)$.

3 Solve $3x + y = 6$.....[1]

and $x^2 + y^2 + 4x + 16y + 28 = 0$....[2]

simultaneously to find the intersection point.

Make y the subject of $[1]$ and substitute into $[2]$:

$x^2 + (6-3x)^2 + 4x + 16(6-3x) + 28 = 0$

$x^2 + 36 - 36x + 9x^2 + 4x + 96 - 48x + 28 = 0$

$10x^2 - 80x + 160 = 0$

$x^2 - 8x + 16 = 0$

$(x-4)^2 = 0$

$x = 4$

Substituting into the linear equation $[1]$ gives:

$y = -6$

The intersection point is (4, –6).

There is only one solution (a repeated root); hence the line must be a tangent to the circle.

4 $y = mx + 1 ....[1]$

$(x-7)^2 + (y-5)^2 = 20 ......[2]$

Using $[1]$, substitute for y in $[2]$:

$(x-7)^2 + (mx + 1 - 5)^2 = 20$

$(x-7)^2 + (mx - 4)^2 = 20$

$x^2 - 14x + 49 + m^2x^2 - 8mx + 16 = 20$

$(1 + m^2)x^2 + x(-14 - 8m) + 45 = 0$

Comparing with $ax^2 + bx + c = 0$:

$a = 1 + m^2$, $b = -14 - 8m$, $c = 45$

For two solutions, $b^2 - 4ac > 0$:

$(-14 - 8m)^2 - 4(1 + m^2)(45) > 0$

$196 + 224m + 64m^2 - 180 - 180m^2 > 0$

$-116m^2 + 224m + 16 > 0$

The graph of $y = -116m^2 + 224m + 16$ is an $\cap$ shaped parabola.

To find the m-intercepts, using the quadratic formula again:

$m = \dfrac{-224 \pm \sqrt{224^2 - 4(-116)(16)}}{2(-116)}$

$m = -\dfrac{2}{29}$ or $m = 2$

Since we require $-116m^2 + 224m + 16 > 0$, we want the part of the $y = -116m^2 + 224m + 16$ graph which is above the m-axis.

Therefore, $-\dfrac{2}{29} < m < 2$

5 $2y - x = 12 ....[1]$

$x^2 + y^2 - 10x - 12y + 36 = 0 ....[2]$

a To find the points A and B, rearrange $[1]$ to give $x = 2y - 12$ and substitute into $[2]$:

$(2y - 12)^2 + y^2 - 10(2y - 12) - 12y + 36 = 0$

$4y^2 - 48y + 144 + y^2 - 20y + 120 - 12y + 36 = 0$

$5y^2 - 80y + 300 = 0$

$y^2 - 16y + 60 = 0$

$(y - 10)(y - 6) = 0$

$y = 10$ or $y = 6$

Substituting each solution into $[2]$ gives:

$x = 8$ or $x = 0$

The coordinates of A and B are: (0, 6) and (8, 10) or vice versa.

b Midpoint of $AB = \left(\dfrac{0 + 8}{2}, \dfrac{6 + 10}{2} \right)$ or (4, 8)

The gradient of $AB = \dfrac{10 - 6}{8 - 0}$ or $\dfrac{1}{2}$

The gradient of the perpendicular bisector of AB is –2, since for perpendicular lines $m_1 \times m_2 = -1$

The equation of the perpendicular bisector of AB is found using $y - y_1 = m(x - x_1)$, $m = -2$ and (4, 8)

$y - 8 = -2(x - 4)$

$y - 8 = -2x + 8$

$y = -2x + 16$

c P and Q can be found by solving simultaneously:

$y = -2x + 16 ......[1]$ and

$x^2 + y^2 - 10x - 12y + 36 = 0 ....[2]$

Using $[1]$ substitute for y in $[2]$:

$x^2 + (-2x + 16)^2 - 10x - 12(-2x + 16) + 36 = 0$

$x^2 + 4x^2 - 64x + 256 - 10x + 24x - 192 + 36 = 0$

$5x^2 - 50x + 100 = 0$

$x^2 - 10x + 20 = 0$

Using the quadratic formula:

$a = 1$, $b = -10$, $c = 20$

$x = \dfrac{--10 \pm \sqrt{(-10)^2 - 4(1)(20)}}{2(1)}$

$x = \dfrac{10 \pm \sqrt{20}}{2}$

$x = 5 + \sqrt{5}$ and $x = 5 - \sqrt{5}$

Substituting $x = 5 + \sqrt{5}$ into $[1]$ gives $6 - 2\sqrt{5}$

Substituting $x = 5 - \sqrt{5}$ into $[1]$ gives $6 + 2\sqrt{5}$

P and Q have coordinates:

$(5 - \sqrt{5},\ 6 + 2\sqrt{5})$ and $(5 + \sqrt{5},\ 6 - 2\sqrt{5})$ or vice versa.

d

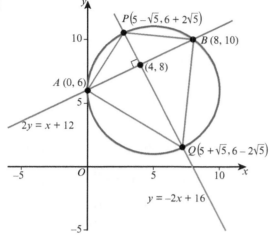

$APBQ$ has to be a kite.

Area of a kite $= \dfrac{1}{2}(AB \times PQ)$

Using Pythagoras:

$AB = \sqrt{(8 - 0)^2 + (10 - 6)^2}$

$AB = \sqrt{80}$

$PQ = \sqrt{\left[\left(5 + \sqrt{5}\right) - \left(5 - \sqrt{5}\right)\right]^2 + \left[\left(6 - 2\sqrt{5}\right) - \left(6 + 2\sqrt{5}\right)\right]^2}$

$\quad = 10$

Area $ABPQ = \dfrac{1}{2} \times \sqrt{80} \times 10$

Area $ABPQ = 20\sqrt{5}$

---

6 Method 1 (Geometric)

$x^2 + y^2 = 25$ has centre $(0, 0)$ and radius 5

We can complete the square for the equation $x^2 + y^2 - 24x - 18y + 125 = 0$:

$(x - 12)^2 - 12^2 + (y - 9)^2 - 9^2 + 125 = 0$

$(x - 12)^2 + (y - 9)^2 = 144 + 81 - 125$

$(x - 12)^2 + (y - 9)^2 = 100$

This circle has centre $(12, 9)$ and radius 10

We can sketch these:

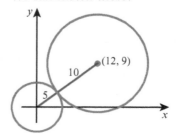

We have to prove that the circles touch.

The length of the line which joins their centres is found by using:

$\sqrt{(x_2 - x_1)^2 + (y_2 - y_1)^2}$ so:

$= \sqrt{(12 - 0)^2 + (9 - 0)^2}$

$= \sqrt{12^2 + 9^2}$

$= \sqrt{225}$

$= 15$

As the radii of the two circles are 5 and 10 and as $5 + 10 = 15$ (the distance between the centres), the two circles touch.

To find the point where they touch, use similar triangles:

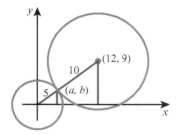

The small triangle has the ratio:

$a : b : 5$

The large triangle has the ratio:

$12 : 9 : 15$

These ratios are the same, so:

$a : b : 5 = 12 : 9 : 15$ or

$a : b : 5 = 4 : 3 : 5$

So, the coordinates of where the two circles touch are at (4, 3).

Method 2 (Algebraic)

We have the equations of the two circles:

$x^2 + y^2 = 25$ ......[1]

$x^2 + y^2 - 24x - 18y + 125 = 0$ ......[2]

Substituting for $x^2 + y^2$ in [2]:

$25 - 24x - 18y + 125 = 0$

$24x + 18y = 150$ or:

$4x + 3y = 25$

If the two circles meet then the intersection points must lie on $4x + 3y = 25$ ....[3]

If we solve simultaneously

$4x + 3y = 25$ ..... [3]

$x^2 + y^2 = 25$ ..... [1]

we find the point(s) where this line meets the circle.

Making x the subject of [3] gives:

$x = \dfrac{25 - 3y}{4}$

If we substitute for x in [1] we get:

$\left(\dfrac{25 - 3y}{4}\right)^2 + y^2 = 25$

$(25 - 3y)^2 + 16y^2 = 400$

$625 - 150y + 9y^2 + 16y^2 = 400$

$25y^2 - 150y + 225 = 0$

$y^2 - 6y + 9 = 0$

$(y - 3)^2 = 0$

$y = 3$

Since there is a single repeated solution, the line is a tangent to the circle.

The x-coordinate of the intersection is

$x = \dfrac{25 - 3(3)}{4}$ or $x = 4$

The touching point is at (4, 3)

If we substitute for x in [2] we get:

$\left(\dfrac{25 - 3y}{4}\right)^2 + y^2 - 24\left(\dfrac{25 - 3y}{4}\right) - 18y + 125 = 0$

$(25 - 3y)^2 + 16y^2 - 96(25 - 3y) - 288y + 2000 = 0$

$625 - 150y + 9y^2 + 16y^2 - 2400$

$+ 288y - 288y + 2000 = 0$

$25y^2 - 150y + 225 = 0$

$y^2 - 6y + 9 = 0$

$(y - 3)^2 = 0$

$y = 3$

Since there is a single repeated solution, the line is a tangent to the circle.

The x-coordinate of the intersection is

$x = \dfrac{25 - 3(3)}{4}$ or $x = 4$

The touching point is at (4, 3)

So the circles both touch at the point (4, 3).

7

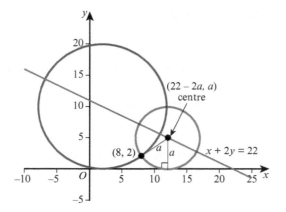

a Looking at the diagram, the distance from the centre of the red circle to the x-axis must equal the distance from the centre of the same circle to the point (8, 2).

The centre of this circle lies on the line $x + 2y = 22$

Let this centre have a y-coordinate a.

Substituting $y = a$ into $x + 2y = 22$ gives:

$x + 2a = 22$

$x = 22 - 2a$

So this circle has a centre $(22 - 2a, a)$

The distance from (8, 2) to $(22 - 2a, a)$ is found using the distance formula:

$$\text{Distance} = \sqrt{(22 - 2a - 8)^2 + (a - 2)^2}$$
$$= \sqrt{(14 - 2a)^2 + (a - 2)^2}$$
$$= \sqrt{196 - 56a + 4a^2 + a^2 - 4a + 4}$$
$$= \sqrt{5a^2 - 60a + 200}$$

This distance has to be equal to a since the centre of the circle is y (or a) units above the x-axis. a is the radius of the circle.

$$a = \sqrt{5a^2 - 60a + 200}$$

Squaring both sides gives:

$a^2 = 5a^2 - 60a + 200$ so:

$4a^2 - 60a + 200 = 0$

$a^2 - 15a + 50 = 0$

$(a - 10)(a - 5) = 0$

$a = 10$ or $a = 5$. There are two solutions, two radii, because both circles satisfy the criteria above.

The centre of the circles are at (2, 10) (blue circle on the diagram) and (12, 5) (the red circle on the diagram).

The radius of the blue circle is 10 and the radius of the red circle is 5.

The equations of both circles are:

$(x - 2)^2 + (y - 10)^2 = 100$ ......[1]

$(x - 12)^2 + (y - 5)^2 = 25$ ....[2]

b To prove that the line $4x + 3y = 88$ is a common tangent to both circles, there are two methods.

Method 1

Use direct substitution to find where the line intersects both circles. This should produce a single repeated root for each equation.

Using $4x + 3y = 88$, make x the subject:

$4x = 88 - 3y$

$x = \dfrac{88 - 3y}{4}$

Substituting for x in [1] gives:

$$\left(\frac{88 - 3y}{4} - 2\right)^2 + (y - 10)^2 = 100$$

$$\left(\frac{88 - 3y}{4} - \frac{8}{4}\right)^2 + (y - 10)^2 = 100$$

$$\left(\frac{80 - 3y}{4}\right)^2 + (y - 10)^2 = 100$$

$(80 - 3y)^2 + 16(y - 10)^2 = 1600$

$(80 - 3y)^2 + 16y^2 - 320y + 1600 = 1600$

$6400 - 480y + 9y^2 + 16y^2 - 320y + 1600 = 1600$

$6400 - 800y + 25y^2 = 0$

$y^2 - 32y + 256 = 0$

$(y - 16)(y - 16) = 0$

$y = 16$ i.e. one repeated root so

$4x + 3y = 88$ is a tangent to the first circle.

Substituting $x = \dfrac{88 - 3y}{4}$ into [2] gives:

$$\left(\dfrac{88 - 3y}{4} - 12\right)^2 + (y - 5)^2 = 25$$

$$\left(\dfrac{88 - 3y}{4} - \dfrac{48}{4}\right)^2 + (y - 5)^2 = 25$$

$$\left(\dfrac{40 - 3y}{4}\right)^2 + (y - 5)^2 = 25$$

$$(40 - 3y)^2 + 16(y - 5)^2 = 400$$

$$1600 - 240y + 9y^2 + 16y^2 - 160y + 400 = 400$$

$$1600 - 400y + 25y^2 = 0$$

$$y^2 - 16y + 64 = 0$$

$$(y - 8)(y - 8) = 0$$

$y = 8$ i.e. one repeated root so

$4x + 3y = 88$ is a tangent to the second circle also.

There is an alternative method to this part which uses the fact that a tangent to a circle will be perpendicular to the radius at that point:

Method 2

We need to find the point on $4x + 3y = 88$ which is closest to the centre of the circle by dropping a perpendicular to the line from the centre. If this point lies on the circle, we know that the line is a tangent.

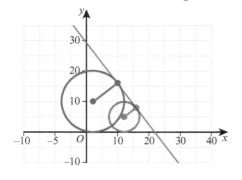

The line $4x + 3y = 88$ when rearranged gives:

$$y = \dfrac{-4}{3}x - \dfrac{88}{3}$$

The gradient of this line is $-\dfrac{4}{3}$

The gradient of a line perpendicular to this has a gradient $\dfrac{3}{4}$

since for perpendicular lines $m_1 \times m_2 = -1$.

The circle with equation $(x - 2)^2 + (y - 10)^2 = 100$ has centre $(2, 10)$

Substituting this point and the gradient into $y - y_1 = m(x - x_1)$ gives:

$$y - 10 = \dfrac{3}{4}(x - 2)$$

$$4y - 40 = 3x - 6$$

$$3x - 4y = -34 \ \ldots\ldots\ldots\ldots [3]$$

$$4x + 3y = 88 \ \ldots\ldots\ldots\ldots... [4]$$

Multiply [3] by 3, [4] by 4 and add:

$$25x = 250$$

$$x = 10$$

Substituting into [4] gives:

$$4(10) + 3y = 88$$

$$y = 16$$

The point $(10, 16)$ also lies on the circle since:

$$(10 - 2)^2 + (16 - 10)^2 = 100$$

$$64 + 36 = 100$$

Hence, the line $4x + 3y = 88$ intersects the circle at one point so it must be a tangent line.

Repeating the same method with the second circle will prove that the line is a tangent to both circles.

1 a Method 1

$$180° = \pi \text{ radians}$$

$$\left(\frac{180}{9}\right)° = \frac{\pi}{9} \text{ radians}$$

$$20° = \frac{\pi}{9} \text{ radians}$$

Method 2

$$20° = \left(20 \times \frac{\pi}{180}\right) \text{ radians}$$

$$20° = \frac{\pi}{9} \text{ radians}$$

l Method 1

$$180° = \pi \text{ radians}$$

$$1° = \frac{\pi}{180°} \text{ radians}$$

$$540° \times 1° = 540° \times \frac{\pi}{180} \text{ radians}$$

$$= 3\pi \text{ radians}$$

Method 2

$$540° = \left(540 \times \frac{\pi}{180}\right) \text{ radians}$$

$$540° = 3\pi \text{ radians}$$

2 g $\pi \text{ radians} = 180°$

$$\frac{3\pi}{10} \text{ radians} = \frac{3}{10} \times 180°$$

$$\frac{3\pi}{10} \text{ radians} = 54°$$

m $\dfrac{5\pi}{4} \text{ radians} = \left(\dfrac{5\pi}{4} \times \dfrac{180}{\pi}\right)°$

$$\frac{5\pi}{4} \text{ radians} = 225°$$

3 d 200°

To change from degrees to radians, multiply by $\dfrac{\pi}{180}$. (Use calculator π.)

$$200° \times \frac{\pi}{180} = 3.49 \text{ radians}$$

4 b 0.8 radians

To change from radians to degrees, multiply by $\dfrac{180}{\pi}$.

$$0.8 \text{ radians} \times \frac{180}{\pi} = 45.8°$$

6 b $\tan (1.5 \text{ rad}) = 14.1$

> You do not need to change the angle to degrees. You should set the angle mode on your calculator to radians.

7 $\tan 1 \text{ radian} = \dfrac{QR}{5}$

$$QR = 5 \times \tan 1$$

$$QR = 5 \times 1.5574\ldots$$

$$QR = 7.79 \text{ cm (to 3 significant figures)}$$

8 We need to solve $\sin x° = \sin x^{\text{radians}}$

As $1 \text{ radian} = \dfrac{180°}{\pi}$, we need to solve

$$\sin x° = \sin \frac{180x°}{\pi}$$

Plotting the sine of angles between 10° and 15° in both degrees and radians on the same axes gives the result.

The intersection point is 12.79° to 2 decimal places.

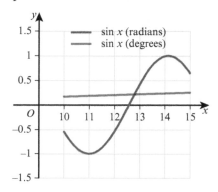

The graph originates from a spreadsheet, part of which is shown in the diagram:

fx	= SIN(A3*3.141/180)

◢	A	B	C	D
1				
2	×	sin x (Radians)	sin x (degrees)	
3	10	−0.544021111	0.173615753	
4	10.1	−0.625070649	0.175333987	
5	10.2	−0.699874688	0.177051687	
6	10.3	−0.76768581	0.178768849	
7	10.4	−0.827826469	0.180485465	
8	10.5	−0.87969576	0.182201533	
9	10.6	−0.922775422	0.183917045	
10	10.7	−0.956635016	0.185631998	
11	10.8	−0.98093623	0.187346385	
12	10.9	−0.995436253	0.189060202	
13	11	−0.999990207	0.190773443	
14	11.1	−0.994552588	0.192486103	
15	11.2	−0.979177729	0.194198177	
16	11.3	−0.95401925	0.19590966	
17	11.4	−0.919328526	0.197620546	
18	11.5	−0.875452175	0.19933083	
19	11.6	−0.822828595	0.201040508	
20	11.7	−0.761983584	0.202749573	
21	11.8	−0.693525085	0.204458021	

EXERCISE 4B

> You will need to recall and apply your knowledge of circle theorems for this and subsequent exercises.

1 b Radius 7 cm and angle $\dfrac{3\pi}{7}$

Arc length $= r\theta$

$$= 7 \times \frac{3\pi}{7}$$

$$= 3\pi \text{ cm}$$

2 a Radius 10 cm and angle 1.3 radians

Arc length $= r\theta$

$$= 10 \times 1.3$$

$$= 13 \text{ cm}$$

3 a Radius 10 cm and arc length 5 cm

Arc length $= r\theta$

$$5 = 10 \times \theta$$

$$\theta = 0.5 \text{ radians}$$

4 Radius $= 158.5 \div 2$

$$= 79.25 \text{ m}$$

Using arc length $= r\theta$

Distance travelled $= 79.25 \times \dfrac{\pi}{16}$

$$= 15.6 \text{ m}$$

5

> Do not confuse the perimeter of a sector with its arc length.

b Perimeter of the sector $= r\theta + 2r$
$$= 5 \times 2.1 + 2 \times 5$$
$$= 20.5 \text{ cm}$$

6 a Tan (angle POQ) $= \dfrac{8}{6}$

$POQ = 0.92729...$
$\qquad = 0.927$ rad(to 3 significant figures)

b $QR = QO - OR$

Using Pythagoras:
$QO = \sqrt{QP^2 + PO^2}$
$\quad = \pm\sqrt{8^2 + 6^2}$
$\quad = 10$ cm (reject negative value as length cannot be negative)

$QR = 10 - 6$
$\quad = 4$ cm

c Perimeter of the shaded area
$= PQ + QR + \text{arc } PR$
$= 8 + 4 + 6 \times 0.92729...$

> If your final answer is to be given to 3 significant figures, always use **more** than 3 significant figures in your working.

$= 17.56377...$

$= 17.6$ cm (to 3 significant figures)

7 a Arc length $AB = r\theta$
$$= 7 \times 2$$
$$= 14 \text{ cm}$$

b Use the cosine rule, $a^2 = b^2 + c^2 - 2bc \cos A$, to find the length of chord AB:

$AB = \pm\sqrt{7^2 + 7^2 - 2(7)(7) \cos 2}$

(Make sure your calculator is in radians.)

$= \pm 11.7805...$ (reject negative value as length cannot be negative)

$AB = 11.8$ cm (to 3 significant figures)

c The perimeter of the shaded segment
$= \text{arc } AB + \text{chord } AB$
$= 14 + 11.7805...$
$= 25.8$ cm (to 3 significant figures)

8 a Using Pythagoras:

the length of $AO = \pm\sqrt{AB^2 + BO^2}$
$\quad = \pm\sqrt{5^2 + 12^2}$
$\quad = 13$ cm (reject negative value as length cannot be negative)

> Special Pythagoras triangles which should be learnt include: 3, 4, 5 triangles; 5, 12, 13 triangles and 7, 24, 25 triangles.

b Angle $AOD = \pi - 2 \times$ angle AOB
$$= \pi - 2 \times \tan^{-1}\left(\frac{5}{12}\right)$$
$$= \pi - 2 \times 0.39479...$$
$$= 2.35201...$$
$$= 2.35 \text{ radians (to 3 significant figures)}$$

c The perimeter of the shaded region
$= \text{arc } AED + AO + OD$
$= 13 \times 2.35201... + 13 + 13$
$= 56.57613...$
$= 56.6$ cm (to 3 significant figures)

9 a Angle $AOC = \pi - \theta$

If the perimeter of sector AOC is twice the perimeter of sector BOC then:
$$10(\pi - \theta) + 10 + 10 = 2 \times (10\theta + 10 + 10)$$
$$10\pi - 10\theta + 20 = 20\theta + 40$$
$$30\theta = 10\pi - 20$$
$$\theta = \frac{\pi - 2}{3} \text{ shown}$$

b

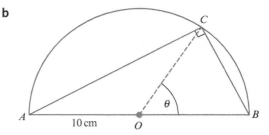

Use triangle OBC and the cosine rule:
$$a^2 = b^2 + c^2 - 2bc \cos A$$
to find the length of chord BC.

$BC = \pm\sqrt{10^2 + 10^2 - 2(10)(10) \cos\left(\dfrac{\pi - 2}{3}\right)}$

(Make sure your calculator is in radians.)

$$= \pm \sqrt{200 - 200 \cos \left(\frac{\pi - 2}{3} \right)}$$

$= 3.78239\ldots$

(reject negative value as length cannot be negative).

Angle ACB is $90°$ (angle in a semicircle).

Using Pythagoras:

$AC^2 = 20^2 - 3.78239\ldots^2$

$AC^2 = 385.69352\ldots$

$AC = 19.63908\ldots$

[AC can also be found by using the cosine rule:

$a^2 = b^2 + c^2 - 2bc \cos A$

Which when rearranged gives:

$$AC = \sqrt{200 - 200 \cos \left[\pi - \left(\frac{\pi - 2}{3} \right) \right]}$$

$$AC = \sqrt{200 - 200 \cos \left(\frac{2\pi + 2}{3} \right)}$$

$AC = \sqrt{200 - 200 \cos (-0.928467)}$ etc

but this method is prone to errors if you are not careful].

Perimeter of triangle $ABC = 3.78239\ldots$
$+ 19.63908\ldots + 20$

$= 43.4$ cm (to 3 significant figures)

10 The wire is made up of two arcs of circles joined by two straight lines. The straight part of the wire runs along two lines that are tangent to both circles. Drawing in the radii of both circles and the straight line joining their centres together with other helpful lines we have:

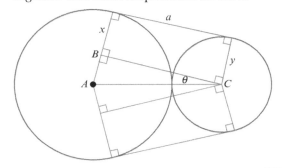

There is a triangle in the diagram which we will use too.

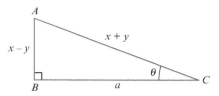

Using Pythagoras:

$a = \sqrt{(x+y)^2 - (x-y)^2}$

$a = \sqrt{x^2 + 2xy + y^2 - (x^2 - 2xy + y^2)}$

$a = \sqrt{x^2 + 2xy + y^2 - x^2 + 2xy - y^2}$

$a = \sqrt{4xy}$ or $a = 2\sqrt{xy}$

Using trigonometry:

$$\sin \theta = \frac{x - y}{x + y}$$

$$\theta = \sin^{-1} \left(\frac{x - y}{x + y} \right) *$$

To find the length of the arcs,

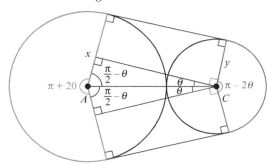

The reflex angle at A is $2\pi - \left(\frac{\pi}{2} - \theta \right) - \left(\frac{\pi}{2} - \theta \right)$

$= 2\pi - \frac{\pi}{2} + \theta - \frac{\pi}{2} + \theta$

$= \pi + 2\theta$

The obtuse angle at B is $2\pi - \frac{\pi}{2} - \frac{\pi}{2} - \theta - \theta$

$= \pi - 2\theta$

Arc length $= r\theta$

Length of the left arc is $x(\pi + 2\theta)$

Length of the right arc is $y(\pi - 2\theta)$

Total length of the belt is:

$a + a + x(\pi + 2\theta) + y(\pi - 2\theta)$

$= 2\sqrt{xy} + 2\sqrt{xy} + x\pi + y\pi + 2x\theta - 2y\theta$

Adding the first two terms, factorising the next two terms and factorising the last two terms gives:

$4\sqrt{xy} + \pi(x + y) + 2\theta(x - y)$

Substituting for θ from * gives:

$4\sqrt{xy} + \pi(x + y) + 2(x - y)\sin^{-1}\left(\dfrac{x - y}{x + y}\right)$ shown

EXERCISE 4C

1 a radius 12 cm and angle $\dfrac{\pi}{6}$ radian

Area of sector $= \dfrac{1}{2}r^2\theta$

$= \dfrac{1}{2} \times 12^2 \times \dfrac{\pi}{6}$

$= 12\pi$ cm^2

2 a Area of sector $= \dfrac{1}{2}r^2\theta$

$= \dfrac{1}{2} \times 34^2 \times 1.5$

$= 867$ cm^2

3 a radius 4 cm and area 9 cm^2

Area of sector $= \dfrac{1}{2}r^2\theta$

$9 = \dfrac{1}{2} \times 4^2 \times \theta$

$\theta = 1.125$ radians

4 a Arc length $= r\theta$

$10 = 8\theta$

$\theta = 1.25$ radians

b Area of sector $= \dfrac{1}{2}r^2\theta$

$= \dfrac{1}{2} \times 8^2 \times 1.25$

$= 40$ cm^2

5 a Arc length $= r\theta$

$7 = 4\theta$

$\theta = \dfrac{7}{4}$ or 1.75 radians

So, angle $POQ = 1.75$ radians

b Triangle POX is right angled (angle between tangent and radius is 90°).

Angle POX is $\dfrac{1.75}{2} = 0.875$ radians

Using trigonometry,

$\tan 0.875 = \dfrac{PX}{4}$

$PX = 4 \times \tan 0.875$

Remember your calculator needs to be in radians.

$PX = 4.7896...$ cm

$PX = 4.79$ cm (to 3 significant figures)

c Area shade $=$ Area $OPXQ -$ area of sector OPQ

Using area of a $\Delta = \dfrac{1}{2} \times$ base $\times$ perpendicular height and area of a sector $= \dfrac{1}{2}r^2\theta$:

Area shaded $= 2 \times$ area of $\Delta OPX - \dfrac{1}{2} \times 4^2 \times 1.75$

$= 2 \times \dfrac{1}{2} \times 4 \times 4.7896...$

$- \dfrac{1}{2} \times 4^2 \times 1.75$

$= 19.158... - 14$

$= 5.16$ cm^2 (to 3 significant figures)

6 Shaded region $=$ Area $\Delta OQR -$ area of sector OPR

Use area of a $\Delta = \dfrac{1}{2} \times$ base $\times$ perpendicular height and area of a sector $= \dfrac{1}{2}r^2\theta$.

To find the area of ΔOQR, first find RQ.

Triangle OQR is right angled at R

$\tan ROQ = \dfrac{RQ}{8}$

$\tan \dfrac{\pi}{3} = \dfrac{RQ}{8}$ (use radians)

$\sqrt{3} = \dfrac{RQ}{8}$

$RQ = 8\sqrt{3}$

Angle $BAC = 0.643501\ldots$ radians

Angle $BCA = \pi - \dfrac{\pi}{2} - 0.643501\ldots$

$= 0.927295\ldots$ radians

Area of sector $ADE = \dfrac{1}{2}r^2\theta$

Area of sector $ADE = \dfrac{1}{2} \times 6^2 \times 0.643501\ldots$

$= 11.58301\ldots$

Area of sector $FCD = \dfrac{1}{2}r^2\theta$

Area of sector $FCD = \dfrac{1}{2} \times 4^2 \times 0.927295\ldots$

$= 7.41836\ldots$

Area of sector $EBF = \dfrac{1}{2}r^2\theta$

Area of sector $EBF = \dfrac{1}{2} \times 2^2 \times \dfrac{\pi}{2}$

$= \pi$

Area of the three sectors $= 11.58301\ldots$
$+ 7.41836\ldots + \pi$
$= 22.14297\ldots$

Area of triangle $ABC = \dfrac{1}{2} \times 8 \times 6$

$= 24 \text{ cm}^2$

Shaded area $= 24 - 22.14297\ldots$

$= 1.85702\ldots$

$= 1.86 \text{ cm}^2$ (to 3 significant figures)

> Do not evaluate this as the question asked for exact values.

Shaded region $= \dfrac{1}{2} \times 8 \times 8\sqrt{3} - \dfrac{1}{2} \times 8^2 \times \dfrac{\pi}{3}$

$= \left(32\sqrt{3} - \dfrac{32\pi}{3}\right) \text{ cm}^2$

7 a Angles OBP and OAP are right angles (angle between tangent and radius is 90°).

Angle $POA = \dfrac{\pi}{6}$

Using triangle POA:

$\tan \dfrac{\pi}{6} = \dfrac{AP}{5}$

$AP = 5 \tan \dfrac{\pi}{6}$ (use radian mode on your calculator)

$AP = \dfrac{5\sqrt{3}}{3} \text{ cm}$

b Shaded region = area $OAPB$ − area sector OAB

Using area of a $\Delta = \dfrac{1}{2} \times$ base $\times$ perpendicular height and area of a sector $= \dfrac{1}{2}r^2\theta$:

$= 2 \times \dfrac{1}{2} \times 5 \times \dfrac{5\sqrt{3}}{3} - \dfrac{1}{2} \times 5^2 \times \dfrac{\pi}{3}$

$= \dfrac{25\sqrt{3}}{3} - \dfrac{25\pi}{6}$

$= \dfrac{25}{6}(2\sqrt{3} - \pi) \text{ cm}^2$

8 Label the diagram with the letters shown.

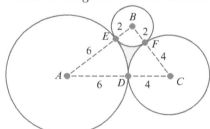

Angle $ABC = 90°$

[Check using Pythagoras,

$AC^2 = AB^2 + BC^2$

$10^2 = 8^2 + 6^2$

$100 = 64 + 36$

$100 = 100$ is true].

$\tan$ angle $BAC = \dfrac{6}{8}$

9

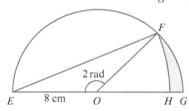

> Be careful! OH is not 8 cm.

a Using area of a triangle $= \dfrac{1}{2}ab\sin C$

the area of triangle $EOF = \dfrac{1}{2} \times 8 \times 8 \times \sin 2$

(use radian mode on your calculator)

$= 29.09751\ldots \text{ cm}^2$

$= 29.1 \text{ cm}^2$ (to 3 significant figures)

b Area sector $FOG = \frac{1}{2}r^2\theta$

$$= \frac{1}{2} \times 8^2 \times (\pi - 2)$$

$$= 36.53096\dots$$

$$= 36.5 \text{ cm}^2 \text{ (to 3 significant figures)}$$

c The radius of sector FEH is EF.

Using cosine rule, $a^2 = b^2 + c^2 - 2bc \cos A$, to find EF:

$$EF^2 = 8^2 + 8^2 - 2 \times 8 \times 8 \times \cos 2$$

(use radian mode on your calculator)

$$EF = \sqrt{181.26679\dots}$$

$$EF = 13.46353\dots$$

ΔEOF is isosceles ($OE = OF$)

Angle $FEH = \dfrac{\pi - 2}{2}$ radians

Area of sector $FEH = \frac{1}{2}r^2\theta$

$$= \frac{1}{2} \times 13.46353\dots^2 \times \left(\frac{\pi - 2}{2}\right)$$

$$= 51.73321\dots$$

$$= 51.7 \text{ cm}^2 \text{ (to 3 significant figures)}.$$

d Shaded area = area of sector FOG − area FOH

Area FOH = area of sector FEH − area of ΔEOF

$$= 51.73321\dots - 29.09751\dots$$

$$= 22.6357\dots \text{ cm}^2$$

Shaded area $= 36.53096\dots - 22.6357\dots$

$$= 13.89526\dots$$

$$= 13.9 \text{ cm}^2 \text{ (to 3 significant figures)}$$

10 a Angle OGF is a right angle (angle between tangent and radius is $90°$).

$OE = EF$

Using ΔOGF and Pythagoras:

$$GF^2 = (2r)^2 - r^2$$

$$GF^2 = 3r^2$$

$$GF = \pm\sqrt{3}\,r \text{ cm}$$

(reject negative value as length cannot be negative).

Using ΔOGF, cosine angle $GOF = \dfrac{r}{2r}$

Angle $GOF = \cos^{-1}\left(\dfrac{1}{2}\right)$ or $\dfrac{\pi}{3}$

$P = \text{Arc } EG + EF + GF$

$P = r \times \dfrac{\pi}{3} + r + \sqrt{3}\,r$

$P = \dfrac{r}{3}(\pi + 3 + 3\sqrt{3})$

Or $P = \dfrac{r}{3}(3 + 3\sqrt{3} + \pi)$ shown.

b Using area of a $\Delta = \frac{1}{2} \times$ base $\times$ perpendicular height:

Area $\Delta OGF = \frac{1}{2} \times GF \times OG$

$$= \frac{1}{2} \times \sqrt{3}\,r \times r$$

$$= \frac{\sqrt{3}\,r^2}{2} \text{ cm}^2$$

Area of sector $OGE = \frac{1}{2}r^2\theta$

$$= \frac{1}{2} \times r^2 \times \frac{\pi}{3}$$

$$= \frac{\pi r^2}{6}$$

Shaded area $= \dfrac{\sqrt{3}\,r^2}{2} - \dfrac{\pi r^2}{6}$

$$= \frac{r^2}{6}(3\sqrt{3} - \pi) \text{ Shown}$$

11 Refer to the lettered diagram shown:

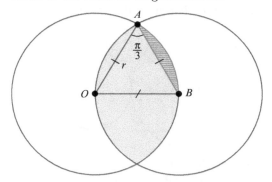

Triangle OAB is equilateral as $OA = AB = OB$

Angle $OAB = \dfrac{\pi}{3}$

Using area of a $\Delta = \frac{1}{2} \times$ base $\times$ perpendicular height:

Area of $\Delta OAB = \frac{1}{2} \times OA \times OB \times \sin OAB$

$$= \frac{1}{2} \times r \times r \times \sin\left(\frac{\pi}{3}\right)$$

$$= \frac{1}{2} \times r \times r \times \frac{\sqrt{3}}{2}$$

$$= \frac{\sqrt{3}}{4} r^2$$

Area of sector $OAB = \frac{1}{2} r^2 \theta$

$$= \frac{1}{2} \times r^2 \times \frac{\pi}{3}$$

$$= \frac{\pi r^2}{6}$$

Area of segment $= \frac{\pi r^2}{6} - \frac{\sqrt{3}}{4} r^2$ cm^2

(shown as orange shading in the diagram)

> Do not confuse **sector** with **segment**.

The shaded area required $= 2 \times$ area of $\Delta OAB + 4$ segments

$$= 2 \times \frac{\sqrt{3}}{4} r^2 + 4 \times \left(\frac{\pi r^2}{6} - \frac{\sqrt{3}}{4} r^2 \right)$$

$$= \frac{\sqrt{3}}{2} r^2 + \frac{2\pi r^2}{3} - \sqrt{3} r^2$$

$$= \frac{2\pi r^2}{3} - \frac{\sqrt{3}}{2} r^2 \text{ cm}^2$$

12 The image in the question is part of a larger diagram:

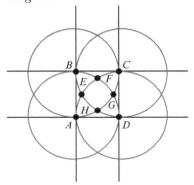

Angle EDF is $\frac{\pi}{6}$ because $DA = DE = DF = DC$ and ΔEDA, ΔFDE, ΔCDF are all congruent triangles. (They are isosceles triangles).

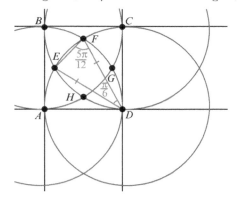

Using area of a $\Delta = \frac{1}{2} \times$ base $\times$ perpendicular height:

ΔFDE has an area $= \frac{1}{2} \times DE \times DF \times \sin FDE$

$$= \frac{1}{2} \times 10 \times 10 \times \sin\left(\frac{\pi}{6}\right)$$

$$= 25 \text{ cm}^2$$

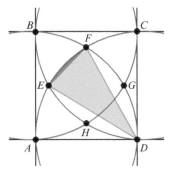

The red segment $= \frac{1}{2} \times 10^2 \times \left(\frac{\pi}{6}\right) - 25$

$$= \frac{25\pi}{3} - 25 \text{ cm}^2$$

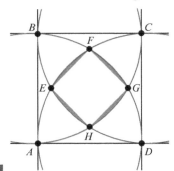

Four red segments
have an area $= 4\left(\dfrac{25\pi}{3} - 25\right)$

$= \dfrac{100\pi}{3} - 100$ cm²

We now have to find the area of the square $EFGH$.

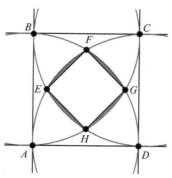

Using $\triangle FDE$,

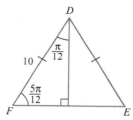

$\cos\dfrac{5\pi}{12} = \dfrac{\frac{1}{2}FE}{10}$ so:

$FE = 2 \times 10 \cos\dfrac{5\pi}{12}$

$= 5\sqrt{6} - 5\sqrt{2}$

Area of square $EFGH = (5\sqrt{6} - 5\sqrt{2})^2$

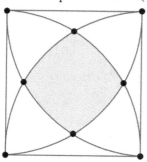

Total area required $= \dfrac{100\pi}{3} - 100 + (5\sqrt{6} - 5\sqrt{2})^{2*}$

$= \dfrac{100\pi}{3} - 100 + 200 - 100\sqrt{3}$

$= 100 + \dfrac{100\pi}{3} - 100\sqrt{3}$

$= 100\left(1 + \dfrac{\pi}{3} - \sqrt{3}\right)$ cm²

$*[(5\sqrt{6} - 5\sqrt{2})(5\sqrt{6} - 5\sqrt{2})$

$= 150 - 25\sqrt{12} - 25\sqrt{12} + 50$

$= 200 - 50\sqrt{12}$

$= 200 - 100\sqrt{3}$]

13 a Angle OPA is a right angle (angle between tangent and radius is 90°).

Angle $POB = x$

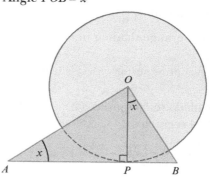

Using $\triangle AOP$, $\tan x = \dfrac{1}{AP}$

$AP = \dfrac{1}{\tan x}$

Using $\triangle AOP$, $\tan x = \dfrac{BP}{1}$

$BP = \tan x$

$AB = AP + PB$

$AB = \tan x + \dfrac{1}{\tan x}$ cm

b Blue shaded area $= \dfrac{1}{2} \times 1^2 \times \dfrac{3\pi}{2}$

$= \dfrac{3\pi}{4}$ cm²

Orange shaded area $= \dfrac{1}{2} \times AB \times OP$

$= \dfrac{1}{2} \times \left(\tan x + \dfrac{1}{\tan x}\right) \times 1$

$= \dfrac{1}{2}\left(\tan x + \dfrac{1}{\tan x}\right)$

If the two shaded areas are equal:

$$\frac{1}{2}\left(\tan x + \frac{1}{\tan x}\right) = \frac{3\pi}{4}$$

$$2\tan x + \frac{2}{\tan x} = 3\pi$$

$2\tan^2 x + 2 = 3\pi \tan x$

$2\tan^2 x - 3\pi \tan x + 2 = 0$

Let $y = \tan x$

So, $2y^2 - 3\pi y + 2 = 0$

Comparing with $ay^2 + by + c = 0$

$a = 2$, $b = -3\pi$, $c = 2$

$$y = \frac{--3\pi \pm \sqrt{(-3\pi)^2 - 4(2)(2)}}{2(2)}$$

$y = 4.48965$ or $y = 0.22273$

$\tan x = 4.48965$ or $\tan x = 0.22273$

$x = 1.35164$ radians

or $x = 0.21915$ radians

14 a Refer to the lettered diagram shown:

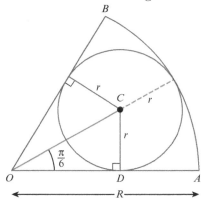

Angle ODC is a right angle (angle between tangent and radius is 90°).

Using triangle OCD,

$$\sin\left(\frac{\pi}{6}\right) = \frac{r}{OC}$$

$$OC = \frac{r}{\sin\left(\frac{\pi}{6}\right)}$$

$OC = 2r$ cm

$R = OC + r$

$R = 2r + r$

$R = 3r$ Shown

b Area of inner circle $= \pi r^2$

Area of sector $= \frac{1}{2} r^2 \theta$

$$= \frac{1}{2} \times (3r)^2 \times \frac{\pi}{3} \text{ or } \frac{3\pi r^2}{2}$$

$$\frac{\text{area of inner circle}}{\text{area of sector}} = \frac{\pi r^2}{\frac{3\pi r^2}{2}}$$

$$= \frac{2}{3} \text{ shown}$$

1 d Use the triangle shown and Pythagoras to find x:

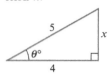

$$x^2 + 4^2 = 5^2$$
$$x = \sqrt{5^2 - 4^2}$$
$$x = 3$$
$$\tan \theta = \frac{3}{4}$$
$$\frac{5}{\tan \theta} = \frac{5}{\frac{3}{4}}$$
$$= \frac{20}{3}$$

2 b Use the triangle shown and Pythagoras:

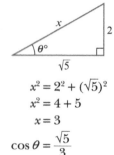

$$x^2 = 2^2 + (\sqrt{5})^2$$
$$x^2 = 4 + 5$$
$$x = 3$$
$$\cos \theta = \frac{\sqrt{5}}{3}$$

3 b Use the triangle below and Pythagoras:

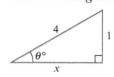

$$x^2 + 1^2 = 4^2$$
$$x = \sqrt{15}$$
$$\tan \theta = \frac{1}{\sqrt{15}}$$
$$\tan \theta = \frac{\sqrt{15}}{15}$$

> It is usual practice to rationalise the denominators of fractions (providing they are numerical) when giving answers.

4 b $\sin^2 \theta = \sin \theta \times \sin \theta$

> $\sin^2\theta$ means $(\sin \theta)^2$

Recall the triangle:

$$\sin^2 \theta = \frac{1}{\sqrt{2}} \times \frac{1}{\sqrt{2}}$$
$$= \frac{1}{2}$$

5 c $1 - 2 \sin^2 \dfrac{\pi}{6} = 1 - 2 \times \sin \dfrac{\pi}{6} \times \sin \dfrac{\pi}{6}$

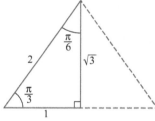

$$= 1 - 2 \times \frac{1}{2} \times \frac{1}{2}$$
$$= \frac{1}{2}$$

6 The two special triangles help to complete the table:

> Learn these 'exact values' triangles as they are very useful.

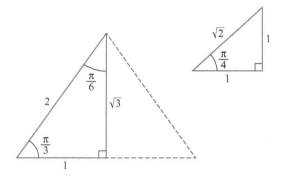

	$\theta = \dfrac{\pi}{4}$	$\theta = \dfrac{\pi}{3}$	$\theta = \dfrac{\pi}{6}$
$\tan\theta$	1	$\sqrt{3}$	$\dfrac{1}{\sqrt{3}}$
$\cos\theta$	$\dfrac{1}{\sqrt{2}}$	$\dfrac{1}{2}$	$\dfrac{\sqrt{3}}{2}$
$\dfrac{1}{\sin\theta}$	$\sqrt{2}$	$\dfrac{2}{\sqrt{3}}$	2

EXERCISE 5B

The acute angle made with the *x*-axis is called the basic angle or reference angle.

1 a

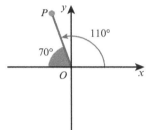

Basic angle is 70°

2 c Basic angle is 50°

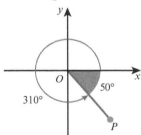

h Basic angle is $\dfrac{\pi}{3}$

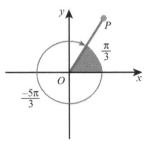

3 b $\theta = -160°$

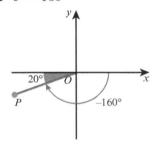

e $\theta = \dfrac{8\pi}{3}$

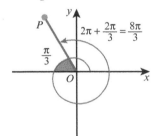

1 c tan 125°

The acute angle made with the x-axis is 55°.

In the second quadrant tan is negative.

tan 125° = −tan 55°

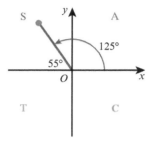

g The acute angle made with the x-axis is $\dfrac{3\pi}{10}$.

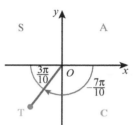

In the third quadrant cos is negative.

$$\cos -\frac{7\pi}{10} = -\cos \frac{3\pi}{10}$$

2 e $\dfrac{4\pi}{3}$ lies in the third quadrant.

$\therefore \sin \dfrac{4\pi}{3}$ is negative

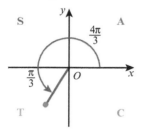

Basic acute angle is $\dfrac{4\pi}{3} - \pi = \dfrac{\pi}{3}$

$\therefore \sin \dfrac{4\pi}{3} = -\sin \dfrac{\pi}{3} = -\dfrac{\sqrt{3}}{2}$

3 $\sin \theta < 0$ means that sin is negative

$\tan \theta < 0$ means that tan is negative

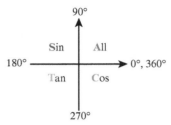

θ is in the 4th quadrant

4 a If θ is obtuse then $90° < \theta < 180°$

i.e. the second quadrant.

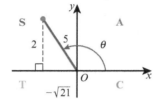

Using Pythagoras, $x^2 = 5^2 - 2^2$

$$x = \pm\sqrt{21}$$

Since $x < 0$, $x = -\sqrt{21}$

$$\cos \theta = \frac{-\sqrt{21}}{5}$$

b $\tan \theta = \dfrac{2}{-\sqrt{21}}$ or $-\dfrac{2}{\sqrt{21}}$

5 $180° \leqslant \theta \leqslant 270°$ is the third quadrant.

$\sin \theta$ is negative in the third quadrant

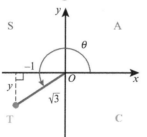

$y^2 + (-1)^2 = (\sqrt{3})^2$

$$y^2 = 2$$

$y = \pm\sqrt{2}$ since $y < 0$, $y = -\sqrt{2}$

$\sin \theta = \dfrac{-\sqrt{2}}{\sqrt{3}}$ or $-\sqrt{\dfrac{2}{3}}$

b $\tan \theta = \dfrac{-\sqrt{2}}{-1}$ or $\sqrt{2}$

6 a $180° \leqslant \theta \leqslant 360°$ are the 3rd and 4th quadrants.

However, tan is positive in the 3rd quadrant so we are looking at the 4th quadrant.

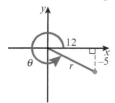

$r^2 = (-5)^2 + 12^2$
$r^2 = \pm\sqrt{169}$
$r^2 = \pm 13$ $r > 0$ by definition
$\quad r = 13$

$\sin \theta = \dfrac{-5}{13}$

b $\cos \theta = \dfrac{12}{13}$

7 c Given $\tan 25° = a$, the right-angled triangle showing the angle 25° is:

$\therefore \cos 65° = \dfrac{a}{\sqrt{a^2 + 1}}$

(you will not be expected to rationalise this answer).

8 b

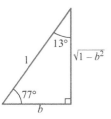

Find the third side of the triangle using Pythagoras:

$\therefore \tan 13° = \dfrac{b}{\sqrt{1 - b^2}}$

(you will not be expected to rationalise this answer).

9 a The second quadrant is where $\sin > 0$ and $\cos < 0$

The diagram shows $\sin A = \dfrac{5}{13}$

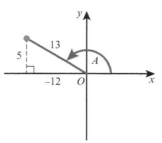

Using Pythagoras, $x^2 = 13^2 - 5^2$
$\quad x = \pm\sqrt{144}$
$\quad x = -12$ since $x < 0$

$\cos A = -\dfrac{12}{13}$

10 a If $\tan A = -\dfrac{2}{3}$ and $\cos B = \dfrac{3}{4}$, then A and B are in the fourth quadrant.

The diagram shows $\tan A = -\dfrac{2}{3}$

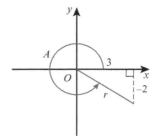

Find r using Pythagoras:
$r^2 = 3^2 + (-2)^2$
$\quad r = \pm\sqrt{13}$ by definition r is positive
$\quad r = \sqrt{13}$

$\sin A = \dfrac{-2}{\sqrt{13}}$

11

	$\theta = 120°$	$\theta = 135°$ [1]	$\theta = 210°$
$\tan \theta$ [2]	$-\sqrt{3}$ [5]	-1	$\dfrac{1}{\sqrt{3}}$
$\sin \theta$	$\dfrac{\sqrt{3}}{2}$ [4]	$\dfrac{1}{\sqrt{2}}$	$\dfrac{1}{2}$
$\dfrac{1}{\cos \theta}$	-2	$-\sqrt{2}$	$-\dfrac{2}{\sqrt{3}}$ [3]

The table shows the original table entries in black, together with the completed entries in red. The worked solutions have been done in the order of the added labels; [1] being the first of the solution etc. This order of working is not the only way to complete the table.

Starting with the middle column labelled [1]:

$\sin \theta$ is positive and $\dfrac{1}{\cos \theta}$ is negative so $\cos \theta$ is negative

So if both are true we are in the second quadrant

Using the diagram and Pythagoras:

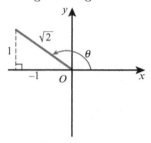

$x^2 = (\sqrt{2})^2 - 1^2$

$x = \pm 1$ but as $x < 0$, $x = -1$

If $\sin \theta = \dfrac{1}{\sqrt{2}}$ then from the 'exact values' triangle,

the basic acute angle is $45°$ and since we are in the second quadrant,

$\theta = 180° - 45°$ or $135°$

so the column [1] is headed by $\theta = 135°$

Also from the triangle, $\tan 45° = 1$, and as $\tan 135° = -1$ so we have filled the spaces labelled [1] and [2]

Now looking at the end column headed

$\theta = 210°$, we can see that $\sin 210° = -\dfrac{1}{2}$

Using the diagram:

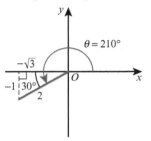

The basic angle is $30°$.

Using Pythagoras:

$x^2 = 2^2 - (-1)^2$

$x = \pm \sqrt{3}$ as $x < 0$, $x = -\sqrt{3}$

So, $\dfrac{1}{\cos \theta}$ becomes $\dfrac{1}{\cos 210°}$ or $\dfrac{1}{-\dfrac{\sqrt{3}}{2}}$ or $-\dfrac{2}{\sqrt{3}}$

which is [3]

Looking at the first column $\theta = 120°$ which is in the second quadrant.

$\dfrac{1}{\cos 120°} = -2$ so $\cos 120° = -\dfrac{1}{2}$

Using the diagram:

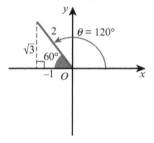

The basic angle is $60°$.

Using Pythagoras:

$y^2 = 2^2 - (-1)^2$

$y = \pm \sqrt{3}$ as $y > 0$, $y = \sqrt{3}$

So, $\sin 120° = \dfrac{\sqrt{3}}{2}$ labelled [4] and

$\tan 120° = \dfrac{\sqrt{3}}{-1}$ or $-\sqrt{3}$ labelled [5]

EXERCISE 5D

> Stretches parallel to the x-axis affect the period of a function.

1 b The graph of $y = \sin x°$ (which has a period 360°) is transformed to the graph of $y = \sin 2x°$ by a stretch parallel to the x-axis stretch factor 2. The period is therefore halved i.e. 180°.

d The graph of $y = \sin x°$ (which has a period 360°) is transformed to the graph of $y = 1 + 2 \sin 3x°$ by:

1 a stretch parallel to the x-axis stretch factor 3 followed by:

2 a stretch parallel to the y-axis stretch factor 2 followed by:

3 A translation by the vector $\begin{pmatrix} 0 \\ 1 \end{pmatrix}$

Only 1. (i.e. the horizontal transformation) affects the period. So, period is $360° \div 3 = 120°$.

> Stretches parallel to the y-axis affect the amplitude of a function.

2 b The graph of $y = \cos x°$ (which has amplitude 1) is transformed to the graph of $y = 5 \cos 2x°$ by:

1 a stretch parallel to the y-axis stretch factor 5 and

2 a stretch parallel to the x-axis stretch factor 2

Only 1. (i.e. the vertical transformation) affects the amplitude. So, amplitude is $1 \times 5 = 5$.

e The graph of $y = \sin x°$ (which has amplitude 1) is transformed to the graph of $y = 4 \sin (2x + 60)°$ by either:

1 Translation $\begin{pmatrix} -60° \\ 0 \end{pmatrix}$ followed by

2 a horizontal stretch factor $\frac{1}{2}$ followed by

3 a vertical stretch factor 4

or:

1 a horizontal stretch factor $\frac{1}{2}$ followed by

2 a translation $\begin{pmatrix} -30° \\ 0 \end{pmatrix}$ and

3 a vertical stretch factor 4.

Only a vertical stretch factor 4 affects the amplitude. So, amplitude is $1 \times 4 = 4$.

3 b $y = \sin \frac{1}{2}x$ for $0° \leqslant x \leqslant 360°$

The graph of $y = \sin x$ (which has amplitude 1 and period 360°) is transformed to the graph $y = \sin \frac{1}{2}x$ by a horizontal stretch factor 2.

This means that all x-coordinates in the original graph are now multiplied by 2, so the period is doubled.

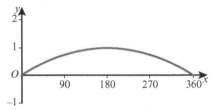

g $y = \sin (x - 45)$ for $0° \leqslant x \leqslant 360°$

The graph of $y = \sin x$ (which has amplitude 1 and period 360°) is transformed to the graph $y = \sin (x - 45)$ by a translation $\begin{pmatrix} 45° \\ 0 \end{pmatrix}$.

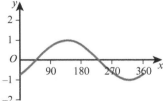

4 a i $y = 2 \sin x$ for $0 \leqslant x \leqslant 2\pi$

The graph of $y = \sin x$ (which has amplitude 1 and period 360°) is transformed to the graph $y = 2 \sin x$ by a vertical stretch factor 2.

The y-coordinates of the original graph are multiplied by 2.

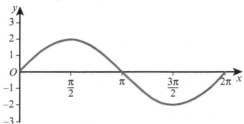

5 **a** The graph of $y = \sin x$ (which has a period 360° and amplitude 1) is transformed to the graph of $y = \sin 2x$ by a stretch parallel to the x-axis stretch factor $\frac{1}{2}$.

The period is therefore halved i.e. 180° (all x-coordinates are divided by 2).

The graph of $y = \cos x$ for $0° \leqslant x \leqslant 360°$ (which has period 360° and amplitude 1) is transformed to the graph of $y = 1 + \cos 2x$ by:

1 A horizontal stretch factor $\frac{1}{2}$ and

2 a translation $\begin{pmatrix} 0 \\ 1 \end{pmatrix}$, in any order.

The period is halved so all original x-coordinates are divided by 2 but the amplitude is unchanged. All original y-coordinates are moved up one unit.

The graphs now look like:

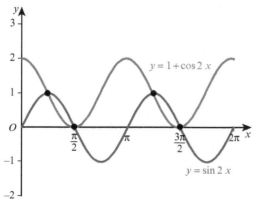

b There are 4 solutions to the equation $\sin 2x = 1 + \cos 2x$ for $0° \leqslant x \leqslant 360°$.

8 This graph is based upon the graph of $y = \sin x$ and has been through the following transformations:

1 a horizontal stretch factor $\frac{1}{b}$ and

2 a vertical stretch factor a and

3 a translation $\begin{pmatrix} 0 \\ c \end{pmatrix}$.

Drawing a horizontal line at $y = 5$ gives the value of c since this represents the translation $\begin{pmatrix} 0 \\ c \end{pmatrix}$.

The amplitude of the graph is now 4 so this is represented by a vertical stretch factor 4. So, $a = 4$.

The period is now π so it has been halved, so $b = 2$.

10 a The graph of $y = \sin x$ (which has amplitude 1 and period 2π) is transformed to the graph $y = 2 \sin x$ by a vertical stretch factor 2.

All y-coordinates of the original graph are multiplied by 2.

The maximum turning point on $y = \sin x$ for $-\pi \leqslant x \leqslant \pi$ is at $\left(\frac{\pi}{2}, 1 \right)$.

The maximum turning point on $y = 2 \sin x$ for $-\pi \leqslant x \leqslant \pi$ is at $\left(\frac{\pi}{2}, 2 \right)$.

The graph of $y = 2 \sin x$ for $-\pi \leqslant x \leqslant \pi$ is shown:

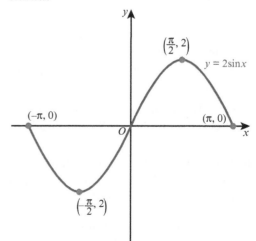

b

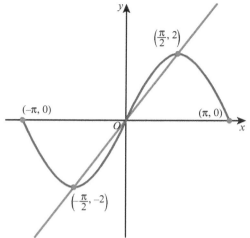

The straight line $y = kx$ must intersect the graph at its maximum point i.e. $\left(\dfrac{\pi}{2}, 2\right)$

Its equation is found by substituting $x = \dfrac{\pi}{2}$ and $y = 2$ into $y = kx$.

So, $2 = k \times \dfrac{\pi}{2}$ so $k = \dfrac{4}{\pi}$

c Using the symmetry of the curve, the line also intersects the curve at $\left(-\dfrac{\pi}{2}, -2\right)$.

11 The graph of $y = \tan x$ has been transformed to the graph of $y = a \tan bx + c$ by:

1 a horizontal stretch factor $\dfrac{1}{b}$

2 a vertical stretch factor a (1 and 2 can be done in any order); then:

3 a translation $\begin{pmatrix} 0 \\ c \end{pmatrix}$

Dealing with the transformations in turn gives:

1 The graph shows that the period is unchanged so, $b = 1$. (Period of a tan x graph is π radians).

i.e. $y = \tan 1x$ or just $y = \tan x$

2 a vertical stretch factor a transforms $y = \tan x$ to $y = 3$ and the point P originally at $\left(\dfrac{\pi}{4}, 1\right)$ is transformed to $P\left(\dfrac{\pi}{4}, 3\right)$ so $a = 3$

i.e. $y = 3 \tan x$

3 The translation 5 units vertically i.e. by $\begin{pmatrix} 0 \\ 5 \end{pmatrix}$ transforms $\left(\dfrac{\pi}{4}, 3\right)$ to $P\left(\dfrac{\pi}{4}, 8\right)$ so $c = 5$

$y = 3 \tan x + 5$

So $a = 3$, $b = 1$, $c = 5$

> Given $y = \sin bx$ or $y = \cos bx$, period $= \dfrac{2\pi}{b}$ $\left[\text{or period} = \dfrac{360°}{b}\right]$.
>
> Given $y = \tan bx$, period $= \dfrac{\pi}{b}$ $\left[\text{or period} = \dfrac{180°}{b}\right]$.

12 a $f(x) = a + b \sin x$ for $0 \leqslant x \leqslant 2\pi$

Substituting $x = 0$ into $f(x)$ gives:

$f(0) = a + b \sin 0$

So $a + b \sin 0 = 3$

$a = 3$

Substituting $x = \dfrac{7\pi}{6}$ into $f(x)$ gives:

$f\left(\dfrac{7\pi}{6}\right) = 3 + b \sin \dfrac{7\pi}{6}$

So $3 + b \sin \dfrac{7\pi}{6} = 2$

$-1 = b \sin \dfrac{7\pi}{6}$

$-\dfrac{1}{2}b = -1$

$b = 2$

b We are required to find the range of f therefore we are looking at the values of $f(x)$ given the graph of $f(x) = 3 + 2 \sin x$

Now, $f(x) = \sin x$ has an amplitude 1, but after a vertical stretch factor 2, $f(x) = 2 \sin x$ and the amplitude is now 2.

So all original y-coordinates are multiplied by 2.

Following this, the vertical translation 3 units up or $\begin{pmatrix} 0 \\ 3 \end{pmatrix}$ means that the y-coordinates are now increased by 3.

The maximum and minimum points of the graph of $f(x) = \sin x$ for $0 \leqslant x \leqslant 2\pi$ are at $\left(\dfrac{\pi}{2}, 1\right)$ and $\left(\dfrac{3\pi}{2}, -1\right)$ respectively.

After the two transformations, they now become:

maximum $\left(\dfrac{\pi}{2}, 1 \times 2 + 3\right)$ or $\left(\dfrac{\pi}{2}, 5\right)$.

minimum $\left(\dfrac{3\pi}{2}, -1 \times 2 + 3\right)$ or $\left(\dfrac{3\pi}{2}, 1\right)$.

So, $1 \leqslant f(x) \leqslant 5$

13 a $f(x) = a - b\cos x$ for $0° \leqslant x \leqslant 360°$

$f(x) = \cos x$ becomes $f(x) = a - b\cos x$ after three transformations:

1 a vertical stretch factor b (all y-coordinates are multiplied by b) and

2 a reflection in the x-axis i.e. the new y-coordinates are now $\times -1$ (these two transformations can be done in any order), followed by

3 translation a units i.e. by $\begin{pmatrix} 0 \\ a \end{pmatrix}$ (the new y-coordinates are now increased by a units).

ALSO since there are only a combination of vertical transformations involved, the period (and therefore the x-coordinates) of all points on the graph during the process remain unchanged.

The maximum and minimum points of the graph of $f(x) = \cos x$ for $0 \leqslant x \leqslant 2\pi$ are at $(0, 1)$ and $(\pi, -1)$ respectively.

After the three transformations $(0, 1)$ becomes $(0, (1 \times b) \times -1 + a)$

So $(1 \times b) \times -1 + a = -2$ which simplified gives:

$a - b = -2$ ....[1]

$(\pi, -1)$ becomes $(\pi, (-1 \times b) \times -1 + a)$

So $(-1 \times b) \times -1 + a = 8$ which simplified gives:

$a + b = 8$ ....[2]

Adding [1] and [2] gives $2a = 6$, so $a = 3$ and $b = 5$.

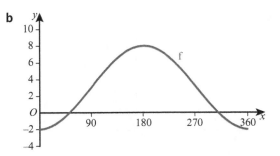

b

14 $f(x) = a + b\sin cx$ for $0° \leqslant x \leqslant 360°$

$f(x) = \sin x$ becomes $f(x) = a + b\sin cx$ after three transformations:

1 a horizontal stretch factor c (all x-coordinates are multiplied by $\dfrac{1}{c}$) and

2 a vertical stretch factor b i.e. the new y-coordinates are now $\times b$ (these two transformations can be done in any order), followed by

3 translation a units i.e. by $\begin{pmatrix} 0 \\ a \end{pmatrix}$ (the new y-coordinates are now increased by a units).

The maximum and minimum points of the graph of $f(x) = \sin x$ for $0 \leqslant x \leqslant 2\pi$ are at $\left(\dfrac{\pi}{2}, 1\right)$ and $\left(\dfrac{3\pi}{2}, -1\right)$ respectively.

After the three transformations:

$\left(\dfrac{\pi}{2}, 1\right)$ becomes $\left(\dfrac{\pi}{2} \times \dfrac{1}{c}, 1 \times b + a\right)$

So, $1 \times b + a = 9$ which simplified gives:

$a + b = 9$ ....[1]

$\left(\dfrac{3\pi}{2}, -1\right)$ becomes $\left(\dfrac{3\pi}{2} \times \dfrac{1}{c}, -1 \times b + a\right)$

So $-1 \times b + a = 1$ which simplified gives:

$a - b = 1$ ....[2]

Adding [1] and [2] gives $2a = 10$ so $a = 5$ and $b = 4$

Period of a sine graph is found by using:

Period $= \dfrac{360°}{c}$ (see Commentary)

$120° = \dfrac{360°}{c}$ so $c = 3$

$\therefore\ a = 5,\ b = 4,\ c = 3$

15 $f(x) = A + 5\cos Bx$ for $0° \leqslant x \leqslant 120°$

$f(x) = \cos x$ becomes $f(x) = A + 5\cos Bx$ after three transformations:

1 a horizontal stretch factor $\dfrac{1}{B}$ (all x-coordinates are multiplied by $\dfrac{1}{B}$)

2 a vertical stretch factor 5 i.e. the new y-coordinates are now $\times 5$ (these two transformations can be done in any order), followed by

3 translation A units i.e. by $\begin{pmatrix} 0 \\ A \end{pmatrix}$ (the new y-coordinates are now increased by A units).

The maximum and minimum points of the graph of $f(x) = \cos x$ for $0 \leqslant x \leqslant 360°$ are at $(0, 1)$ and $(180, -1)$ respectively.

After the three transformations $(0, 1)$ becomes

$\left(0 \times \dfrac{1}{B}, 1 \times 5 + A\right)$

So $1 \times 5 + A = 7$ which simplified gives:

$A = 2$

Period $= \dfrac{360}{B}$ so

$\dfrac{360}{B} = 60 \; B = 6$

b The amplitude is only affected by transformation 2 i.e. the vertical stretch factor 5, so the amplitude (which was 1 for $y = \cos x$) is now 5.

c

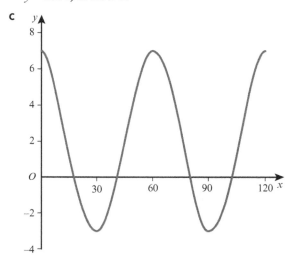

16 The sketch may help:

Looking at the sequence of graphs:

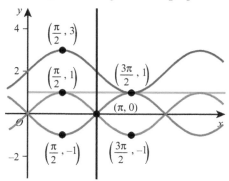

If $y = \sin x$ is reflected in $x = \pi$, its equation becomes $y = -\sin x$.

If the new graph is reflected in $y = 1$ the equation of the resulting function is:

$y = 2 + \sin x$

17 Looking at the sequence of graphs:

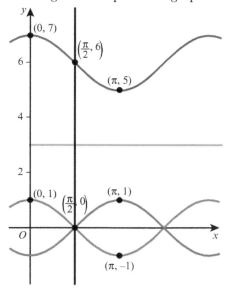

$y = \cos x$ reflected in the line $x = \dfrac{\pi}{2}$ has the equation $y = -\cos x$.

If the new graph is reflected in the line $y = 3$ the equation of the resulting function is:

$y = 6 + \cos x$

Recall the two exact value triangles (in degrees or radians) to help you answer questions 1–3.

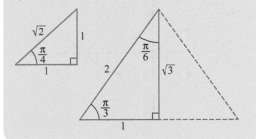

1 b $\sin^{-1}\left(\dfrac{1}{2}\right)$ means the angle whose sine is $\dfrac{1}{2}$ where $-90° \leqslant$ angle $\leqslant 90°$.

Hence, $\sin^{-1}\dfrac{1}{2} = 30°$.

2 e $\cos^{-1}\left(-\dfrac{1}{2}\right)$ means the angle whose cosine is $-\dfrac{1}{2}$ where $0° \leqslant$ angle $\leqslant \pi$

Hence, $\cos^{-1}\left(-\dfrac{1}{2}\right) = \dfrac{2\pi}{3}$

3 a $\cos^{-1}\left(\dfrac{3}{5}\right)$ means the angle θ whose cosine is $\left(\dfrac{3}{5}\right)$ where $0° \leqslant$ angle $\leqslant 180°$.

However, this does not use one of the exact triangles above and we are not allowed to use a calculator.

Cosine is positive in the first quadrant, so using the triangle shown and Pythagoras, calculate the unknown side i.e. 4.

$\sin\theta = \dfrac{4}{5}$ so $\sin^2\theta = \left(\dfrac{4}{5}\right)^2$ or $\dfrac{16}{25}$

b Using the same triangle as in **a**:

$\tan\theta = \dfrac{4}{3}$ so $\tan^2\theta = \left(\dfrac{4}{3}\right)^2$ or $\dfrac{16}{9}$

4 a The graph of $f(x) = \sin x$ has been transformed to the graph of $f(x) = 3\sin x - 4$ by:

- a vertical stretch factor 3 (the range is now $-3 \leqslant x \leqslant 3$), followed by:

- a translation $\begin{pmatrix} 0 \\ -4 \end{pmatrix}$ (the range is now $-7 \leqslant f(x) \leqslant -1$).

Answer is $-7 \leqslant f(x) \leqslant -1$
(Neither of the transformations affected the domain.)

b $f(x) = 3\sin x - 4$
$y = 3\sin x - 4$
$x = 3\sin y - 4$
$3\sin y = x + 4$
$\sin y = \left(\dfrac{x+4}{3}\right)$
$y = \sin^{-1}\left(\dfrac{x+4}{3}\right)$
$f^{-1}(x) = \sin^{-1}\left(\dfrac{x+4}{3}\right)$

5 a The graph of $f(x) = \cos x$ has been transformed to the graph of $f(x) = 4 - 2\cos x$ by:

- a vertical stretch factor 2 (the range is now $-2 \leqslant x \leqslant 2$), followed by:

- a reflection in the x-axis (this does not alter the range), followed by:

- a translation $\begin{pmatrix} 0 \\ 4 \end{pmatrix}$, the range is now $2 \leqslant f(x) \leqslant 6$ (the domain is unaltered i.e. $0 \leqslant x \leqslant \pi$).

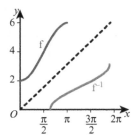

b Looking at the graph, f is one-one, therefore it has an inverse.

$$f(x) = 4 - 2 \cos x$$
$$y = 4 - 2 \cos x$$
$$x = 4 - 2 \cos y$$
$$2 \cos y = 4 - x$$
$$\cos y = \frac{4 - x}{2}$$
$$y = \cos^{-1}\left(\frac{4 - x}{2}\right)$$
$$f^{-1}(x) = \cos^{-1}\left(\frac{4 - x}{2}\right)$$

c see sketch

6 a The graph of $f(x) = \sin x$ has been transformed to the graph of $f(x) = 5 - 2 \sin x$ by:

• a vertical stretch factor 2 (the domain is still $\frac{\pi}{2} \le x \le p$, the range is now $-2 \le x \le 2$), followed by:

• a reflection in the x-axis (the domain is still $\frac{\pi}{2} \le x \le p$, this does not alter the range), followed by:

• a translation $\begin{pmatrix} 0 \\ 5 \end{pmatrix}$ (the domain is still $\frac{\pi}{2} \le x \le p$, the range is now $3 \le f(x) \le 7$).

The sketch of the function $f(x) = 5 - 2 \sin x$ for the domain $x \ge \frac{\pi}{2}$ is shown:

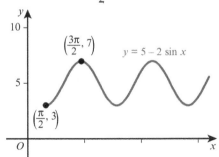

Function f has an inverse only if it is one to one.

Looking at the graph, the maximum value of x for this to be true is $\frac{3\pi}{2}$

So, $p = \frac{3\pi}{2}$

b
$$f(x) = 5 - 2 \sin x$$
$$y = 5 - 2 \sin x$$
$$x = 5 - 2 \sin y$$
$$2 \sin y = 5 - x$$
$$\sin y = \frac{5 - x}{2}$$
$$y = \sin^{-1}\left(\frac{5 - x}{2}\right)$$
$$f^{-1}(x) = \sin^{-1}\left(\frac{5 - x}{2}\right)$$

The domain of f^{-1} is the same as the range of f, i.e. the domain is $3 \le x \le 7$.

7 The graph of $f(x) = \cos x$ has been transformed to the graph of $f(x) = 4 \cos\left(\frac{x}{2}\right) - 5$ by:

• a horizontal stretch factor 2, the domain is now $0 \le x \le 4\pi$.

• a vertical stretch factor 4 (the range is now $-4 \le x \le 4$), followed by:

• a translation $\begin{pmatrix} 0 \\ -5 \end{pmatrix}$, the range is now $-9 \le f(x) \le -1$ (the domain is unaltered i.e. $0 \le x \le 4\pi$).

So the range of f is $-9 \le f(x) \le -1$.

b
$$f(x) = 4 \cos\left(\frac{x}{2}\right) - 5$$
$$y = 4 \cos\left(\frac{x}{2}\right) - 5$$
$$x = 4 \cos\left(\frac{y}{2}\right) - 5$$
$$4 \cos\left(\frac{y}{2}\right) = x + 5$$
$$\cos\left(\frac{y}{2}\right) = \frac{x + 5}{4}$$
$$\frac{y}{2} = \cos^{-1}\left(\frac{x + 5}{4}\right)$$
$$y = 2 \cos^{-1}\left(\frac{x + 5}{4}\right)$$
$$f^{-1}(x) = 2 \cos^{-1}\left(\frac{x + 5}{4}\right)$$

The range of $f^{-1}(x)$ is the same as the domain of f, i.e. $0 \le f^{-1}(x) \le 2\pi$

1 c $\cos x = 0.7$ for $0° \leqslant x \leqslant 360°$

The graph of $y = \cos x$ and $y = 0.7$ for the domain $0° \leqslant x \leqslant 360°$ is shown:

$x = \cos^{-1} 0.7$

$x = 45.57°$

One solution is $45.6°$

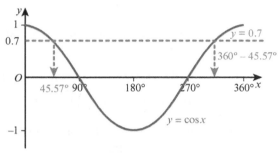

The sketch graph shows there are two values of x, between $0°$ and $360°$, for which $\cos x = 0.7$.

Using the symmetry of the curve, the second value is $(360° - 45.57°) = 314.43°$

Hence the solution of $\cos x = -0.7$ for $0° \leqslant x \leqslant 360°$ is

$x = 45.6$ or $314.4°$ (correct to 1 decimal place)

f $\tan x = -2$

$\tan^{-1}(-2) = -63.43°$ (this is outside $0° \leqslant x \leqslant 360°$)

The sketch graph shows there are two values of x, between $0°$ and $360°$, for which $\tan x = -2$.

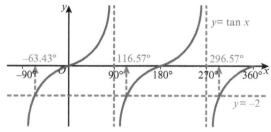

Using the symmetry of the curve,

the first value is $(180° - 63.43°) = 116.57°$

the second value is $(360° - 63.43°) = 296.57°$

Hence the solution of $\tan x = -2$ for $0° \leqslant x \leqslant 360°$ is

$x = 116.6$ or $296.6°$ (correct to 1 decimal place)

2 d $\sin x = -0.7$

$x = \sin^{-1}(-0.7)$

$x = -0.775$ radians (this is outside $0 \leqslant x \leqslant 2\pi$)

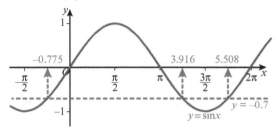

The sketch graph shows there are two values of x, between 0 and 2π, for which $\sin x = -0.7$.

Using the symmetry of the curve,

the first value is $(\pi + 0.775) = 3.917$ radians

the second value is $(2\pi - 0.775) = 5.508$ radians

Hence the solution of $\sin x = -0.7$ for $0 \leqslant x \leqslant 2\pi$ is

$x = 3.92$ or 5.51 radians (correct to 3 significant figures)

g $4 \sin x = 3$ for $0 \leqslant x \leqslant 2\pi$

$x = \sin^{-1} 0.75$

$x = 0.848$ radians

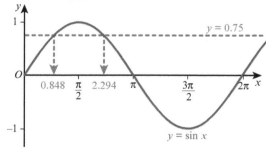

The sketch graph shows there are two values of x, between 0 and 2π, for which $\sin x = 0.75$.

Using the symmetry of the curve,
the second value is $(\pi - 0.848) = 2.294$
radians (to 3 decimal places).

Hence the solution of $\sin x = 0.75$ for
$0 \leqslant x \leqslant 2\pi$ is
$x = 0.848$ or 2.29 radians (correct to 3
significant figures).

3 a $\cos 2x = 0.6$ for $0° \leqslant x \leqslant 180°$

Let $2x = A$
$$A = \cos^{-1} 0.6$$
$$A = 53.13°$$
The sketch graph shows there are two values of
x, between $0°$ and $360°$, for which $\cos A = 0.6$.

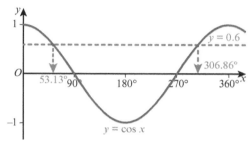

Using the symmetry of the curve,
the second value is $(360° - 53.13°) = 306.86°$
Using $x = 2A$
$2A = 53.13°$ and $2A = 306.86°$
$x = 26.6°$ and $x = 153.4°$ (correct to 1 decimal
place)

g $4 + 2\tan 2x = 0$ for $0° \leqslant x \leqslant 180°$

$\tan 2x = -2$
Let $2x = A$
$$A = \tan^{-1}(-2)$$
$$A = -63.43°$$

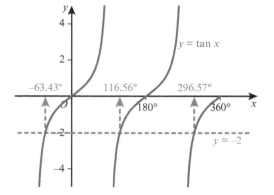

The sketch graph shows there are two
values of x, between $0°$ and $360°$, for which
$\tan x = -2$.

Using the symmetry of the curve,
the first value is $(180° - 63.43°) = 116.57°$
The second value is $(360° - 63.43°) = 296.57°$
Using $x = 2A$
$2A = 116.57°$ and $2A = 296.57°$
$x = 58.3°$ and $x = 148.3°$ (correct to 1
decimal place).

4 d $3\sin(2x - 4) = 2$ for $0 < x < \pi$

Let $2x - 4 = A$
$3\sin A = 2$
$$A = \sin^{-1}\left(\frac{2}{3}\right)$$
$$A = 0.7297 \text{ radians.}$$
Looking at the sketch and using the
symmetry of the curve:

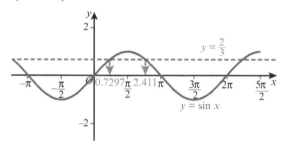

$x = 0.7297$ $\quad\quad x = \pi - 0.7297$
$\quad\quad\quad\quad\quad\quad = 2.411$
$x = -\pi - 0.7297$ $\quad x = 2\pi + 0.7297$
$x = -3.871$ $\quad\quad x = 7.012$
Using $2x - 4 = A$,
$2x - 4 = 0.7297$ $\quad 2x - 4 = 2.411$
$x = \frac{1}{2}(0.7297 + 4)$ $\quad A = \frac{1}{2}(2.411 + 4)$
$x = 2.36$ $\quad\quad\quad A = 3.21$
$2x - 4 = -3.871$ $\quad 2x - 4 = 7.012$
$x = \frac{1}{2}(-3.871 + 4)$ $\quad x = \frac{1}{2}(7.012 + 4)$
$x = 0.0643$ $\quad\quad x = 5.51$
Hence the solution of $3\sin(2x - 4) = 2$ for
$0 < x < \pi$ is
$x = 0.0643$ or 2.36 or 3.21 or 5.51 radians
(to 3 significant figures).

e $2 \tan \left(\dfrac{x}{2}\right) + \sqrt{3} = 0$ for $0° \leqslant x \leqslant 540°$

Let $A = \dfrac{x}{2}$

$2 \tan A + \sqrt{3} = 0$

$\tan A = -\dfrac{\sqrt{3}}{2}$

$A = \tan^{-1}\left(-\dfrac{\sqrt{3}}{2}\right) = -40.89°$

Looking at the sketch and using the symmetry of the curve:

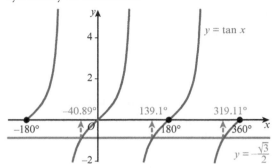

the first value is $(180° - 40.89°) = 139.11°$
the second value is $(360° - 40.89°) = 319.11°$

Using $A = \dfrac{x}{2}$

$x = 139.11° \times 2$

$x = 278.22°$

[Note: $x = 319.11 \times 2$ i.e. $x = 638.22°$ is out of range $0° \leqslant x \leqslant 540°$]

$x = 278.2°$ (correct to 1 decimal place)

> Sometimes with more complex equations, it is difficult to tell if the domain of your sketch will result in finding all the possible solutions. Widening the domain in your diagram will ensure that no solutions are missed.

5 d $3 \cos 2x - 4 \sin 2x = 0$ for $0° \leqslant x \leqslant 360°$

Divide both sides by $\cos 2x$ and use

$\tan \theta = \dfrac{\sin \theta}{\cos \theta}$

$3 - 4 \tan 2x = 0$

$4 \tan 2x = 3$

Let $A = 2x$

$\tan A = 0.75$

$\tan^{-1} 0.75 = A$

$A = 36.86...°$

Using the symmetry of the curve, the second value is
$A = (180° + 36.86...°) = 216.86...°$
the third value is
$A = (360° + 36.86...°) = 396.86...°$
the fourth value is
$A = (540° + 36.86...°) = 576.86...°$
As $A = 2x$:

$2x = 36.86...°$

$x = 18.4°$

$2x = 216.86...°$

$x = 108.4°$

$2x = 396.86...°$

$x = 198.4°$

$2x = 576.86...°$

$x = 288.4°$

Solutions are: $18.4°$, $108.4°$, $198.4°$, $288.4°$ to 1 decimal place

6 $4 \sin (2x + 0.3) - 5 \cos (2x + 0.3) = 0$ for $0 \leqslant x \leqslant \pi$

Dividing both sides by $\cos (2x + 0.3)$ gives:

$\dfrac{4 \sin (2x + 0.3)}{\cos (2x + 0.3)} - \dfrac{5 \cos (2x + 0.3)}{\cos (2x + 0.3)} = 0$

Using $\tan \theta = \dfrac{\sin \theta}{\cos \theta}$ gives:

$4 \tan (2x + 0.3) - 5 = 0$

$\tan (2x + 0.3) = 1.25$

Let $A = 2x + 0.3$

$\tan A = 1.25$

$A = \tan^{-1} 1.25$

$A = 0.8960...$

Using the symmetry of the curve:

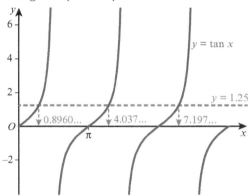

the second value is

$A = (\pi + 0.8960...) = 4.037...$ radians

the third value is $A = (2\pi + 0.8960...) = 7.179...$ radians

As $A = 2x + 0.3$

$2x + 0.3 = 0.8960...$

$\quad x = 0.298...$ radians.

$2x + 0.3 = 4.037...$

$\quad x = 1.87...$ radians

$2x + 0.3 = 7.179...$

$\quad x = 3.43...$ (out of range $0 \leqslant x \leqslant \pi$)

Solutions are 0.298 radians and 1.87 radians.

7 c $\tan^2 x = 5 \tan x$ for $0° \leqslant x \leqslant 360°$.

> Do not be tempted to divide throughout by $\tan x$ as it will lose some solutions.

$\qquad \tan^2 x = 5 \tan x$

$\tan^2 x - 5 \tan x = 0$

$\tan x(\tan x - 5) = 0$

$\tan x = 0$ or $\tan x - 5 = 0$

If $\tan x = 0$ then $x = 0°, 180°, 360°$ (the period of tan is $180°$).

If $\tan x - 5 = 0$ then looking at the sketch:

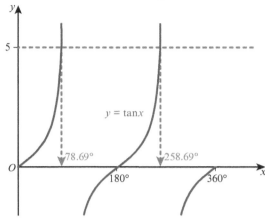

$\tan x = 5$ so $x = 78.69°$ and

$180° + 78.69° = 258.69°$

Solutions are: $0°, 78.7°, 180°, 258.7°, 360°$

e $2 \sin x \cos x = \sin x$

> Do not divide throughout by $\sin x$ as this will lose some solutions.

$2 \sin x \cos x - \sin x = 0$

$\sin x(2 \cos x - 1) = 0$

$\sin x = 0$ so $x = 0°, 180°, 360°$

$2 \cos x - 1 = 0$

$x = \cos^{-1}\left(\dfrac{1}{2}\right)$ so $x = 60°, 300°$ (cos is positive in the first and fourth quadrants).

Solutions are: $0°, 60°, 180°, 300°, 360°$

8 a $4 \cos^2 x = 1$ for $0° \leqslant x \leqslant 360°$

$\cos^2 x = \dfrac{1}{4}$

$\cos x = \pm \dfrac{1}{2}$

If $\cos x = \dfrac{1}{2}$ then $x = 60°, 300°$ (cos is positive in the first and fourth quadrants).

If $\cos x = -\dfrac{1}{2}$ then $x = 180° - 60°$ or $120°$ (cos is negative in the second and third quadrants)

and $x = 180° + 60°$ or $240°$

Solutions are: $60°, 120°, 240°, 300°$

b $4\tan^2 x = 9$

$$\tan^2 x = \frac{9}{4}$$

$$\tan x = \pm\frac{3}{2}$$

If $\tan x = \frac{3}{2}$ then $x = 56.30...°$

$$x = 180° + 56.30...°$$
$$= 236.30...°$$

If $\tan x = -\frac{3}{2}$ then $x = -56.30$ (out of range)

$$x = 180° - 56.30...°$$
$$x = 123.70...°$$
$$x = 360° - 56.30...°$$
$$x = 303.7°$$

Solutions are: $56.3°$, $123.7°$, $236.3°$, $303.7°$
(to 1 decimal place)

> It is essential to be able to recall and use sketches of sin, cos and tan functions, showing their amplitudes, periods, axis intercepts and asymptotes (if applicable).

9 a $2\sin^2 x + \sin x - 1 = 0$ for $0° \leqslant x \leqslant 360°$

Factorising gives:
$(2\sin x - 1)(\sin x + 1) = 0$
If $2\sin x - 1 = 0$

$\sin x = \frac{1}{2}$ so $x = 30°$ or $150°$

If $\sin x + 1 = 0$
$\sin x = -1$ so $x = 270°$
Solutions are: $30°$, $150°$, $270°$

f $\cos x + 5 = 6\sin^2 x$ for $0° \leqslant x \leqslant 360°$

$6\sin^2 x - \cos x - 5 = 0$
Using the identity: $\sin^2 x + \cos^2 x \equiv 1$
and rearranging: $\sin^2 x \equiv 1 - \cos^2 x$
multiplying by 6 gives: $6\sin^2 x \equiv 6 - 6\cos^2 x$
then substituting gives:
$6 - 6\cos^2 x - \cos x - 5 = 0$
$6\cos^2 x + \cos x - 1 = 0$

Factorising:
$(3\cos x - 1)(2\cos x + 1) = 0*$
Either: $3\cos x - 1 = 0$ or $2\cos x + 1 = 0$

$\cos x = \frac{1}{3}$ or $\cos x = -\frac{1}{2}$

If $\cos x = \frac{1}{3}$

$x = 70.52...°$ or $360° - 70.52...° = 289.47°$
Or: $2\cos x + 1 = 0$

$$\cos x = -\frac{1}{2}$$

$x = 120°$, $240°$
Solutions: $70.5°$, $120°$, $240°$, $289.5°$

$*$ At this stage you could use the quadratic formula to solve the equation by letting $y = \cos x$

So, $6y^2 + y - 1 = 0$

Comparing with $ay^2 + by + c = 0$:
$a = 6$, $b = 1$, $c = -1$

$$y = \frac{-1 \pm \sqrt{1^2 - 4(6)(-1)}}{2(6)}$$

$$y = \frac{-1 \pm \sqrt{25}}{12}$$

$y = \frac{1}{3}$ or $y = -\frac{1}{2}$

So, $\cos x = \frac{1}{3}$ or $\cos x = -\frac{1}{2}$ now continue as before.

10 a $4\tan x = 3\cos x$ for $0 \leqslant x \leqslant 2\pi$

$4\tan x = 3\cos x$

rewrite $\tan x$ as $\frac{\sin x}{\cos x}$ and substitute:

$4\frac{\sin x}{\cos x} = 3\cos x$

$4\sin x = 3\cos^2 x$

Using the identity: $\sin^2 x + \cos^2 x \equiv 1$
Rearrange to give: $\cos^2 x \equiv 1 - \sin^2 x$
Then substitute for $\cos^2 x$:
$$4\sin x = 3(1 - \sin^2 x)$$
$$4\sin x = 3 - 3\sin^2 x$$

$3\sin^2 x + 4\sin x - 3 = 0$
Let $y = \sin x$
$3y^2 + 4y - 3 = 0$

Using the quadratic formula:

$a = 3$, $b = 4$, $c = -3$

$$y = \frac{-4 \pm \sqrt{4^2 - 4(3)(-3)}}{2(3)}$$

$$y = \frac{-4 \pm \sqrt{52}}{6}$$

So $\sin x = \dfrac{-4 \pm \sqrt{52}}{6}$

Either $\sin x = 0.53518\ldots$

or $\sin x = -1.8685$ (reject as sine cannot be less than -1)

So, $\sin x = 0.53518$

$x = 0.5647$ radians or $\pi - 0.5647 = 2.576\ldots$ radians

Solutions: 0.565 radians and 2.58 radians.

b $2\cos^2 x + 5\sin x = 4$

Using the identity: $\sin^2 x + \cos^2 x \equiv 1$

Rearrange to give: $\cos^2 x \equiv 1 - \sin^2 x$

then substitute for $\cos^2 x$:

$2(1 - \sin^2 x) + 5\sin x = 4$

$2 - 2\sin^2 x + 5\sin x = 4$

$2\sin^2 x - 5\sin x + 2 = 0$

$(2\sin x - 1)(\sin x - 2) = 0$

Either $\sin x - 2 = 0$ or $2\sin x - 1 = 0$

$\sin x - 2 = 0$

$\sin x = 2$ (no solutions since $\sin x$ cannot be greater than 1)

or $2\sin x - 1 = 0$

$\sin x = 0.5$

$x = \dfrac{\pi}{6}$ or $x = \pi - \dfrac{\pi}{6}$ or $\dfrac{5\pi}{6}$

Solutions are: $\dfrac{\pi}{6}$ radians and $\dfrac{5\pi}{6}$ radians.

11 $\sin^2 x + 3\sin x\cos x + 2\cos^2 x = 0$ for $0 \leqslant x \leqslant 2\pi$

$(\cos x + \sin x)(2\cos x + \sin x) = 0$

Either $\cos x + \sin x = 0$

Or $2\cos x + \sin x = 0$

If $\cos x + \sin x = 0$ then dividing by $\cos x$ gives:

$1 + \tan x = 0$

$\tan x = -1$

$x = -\dfrac{\pi}{4}$

Using the symmetry of the tan curve:

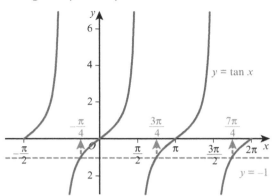

$x = \pi - \dfrac{\pi}{4}$ or $\dfrac{3\pi}{4}$

$x = 2\pi - \dfrac{\pi}{4}$ or $\dfrac{7\pi}{4}$

If $2\cos x + \sin x = 0$ then dividing by $\cos x$ gives:

$2 + \tan x = 0$

$\tan x = -2$

$x = -1.107$

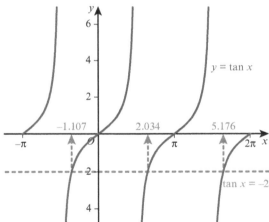

Using the symmetry of the tan curve:

$x = \pi - 1.107$ or 2.034 radians

$x = 2\pi - 1.107$ or 5.176 radians

Solutions: 2.03, $\dfrac{\pi}{4}$, 5.18, $\dfrac{7\pi}{4}$ radians

1 $2\sin^2 x - 7\cos^2 x + 4$ ....[1]

Using the identity: $\sin^2 x + \cos^2 x \equiv 1$

Rearranging gives:

$\cos^2\theta \equiv 1 - \sin^2\theta$

Multiplying by 7 gives:

$7\cos^2 x \equiv 7 - 7\sin^2 x$

Substituting into [1] gives:

$2\sin^2 x - (7 - 7\sin^2 x) + 4$

$2\sin^2 x - 7 + 7\sin^2 x + 4$

Answer: $9\sin^2 x - 3$ is $2\sin^2 x - 7\cos^2 x + 4$ expressed in terms of $\sin x$.

2 e $\dfrac{\cos^2 x - \sin^2 x}{\cos x + \sin x} + \sin x \equiv \cos x$

Starting with the left-hand side and writing the numerator as the difference of two squares:

$= \dfrac{(\cos x + \sin x)(\cos x - \sin x)}{\cos x + \sin x} + \sin x$

Cancelling gives:

$= (\cos x - \sin x) + \sin x$

$= \cos x$ proved

f $\cos^4 x + \sin^2 x\cos^2 x \equiv \cos^2 x$

Factorising the left-hand side gives:

$= \cos^2 x(\cos^2 x + \sin^2 x)$

Substituting by using the identity:

$\sin^2 x + \cos^2 x \equiv 1$ gives:

$= \cos^2 x \times (1)$

$= \cos^2 x$ proved

3 b $2(1 + \cos x) - (1 + \cos x)^2 \equiv \sin^2 x$

> Be careful with the minus sign in front of brackets.

Left-hand side:

$= 2(1 + \cos x) - [(1 + \cos x)^2]$

$= 2 + 2\cos x - [(1 + \cos x)(1 + \cos x)]$

$= 2 + 2\cos x - [1 + 2\cos x + \cos^2 x]$

$= 2 + 2\cos x - 1 - 2\cos x - \cos^2 x$

$= 1 - \cos^2 x$

$= \sin^2 x$ proved

[Since using the identity: $\sin^2\theta + \cos^2\theta \equiv 1$ and rearranging gives: $1 - \cos^2 x \equiv \sin^2\theta$]

4 c $\tan^2 x - \sin^2 x \equiv \tan^2 x\sin^2 x$

Left-hand side:

$= \dfrac{\sin^2 x}{\cos^2 x} - \sin^2 x$

$= \dfrac{\sin^2 x}{\cos^2 x} - \dfrac{\sin^2 x}{1}$

Multiplying top and bottom of the second fraction by $\cos^2 x$:

$= \dfrac{\sin^2 x}{\cos^2 x} - \dfrac{\sin^2 x\cos^2 x}{\cos^2 x}$

$= \dfrac{\sin^2 x - \sin^2 x\cos^2 x}{\cos^2 x}$

Factorising:

$= \dfrac{\sin^2 x(1 - \cos^2 x)}{\cos^2 x}$

$= \dfrac{\sin^2 x}{\cos^2 x} \times (1 - \cos^2 x)$

Using the identity: $\sin^2 x + \cos^2 x \equiv 1$ and rearranging gives: $\sin^2\theta \equiv 1 - \cos^2 x$

So, substituting for $1 - \cos^2 x$ gives:

$= \dfrac{\sin^2 x}{\cos^2 x} \times \sin^2 x$

$= \tan^2 x\sin^2 x$ proved

5 c $\dfrac{\cos^4 x - \sin^4 x}{\cos^2 x} \equiv 1 - \tan^2 x$

Left-hand side:

Writing the numerator as the difference between two squares:

$= \dfrac{(\cos^2 x - \sin^2 x)(\cos^2 x + \sin^2 x)}{\cos^2 x}$

Using the identity: $\sin^2 x + \cos^2 x \equiv 1$, the second bracket in the numerator becomes 1

So the expression becomes:

$= \dfrac{(\cos^2 x - \sin^2 x)}{\cos^2 x}$

Splitting into two fractions:

$= \dfrac{\cos^2 x}{\cos^2 x} - \dfrac{\sin^2 x}{\cos^2 x}$

$= 1 - \tan^2 x$ proved

f $\left(\dfrac{1}{\sin x} - \dfrac{1}{\tan x}\right)^2 \equiv \dfrac{1-\cos x}{1+\cos x}$

Left-hand side:

Using $\tan x \equiv \dfrac{\sin x}{\cos x}$

$= \left(\dfrac{1}{\sin x} - \dfrac{1}{\frac{\sin x}{\cos x}}\right)^2$

$= \left(\dfrac{1}{\sin x} - \dfrac{\cos x}{\sin x}\right)^2$

$= \left(\dfrac{1-\cos x}{\sin x}\right)^2$

$= \dfrac{(1-\cos x)^2}{\sin^2 x}$

Using the identity: $\sin^2 x + \cos^2 x \equiv 1$
Rearranging gives: $\sin^2 x \equiv 1 - \cos^2 x$
Substituting for $\sin^2 x$ in the denominator:

$= \dfrac{(1-\cos x)^2}{1-\cos^2 x}$

Writing the denominator as the difference between two squares:

$= \dfrac{(1-\cos x)^2}{(1-\cos x)(1+\cos x)}$

$= \dfrac{1-\cos x}{1+\cos x}$ proved

6 d $\dfrac{\sin x}{1+\cos x} + \dfrac{1+\cos x}{\sin x} \equiv \dfrac{2}{\sin x}$

Left-hand side:
Adding the fractions:

$= \dfrac{(\sin x)^2}{\sin x(1+\cos x)} + \dfrac{(1+\cos x)^2}{\sin x(1+\cos x)}$

Remember $(\sin x)^2$ is the same as $\sin^2 x$.

$= \dfrac{\sin^2 x + (1+\cos x)^2}{\sin x(1+\cos x)}$

$= \dfrac{\sin^2 x + 1 + 2\cos x + \cos^2 x}{\sin x(1+\cos x)}$

Using the identity $\sin^2 x + \cos^2 x \equiv 1$ to simplify the numerator gives:

$= \dfrac{2+2\cos x}{\sin x(1+\cos x)}$

$= \dfrac{2(1+\cos x)}{\sin x(1+\cos x)}$

$= \dfrac{2}{\sin x}$ proved

7 $(1+\cos x)^2 + (1-\cos x)^2 + 2\sin^2 x$
$= 1 + 2\cos x + \cos^2 x + 1 - 2\cos x + \cos^2 x + 2\sin^2 x$
$= 2 + 2\cos^2 x + 2\sin^2 x$
$= 2(1+\cos^2 x + \sin^2 x)$

Using the identity: $\sin^2 x + \cos^2 x \equiv 1$ gives:
$= 2(1+1)$
$= 4$ this is the constant value (as it does not contain a variable).

8 a $7\sin^2 x + 4\cos^2 x$

Using the identity $\sin^2 x + \cos^2 x \equiv 1$ and rearranging gives:
$\cos^2 x \equiv 1 - \sin^2 x$
Multiplying by 4 gives:
$4\cos^2 x = 4 - 4\sin^2 x$
Substituting for $4\cos^2 x$ gives:
$7\sin^2 x + 4 - 4\sin^2 x$
Simplifying gives:
$4 + 3\sin^2 x$

b Let $f(x) = 4 + 3\sin^2 x$

Given the graph of $h(x) = \sin x$ for the domain $0 \le x \le 2\pi$
the range is $-1 \le h(x) \le 1$
The graph of $g(x) = \sin^2 x$ has the range $0 \le g(x) \le 1$
The graph of $g(x)$ is transformed to $f(x) = 3\sin^2 x + 4$
by a vertical stretch factor 3 followed by a translation $\begin{pmatrix}0\\4\end{pmatrix}$.
After the stretch (the y-coordinates are multiplied by 3) and the translation (the y-coordinates are increased by 4), the range is $0 \times 3 + 4 \le f(x) \le 1 \times 3 + 4$
i.e. $4 \le f(x) \le 7$

9 a $4\sin\theta - \cos^2\theta$

Using the identity $\sin^2\theta + \cos^2\theta \equiv 1$ and rearranging gives:
$\cos^2\theta \equiv 1 - \sin^2\theta$
Substituting for $\cos^2 x$ gives:
$4\sin\theta - (1-\sin^2\theta)$ expand and rearrange:
$\sin^2\theta + 4\sin\theta - 1$ complete the square:
$(\sin\theta + 2)^2 - 2^2 - 1$

> Be careful not to confuse $\sin \theta + 2$ with $\sin(\theta + 2)$.

$(\sin \theta + 2)^2 - 5$

b Let $d(\theta) = (\sin \theta + 2)^2 - 5$

Given the graph of $h(\theta) = \sin \theta$ for the domain $0 \leqslant \theta \leqslant 2\pi$, the range is $-1 \leqslant h(\theta) \leqslant 1$

The graph of $g(\theta) = \sin \theta + 2$ is a translation of $h(\theta)$ by $\begin{pmatrix} 0 \\ 2 \end{pmatrix}$ which now has the range

$-1 + 2 \leqslant g(\theta) \leqslant 1 + 2$ or $1 \leqslant g(\theta) \leqslant 3$

The graph of $f(\theta) = (\sin \theta + 2)^2$ has the range:

$1^2 \leqslant f(\theta) \leqslant 3^2$ or $1 \leqslant f(\theta) \leqslant 9$

The graph of $d(\theta) = (\sin \theta + 2)^2 - 5$ is the graph of $f(\theta)$ translated $\begin{pmatrix} 0 \\ -5 \end{pmatrix}$.

Its range is now: $1 - 5 \leqslant d(\theta) \leqslant 9 - 5$ or $-4 \leqslant d(\theta) \leqslant 4$

The maximum and minimum values are 4 and -4 respectively.

10 a $a = \dfrac{1 - \sin \theta}{2 \cos \theta}$

Multiplying both sides by $2 \cos \theta$:

$a(2 \cos \theta) = 1 - \sin \theta$

Dividing both sides by a:

$2 \cos \theta = \dfrac{1 - \sin \theta}{a}$

Dividing both sides by $1 - \sin \theta$:

$\dfrac{2 \cos \theta}{1 - \sin \theta} = \dfrac{1}{a}$

Dealing with the left-hand side:

Multiplying top and bottom by $(1 + \sin \theta)$ gives:

$\dfrac{2 \cos \theta(1 + \sin \theta)}{(1 - \sin \theta)(1 + \sin \theta)} = \dfrac{1}{a}$

$\dfrac{2 \cos \theta(1 + \sin \theta)}{1 - \sin^2 \theta} = \dfrac{1}{a}$

Using the identity $\sin^2 \theta + \cos^2 \theta \equiv 1$ and rearranging gives:

$\cos^2 \theta \equiv 1 - \sin^2 \theta$

Substituting for $\cos^2 \theta$ gives:

$\dfrac{2 \cos \theta(1 + \sin \theta)}{\cos^2 \theta} = \dfrac{1}{a}$

Dividing top and bottom by $\cos \theta$ gives:

$\dfrac{1}{a} = \dfrac{2(1 + \sin \theta)}{\cos \theta}$ shown.

b Using $a = \dfrac{1 - \sin \theta}{2 \cos \theta}$

$2a \cos \theta = 1 - \sin \theta$

$\cos \theta = \dfrac{1 - \sin \theta}{2a} \quad \dots \dots [1]$

Using $\dfrac{1}{a} = \dfrac{2(1 + \sin \theta)}{\cos \theta}$

$\dfrac{\cos \theta}{a} = 2(1 + \sin \theta)$

$\cos \theta = 2a(1 + \sin \theta) \dots [2]$

Equating $[1]$ and $[2]$:

$\dfrac{1 - \sin \theta}{2a} = 2a(1 + \sin \theta)$

$1 - \sin \theta = 4a^2(1 + \sin \theta)$

$1 - \sin \theta = 4a^2 + 4a^2 \sin \theta$

$1 - 4a^2 = 4a^2 \sin \theta + \sin \theta$

$1 - 4a^2 = \sin \theta(4a^2 + 1)$

$\sin \theta = \dfrac{1 - 4a^2}{1 + 4a^2}$

Using: $a = \dfrac{1 - \sin \theta}{2 \cos \theta}$

$2a \cos \theta = 1 - \sin \theta$

$\sin \theta = 1 - 2a \cos \theta \dots [3]$

Using: $\dfrac{1}{a} = \dfrac{2(1 + \sin \theta)}{\cos \theta}$

$\dfrac{\cos \theta}{a} = 2(1 + \sin \theta)$

$\cos \theta = 2a(1 + \sin \theta)$

$\cos \theta = 2a + 2a \sin \theta$

$\cos \theta - 2a = 2a \sin \theta$

$\sin \theta = \dfrac{\cos \theta - 2a}{2a} \dots [4]$

Equating $[3]$ and $[4]$:

$1 - 2a \cos \theta = \dfrac{\cos \theta - 2a}{2a}$

$2a(1 - 2a \cos \theta) = \cos \theta - 2a$

$2a - 4a^2 \cos \theta = \cos \theta - 2a$

$4a = \cos \theta + 4a^2 \cos \theta$

$4a = \cos \theta(1 + 4a^2)$

$\cos \theta = \dfrac{4a}{1 + 4a^2}$

EXERCISE 5H

1 a $\cos\theta + \sin\theta = 5\cos\theta$

Dividing both sides by $\cos\theta$ gives:

$1 + \dfrac{\sin\theta}{\cos\theta} = 5$

Using $\tan\theta = \dfrac{\sin\theta}{\cos\theta}$

$1 + \tan\theta = 5$

$\quad \tan\theta = 4$

b $\theta = \tan^{-1} 4$

$\theta = 75.96°$

The second solution is
$180° + 75.96° = 255.96°$

Solutions are: $76.0°, 256.0°$ (to 1 decimal place)

2 a $3\sin^2\theta + 5\sin\theta\cos\theta = 2\cos^2\theta$

Divide both sides by $\cos^2\theta$:

$\dfrac{3\sin^2\theta}{\cos^2\theta} + \dfrac{5\sin\theta\cos\theta}{\cos^2\theta} = \dfrac{2\cos^2\theta}{\cos^2\theta}$

Using $\tan\theta = \dfrac{\sin\theta}{\cos\theta}$

$3\tan^2\theta + 5\tan\theta = 2$

$3\tan^2\theta + 5\tan\theta - 2 = 0$ shown

b Using $3\tan^2\theta + 5\tan\theta - 2 = 0$

Factorising the left-hand side gives:
$(3\tan\theta - 1)(\tan\theta + 2) = 0$

Either: $3\tan\theta - 1 = 0$

$\tan\theta = \dfrac{1}{3}$

$\theta = 18.43…°$

There are no other solutions in the range

$0° \leqslant \theta \leqslant 180°$ which satisfy $\tan\theta = \dfrac{1}{3}$

Or: $\tan\theta + 2 = 0$

$\quad \tan\theta = -2$

$\quad\quad \theta = -63.43…°$

Using the sketch:

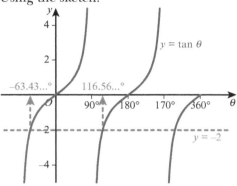

The first solution is
$180° - 63.43…° = 116.56…°$

Solutions are: $18.4°, 116.6°$ (to 1 decimal place)

3 a Given: $8\sin^2\theta + 2\cos^2\theta - \cos\theta = 6$

There is no $\sin\theta$ in the new form.

Using the identity $\sin^2\theta + \cos^2\theta \equiv 1$
rearranging gives:
$\sin^2\theta = 1 - \cos^2\theta$

Substituting for $\sin^2\theta$ gives:
$8(1 - \cos^2\theta) + 2\cos^2\theta - \cos\theta = 6$

$8 - 8\cos^2\theta + 2\cos^2\theta - \cos\theta = 6$

$8 - 6\cos^2\theta - \cos\theta = 6$

Rearranging:
$6\cos^2\theta + \cos\theta - 2 = 0$ shown

b Factorising the left-hand side gives:
$(3\cos\theta + 2)(2\cos\theta - 1) = 0$

Either: $3\cos\theta + 2 = 0$

$\cos\theta = -\dfrac{2}{3}$

$\theta = 131.81°$

Using the sketch:

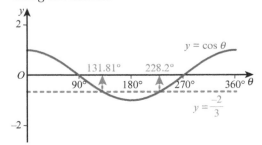

The second solution is 228.2°

Or: $2\cos\theta - 1 = 0$

$$\cos\theta = \frac{1}{2}$$

$$\theta = 60°$$

The other solution in the range

$0° \leqslant \theta \leqslant 360°$ for which $\cos\theta = \frac{1}{2}$ is:

$\theta = 360° - 60°$ or $300°$ (cos is positive in the fourth quadrant)

The solutions are:
$60°, 131.8°, 228.2°, 300°$

4 a $4\sin^4\theta + 14 = 19\cos^2\theta$

> Looking at the right-hand side, there are no $\cos\theta$ terms.

Using the identity $\sin^2\theta + \cos^2\theta \equiv 1$ rearranging gives:
$\cos^2\theta \equiv 1 - \sin^2\theta$

Substituting for $\cos^2\theta$ into the original equation gives:
$4\sin^4\theta + 14 = 19(1 - \sin^2\theta)$
$4\sin^4\theta + 14 = 19 - 19\sin^2\theta$
Substitute $x = \sin^2\theta$
$4x^2 + 14 = 19 - 19x$
$4x^2 + 19x - 5 = 0$ shown

---

b Factorising the left-hand side gives:
$(4x - 1)(x + 5) = 0$
Either: $x + 5 = 0$
$\sin^2\theta + 5 = 0$
$\sin^2\theta = -5$ No real solutions.
Or: $4x - 1 = 0$
$$x = \frac{1}{4}$$
So, $\sin^2\theta = \frac{1}{4}$
$$\sin\theta = \pm\frac{1}{2}$$
Using the sketch:

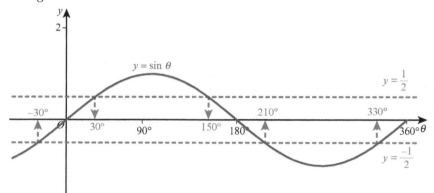

If $\sin\theta = \frac{1}{2}$ then $\theta = 30°$ and $150°$

If $\sin\theta = -\frac{1}{2}$ then $\theta = 210°$ and $330°$

Solutions are: $30°, 150°, 210°, 330°$

> Sin is positive in the first and second quadrants. Sin is negative in the second and fourth quadrants.

5 a Write $\sin\theta\tan\theta = 3$ in the form
$\cos^2\theta + 3\cos\theta - 1 = 0$.

> There are no $\sin\theta$ nor $\tan\theta$ terms in the rewritten form.

Using $\tan\theta = \dfrac{\sin\theta}{\cos\theta}$ and substituting gives:

$\sin\theta \times \dfrac{\sin\theta}{\cos\theta} = 3$

$\dfrac{\sin^2\theta}{\cos\theta} = 3$

$\sin^2\theta = 3\cos\theta$

Using the identity $\sin^2\theta + \cos^2\theta \equiv 1$ and rearranging gives:
$\sin^2\theta \equiv 1 - \cos^2\theta$
Substituting for $\sin^2\theta$ gives:
$1 - \cos^2\theta = 3\cos\theta$
Rearranging gives:
$\cos^2\theta + 3\cos\theta - 1 = 0$ shown

b $\cos^2\theta + 3\cos\theta - 1 = 0$

The left-hand side will not factorise, so using the quadratic formula and comparing with $ax^2 + bx + c = 0$ and letting $x = \cos\theta$:
$x^2 + 3x - 1 = 0$
$a = 1, b = 3, c = -1$
$x = \dfrac{-b \pm \sqrt{b^2 - 4ac}}{2a}$
$x = \dfrac{-3 \pm \sqrt{3^2 - 4(1)(-1)}}{2(1)}$
$x = \dfrac{-3 \pm \sqrt{13}}{2}$
$x = -3.3027$ or $x = 0.3027$
So, $\cos\theta = -3.3027$ (No solutions as $-1 \leqslant \cos\theta \leqslant 1$)
or $\cos\theta = 0.3027$
$\qquad \theta = 72.38°$
As cos is positive in the fourth quadrant, the second solution is $360° - 72.38° = 287.62°$
Solutions are: $72.4°, 287.6°$ (to 1 decimal place)

6 a $5(2\sin\theta - \cos\theta) = 4(\sin\theta + 2\cos\theta)$
Expanding brackets:
$10\sin\theta - 5\cos\theta = 4\sin\theta + 8\cos\theta$
$6\sin\theta = 13\cos\theta$

Dividing both sides by $\cos\theta$ and using
$\tan\theta = \dfrac{\sin\theta}{\cos\theta}$ gives:
$6\tan\theta = 13$
$\tan\theta = \dfrac{13}{6}$ shown.

b $\theta = \tan^{-1}\dfrac{13}{6}$
$\theta = 65.22°$
The second solution is $180° + 65.22°$ (as tan is positive in the third quadrant).
Solutions are: $65.2°, 245.2°$ (to 1 decimal place)

7 a $\dfrac{\sin\theta}{1 + \cos\theta} + \dfrac{1 + \cos\theta}{\sin\theta} \equiv \dfrac{2}{\sin\theta}$.
Left-hand side:
Adding the fractions:
$= \dfrac{(\sin\theta)^2}{\sin\theta(1 + \cos\theta)} + \dfrac{(1 + \cos\theta)^2}{\sin\theta(1 + \cos\theta)}$
$= \dfrac{\sin^2\theta + (1 + \cos\theta)^2}{\sin\theta(1 + \cos\theta)}$
$= \dfrac{\sin^2\theta + 1 + 2\cos\theta + \cos^2\theta}{\sin\theta(1 + \cos\theta)}$
Using the identity $\sin^2\theta + \cos^2\theta \equiv 1$ to simplify the numerator gives:
$= \dfrac{2 + 2\cos\theta}{\sin\theta(1 + \cos\theta)}$
$= \dfrac{2(1 + \cos\theta)}{\sin\theta(1 + \cos\theta)}$
$= \dfrac{2}{\sin\theta}$ proved

b $\dfrac{2}{\sin\theta} = 1 + 3\sin\theta$
$2 = \sin\theta + 3\sin^2\theta$
$3\sin^2\theta + \sin\theta - 2 = 0$
Factorising:
$(3\sin\theta - 2)(\sin\theta + 1) = 0$
Either: $\sin\theta + 1 = 0$
$\qquad \sin\theta = -1$
$\qquad \theta = 270°$
Or: $3\sin\theta - 2 = 0$
$\qquad \sin\theta = \dfrac{2}{3}$
$\qquad \theta = 41.81°$

As sin is positive in the first and second quadrants, the second solution is
$180° − 41.81° = 138.19°$
Solutions are: $41.8°$, $138.2°$, $270°$

8 a $\dfrac{\cos \theta}{\tan \theta(1 + \sin \theta)} \equiv \dfrac{1}{\sin \theta} - 1.$

Left-hand side:
Multiplying top and bottom by $(1 - \sin \theta)$

$= \dfrac{\cos \theta(1 - \sin \theta)}{\tan \theta(1 + \sin \theta)(1 - \sin \theta)}$

Expanding denominator:

$= \dfrac{\cos \theta(1 - \sin \theta)}{\tan \theta(1 - \sin^2 \theta)}$

Using the identity $\sin^2 \theta + \cos^2 \theta \equiv 1$ and rearranging gives:
$1 - \sin^2 \theta \equiv \cos^2 \theta$
Substituting for $1 - \sin^2 \theta$ in the denominator gives:

$= \dfrac{\cos \theta(1 - \sin \theta)}{\tan \theta \cos^2 \theta}$

Dividing top and bottom by $\cos \theta$ gives:

$= \dfrac{1 - \sin \theta}{\tan \theta \cos \theta}$

Using $\tan \theta = \dfrac{\sin \theta}{\cos \theta}$ and substituting gives:

$= \dfrac{1 - \sin \theta}{\dfrac{\sin \theta}{\cos \theta} \times \cos \theta}$

$= \dfrac{1 - \sin \theta}{\sin \theta}$

$= \dfrac{1}{\sin \theta} - 1$ shown.

b $\dfrac{1}{\sin \theta} - 1 = 1$

$\dfrac{1}{\sin \theta} = 2$

$2 \sin \theta = 1$

$\sin \theta = \dfrac{1}{2}$

Sin is positive in the first and second quadrants so:
$\theta = 30°$ and $\theta = 180° − 30°$ or $150°$
Solutions are: $30°$ and $150°$

9 a $\dfrac{1}{1 + \sin \theta} + \dfrac{1}{1 - \sin \theta} \equiv \dfrac{2}{\cos^2 \theta}.$

Left-hand side:
Adding fractions gives:

$= \dfrac{1 - \sin \theta}{(1 - \sin \theta)(1 + \sin \theta)} + \dfrac{1 + \sin \theta}{(1 - \sin \theta)(1 + \sin \theta)}$

$= \dfrac{1 - \sin \theta + 1 + \sin \theta}{(1 - \sin \theta)(1 + \sin \theta)}$

$= \dfrac{2}{1 - \sin^2 \theta}$

Using the identity $\sin^2 \theta + \cos^2 \theta \equiv 1$ and rearranging gives:
$1 - \sin^2 \theta \equiv \cos^2 \theta$
Substituting for $1 - \sin^2 \theta$ gives:

$\dfrac{2}{\cos^2 \theta}$ shown.

b $\cos \theta \times \dfrac{2}{\cos^2 \theta} = 5$

Simplifying the left-hand side gives:

$\dfrac{2}{\cos \theta} = 5$

$2 = 5 \cos \theta$

$\cos \theta = 0.4$

$\theta = 66.42...°$

Cos is positive in the first and fourth quadrants so the second solution is
$360° − 66.42...° = 293.57...°$
Solutions are: $66.4°$ and $293.6°$

10 a $\left(\dfrac{1}{\sin \theta} + \dfrac{1}{\tan \theta}\right)^2 \equiv \dfrac{1 + \cos \theta}{1 - \cos \theta}.$

Left-hand side:

$= \left(\dfrac{1}{\sin \theta} + \dfrac{1}{\tan \theta}\right)^2$

Using $\tan \theta = \dfrac{\sin \theta}{\cos \theta}$ and substituting gives:

$\left(\dfrac{1}{\sin \theta} + \dfrac{1}{\dfrac{\sin \theta}{\cos \theta}}\right)^2$

$= \left(\dfrac{1}{\sin \theta} + \dfrac{\cos \theta}{\sin \theta}\right)^2$

Adding fractions gives:

$= \left(\dfrac{1 + \cos \theta}{\sin \theta}\right)^2$

Squaring gives:

$$= \frac{(1 + \cos\theta)(1 + \cos\theta)}{\sin^2\theta}$$

Using the identity $\sin^2\theta + \cos^2\theta \equiv 1$ and rearranging gives:

$$\sin^2\theta \equiv 1 - \cos^2\theta$$

Substituting for $\sin^2\theta$ in the denominator gives:

$$= \frac{(1 + \cos\theta)(1 + \cos\theta)}{1 - \cos^2\theta}$$

Writing the denominator as the difference of two squares gives:

$$= \frac{(1 + \cos\theta)(1 + \cos\theta)}{(1 - \cos\theta)(1 + \cos\theta)}$$

Dividing top and bottom by $(1 + \cos\theta)$ gives:

$$\frac{1 + \cos\theta}{1 - \cos\theta} \text{ shown.}$$

b $\dfrac{1 + \cos\theta}{1 - \cos\theta} = 2$

$$1 + \cos\theta = 2(1 - \cos\theta)$$
$$1 + \cos\theta = 2 - 2\cos\theta$$
$$3\cos\theta = 1$$
$$\cos\theta = \frac{1}{3}$$
$$\theta = 70.52\ldots°$$

Cos is positive in the first and fourth quadrants so the second solution is $360° - 70.52\ldots° = 289.47\ldots°$

Solutions are: $70.5°$ and $289.5°$

11 a $\cos^4\theta - \sin^4\theta \equiv 2\cos^2\theta - 1$.

Left-hand side:
Write as the difference of two squares:
$$= (\cos^2\theta - \sin^2\theta)(\cos^2\theta + \sin^2\theta)$$

Using the identity $\cos^2\theta + \sin^2\theta \equiv 1$ to simplify the second bracket gives:
$$(\cos^2\theta - \sin^2\theta)(1)$$

and as: $\sin^2\theta \equiv 1 - \cos^2\theta$

Substituting for $\sin^2\theta$ gives:
$$\cos^2\theta - (1 - \cos^2\theta)$$
$$= \cos^2\theta - 1 + \cos^2\theta$$
$$= 2\cos^2\theta - 1 \text{ shown.}$$

b $2\cos^2\theta - 1 = \dfrac{1}{2}$

$$2\cos^2\theta = \frac{3}{2}$$
$$\cos^2\theta = \frac{3}{4}$$
$$\cos\theta = \pm\sqrt{\frac{3}{4}}$$
$$\cos\theta = \pm\frac{\sqrt{3}}{2}$$

The positive root gives: $\theta = 30°$ and $360° - 30° = 330°$ (since cos is positive in the first and fourth quadrants)

The negative root gives: $\theta = 150°$ and using symmetry of the cos curve, $\theta = 360° - 150°$ or $210°$

Solutions are: $30°, 150°, 210°, 330°$

1 b $(1-x)^4$

The index is 4 so use the row for $n = 4$ in Pascal's triangle: $(1, 4, 6, 4, 1)$

$(1-x)^4 = 1(1)^4 + 4(1)^3(-x) + 6(1)^2(-x)^2 + 4(1)^1(-x)^3 + 1(1)(-x)^4$

$\qquad = 1 - 4x + 6x^2 - 4x^3 + x^4$

> Be careful! Do not to forget to include the '−' sign in the brackets.

f $(2x + 3y)^3$

The index is 3 so use the row for $n = 3$ in Pascal's triangle: $(1, 3, 3, 1)$

$(2x + 3y)^3 = 1(2x)^3 + 3(2x)^2(3y) + 3(2x)(3y)^2 + 1(3y)^3$

$\qquad = 8x^3 + 36x^2y + 54xy^2 + 27y^3$

2 c $(3 - x)^5$

The index is 5 so use the row for $n = 5$ in Pascal's triangle: $(1, 5, 10, 10, 5, 1)$

$(3 - x)^5 = 1(3)^5 + 5(3)^4(-x) + 10(3)^3(-x)^2 + 10(3)^2(-x)^3 + 5(3)(-x)^4 + 1(-x)^5$

$\qquad = 243 - 405x + 270x^2 - 90x^3 + 15x^4 - x^5$

Answer: -90

> It is not necessary to write down all the terms if you are asked for one specific term of a series.

f $(2x - 1)^4$

The index is 4 so use the row for $n = 4$ in Pascal's triangle: $(1, 4, 6, 4, 1)$

The term containing x^3 is $4(2x)^3(-1)^1$ or $-32x^3$

Answer: -32

> Be careful! In Question 2f an answer $-32x^3$ would not be correct.

3 $(3 + x)^5 + (3 - x)^5 = A + Bx^2 + Cx^4$

$\qquad (3 + x)^5 = 1(3)^5 + 5(3)^4(x) + 10(3)^3(x)^2 + 10(3)^2(x)^3 + 5(3)(x)^4 + 1(x)^5$

$\qquad\qquad = 243 + 405x + 270x^2 + 90x^3 + 15x^4 + x^5$

$\qquad (3 - x)^5 = 243 - 405x + 270x^2 - 90x^3 + 15x^4 - x^5$

$(3 + x)^5 + (3 - x)^5 = 486 + 540x^2 + 30x^4$

$A = 486,\ B = 540,\ C = 30$

4 Given: $(3 + ax)^4 = 1(3)^4 + 4(3)^3(ax) + 6(3)^2(ax)^2 + 4(3)^1(ax)^3 + 1(1)(ax)^4$

$\qquad\qquad = 81 + 108ax + 54a^2x^2 + 12a^3x^3 + a^4x^4$

The coefficient of x^2 is $54a^2$

$54a^2 = 216$

$\quad a^2 = 4$

$\quad\ a = \pm 2$

5 a $(2 + x)^4 = 1(2)^4 + 4(2)^3(x) + 6(2)^2(x)^2 + 4(2)^1(x)^3 + 1(x)^4$
$\qquad = 16 + 32x + 24x^2 + 8x^3 + x^4$

$\left(2 + \sqrt{3}\right)^4$ uses the above expansion but substitutes $x = \sqrt{3}$

$\qquad = 16 + 32\sqrt{3} + 24\left(\sqrt{3}\right)^2 + 8\left(\sqrt{3}\right)^3 + \left(\sqrt{3}\right)^4$
$\qquad = 16 + 32\sqrt{3} + 72 + 24\sqrt{3} + 9$
$\qquad = 97 + 56\sqrt{3}$

6 a $(1 + x)^3 = 1(1)^3 + 3(1)^2(x) + 3(1)^1(x)^2 + 1(x)^3$
$\qquad = 1 + 3x + 3x^2 + x^3$

b i $\left(1 + \sqrt{5}\right)^3$ is found by substituting $x = \sqrt{5}$ into **a**, i.e.

$\qquad = 1 + 3\sqrt{5} + 3\left(\sqrt{5}\right)^2 + \left(\sqrt{5}\right)^3$
$\qquad = 1 + 3\sqrt{5} + 15 + 5\sqrt{5}$
$\qquad = 16 + 8\sqrt{5}$

ii $(1 - x)^3 = 1 - 3x + 3x^2 - x^3$

$\left(1 - \sqrt{5}\right)^3 = 1 - 3\sqrt{5} + 15 - 5\sqrt{5}$
$\qquad\qquad = 16 - 8\sqrt{5}$

c $16 + 8\sqrt{5} + 16 - 8\sqrt{5}$
$\quad = 32$

7 $(1 + x)(2 + 3x)^4$.

$(2 + 3x)^4 = 1(2)^4 + 4(2)^3(3x) + 6(2)^2(3x)^2 + 4(2)^1(3x)^3 + 1(3x)^4$
$\qquad\qquad = 16 + 96x + 216x^2 + 216x^3 + 81x^4$
$(1 + x)(2 + 3x)^4 = (1 + x)(16 + 96x + 216x^2 + 216x^3 + 81x^4)$
$\qquad\qquad = 16 + 96x + 216x^2 + 216x^3 + 81x^4 + 16x + 96x^2 + 216x^3 + 216x^4 + 81x^5$
$\qquad\qquad = 16 + 112x + 312x^2 + 432x^3 + 297x^4 + 81x^5$

8 a Expand $(x^2 - 1)^4 = 1[x^2]^4 + 4[x^2]^3(-1) + 6[x^2]^2(-1)^2 + 4[x^2]^1(-1)^3 + 1(-1)^4$
$\qquad\qquad = x^8 - 4x^6 + 6x^4 - 4x^2 + 1$

b $(1 - 2x^2)(x^8 - 4x^6 + 6x^4 - 4x^2 + 1)$

The term in x^6 comes from the products: $1 \times (-4x^6) + (-2x^2) \times (6x^4)$

so, $-4x^6 - 12x^6$ or $-16x^6$

The coefficient of x^6 is -16

Answer: -16

9 $\left(3x - \dfrac{2}{x}\right)^4$

$= 1(3x)^4 + 4(3x)^3\left(-\dfrac{2}{x}\right) + 6(3x)^2\left(-\dfrac{2}{x}\right)^2 + 4(3x)^1\left(-\dfrac{2}{x}\right)^3 + 1\left(-\dfrac{2}{x}\right)^4$

$= 81x^4 - 216x^2 + 216 - \dfrac{96}{x^2} + \dfrac{16}{x^4}$

The coefficient of x^2 is -216

10 $\left(x^2 - \dfrac{3}{x^2}\right)^4$

The independent term does not involve x.

$= 1(x^2)^4 + 4(x^2)^3\left(-\dfrac{3}{x^2}\right) + 6(x^2)^2\left(-\dfrac{3}{x^2}\right)^2 + 4(x^2)\left(-\dfrac{3}{x^2}\right)^3 + 1\left(-\dfrac{3}{x^2}\right)^4$

$= x^8 - 12x^4 + 54 - \dfrac{108}{x^4} + \dfrac{81}{x^8}$

The term independent of x is 54.

11 a $(1 + y)^4 = 1(1)^4 + 4(1)^3(y) + 6(1)^2(y)^2 + 4(1)^1(y)^3 + 1(1)(y)^4$
$\qquad\qquad = 1 + 4y + 6y^2 + 4y^3 + y^4$

So the first three terms are $1 + 4y + 6y^2$.

b $(1 + 5x - 2x^2)^4 = 1 + 4(5x - 2x^2) + 6(5x - 2x^2)^2 + 4(5x - 2x^2)^3 + (5x - 2x^2)^4$

The coefficient of x^2 is found from the products:

$4 \times -2x^2$ and $6 \times 5x \times 5x$

$-8x^2 + 150x^2$ or $142x^2$

Answer: 142

12 $(1 + ax)^4 = 1(1)^4 + 4(1)^3(ax) + 6(1)^2(ax)^2 + 4(1)^1(ax)^3 + 1(1)(ax)^4$

The term in x^2 is $6(ax)^2$ or $6a^2x^2$

$\left(1 + \dfrac{ax}{3}\right)^3 = 1(1)^3 + 3(1)^2\left(\dfrac{ax}{3}\right) + 3(1)^1\left(\dfrac{ax}{3}\right)^2 + 1\left(\dfrac{ax}{3}\right)^3$

The term in x is $3(1)^2\left(\dfrac{ax}{3}\right)$ or ax

So, $6a^2 = 30 \times a$ so $a = 5$

13 $\left(3x^4 + \dfrac{1}{x}\right)^4 = 1(3x^4)^4 + 4(3x^4)^3\left(\dfrac{1}{x}\right) + 6(3x^4)^2\left(\dfrac{1}{x}\right)^2 + 4(3x^4)^1\left(\dfrac{1}{x}\right)^3 + 1(1)\left(\dfrac{1}{x}\right)^4$

$\qquad\qquad = 81x^{16} + 108x^{11} + 54x^6 + 12x + \dfrac{1}{x^4}$

The power which has the greatest coefficient is x^{11}.

14 a $(x + y)^5 = 1(x)^5 + 5(x)^4(y) + 10(x)^3(y)^2 + 10(x)^2(y)^3 + 5(x)(y)^4 + 1(y)^5$
$\qquad\qquad = x^5 + 5x^4y + 10x^3y^2 + 10x^2y^3 + 5xy^4 + y^5$

b $\left(10\dfrac{1}{4}\right)^5 = (10 + 0.25)^5$

$= 10^5 + 5 \times 10^4 \times 0.25 + 10 \times 10^3 \times 0.25^2 + 10 \times 10^2 \times 0.25^3 + 5 \times 10 \times 0.25^4 + 0.25^5$

$= 100\,000 + \dfrac{50\,000}{4} + \dfrac{10\,000}{16} + \dfrac{1000}{64} + \dfrac{50}{256} + \dfrac{1}{1024}$

$= 100\,000 + 12500 + 625 + \ldots$ (ignoring the last 3 terms as these are less than 50)

$= 113\,125$

$= 113\,000$ to the nearest hundred

15 a

$$\left(x^2 + \frac{1}{x}\right)^4 = 1(x^2)^4 + 4(x^2)^3\left(\frac{1}{x}\right) + 6(x^2)^2\left(\frac{1}{x}\right)^2 + 4(x^2)^1\left(\frac{1}{x}\right)^3 + 1\left(\frac{1}{x}\right)^4$$

$$= x^8 + 4x^5 + 6x^2 + \frac{4}{x} + \frac{1}{x^4}$$

$$\left(x^2 - \frac{1}{x}\right)^4 = x^8 - 4x^5 + 6x^2 - \frac{4}{x} + \frac{1}{x^4}$$

$$\left(x^2 + \frac{1}{x}\right)^4 - \left(x^2 - \frac{1}{x}\right)^4 = 8x^5 + \frac{8}{x}$$

$$= px^5 + \frac{q}{x}$$

$\therefore\ p = 8$ and $q = 8$

b Substituting $x^2 = 2$ and so $x = \pm\sqrt{2}$ (reject the $-\sqrt{2}$ to be consistent with the signs in the brackets)

$$\left(2 + \frac{1}{\sqrt{2}}\right)^4 - \left(2 - \frac{1}{\sqrt{2}}\right)^4 = 8x^5 + \frac{8}{x}$$

Which becomes: $8 \times \left(\sqrt{2}\right)^5 + \dfrac{8}{\sqrt{2}}$

Evaluating this gives: $32\sqrt{2} + \dfrac{8\sqrt{2}}{2}$

$$= 32\sqrt{2} + 4\sqrt{2}$$

$$= 36\sqrt{2}$$

16 a $y^3 = \left(x + \dfrac{1}{x}\right)^3$

$$= 1(x)^3 + 3(x)^2\left(\frac{1}{x}\right) + 3(x)^1\left(\frac{1}{x}\right)^2 + 1\left(\frac{1}{x}\right)^3$$

$$= x^3 + 3x + \frac{3}{x} + \frac{1}{x^3}$$

$$= x^3 + \frac{1}{x^3} + 3x + \frac{3}{x}$$

$$= x^3 + \frac{1}{x^3} + 3\left(1 + \frac{1}{x}\right)$$

So, $y^3 = x^3 + \dfrac{1}{x^3} + 3y$

$$x^3 + \frac{1}{x^3} = y^3 - 3y$$

b $y^5 = \left(x + \dfrac{1}{x}\right)^5$

$$= 1(x)^5 + 5(x)^4\left(\frac{1}{x}\right) + 10(x)^3\left(\frac{1}{x}\right)^2 + 10(x)^2\left(\frac{1}{x}\right)^3 + 5(x)\left(\frac{1}{x}\right)^4 + 1\left(\frac{1}{x}\right)^5$$

$$= x^5 + 5x^3 + 10x + \frac{10}{x} + \frac{5}{x^3} + \frac{1}{x^5}$$

$$= x^5 + \frac{1}{x^5} + 5x^3 + \frac{10}{x} + 10x + \frac{5}{x^3}$$

$$y^5 = x^5 + \frac{1}{x^5} + 5\left(x^3 + \frac{1}{x^3}\right) + 10\left(x + \frac{1}{x}\right)$$

$$y^5 = x^5 + \frac{1}{x^5} + 5(y^3 - 3y) + 10y$$

$$y^5 = x^5 + \frac{1}{x^5} + 5y^3 - 15y + 10y$$

$$y^5 = x^5 + \frac{1}{x^5} + 5y^3 - 5y$$

$$x^5 + \frac{1}{x^5} = y^5 - 5y^3 + 5y$$

EXERCISE 6B

1 a $\dbinom{7}{3} = \dfrac{7 \times 6 \times 5}{3 \times 2 \times 1} = \dfrac{210}{6} = 35$

2 a $\dbinom{n}{2} = \dfrac{n \times (n-1)}{2 \times 1} = \dfrac{n(n-1)}{2}$

3 a $\dbinom{n}{r} = \dfrac{n!}{r!(n-r)!}$

$\dbinom{10}{2} = \dfrac{10!}{2!(10-2)!}$

$= 45$

4 f $(2-x)^{13} = \dbinom{13}{0}2^{13} + \dbinom{13}{1}2^{12}(-x)^1$

$\qquad + \dbinom{13}{2}2^{11}(-x)^2 \dots$

$\qquad = 8192 - 53\,248x + 159\,744x^2$

5 b Given $(1+3x)^{12}$, the term containing x^3 is:

$\dbinom{12}{3}(1)^9(3x)^3 = 5940x^3$

The coefficient of x^3 is 5940.

6 Given $(2x+1)^{12}$, the term containing x^4 is:

$\dbinom{12}{8}(2x)^4 1^8 = 7920x^3$

The coefficient of x^4 is 7920

7 Given $(5-2x)^8$ the term containing x^5 is:

$\dbinom{8}{5}5^3(-2x)^5 = -224\,000x^5$

8 Given $(x-2y)^{13}$

$\dbinom{13}{5}x^8(-2y)^5 = 1287x^8 \times -32y^5 = -41\,184x^8y^5$

The coefficient is $-41\,184$.

9 The independent term does not involve x.
The x terms cancel each other out when the power of x is double the power of $\dfrac{3}{x^2}$.

Also, the sum of these powers must be 12.

So, $\left(x - \dfrac{3}{x^2}\right)^{12} = \dbinom{12}{4}x^8\left(-\dfrac{3}{x^2}\right)^4 + \dots$

$\qquad = 495x^8 \times \dfrac{81}{x^8}$

$\qquad = 40\,095$

10 a $(1-x)(2+x)^7 = (1-x)\left[\binom{7}{0}2^7 + \binom{7}{1}2^6(x)^1 + \binom{7}{2}2^5(x)^2 + \ldots\right]$

$= (1-x)[128 + 448x + 672x^2 + \ldots]$
$= 128 + 448x + 672x^2 - 128x - 448x^2 + \ldots$
$= 128 + 320x + 224x^2$

b $(1+2x)(1-3x)^{10} = (1+2x)\left[\binom{10}{0}1^{10} + \binom{10}{1}1^9(-3x)^1 + \binom{10}{2}1^8(-3x)^2 + \ldots\right]$

$= (1+2x)[1 - 30x + 405x^2 - \ldots]$
$= 1 - 30x + 405x^2 + 2x - 60x^2 + \ldots$
$= 1 - 28x + 345x^2$

c $(1+x)\left(1-\dfrac{x}{2}\right)^8 = (1+x)\left[\binom{8}{0}1^8 + \binom{8}{1}1^7\left(-\dfrac{x}{2}\right)^1 + \binom{8}{2}1^6\left(-\dfrac{x}{2}\right)^2 + \ldots\right]$

$= (1+x)[1 - 4x + 7x^2 + \ldots]$
$= 1 - 4x + 7x^2 + x - 4x^2 \ldots$
$= 1 - 3x + 3x^2$

11 a $(2+x)^{10} = \binom{10}{0}2^{10} + \binom{10}{1}2^9(x)^1 + \binom{10}{2}2^8(x)^2 + \ldots$

$= 1024 + 5120x + 11\,520x^2$

b $(2+2y-3y^2)^{10} = 1024 + 5120(2y-3y^2) + 11\,520(2y-3y^2)^2$
$= 1024 + 10\,240y - 15\,360y^2 + 46\,080y^2$

(We ignore higher powers of y as only the first three terms are required i.e. the terms containing y^0, y^1 and y^2.)

$= 1024 + 10\,240y + 30\,720y^2$

12 a $\left(1-\dfrac{x}{2}\right)^8 = \binom{8}{0}1^8 + \binom{8}{1}1^7\left(-\dfrac{x}{2}\right)^1 + \binom{8}{2}1^6\left(-\dfrac{x}{2}\right)^2 + \ldots$

$= 1 - 4x + 7x^2$

b $(2+3x-x^2)\left(1-\dfrac{x}{2}\right)^8 = (2+3x-x^2)(1 - 4x + 7x^2 - \ldots)$

Term required is $= 2 \times 7x^2 + 3x \times (-4x) + (-x^2) \times 1$
$= 14x^2 - 12x^2 - 1x^2$
$= 1x^2$

Answer is 1.

13 $(2-3x)^4(1+2x)^{10}$

$= \left[\binom{4}{0}2^4 + \binom{4}{1}2^3(-3x)^1 + \binom{4}{2}2^2(-3x)^2 \ldots\right]\left[\binom{10}{0}1^{10} + \binom{10}{1}1^9(2x)^1 + \binom{10}{2}1^8(2x)^2 \ldots\right]$

$= [16 - 96x + 216x^2][1 + 20x + 180x^2]$
$= 16 + 320x + 2880x^2 - 96x - 1920x^2 + 216x^2$
$= 16 + 224x + 1176x^2$

14 $([1 + (ax + bx^2)])^7 = \binom{7}{0}1^7 + \binom{7}{1}1^6(ax + bx^2)^1 + \binom{7}{2}1^5(ax + bx^2)^2 + \binom{7}{3}1^4(ax + bx^2)^3 \dots$

$= 1 + 7ax + 7bx^2 + 21a^2x^2 + 21abx^3 + 21abx^3 + 35a^3x^3 + \dots$ compare this with:

$= 1 - 14x + 91x^2 + px^3$ to find the values of a, b and p.

Equating the coefficient of x gives: $7a = -14$ so $a = -2$

Equating the coefficient of x^2 gives: $7b + 21a^2 = 91$

$7b + 21(-2)^2 = 91$

$7b + 84 = 91$

$7b = 7$

$b = 1$

Equating the coefficient of x^3 gives: $42ab + 35a^3 = p$

$p = 42 \times (-2) \times 1 + 35(-2)^3$

$p = -364$

Solutions: $a = -2$, $b = 1$, $p = -364$

15 $(1 + x)\left(2 - \dfrac{x}{4}\right)^n = (1 + x)\left[\binom{n}{0}2^n + \binom{n}{1}2^{n-1}\left(-\dfrac{x}{4}\right)^1 + \binom{n}{2}2^{n-2}\left(-\dfrac{x}{4}\right)^2 \dots\right]$

$= (1 + x)\left[2^n - \dfrac{2^{n-1}nx}{4} + \dfrac{2^{n-2}n(n-1)}{2 \times 1} \times \dfrac{x^2}{16} \dots\right]$

$= 2^n - \dfrac{2^{n-1}nx}{4} + \dfrac{2^{n-2}n(n-1)}{2 \times 1} \times \dfrac{x^2}{16} + 2^n x - \dfrac{2^{n-1}nx^2}{4} + \dots$

$= 2^n - \dfrac{2^{n-1}nx}{2^2} + \dfrac{2^{n-2}n(n-1)x^2}{2^5} + 2^n x - \dfrac{2^{n-1}nx^2}{2^2} + \dots$

$= 2^n - 2^{n-3}nx + 2^{n-7}n(n-1)x^2 + 2^n x - 2^{n-3}nx^2 + \dots$

$p = 2^n$

There is no 'x' term so $-2^{n-3}n + 2^n = 0$

$2^{n-3}n = 2^n$

Divide both sides by 2^{n-3} gives:

$n = 2^3$

$n = 8$

So, $p = 2^8$

$p = 256$

$q = 2^{n-7}n(n-1) - 2^{n-3}n$

$q = 2^{8-7} \times 8 \times (8-1) - 2^{8-3} \times 8$

$q = 112 - 256$

$q = -144$

EXERCISE 6C

1 nth term $= a + (n-1)d$
$\quad$ 7th term $= a + (7-1)d$
$\quad\quad\quad = a + 6d$
$\quad$ 19th term $= a + (19-1)$
$\quad\quad\quad = a + 18d$

2 **a** First find the number of terms in the series:
$\quad$ Use nth term $= a + (n-1)d$
$\quad\quad 97 = 13 + (n-1) \times 4$
$\quad\quad 84 = (n-1) \times 4$
$\quad\quad n = \dfrac{84}{4} + 1$
$\quad n = 22$ so there are 22 terms.

$\quad$ Now use $S_n = \dfrac{n}{2}(a+l)$
$\quad\quad S_{22} = \dfrac{22}{2}(13 + 97)$
$\quad\quad S_{22} = 1210$
$\quad$ The sum of the series is 1210.

3 **c** First find the common difference:
$\quad d = \dfrac{1}{2} - \dfrac{1}{3}$ or $\dfrac{1}{6}$
$\quad S_n = \dfrac{n}{2}[2a + (n-1)d]$
$\quad S_{20} = \dfrac{20}{2}\left[2 \times \dfrac{1}{3} + (20-1)\dfrac{1}{6}\right]$
$\quad S_{20} = 10\left[\dfrac{2}{3} + \dfrac{19}{6}\right]$
$\quad S_{20} = 38\dfrac{1}{3}$

4 $S_n = \dfrac{n}{2}[2a + (n-1)d]$
$\quad S_{20} = \dfrac{20}{2}[2 \times 15 + (20-1)d]$
$\quad 1630 = 10[30 + 19d]$
$\quad 163 = 30 + 19d$
$\quad d = \dfrac{133}{19}$ or $d = 7$
$\quad$ The common difference is 7.

5 **a** Using nth term $= a + (n-1)d$
$\quad\quad 78 = -27 + (16-1)d$
$\quad\quad 78 + 27 = 15d$
$\quad\quad d = 7$
$\quad$ The common difference is 7.
$\quad$ Use nth term $= a + (n-1)d$
$\quad\quad 169 = -27 + (n-1) \times 7$
$\quad\quad 196 = 7(n-1)$
$\quad\quad n = 29$
$\quad$ There are 29 terms.

$\quad$ **b** Use $S_n = \dfrac{n}{2}(a+l)$
$\quad\quad S_{29} = \dfrac{29}{2}(-27 + 169)$
$\quad\quad S_{29} = 2059$

6   The common difference $d = 139 - 146$
$\quad\quad\quad d = -7$
$\quad$ Using nth term $= a + (n-1)d$ to find n:
$\quad\quad -43 = 146 + (n-1) \times -7$
$\quad\quad -189 = -7(n-1)$
$\quad\quad n = 28$
$\quad$ Using $S_n = \dfrac{n}{2}(a+l)$:
$\quad\quad S_{28} = \dfrac{28}{2}(146 + (-43))$
$\quad\quad S_{28} = 1442$
$\quad$ Sum of all the terms is 1442.

7   Common difference $d = 9 - 2$
$\quad\quad\quad = 7$
$\quad$ Using nth term $= a + (n-1)d$ to find n:
$\quad\quad = 2 + (n-1) \times 7$
$\quad$ As the last or nth term is greater than 150:
$\quad 2 + (n-1) \times 7 > 150$
$\quad\quad n - 1 > \dfrac{148}{7}$
$\quad\quad n > 21\dfrac{1}{7} + 1$
$\quad\quad n > 22\dfrac{1}{7}$
$\quad$ The smallest that n could be is 23.

To find the value of the 23rd term use nth term
$= a + (n-1)d$:
The 23rd term $= 2 + 22 \times 7$
$$= 156$$
Using $S_n = \frac{n}{2}(a+l)$:
$$S_{23} = \frac{23}{2}(2 + 156)$$
$$S_{23} = 1817$$
The sum of all the terms is 1817.

8 1st term $= 15$

2nd term $= 15 + d$

3rd term $= 15 + 2d$

4th term $= 15 + 3d$

5th term $= 15 + 4d$
$$S_n = 75 + 10d$$
$$79 = 75 + 10d$$
$$d = 0.4$$
Find the number of terms using nth term
$= a + (n-1)d$:
$$27 = 15 + (n-1) \times 0.4$$
$$n - 1 = \frac{12}{0.4}$$
$$n = 31$$
The number of terms in this progression is 31.

9 First term: $a = 105$

Last term $l = 294$

Common difference $d = 7$

Using nth term $= a + (n-1)d$:
$$294 = 105 + 7(n-1)$$
$$189 = 7(n-1)$$
$$n - 1 = 27$$
$$n = 28$$
There are 28 terms between 100 and 300 which
are divisible by 7.

Using $S_n = \frac{n}{2}(a+l)$
$$S_{28} = \frac{28}{2}(105 + 294)$$
$$= 5586$$

10 $a = 2$, $l = 17$ $S_n = 500$

Using nth term $= a + (n-1)d$:

$$17 = 2 + 10d$$
$$d = 1.5$$
Using $S_n = \frac{n}{2}[2a + (n-1)d]$:
$$500 = \frac{n}{2}[2 \times 2 + (n-1) \times 1.5]$$
$$1000 = n[4 + 1.5n - 1.5]$$
$$1000 = 2.5n + 1.5n^2$$
$$2000 = 5n + 3n^2$$
$$3n^2 + 5n - 2000 = 0$$
Comparing this to $an^2 + bn + c = 0$:
$$a = 3, b = 5, c = -2000$$
$$n = \frac{-5 \pm \sqrt{5^2 - 4(3)(-2000)}}{2(3)}$$
$$n = \frac{-5 \pm \sqrt{24025}}{6}$$
$$n = \frac{-5 + 155}{6} \text{ or } n = \frac{-5 - 155}{6} \text{ (reject as the}$$
number of terms cannot be negative)
$$n = 25$$
There are 25 terms in this progression.

11 $S_{16} = 8000$

1st payment $= 200$

5th payment $= 200 + 4d$

Using $S_n = \frac{n}{2}[2a + (n-1)d]$:
$$8000 = \frac{16}{2}(2 \times 200 + (16-1) \times d)$$
$$8000 = \frac{16}{2}(2 \times 200 + (16-1) \times d)$$
$$8000 = 8(400 + 15d)$$
$$15d = 600$$
$$d = 40$$
5th payment $= 200 + 4 \times 40$
$$= \$360$$

12 The 6th term $= -3$, $S_{10} = -10$

a Using nth term $= a + (n-1)d$:
$$-3 = a + (6-1)d$$
$$-3 = a + 5d \text{ ......[1]}$$
Using $S_n = \frac{n}{2}[2a + (n-1)d]$:
$$-10 = \frac{10}{2}[2a + (10-1)d]$$
$$-10 = 5[2a + 9d]$$
$$-2 = 2a + 9d \text{ ....[2]}$$

Using $[1]$ and $[2]$, multiplying $[1]$ by 2 then subtracting:

$-6 = 2a + 10d$

$-2 = 2a + 9d$

$-4 = d$

$d = -4$

Substituting $d = -4$ into $[1]$ gives:

$-3 = a + 5(-4)$

$a = 17$

The first term is 17 and the common difference is -4.

b Using nth term $= a + (n-1)d$

$-59 = 17 + (n-1) \times -4$

$-76 = -4n + 4$

$4n = 80$

$n = 20$

13 $S_1 = 4(1)^2 + 3(1)$

$S_1 = 7$ (this is the first term of the series)

$S_2 = 4(2)^2 + 3(2)$

$S_2 = 22$

As $S_n - S_{n-1} =$ common difference,

The second term is $22 - 7 = 15$

The common difference is $15 - 7 = 8$.

14 $S_n - S_{n-1} =$ common difference,

$S_1 = 12(1) - 2(1)^2$

$S_1 = 10$

The first term is 10.

$S_2 = 12(2) - 2(2)^2$

$S_2 = 16$

Using $S_n - S_{n-1} =$ common difference,

The second term is $16 - 10 = 6$

The common difference is $6 - 10 = -4$.

15 $S_n = \frac{1}{4}(5n^2 - 17n)$

$S_1 = \frac{1}{4}(5(1)^2 - 17(1))$

$S_1 = -3$

The first term is -3.

$S_2 = \frac{1}{4}(5(2)^2 - 17(2))$

$S_2 = -3.5$

The second term is $-3.5 - (-3)$ or -0.5

The common difference is $-0.5 - (-3)$ or 2.5

nth term $= a + (n-1)d$

$= -3 + (n-1)2.5$

$= -3 + 2.5n - 2.5$

$= 2.5n - 5.5$ or $\frac{1}{2}(5n - 11)$

16 $n = 10$

First sector angle is a degrees

Tenth sector angle $= 7a$ degrees

$360 = \frac{10}{2}(a + 7a)$

$360 = 5a + 35a$

$40a = 360$

$a = 9$

The smallest sector is $9°$.

17 a $S_n = \frac{n}{2}[2a + (n-1)d]$

$S_{20} = \frac{20}{2}[2a + (20-1)d]$

$S_{20} = 10[2a + 19d]$

$S_{20} = 20a + 190d$

$S_5 = \frac{5}{2}[2a + (5-1)d]$

$S_5 = 5a + 10d$

$S_{20} = 7 \times S_5$

So, $20a + 190d = 7(5a + 10d)$

$20a + 190d = 35a + 70d$

$15a = 120d$

$a = 8d$

b The 65th term $= a + (65-1)d$

$= a + 64d$

Now substitute $d = \frac{1}{8}a$

$= a + 64 \times \frac{1}{8}a$

$= 9a$

18 Using nth term $= a + (n-1)d$:

The third term $= a + (3-1)d$

$= a + 2d$

The tenth term $= a + (10-1)d$

$= a + 9d$

$a + 9d = 3(a + 2d)$

$a + 9d = 3a + 6d$

$a = 1.5d$

Using $S_n = \frac{n}{2}[2a + (n-1)d]$:

$S_{10} = \frac{10}{2}[2(1.5d) + (10-1)d]$

$S_{10} = 5[3d + 9d]$

$\quad\ = 60d$

$S_3 = \frac{3}{2}[2(1.5d) + (3-1)d]$

$S_3 = \frac{3}{2}[3d + 2d]$

$S_3 = 7.5d$

So, $\dfrac{S_{10}}{S_3} = \dfrac{60d}{7.5d}$ or 8

Therefore the sum of the first 10 terms is 8 times the sum of the first 3 terms.

19 a Common difference is $1 - \sin^2 x$

$\sin^2 x + \cos^2 x \equiv 1$

So, $1 - \sin^2 x \equiv \cos^2 x$

Using nth term $= a + (n-1)d$:

the fifth term $= \sin^2 x + (5-1)d$

$\qquad\qquad\quad = \sin^2 x + 4(1 - \sin^2 x)$

$\qquad\qquad\quad = \sin^2 x + 4 - 4\sin^2 x$

$\qquad\qquad\quad = 4 - 3\sin^2 x$

b Using $S_n = \frac{n}{2}[2a + (n-1)d]$:

$S_{10} = \frac{10}{2}[2\sin^2 x + (10-1)(1 - \sin^2 x)]$

$S_{10} = 5[2\sin^2 x + 9 - 9\sin^2 x]$

$S_{10} = 5[9 - 7\sin^2 x]$

$S_{10} = 45 - 35\sin^2 x$

As $\sin^2 x + \cos^2 x \equiv 1$,

$\sin^2 x \equiv 1 - \cos^2 x$

$S_{10} = 45 - 35(1 - \cos^2 x)$

$S_{10} = 45 - 35 + 35\cos^2 x$

$S_{10} = 10 + 35\cos^2 x$ shown

20 a The sum of the digits of the integers from 19 to 21 is:

$(1+9) + (2+0) + (2+1) = 15$ shown.

b Each number is made up of a digit in the 'units' column and a digit in the 'tens' column.

The numbers range from 01 to 99.

The sum of all the digits in the **units** column is found by using $S_n = \frac{n}{2}(a+l)$:

Total of digits $= \dfrac{10}{2}(0+9) \times 10 = 450$

The sum of all the digits in the **tens** column is found by using $S_n = \frac{n}{2}(a+l)$:

Total of digits $= \dfrac{10}{2}(0+9) \times 10 = 450$

Total of all digits $= 450 + 450$

$\qquad\qquad\qquad\quad = 900$

EXERCISE 6D

1 c $81, -27, 9, -3, \dots$

$\dfrac{-27}{81} = \dfrac{9}{-27} = \dfrac{-3}{9} = -\dfrac{1}{3}$

The common ratio is consistent so this is a geometric progression.

The 8th term is $81\left(-\dfrac{1}{3}\right)^{8-1} = -\dfrac{1}{27}$

e $1, 0.4, 0.16, 0.64, \dots$

$\dfrac{0.4}{1} = 0.4, \dfrac{0.16}{0.4} = 0.4, \dfrac{0.64}{0.16} = 4$

The common ratio is inconsistent so this is not a geometric progression.

2 Using nth term $= ar^{n-1}$:

Sixth term $= ar^{6-1}$

$\qquad\qquad = ar^5$

15th term $= ar^{14}$

3 $a = 270$

Fourth term $= ar^{4-1}$

$ar^{4-1} = 80$

So, $270r^3 = 80$

$$r^3 = \frac{80}{270}$$

$$r = \frac{2}{3}$$

4 $a = 50$

Using nth term $= ar^{n-1}$:

Second term is $ar^{2-1} = -30$

$ar = -30$

So, $50r = -30$

$r = -0.6$

The fourth term $= ar^{n-1}$

$$= 50 \times -0.6^{4-1}$$

$$= -10.8$$

5 Using nth term $= ar^{n-1}$:

The second term $= ar^{2-1}$

$\therefore$ $ar = 12$ ....[1]

The fourth term $= ar^{4-1}$

$\therefore$ $ar^3 = 27$ ....[2]

Dividing [2] by [1] gives:

$$\frac{ar^3}{ar} = \frac{27}{12}$$

$$r^2 = \frac{9}{4}$$

$r = \pm\frac{3}{2}$ (reject negative value)

$$r = \frac{3}{2}$$

As $ar = 12$,

$a = 12 \div \frac{3}{2}$

First term $= 8$

6 Using nth term $= ar^{n-1}$:

The 1st term is a

2nd term $ar = a - 16$ ......[1]

Sum of 2nd and 3rd terms:

$84 = ar + ar^2$ ....[2]

Using [1] and substituting for ar in [2] gives:

$84 = a - 16 + ar^2$ ....[3]

As $\frac{a-16}{a} = r$ ....[4] [from equation [1]]

Using [4], substituting for r in [3] gives:

$$84 = a - 16 + a\left(\frac{a-16}{a}\right)^2 \quad ......[3]$$

$$84 = a - 16 + \frac{(a-16)^2}{a}$$

$$84a = a^2 - 16a + (a-16)^2$$

$$84a = a^2 - 16a + a^2 - 32a + 256$$

$$2a^2 - 132a + 256 = 0$$

$$a^2 - 66a + 128 = 0$$

$$(a-64)(a-2) = 0$$

$a = 2$ or 64

If $a = 2$, the second term would be -14 so reject $a = 2$.

So $a = 64$.

The first term is 64.

7
$$\frac{4}{x} = \frac{x+6}{4}$$

$$16 = x(x+6)$$

$$16 = x^2 + 6x$$

$$x^2 + 6x - 16 = 0$$

$$(x+8)(x-2) = 0$$

$x = -8$ or $x = 2$

8 **c** $1 - 2 + 4 - 8 + ...$

$$r = \frac{-2}{1} \text{ or } -2$$

Using: $S_n = \frac{a(r^n - 1)}{r - 1}$

$$S_8 = \frac{1[(-2)^8 - 1]}{-2 - 1}$$

$$S_8 = -85$$

9 $r = \frac{1}{0.5}$ or 2

Smallest number of terms (n) that will give a sum greater than $1\,000\,000$ is found by using:

$$S_n = \frac{a(r^n - 1)}{r - 1}$$

i.e. $\frac{0.5(2^n - 1)}{2 - 1} > 1\,000\,000$

$$0.5(2^n - 1) > 1\,000\,000$$

$$2^n - 1 > 2\,000\,000$$

$$2^n > 2\,000\,001$$

You will learn another method for solving equations of this type using logarithms in Pure Mathematics 2 & 3

As $2^{20} = 1\,048\,576$ and $2^{21} = 2\,097\,152$,

$n = 21$

Smallest number of terms is 21.

10 a Let n be the number of **impacts**.

Initially (after no impacts i.e. $n = 0$), the height it rises to is 8 m

So, first term $n = 0$: $a\left(\dfrac{3}{4}\right)^0 = 8$

Second term: $n = 1$: $ar = 8 \times \left(\dfrac{3}{4}\right)^1$ or 6

After the nth impact the ball rises $8\left(\dfrac{3}{4}\right)^n$

b At the first impact, the ball has already travelled 16 m, so $a = 16$.

Using $S_n = \dfrac{a(1 - r^n)}{1 - r}$:

At the 5th impact it has travelled a total distance of:

$$S_5 = \frac{16\left[1 - \left(\dfrac{3}{4}\right)^5\right]}{1 - \dfrac{3}{4}}.$$

$= 48.8125$ m

11 a 2nd term $= ar$ or 24

3rd term $= ar^2$ or $12(x + 1)$

So, dividing 3rd term by the 2nd term gives:

$$\frac{ar^2}{ar} = \frac{12(x + 1)}{24}$$

$$r = \frac{x + 1}{2}$$

The first term is $ar \div r = a$

So, $a = 24 \div \dfrac{x + 1}{2}$

Or $a = \dfrac{48}{x + 1}$

b $\dfrac{48}{x + 1} + 24 + 12(x + 1) = 76$

Multiply both sides by $x + 1$:

$48 + 24(x + 1) + 12(x + 1)(x + 1) = 76(x + 1)$

$48 + 24x + 24 + 12x^2 + 24x + 12 = 76x + 76$

$12x^2 - 28x + 8 = 0$

$3x^2 - 7x + 2 = 0$

$(3x - 1)(x - 2) = 0$

$(3x - 1)(x - 2) = 0$

Either $3x - 1 = 0$ so $x - 2 = 0$

$x = \dfrac{1}{3}$ or 2

12 3rd term $= ar^2$, 1st term $= a$

$ar^2 = 9a$

$r^2 = \pm 3$

Using $S_n = \dfrac{a(r^n - 1)}{r - 1}$:

$n = 4$, $r = 3$

$S_4 = \dfrac{a(3^4 - 1)}{3 - 1}$

$S_4 = ka$

$ka = \dfrac{a(3^4 - 1)}{3 - 1}$

$k = 40$

Using $S_n = \dfrac{a(r^n - 1)}{r - 1}$:

$n = 4$, $r = -3$

$S_4 = \dfrac{a[(-3)^4 - 1]}{-3 - 1}$

$S_4 = ka$

$ka = \dfrac{a[(-3)^4 - 1]}{-3 - 1}$

$k = -20$

13 a $r = 1.1$, $a = 10\,000$, $n = 6$

The value in 2016 $= 10\,000 \times 1.1^6$

$= \$17\,715.61$

b 2010 to 2016 inclusive $= 7$ years

Using $S_n = \dfrac{a(r^n - 1)}{r - 1}$

$n = 7$, $r = 1.1$

$S_7 = \dfrac{10\,000(1.1^7 - 1)}{1.1 - 1}$

$= \$94\,871.71$

14 Using $S_n = \dfrac{a(r^n - 1)}{r - 1}$:

$S_{3n} = \dfrac{a(r^{3n} - 1)}{r - 1}$

$S_{2n} = \dfrac{a(r^{2n} - 1)}{r - 1}$

$$\frac{S_{3n} - S_{2n}}{S_n} = \frac{\dfrac{a(r^{3n} - 1)}{r - 1} - \dfrac{a(r^{2n} - 1)}{r - 1}}{\dfrac{a(r^n - 1)}{r - 1}}$$

Multiplying top and bottom (on the right-hand side) by $r - 1$:

$$= \frac{a(r^{3n} - 1) - a(r^{2n} - 1)}{a(r^n - 1)}$$

Dividing all terms by a gives:

$$= \frac{(r^{3n} - 1) - (r^{2n} - 1)}{(r^n - 1)}$$

$$= \frac{r^{3n} - r^{2n}}{r^n - 1}$$

$$= \frac{r^{2n}(r^n - 1)}{r^n - 1}$$

$$= r^{2n} \text{ shown}$$

15 Split the sequence up into two geometric sequences and add each sequence to n terms:

1st sequence is $1, 3, 9, 27, 81, \ldots$

Using $S_n = \dfrac{a(r^n - 1)}{r - 1}$: $a = 1, r = 3, n = n$

$$S_n = \frac{1(3^n - 1)}{3 - 1}$$

$$S_n = \frac{3^n - 1}{2}$$

2nd sequence is $1, \dfrac{1}{3}, \dfrac{1}{9}, \dfrac{1}{27}, \dfrac{1}{81}, \ldots$

Using $S_n = \dfrac{a(1 - r^n)}{1 - r}$: $a = 1, r = \dfrac{1}{3}, n = n$

$$S_n = \frac{1\left[1 - \left(\dfrac{1}{3}\right)^n\right]}{1 - \dfrac{1}{3}}$$

As $\left(\dfrac{1}{3}\right)^n = (3^{-1})^n = 3^{-n}$,

$$S_n = \frac{1 - 3^{-n}}{\dfrac{2}{3}}$$

Multiplying top and bottom by 3 gives:

$$S_n = \frac{3 - 3 \times 3^{-n}}{2}$$

$$S_n = \frac{3 - 3^{1-n}}{2}$$

Adding both S_n expressions gives:

$$S_{2n} = \frac{3^n - 1}{2} + \frac{3 - 3^{1-n}}{2}$$

$$S_{2n} = \frac{3^n - 1 + 3 - 3^{1-n}}{2}$$

$$S_{2n} = \frac{2 + 3^n - 3^{1-n}}{2}$$

or $S_{2n} = \dfrac{1}{2}(2 + 3^n - 3^{1-n})$ shown

16 $S_n = 1 + 11 + 111 + 1111 + 11\,111 + \ldots$

$9S_n = 9 + 99 + 999 + 9999 + 99\,999 + \ldots$

$9S_n = (10 - 1) + (100 - 1) + (1000 - 1) + \ldots$

$9S_n = 10 + 100 + 1000 + \ldots - n$

Using $S_n = \dfrac{a(r^n - 1)}{r - 1}$: $a = 10, r = 10, n = n$

$$9S_n = \frac{10(10^n - 1)}{10 - 1} - n$$

$$S_n = \frac{10(10^n - 1)}{9(10 - 1)} - \frac{n}{9}$$

$$S_n = \frac{10^{n+1} - 10}{81} - \frac{9n}{81}$$

$$S_n = \frac{10^{n+1} - 10 - 9n}{81} \text{ shown}$$

1 a Using $S_\infty = \dfrac{a}{1 - r}$: $a = 40, r = \dfrac{-20}{40}$ or -0.5

$$S_\infty = \frac{40}{1 - -0.5}$$

$$= 26\frac{2}{3}$$

2 Using $S_\infty = \dfrac{a}{1 - r}$: $a = 1, r = \dfrac{0.5^2}{1}$ or 0.25

$$S_\infty = \frac{1}{1 - 0.25}$$

$$= \frac{4}{3}$$

3 Using $S_\infty = \dfrac{a}{1 - r}$: $a = 8, r = \dfrac{6}{8}$ or 0.75

$$S_\infty = \frac{8}{1 - 0.75}$$

$$S_\infty = 32$$

4 The first term $a = 270$

The fourth term is $ar^3 = 80$

So, $270r^3 = 80$

$$r^3 = \frac{8}{27}$$

$$r = \frac{2}{3}$$

Using $S_\infty = \frac{a}{1-r}$:

$$S_\infty = \frac{270}{1 - \frac{2}{3}}$$

$$S_\infty = 810$$

5 a $0.\dot{5}\dot{7} = \frac{57}{100} + \frac{57}{10\,000} + \frac{57}{1\,000\,000} + \ldots$

   b $a = \frac{57}{100}$, $r = \frac{1}{100}$

   Using $S_\infty = \frac{a}{1-r}$:

$$S_\infty = \frac{\frac{57}{100}}{1 - \frac{1}{100}}$$

$$S_\infty = \frac{19}{33} \text{ shown}$$

**6 ** $a = 150$, $S_\infty = 200$

   Using $S_\infty = \frac{a}{1-r}$:

$$200 = \frac{150}{1-r}$$

$$200(1-r) = 150$$

$$200 - 200r = 150$$

$$200r = 50$$

$$r = 0.25$$

   Using $S_n = \frac{a(1-r^n)}{1-r}$:

$$S_4 = \frac{150(1 - 0.25^4)}{1 - 0.25}$$

$$S_4 = 199.21875$$

The sum of the first four terms is 199.21875.

**7 ** $ar = 4.5$, $S_\infty = 18$

   Using $S_\infty = \frac{a}{1-r}$:

$$18 = \frac{a}{1-r}$$

$$18(1-r) = a$$

$$18 - 18r = a \ \ldots\ldots\ldots\ldots\ldots [1]$$

As $ar = 4.5$, $a = \frac{4.5}{r}$ $\ldots\ldots [2]$

Substituting for a in $[1]$ gives:

$$18 - 18r = \frac{4.5}{r}$$

$$18r - 18r^2 = 4.5$$

$$18r^2 - 18r + 4.5 = 0$$

Comparing this to $ar^2 + br + c = 0$, where $a = 18$, $b = -18$, $c = 4.5$ and using the quadratic formula:

$$r = \frac{--18 \pm \sqrt{(-18)^2 - 4(18)(4.5)}}{2(18)}$$

$$r = \frac{18}{36} \text{ or } 0.5$$

As $a = \frac{4.5}{r}$ $\ldots\ldots$ [2] and $r = 0.5$

The first term $= \frac{4.5}{0.5}$ or 9.

**8 ** $0.315151515 \ldots\ldots = \frac{3}{10} + \frac{15}{1000} + \frac{15}{100\,000} + \ldots$

The right-hand side is made up of $\frac{3}{10}$ plus an infinite geometric sequence with $a = \frac{15}{1000}$ and $r = \frac{1}{100}$.

i.e. $\dfrac{3}{10} + \dfrac{\frac{15}{1000}}{1 - \frac{1}{100}}$

$$= \frac{3}{10} + \frac{1}{66}$$

$$= \frac{52}{165}$$

9 a $ar = 9$, $ar^3 = 4$

   Dividing gives:

$$\frac{ar^3}{ar} = \frac{4}{9}$$

$$r^2 = \frac{4}{9}$$

$$r = \pm\frac{2}{3} \text{ (reject the negative value)}$$

$$r = \frac{2}{3}$$

The first term a is found from substituting $r = \frac{2}{3}$ into $ar = 9$:

$$a \times \frac{2}{3} = 9$$

$$a = 13.5$$

b Using $S_\infty = \dfrac{a}{1-r}$

$$S_\infty = \dfrac{13.5}{1 - \dfrac{2}{3}}$$

$$S_\infty = 40.5$$

10 a $ar^2 = 16$, $ar^5 = -\dfrac{1}{4}$

Dividing gives: $\dfrac{ar^5}{ar^2} = \dfrac{-\dfrac{1}{4}}{16}$

$$r^3 = -\dfrac{1}{64}$$

$$r = -\dfrac{1}{4}$$

Substituting $r = -\dfrac{1}{4}$ into $ar^2 = 16$ gives:

$$a \times \left(-\dfrac{1}{4}\right)^2 = 16$$

$$\dfrac{1}{16}a = 16$$

$$a = 256$$

b Using $S_\infty = \dfrac{a}{1-r}$

$$S_\infty = \dfrac{256}{1 - -\dfrac{1}{4}}$$

$$S_\infty = 204.8$$

11 a $a = 135$, $ar = k$, $ar^2 = 60$

So, $\dfrac{ar}{a} = \dfrac{k}{135}$

$$r = \dfrac{k}{135}$$

$$\dfrac{ar^2}{ar} = \dfrac{60}{k}$$

$$r = \dfrac{60}{k}$$

$$\dfrac{60}{k} = \dfrac{k}{135}$$

$$k^2 = 8100$$

$$k = \pm 90$$

Reject negative value as all terms are positive.

$$k = 90$$

$$r = \dfrac{60}{90} \text{ or } \dfrac{2}{3}$$

b Using $S_\infty = \dfrac{a}{1-r}$: $a = 135$, $r = \dfrac{2}{3}$

$$S_\infty = \dfrac{135}{1 - \dfrac{2}{3}}$$

$$S_\infty = 405$$

12 a $a = k+12$, $ar = k$, $ar^2 = k-9$

So, $\dfrac{ar}{a} = \dfrac{k}{k+12}$

$$r = \dfrac{k}{k+12}$$

$$\dfrac{ar^2}{ar} = \dfrac{k-9}{k}$$

$$r = \dfrac{k-9}{k}$$

$$\dfrac{k}{k+12} = \dfrac{k-9}{k}$$

$$k^2 = (k+12)(k-9)$$

$$k^2 = k^2 + 3k - 108$$

$$3k = 108$$

$$k = 36$$

Substituting $k = 36$ into $r = \dfrac{k}{k+12}$ gives:

$$r = \dfrac{36}{48} \text{ or } \dfrac{3}{4}$$

b Using $S_\infty = \dfrac{a}{1-r}$: $a = 48$, $r = \dfrac{3}{4}$

$$S_\infty = \dfrac{48}{1 - \dfrac{3}{4}}$$

$$S_\infty = 192$$

13 $ar^3 = 48$, $S_\infty = 5a$

Using $S_\infty = \dfrac{a}{1-r}$:

$$5a = \dfrac{a}{1-r}$$

Dividing both sides by a gives:

$$5 = \dfrac{1}{1-r}$$

$$5(1-r) = 1$$

$$5 - 5r = 1$$

$$5r = 4$$

$$r = \dfrac{4}{5}$$

So, if $ar^3 = 48$, substituting for r gives:

$$a\left(\frac{4}{5}\right)^3 = 48$$

$$a = 48 \div \left(\frac{4}{5}\right)^3$$

$$a = 93.75$$

First term is 93.75.

14 Using $S_n = \dfrac{a(1-r^n)}{1-r}$: $n = 3$, $S_n = 3.92$

$$3.92 = \frac{a(1-r^3)}{1-r}$$

$$3.92(1-r) = a(1-r^3)$$

$$1 - r = \frac{a(1-r^3)}{3.92} \quad \text{........[1]}$$

Using $S_\infty = \dfrac{a}{1-r}$: $S_\infty = 5$

$$5 = \frac{a}{1-r}$$

$$5(1-r) = a$$

$$1 - r = \frac{a}{5} \quad \text{...................[2]}$$

Equating [1] and [2]:

$$\frac{a(1-r^3)}{3.92} = \frac{a}{5}$$

Dividing both sides by a:

$$\frac{(1-r^3)}{3.92} = \frac{1}{5}$$

$$1 - r^3 = \frac{3.92}{5}$$

$$r^3 = \frac{27}{125}$$

$$r = \frac{3}{5}$$

Substituting $r = \dfrac{3}{5}$ into [2] gives:

$$1 - \frac{3}{5} = \frac{a}{5}$$

$$a = 2$$

15 $a = 1$, $ar = 2\cos x$ where $0 < x < \dfrac{\pi}{2}$.

The progression is convergent if $-1 < r < 1$.

$$\frac{ar}{a} = \frac{2\cos x}{1}$$

$$r = 2\cos x$$

So, $-1 < 2\cos x < 1$.

Solving $2\cos x < 1$:

$$\cos x < \frac{1}{2}$$

Given the domain $0 < x < \dfrac{\pi}{2}$:

$$\frac{\pi}{3} < x < \frac{\pi}{2}$$

Solving: $2\cos x > -1$

$$\cos x > -\frac{1}{2}$$

Given the domain $0 < x < \dfrac{\pi}{2}$, cos is positive in this domain.

Solution: $\dfrac{\pi}{3} < x < \dfrac{\pi}{2}$

16 a

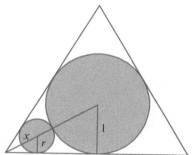

The radius of the large circle is 1.

Let the radius of the small circle be r, and the hypotenuse of the small right-angled triangle be x.

$$\therefore \sin 30° = \frac{1}{2} = \frac{r}{x}$$

So, $x = 2r$

So, for a 30° right-angled triangle the hypotenuse is twice the height.

The hypotenuse of the big right-angled triangle is given by $x + r + 1$:

$$x + r + 1 = 2$$

$$2r + r + 1 = 2$$

$$r = \frac{1}{3}$$

Circumference of the large circle is

$$2\pi \times 1 = 2\pi$$

Radius of each subsequent circle is $\dfrac{1}{3}$ of the radius of the previous circle.

So the sum of the circumferences is:

$$2\pi\left(\frac{1}{3}\right) + 2\pi\left(\frac{1}{9}\right) + \ldots = 2\pi\left(\frac{1}{3} + \frac{1}{9} + \ldots\right)$$

Using the sum to infinity for a geometric progression:

$S_\infty = \dfrac{a}{1 - r}$ where the first term $a = \dfrac{1}{3}$, and the common ratio $r = \dfrac{1}{3}$, we get

$$S_\infty = \frac{1}{3} + \frac{1}{9} + \ldots = \frac{\frac{1}{3}}{\frac{2}{3}} = \frac{1}{2}$$

Hence the sum of the circumferences of **all** the circles excluding the large circle is:

$2\pi \times \dfrac{1}{2} \times 3$ or 3π.

The total circumference of all the circles is $2\pi + 3\pi$ or 5π.

b The sum of all the areas of the circles is area of large circle + area of all the smaller circles.

Area of large circle $= \pi \times 1^2$ or π

Now looking at the smaller circles:

The radius of each smaller circle is $\dfrac{1}{3}$ of the radius of the previous circle.

$$\therefore \pi\left(\frac{1}{3}\right)^2 + \pi\left(\frac{1}{9}\right)^2 + \ldots = \pi \times 1^2\left(\frac{1}{9} + \frac{1}{81} + \ldots\right)$$

Using the sum to infinity for a geometric progression:

$S_\infty = \dfrac{a}{1 - r}$ where the first term $a = \dfrac{1}{9}$, and the common ratio $r = \dfrac{1}{9}$, we get

$$\frac{1}{9} + \frac{1}{81} + \ldots = \frac{\frac{1}{9}}{\frac{8}{9}} = \frac{1}{8}$$

Hence the infinite set of smaller circles must represent exactly $\dfrac{3}{8}$ the area of the large red circle $= \dfrac{3}{8}\pi$

Total area of all the circles is $\pi + \dfrac{3}{8}\pi = \dfrac{11\pi}{8}$

17 a Each side of the green triangle is exactly $\dfrac{1}{3}$ the size of a side of the large blue triangle.

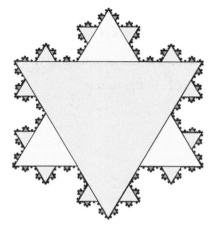

If each side of the original triangle is 3, after one iteration, each side becomes 4.

The perimeter of the original triangle was 9, it now becomes 12.

So the perimeter after each iteration is multiplied by $\dfrac{12}{9}$ or $\dfrac{4}{3}$.

After n iterations, the perimeter has become $\left(\dfrac{4}{3}\right)^n$ times the original perimeter.

The sequence is:

$$\left(\frac{4}{3}\right)^1, \left(\frac{4}{3}\right)^2, \left(\frac{4}{3}\right)^3, \ldots$$

As the number of iterations are unbounded, the perimeter will keep on enlarging as n tends to infinity.

b The area inside the Koch snowflake is the summation of infinitely many equilateral triangles (see diagram in part **a**).

Each side of the green triangle is exactly $\dfrac{1}{3}$ the size of a side of the large blue triangle, and therefore has exactly $\dfrac{1}{9}$ the area.

Each yellow triangle has $\dfrac{1}{9}$ the area of a green triangle etc.

If the blue triangle is 1 unit of area, the total area of the snowflake is:

$$1 + 3\left(\frac{1}{9}\right) + 12\left(\frac{1}{9}\right)^2 + 48\left(\frac{1}{9}\right)^3 + \ldots$$

Excluding the initial 1, this series is geometric with constant ratio $r = \frac{4}{9}$.

The first term of the geometric series is $a = 3\left(\frac{1}{9}\right) = \frac{1}{3}$, so the sum is:

$$1 + \frac{a}{1-r} = 1 + \frac{\frac{1}{3}}{1 - \frac{4}{9}} = \frac{8}{5}$$

So, Koch snowflake has $\frac{8}{5}$ of the area of the original triangle.

1 a Arithmetic: first term = 16, second term = 24

$d = 24 - 16$ or 8

Using nth term $= a + (n-1)d$:

8th term $= 16 + (8-1)8$

$\qquad = 72$

$S_n = \frac{n}{2}(a+l)$, $a = 16$, $l = 72$,

$S_8 = \frac{8}{2}(16 + 72)$

$\quad = 352$

Sum of first eight terms is 352.

b $a = 16$, $ar = 24$

$\frac{ar}{a} = \frac{24}{16}$

$r = 1.5$

Using $S_n = \frac{a(r^n - 1)}{r-1}$: $n = 8$, $a = 16$, $r = 1.5$

$S_8 = \frac{16(1.5^8 - 1)}{1.5 - 1}$

$\quad = 788.125$

Sum of first eight terms is 788.125.

2 a $a = 20$, $ar = 16$

$\frac{ar}{a} = \frac{16}{20}$

$r = 0.8$

Using $S_\infty = \frac{a}{1-r}$: $a = 20$, $r = 0.8$

$S_\infty = \frac{20}{1 - 0.8}$

$S_\infty = 100$

b 1st term = 20, 2nd term = 16

$d = 16 - 20$ or -4

Use $S_n = \frac{n}{2}[2a + (n-1)d]$

$-160 = \frac{n}{2}[2 \times 20 + (n-1) \times -4]$

$-320 = n[40 - 4n + 4]$

$-320 = 44n - 4n^2$

$4n^2 - 44n - 320 = 0$

$n^2 - 11n - 80 = 0$

$(n - 16)(n + 5) = 0$

$n = 16$ or $n = -5$ reject

There are 16 terms.

3 a For the geometric progression:

The 1st term is $a = 12$

The 2nd term is $12r$

The 3rd term is $12r^2$

For the arithmetic progression:

The 1st term is $a = 12$

The 4th term is $12 + 3d$

The 10th term is $12 + 9d$

$12 + 3d = 12r$ ....[1]

$12 + 9d = 12r^2$ ....[2]

Multiplying [1] by 3 then subtracting [2] gives:

$\qquad 36 + 9d = 36r$

$\qquad 12 + 9d = 12r^2$

$\qquad\qquad 24 = 36r - 12r^2$

$12r^2 - 36r + 24 = 0$

$\qquad r^2 - 3r + 2 = 0$

$\qquad (r - 2)(r - 1) = 0$

$r = 2$ or $r = 1$ reject

$r = 2$

b Geometric: 6th term $= ar^{n-1}$
$$= 12 \times 2^{6-1}$$
$$= 384$$
Arithmetic: Using $[1]$ $12 + 3d = 12 \times 2$
$$3d = 12$$
$$d = 4$$
Using nth term $= a + (n-1)d$:
6th term $= 12 + (6-1) \times 4$
$$= 32$$

4 Geometric progression $n = 8$, $a = 256$, $r = \dfrac{1}{2}$ or 0.5

Using $S_n = \dfrac{a(1 - r^n)}{1 - r}$:

$$S_8 = \frac{256(1 - 0.5^8)}{1 - 0.5}$$

$$S_8 = 510$$

Arithmetic progression $n = 51$, $d = \dfrac{1}{2}$ or 0.5

Use $S_n = \dfrac{n}{2}[2a + (n-1)d]$:

$$S_{51} = \frac{51}{2}[2a + (51 - 1) \times 0.5]$$

$$S_{51} = \frac{51}{2}[2a + 25]$$

So, $510 = \dfrac{51}{2}[2a + 25]$

$$20 = 2a + 25$$
$$a = -2.5$$

Using nth term $= a + (n-1)d$:
The last term $= -2.5 + (51 - 1) \times 0.5$
The last term $= 22.5$

5 a For the geometric progression:
The 1st term is $a = 100$
The 2nd term is $100r$
The 3rd term is $100r^2$
For the arithmetic progression:
The 1st term is $a = 100$
The 6th term is $100 + 5d$
The 9th term is $100 + 8d$
$100 + 5d = 100r \dots\dots[1]$
$100 + 8d = 100r^2 \dots\dots[2]$

Multiplying $[1]$ by 8, $[2]$ by 5 then subtracting $[2]$ gives:
$$800 + 40d = 800r$$
$$500 + 40d = 500r^2$$
So, $300 = 800r - 500r^2$
$$500r^2 - 800r + 300 = 0$$
$$5r^2 - 8r + 3 = 0$$
$$(5r - 3)(r - 1) = 0$$
Either $r - 1 = 0$ so $r = 1$ reject
or $5r - 3 = 0$
$$r = \frac{3}{5}$$

b Geometric 5th term $= ar^{n-1}$
$$= 100 \times \left(\frac{3}{5}\right)^{5-1}$$
$$= 12.96$$
Arithmetic, using $[1]$: $100 + 5d = 100 \times \dfrac{3}{5}$
$$5d = -40$$
$$d = -8$$
Using nth term $= a + (n-1)d$:
5th term $= 100 + (5 - 1) \times -8$
$$= 68$$

6 a $a = 16$, $S_{20} = 1080$
Using $S_n = \dfrac{n}{2}[2a + (n-1)d]$:
$$1080 = \frac{20}{2}[2 \times 16 + (20 - 1)d]$$
$$108 = 32 + 19d$$
$$19d = 76$$
$$d = 4$$
The common difference is 4.

b For the geometric progression:
The 1st term is $a = 16$
The 2nd term is $16r$
The 3rd term is $16r^2$
For the arithmetic progression:
The 1st term is 16
The 3rd term is $16 + 2 \times 4$ or 24
The nth term is $16 + (n-1) \times 4$
$$= 16 + 4n - 4$$
$$= 12 + 4n$$
So, $24 = 16r$
$$r = 1.5$$

Also, $12 + 4n = 16r^2$

$12 + 4n = 16 \times 1.5^2$

$12 + 4n = 36$

$\qquad n = 6$

The common ratio of the geometric progression is 1.5 and the value of n is 6.

7 a If the progression is arithmetic, first term $a = 2x$ and the second term is x^2, $d = 15$

So $x^2 - 2x = 15$

$x^2 - 2x - 15 = 0$

$(x - 5)(x + 3) = 0$

$x = 5$ or $x = -3$

If $x = 5$, the third term is $x^2 + 15$ which is $5^2 + 15 = 40$

If $x = -3$, the third term is $x^2 + 15$ which is $(-3)^2 + 15 = 24$

The possible values for the third term are 24 and 40.

b If the progression is geometric,

1st term $a = 2x$

2nd term $ar = x^2$

3rd term $ar^2 = -\dfrac{1}{16}$

$\dfrac{ar}{a} = \dfrac{x^2}{2x}$

$r = \dfrac{x}{2}$

and $\dfrac{ar^2}{ar} = \dfrac{-\dfrac{1}{16}}{x^2}$

$r = -\dfrac{1}{16x^2}$

$\dfrac{x}{2} = -\dfrac{1}{16x^2}$

$x^3 = -\dfrac{1}{8}$

$x = -\dfrac{1}{2}$

The first term is $2 \times -\dfrac{1}{2} = -1$

$r = \dfrac{x}{2}$ or $\dfrac{-\dfrac{1}{2}}{2}$ or $-\dfrac{1}{4}$

Using $S_\infty = \dfrac{a}{1-r}$: $a = -1, r = -\dfrac{1}{4}$

$S_\infty = \dfrac{-1}{1 - -\dfrac{1}{4}}$

$S_\infty = -\dfrac{4}{5}$

1 a $C = (x_1, y_1)$ $F = (x_2, y_2)$
$C = (0.8, 1.44)$ $F = (1, 2)$

Gradient of chord $CF = \dfrac{y_2 - y_1}{x_2 - x_1}$

$= \dfrac{2 - 1.44}{1 - 0.8}$

$= \dfrac{0.56}{0.2}$ or 2.8

$D = (x_1, y_1)$ $F = (x_2, y_2)$
$D = (0.95, 1.8525)$ $F = (1, 2)$

Gradient of chord $DF = \dfrac{y_2 - y_1}{x_2 - x_1}$

$= \dfrac{2 - 1.8525}{1 - 0.95}$

$= \dfrac{0.1475}{0.05}$ or 2.95

$E = (x_1, y_1)$ $F = (x_2, y_2)$
$E = (0.99, 1.9701)$ $F = (1, 2)$

Gradient of chord $EF = \dfrac{y_2 - y_1}{x_2 - x_1}$

$EF = \dfrac{2 - 1.9701}{1 - 0.99}$

$EF = \dfrac{0.0299}{0.01}$ or 2.99

b The values are moving closer to 3.

2 b $y = x^2 - 2x + 3$ at $(0, 3)$
$A = (x_1, y_1)$ $F = (x_2, y_2)$
$A = (0.5, 2.25)$ $F = (0, 3)$

Choosing values of x between 0 and 0.5 inclusive which differ by 0.1

Gradient of chord $AF = \dfrac{y_2 - y_1}{x_2 - x_1}$

$= \dfrac{3 - 2.25}{0 - 0.5}$

$= \dfrac{0.75}{-0.5}$ or -1.5

$B = (x_1, y_1)$ $F = (x_2, y_2)$
$B = (0.4, 2.36)$ $F = (0, 3)$

Gradient of chord $BF = \dfrac{y_2 - y_1}{x_2 - x_1}$

$= \dfrac{3 - 2.36}{0 - 0.4}$

$= \dfrac{0.64}{-0.4}$ or -1.6

$C = (x_1, y_1)$ $F = (x_2, y_2)$
$C = (0.3, 2.49)$ $F = (0, 3)$

Gradient of chord $CF = \dfrac{y_2 - y_1}{x_2 - x_1}$

$= \dfrac{3 - 2.49}{0 - 0.3}$

$= \dfrac{0.51}{-0.3}$ or -1.7

$D = (x_1, y_1)$ $F = (x_2, y_2)$
$D = (0.2, 2.64)$ $F = (0, 3)$

Gradient of chord $DF = \dfrac{y_2 - y_1}{x_2 - x_1}$

$= \dfrac{3 - 2.64}{0 - 0.2}$

$= \dfrac{0.36}{-0.2}$ or -1.8

$E = (x_1, y_1)$ $F = (x_2, y_2)$
$E = (0.1, 2.81)$ $F = (0, 3)$

Gradient of chord $EF = \dfrac{y_2 - y_1}{x_2 - x_1}$

$= \dfrac{3 - 2.81}{0 - 0.1}$

$= \dfrac{0.19}{-0.1}$ or -1.9

The gradients appear to be getting close to the value -2 as the sequence of the gradients of the chords show.

3 d $\dfrac{d}{dx}\left(\dfrac{1}{x}\right) = \dfrac{d}{dx}(x^{-1})$

$\qquad = -1x^{-1-1}$

$\qquad = -1x^{-2}$ or $\dfrac{-1}{x^2}$

> It is useful to be able to change terms which contain fractions and indices into alternative forms.

f $\dfrac{d}{dx}\left(\sqrt[3]{x^2}\right) = \dfrac{d}{dx}\left(x^{\frac{2}{3}}\right)$

$\qquad = \dfrac{2}{3}x^{\frac{2}{3}-1}$

$\qquad = \dfrac{2}{3}x^{-\frac{1}{3}}$ or $= \dfrac{2}{3x^{\frac{1}{3}}}$ or $\dfrac{2}{3\sqrt[3]{x}}$

4 e $f(x) = \dfrac{5}{3x^2}$

$\qquad f(x) = \dfrac{5}{3}x^{-2}$

$\qquad f'(x) = -2 \times \dfrac{5}{3}x^{-2-1}$

$\qquad f'(x) = -\dfrac{10}{3}x^{-3}$ or $\dfrac{-10}{3x^3}$ or $-\dfrac{10}{3x^3}$

h $f(x) = \dfrac{2x\sqrt{x}}{3x^3}$

First simplify fraction:

As $2x\sqrt{x} = 2 \times x^1 \times x^{\frac{1}{2}}$ or $2x^{\frac{3}{2}}$

$\qquad f(x) = \dfrac{2x^{\frac{3}{2}}}{3x^3}$

$\qquad f(x) = \dfrac{2}{3}x^{-\frac{3}{2}}$

$\qquad f'(x) = -\dfrac{3}{2} \times \dfrac{2}{3}x^{-\frac{3}{2}-1}$

$\qquad f'(x) = -x^{-\frac{5}{2}}$ or $-\dfrac{1}{x^{\frac{5}{2}}}$ or $-\dfrac{1}{\sqrt{x^5}}$

> Remember, if differentiating a constant, the answer is always 0.

5 e $y = (2x^2 - 3)^2$

Expand brackets:

$\qquad y = (2x^2 - 3)(2x^2 - 3)$

$\qquad y = 4x^4 - 12x^2 + 9$

$\qquad \dfrac{dy}{dx} = 16x^3 - 24x$

> You will learn another way to differentiate expressions like this in the next section.

h $y = 3x + \dfrac{5}{x} - \dfrac{1}{2\sqrt{x}}$

Write this as:

$\qquad y = 3x + 5x^{-1} - \dfrac{1}{2}x^{-\frac{1}{2}}$

$\qquad \dfrac{dy}{dx} = 3 + -1 \times 5x^{-2} - \left(\dfrac{1}{2} \times -\dfrac{1}{2}x^{-\frac{1}{2}-1}\right)$

$\qquad \dfrac{dy}{dx} = 3 - 5x^{-2} - \left(-\dfrac{1}{4}x^{-\frac{3}{2}}\right)$

$\qquad \dfrac{dy}{dx} = 3 - \dfrac{5}{x^2} + \dfrac{1}{4x^{\frac{3}{2}}}$

Or $\dfrac{dy}{dx} = 3 - \dfrac{5}{x^2} + \dfrac{1}{4\sqrt{x^3}}$

6 c $y = \dfrac{3x - 2}{x^2}$

Rewrite fraction as:

$\qquad y = 3x^{-1} - 2x^{-2}$

$\qquad \dfrac{dy}{dx} = -3x^{-2} - (2 \times -2x^{-2-1})$

$\qquad \dfrac{dy}{dx} = -3x^{-2} + 4x^{-3}$

$\qquad \dfrac{dy}{dx} = -\dfrac{3}{x^2} + \dfrac{4}{x^3}$

At $x = -2$,

$\qquad \dfrac{dy}{dx} = -\dfrac{3}{(-2)^2} + \dfrac{4}{(-2)^3}$

$\qquad \dfrac{dy}{dx} = -\dfrac{3}{4} + \dfrac{4}{-8}$

$\qquad \dfrac{dy}{dx} = -\dfrac{3}{4} - \dfrac{1}{2}$

$\qquad \dfrac{dy}{dx} = -\dfrac{5}{4}$

7 $y = (2x - 5)(x + 4)$

Expand brackets:

$y = 2x^2 + 3x - 20$

$\dfrac{dy}{dx} = 4x + 3$

At $x = 3$,

$\dfrac{dy}{dx} = 4(3) + 3$

$\dfrac{dy}{dx} = 15$

The gradient is 15.

8 $xy = 12$

Make y subject:

$y = \dfrac{12}{x}$

$y = 12x^{-1}$

$\dfrac{dy}{dx} = -12x^{-2}$ or $-\dfrac{12}{x^2}$

At $x = 2$, $\dfrac{dy}{dx} = -\dfrac{12}{2^2}$ or -3

9 At the y-intercept, $x = 0$

$y = 5x^2 - 8x + 3$

$\dfrac{dy}{dx} = 10x - 8$

At $x = 0$, gradient of the curve is:

$\dfrac{dy}{dx} = 10(0) - 8$ or -8

> It is a common mistake to misinterpret the next question. Do not confuse 'Find the gradient at the point where $x = 9$' with 'Find the point(s) where the gradient is 9'.

10 $y = x^3 - 3x - 8$

$\dfrac{dy}{dx} = 3x^2 - 3$

Solving $3x^2 - 3 = 9$ gives the coordinates where the gradient is 9.

$3x^2 = 12$

$x^2 = 4$

$x = \pm 2$

If $x = 2$ then substituting back into the equation of the curve gives:

$y = x^3 - 3x - 8$

$y = 2^3 - 3(2) - 8$

$y = -6$

If $x = -2$ then

$y = x^3 - 3x - 8$ becomes:

$y = (-2)^3 - 3(-2) - 8$

$y = -10$

The points are at $(-2, -10)$ and $(2, -6)$.

11 The curve crosses the x-axis where $y = 0$.

So $y = \dfrac{5x - 10}{x^2}$ becomes:

$0 = \dfrac{5x - 10}{x^2}$

$5x - 10 = 0$

$x = 2$

Rewrite $y = \dfrac{5x - 10}{x^2}$:

$y = \dfrac{5x}{x^2} - \dfrac{10}{x^2}$ or $y = 5x^{-1} - 10x^{-2}$

$\dfrac{dy}{dx} = -5x^{-2} + 20x^{-3}$

or $\dfrac{dy}{dx} = \dfrac{-5}{x^2} + \dfrac{20}{x^3}$

Substituting $x = 2$ into $\dfrac{dy}{dx}$ gives:

$\dfrac{dy}{dx} = -\dfrac{5}{2^2} + \dfrac{20}{2^3}$

$= -\dfrac{5}{4} + \dfrac{20}{8}$

$= \dfrac{5}{4}$

The gradient at where the curve crosses the y-axis is $\dfrac{5}{4}$

12 a Solve $y = x^2 - 4x - 5$ and $y = 1 - 3x$ simultaneously to find A and B

$\therefore\ x^2 - 4x - 5 = 1 - 3x$

$x^2 - x - 6 = 0$

$(x - 3)(x + 2) = 0$

$x = 3$ or $x = -2$

If $x = 3$ then substituting into the linear equation gives the y-coordinate.

$y = 1 - 3x$
$y = 1 - 3(3)$
$y = -8$

If $x = -2$ substituting into the linear equation gives the y-coordinate.

$y = 1 - 3x$
$y = 1 - 3(-2)$
$y = 7$

Points A and B are at $(-2, 7)$ and $(3, -8)$

b Differentiating the equation of the curve i.e. $y = x^2 - 4x - 5$ gives:

$$\frac{dy}{dx} = 2x - 4$$

At $x = 3$, $\frac{dy}{dx} = 2(3) - 4$ or 2

At $x = -2$, $\frac{dy}{dx} = 2(-2) - 4$ or -8

The gradients at A and B on the curve are 2 and -8.

13 Given $y = ax^2 + bx$

Substituting $x = 3$ and $y = -3$ gives:

$-3 = a(3)^2 + b(3)$
$-3 = 9a + 3b$
$3a + b = -1$ ....[1]

$$\frac{dy}{dx} = 2ax + b$$

Substituting $x = 3$ into $\frac{dy}{dx} = 2ax + b$ gives:

$$\frac{dy}{dx} = 2a(3) + b$$

At $x = 3$, $\frac{dy}{dx} = 5$

So, $6a + b = 5$ .....[2]

Subtracting [2] from [1] gives:

$-3a = -6$
$a = 2$

Substituting $a = 2$ into [1] gives:

$3a + b = -1$
$3(2) + b = -1$
$b = -7$

Solution: $a = 2$, $b = -7$

14 Given $y = x^3 + ax^2 + bx + 7$

Substituting $x = 1$ and $y = 5$ gives:

$1^3 + a(1)^2 + b(1) + 7 = 5$
$a + b = -3$ ....[1]

$$\frac{dy}{dx} = 3x^2 + 2ax + b$$

At $x = 1$, $\frac{dy}{dx} = -5$ so:

$-5 = 3(1)^2 + 2a(1) + b$
$2a + b = -8$ ....[2]

Subtracting [2] from [1] gives:

$-a = 5$
$a = -5$

Substituting $a = -5$ into [1] gives:

$-5 + b = -3$
$b = 2$

Solution: $a = -5$, $b = 2$

15 Given $y = ax + \dfrac{b}{x^2}$

Rewrite as: $y = ax + bx^{-2}$

$$\frac{dy}{dx} = a - 2bx^{-3} \text{ or } \frac{dy}{dx} = a - \frac{2b}{x^3}$$

Substituting $x = 1$ and $\frac{dy}{dx} = 16$ gives:

$16 = a - \dfrac{2b}{1^3}$

$16 = a - 2b$ ....[1]

Substituting $x = -1$ and $\frac{dy}{dx} = -8$ gives:

$-8 = a - \dfrac{2b}{(-1)^3}$

$-8 = a + 2b$ ....[2]

Subtracting [2] from [1] gives:

$24 = -4b$

$b = -6$

Substituting $b = -6$ into [1] gives:

$16 = a - 2(-6)$

$a = 4$

Solution: $a = 4, b = -6$

16 Given $y = x^3 + ax^2 + bx + 3$

Differentiating gives:

$\dfrac{dy}{dx} = 3x^2 + 2ax + b$

Substituting $x = 1$ and $\dfrac{dy}{dx} = 0$ gives:

$0 = 3(1)^2 + 2a(1) + b$

$2a + b = -3$ ....[1]

Substituting $x = 6$ and $\dfrac{dy}{dx} = 0$ gives:

$0 = 3(6)^2 + 2a(6) + b$

$12a + b = -108$ ....[2]

Subtracting [2] from [1] gives:

$-10a = 105$

$a = -10.5$

Substituting $a = -10.5$ into [1] gives:

$2(-10.5) + b = -3$

$b = 18$

Solution: $a = -10.5, b = 18$

17 Given $y = 2x^3 - 3x^2 - 36x + 5$

Differentiating gives:

$\dfrac{dy}{dx} = 6x^2 - 6x - 36$

We want $\dfrac{dy}{dx} < 0$ so:

$6x^2 - 6x - 36 < 0$

$x^2 - x - 6 < 0$

Factorising the left-hand side of the inequality:

$(x - 3)(x + 2) < 0$

The graph of $y = (x - 3)(x + 2)$ is a $\cup$ shaped parabola.

The x-intercepts are at $x = 3$ and $x = -2$.

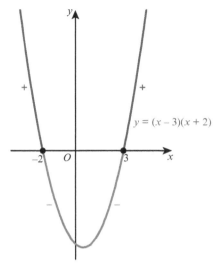

For $(x - 3)(x + 2) < 0$ we need to find the range of values of x for which the curve is negative (below the x-axis).

The solution is $-2 < x < 3$.

18 Given $y = 4x^3 + 3x^2 - 6x - 9$

Differentiating gives:

$\dfrac{dy}{dx} = 12x^2 + 6x - 6$

We want $\dfrac{dy}{dx} \geqslant 0$ so:

$\qquad 12x^2 + 6x - 6 \geqslant 0$

Or: $\qquad 2x^2 + x - 1 \geqslant 0$

$\qquad (2x - 1)(x + 1) \geqslant 0$

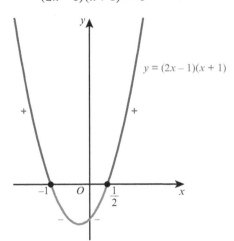

The graph of $y=(2x-1)(x+1)$ is a $\cup$ shaped parabola.

The x-intercepts are at $x=\dfrac{1}{2}$ and $x=-1$.

For $(2x-1)(x+1)\geqslant 0$ we need to find the range of values of x for which the curve is positive (on or above the x-axis).

The solution is $x\leqslant -1$ and $x\geqslant \dfrac{1}{2}$.

19 Given $y=3x^3+6x^2+4x-5$

Differentiating gives:

$$\frac{dy}{dx}=9x^2+12x+4$$

Complete the square:

$$\frac{dy}{dx}=9\left[x^2+\frac{12}{9}x\right]+4$$

$$\frac{dy}{dx}=9\left[\left(x+\frac{12}{18}\right)^2-\left(\frac{12}{18}\right)^2\right]+4$$

$$\frac{dy}{dx}=9\left[\left(x+\frac{2}{3}\right)^2-\left(\frac{2}{3}\right)^2\right]+4$$

$$\frac{dy}{dx}=9\left(x+\frac{2}{3}\right)^2-9\left(\frac{2}{3}\right)^2+4$$

$$\frac{dy}{dx}=9\left(x+\frac{2}{3}\right)^2-4+4$$

$$\frac{dy}{dx}=9\left(x+\frac{2}{3}\right)^2$$

$9\left(x+\dfrac{2}{3}\right)^2$ is always $\geqslant 0$ i.e. it is not negative for any value of x. Shown.

1 f Let $y=5(2x-1)^5$

Use the chain rule to differentiate:

Let $u=2x-1$ so $y=5u^5$

$\dfrac{du}{dx}=2$ and $\dfrac{dy}{du}=25u^4$

$\dfrac{dy}{dx}=\dfrac{dy}{du}\times\dfrac{du}{dx}$

$\quad\ =25u^4\times 2$

$\quad\ =25(2x-1)^4\times 2$

$\quad\ =50(2x-1)^4$

l Let $y=\left(x^2-\dfrac{5}{x}\right)^5$

Use the chain rule to differentiate:

Let $u=x^2-\dfrac{5}{x}$ or x^2-5x^{-1} so $y=u^5$

$\dfrac{du}{dx}=2x+5x^{-2}$ and $\dfrac{dy}{du}=5u^4$

$\dfrac{dy}{dx}=\dfrac{dy}{du}\times\dfrac{du}{dx}$

$\quad\ =5u^4\times(2x+5x^{-2})$

$\quad\ =5\left(x^2-\dfrac{5}{x}\right)^4\times(2x+5x^{-2})$

$\quad\ =5\left(x^2-\dfrac{5}{x}\right)^4\left(2x+\dfrac{5}{x^2}\right)$

This answer may be simplified:

$=5\left(\dfrac{x^3}{x}-\dfrac{5}{x}\right)^4\left(\dfrac{2x^3}{x^2}+\dfrac{5}{x^2}\right)$

$=5\left(\dfrac{x^3-5}{x}\right)^4\left(\dfrac{2x^3+5}{x^2}\right)$

$=5\,\dfrac{(x^3-5)^4}{x^4}\times\dfrac{(2x^3+5)}{x^2}$

$=\dfrac{5(x^3-5)^4(2x^3+5)}{x^6}$

2 c Let $y = \dfrac{8}{3-2x}$

Rewrite as $y = 8(3-2x)^{-1}$

Use the chain rule to differentiate:

Let $u = 3-2x$ so $y = 8u^{-1}$

$\dfrac{du}{dx} = -2$ and $\dfrac{dy}{du} = -8u^{-2}$

$\dfrac{dy}{dx} = \dfrac{dy}{du} \times \dfrac{du}{dx}$

$= -8u^{-2} \times -2$

$= 16u^{-2}$

$= \dfrac{16}{(3-2x)^2}$

h Let $y = \dfrac{7}{(2x^2-5x)^7}$

Rewrite as $y = 7(2x^2-5x)^{-7}$

Use the chain rule to differentiate:

Let $u = 2x^2-5x$ so $y = 7u^{-7}$

$\dfrac{du}{dx} = 4x-5$ and $\dfrac{dy}{du} = -49u^{-8}$

$\dfrac{dy}{dx} = \dfrac{dy}{du} \times \dfrac{du}{dx}$

$= -49u^{-8} \times (4x-5)$

$= -\dfrac{49(4x-5)}{(2x^2-5x)^8}$

This answer may be simplified:

$= -\dfrac{49(4x-5)}{[x(2x-5)]^8}$

$= -\dfrac{49(4x-5)}{x^8(2x-5)^8}$

3 e Let $y = \sqrt[3]{5-2x}$

Rewrite as $y = (5-2x)^{\frac{1}{3}}$

Use the chain rule to differentiate:

Let $u = 5-2x$ so $y = u^{\frac{1}{3}}$

$\dfrac{du}{dx} = -2$ and $\dfrac{dy}{du} = \dfrac{1}{3}u^{-\frac{2}{3}}$

$\dfrac{dy}{dx} = \dfrac{dy}{du} \times \dfrac{du}{dx}$

$= \dfrac{1}{3}u^{-\frac{2}{3}} \times -2$

$= -\dfrac{2}{3u^{\frac{2}{3}}}$

$= -\dfrac{2}{3(5-2x)^{\frac{2}{3}}}$

$= -\dfrac{2}{3\sqrt[3]{(5-2x)^2}}$

h Let $y = \dfrac{6}{\sqrt[3]{2-3x}}$

Rewrite as: $y = 6(2-3x)^{-\frac{1}{3}}$

Use the chain rule to differentiate:

Let $u = 2-3x$ so $y = 6u^{-\frac{1}{3}}$

$\dfrac{du}{dx} = -3$ and $\dfrac{dy}{du} = -\dfrac{1}{3} \times 6u^{-\frac{4}{3}}$

$\dfrac{dy}{dx} = \dfrac{dy}{du} \times \dfrac{du}{dx}$

$= -2u^{-\frac{4}{3}} \times -3$

$= \dfrac{6}{u^{\frac{4}{3}}}$

$= \dfrac{6}{\sqrt[3]{(2-3x)^4}}$

4 $y = (2x-3)^5$

Use the chain rule to differentiate:

Let $u = 2x-3$ so $y = u^5$

$\dfrac{du}{dx} = 2$ and $\dfrac{dy}{du} = 5u^4$

$\dfrac{dy}{dx} = \dfrac{dy}{du} \times \dfrac{du}{dx}$

$= 5u^4 \times 2$

$= 5(2x-3)^4 \times 2$

$= 10(2x-3)^4$

At $x = 2$, gradient of the curve is:

$10(2 \times 2 - 3)^4$ or 10

5 $y = \dfrac{6}{(x-1)^2}$

Rewrite as $y = 6(x-1)^{-2}$

Use the chain rule to differentiate:

Let $u = x-1$ so $y = 6u^{-2}$

$\dfrac{du}{dx} = 1$ and $\dfrac{dy}{du} = -12u^{-3}$

$$\frac{dy}{dx} = \frac{dy}{du} \times \frac{du}{dx}$$
$$= -12u^{-3} \times 1$$
$$= -12u^{-3}$$
$$= -\frac{12}{(x-1)^3}$$

On the y-axis, $x = 0$ so:

$$\text{Gradient} = -\frac{12}{(0-1)^3} \text{ or } 12$$

6 $y = x - \dfrac{3}{x+2}$

$y = 0$ at the points where the curve crosses the x-axis

$$x - \frac{3}{x+2} = 0$$

Multiplying both sides by $(x+2)$ gives:

$$x(x+2) - 3 = 0$$
$$x^2 + 2x - 3 = 0$$
$$(x+3)(x-1) = 0$$

The x-intercepts are $x = -3$ and $x = 1$

So rewriting $y = x - \dfrac{3}{x+2}$ gives:

$$y = x - 3(x+2)^{-1}$$

[If $P = 3(x+2)^{-1}$

Use the chain rule to differentiate:

Let $u = x + 2$ $P = 3u^{-1}$

$$\frac{du}{dx} = 1 \qquad \frac{dP}{du} = -3u^{-2}$$

$$\frac{dP}{dx} = \frac{dP}{du} \times \frac{du}{dx}$$

$$\frac{dP}{dx} = -3u^{-2} \times 1$$

$$\frac{dP}{dx} = -3(x+2)^{-2}]$$

Differentiating y gives:

$$\frac{dy}{dx} = 1 + 3(x+2)^{-2}$$

Substituting $x = -3$ into $\dfrac{dy}{dx} = 1 + 3(x+2)^{-2}$

gives the gradient at $x = -3$

$$\frac{dy}{dx} = 1 + 3(-3+2)^{-2}$$

Gradient is 4.

Substituting $x = 1$ into

$$\frac{dy}{dx} = 1 + 3(x+2)^{-2}$$

gives the gradient at $x = 1$

so $1 + 3(x+2)^{-2}$ or $1 + \dfrac{3}{9}$ or $\dfrac{4}{3}$

Gradient is $\dfrac{4}{3}$.

7 $y = \sqrt{(x^2 - 10x + 26)}$

Rewrite as $y = (x^2 - 10x + 26)^{\frac{1}{2}}$

Use the chain rule to differentiate:

Let $u = x^2 - 10x + 26$ so $y = u^{\frac{1}{2}}$

$$\frac{du}{dx} = 2x - 10 \text{ and } \frac{dy}{du} = \frac{1}{2}u^{-\frac{1}{2}}$$

$$\frac{dy}{dx} = \frac{dy}{du} \times \frac{du}{dx}$$

$$= \frac{1}{2}u^{-\frac{1}{2}} \times (2x - 10)$$

$$= \frac{1}{2(x^2 - 10x + 26)^{\frac{1}{2}}} \times (2x - 10)$$

$$= \frac{x - 5}{\sqrt{x^2 - 10x + 26}}$$

The gradient is zero when:

$$\frac{2x - 10}{\sqrt{x^2 - 10x + 26}} = 0$$

So, $2x - 10 = 0$

$x = 5$

Substituting $x = 5$ into $y = \sqrt{(x^2 - 10x + 26)}$ gives:

$$y = \sqrt{(5^2 - 10(5) + 26)}$$

$$y = 1$$

The coordinates are (5, 1).

8 $y = \dfrac{a}{bx - 1}$ passes through $x = 2, y = 1$

Substitution gives:

$$1 = \frac{a}{2b - 1}$$

$$a = 2b - 1 \ \ldots\ldots\ldots\ldots [1]$$

Rewrite $y = \dfrac{a}{bx - 1}$ as $y = a(bx - 1)^{-1}$

Use the chain rule to find the derivative first:

Let $u = bx - 1$ so $y = au^{-1}$

$\dfrac{du}{dx} = b$ and $\dfrac{dy}{du} = -au^{-2}$

$\dfrac{dy}{dx} = \dfrac{dy}{du} \times \dfrac{du}{dx}$

$\phantom{\dfrac{dy}{dx}} = -au^{-2} \times b$

$\phantom{\dfrac{dy}{dx}} = -abu^{-2}$

$\phantom{\dfrac{dy}{dx}} = -\dfrac{ab}{(bx-1)^2}$

Substitute $x = 2$ to find the gradient at that point:

$\dfrac{dy}{dx} = -\dfrac{ab}{(2b-1)^2}$

So, $-\dfrac{ab}{(2b-1)^2} = -\dfrac{3}{5}$

$5ab = 3(2b-1)^2$ ....[2]

Using [1] substitute for a in [2]:

$\qquad 5(2b-1)b = 3(2b-1)^2$

$\qquad 10b^2 - 5b = 3(2b-1)(2b-1)$

$\qquad 10b^2 - 5b = 12b^2 - 12b + 3$

$\qquad 2b^2 - 7b + 3 = 0$

$\qquad (2b-1)(b-3) = 0$

$b = \dfrac{1}{2}$ or $b = 3$

Substituting $b = \dfrac{1}{2}$ into [1] gives:

$a = 2 \times \dfrac{1}{2} - 1$ or $a = 0$ ($a \neq 0$ as it would not be a curve)

Substitute $b = 3$ into [1] gives:

$a = 2 \times 3 - 1$ or $a = 5$

Solutions: $a = 5$, $b = 3$

EXERCISE 7C

1 **a** $y = x^2 - 3x + 2$

Differentiating gives:

$\dfrac{dy}{dx} = 2x - 3$

When $x = 3$, $\dfrac{dy}{dx} = 2(3) - 3$ or 3

The tangent passes through the point $(3, 2)$ and has a gradient $= 3$

Using $y - y_1 = m(x - x_1)$:

$y - 2 = 3(x - 3)$

$\quad y = 3x - 7$

c $y = \dfrac{x^3 - 5}{x}$

So, $y = x^2 - 5x^{-1}$

Differentiating gives:

$\dfrac{dy}{dx} = 2x + 5x^{-2}$ or $\dfrac{dy}{dx} = 2x + \dfrac{5}{x^2}$

When $x = -1$, $\dfrac{dy}{dx} = 2(-1) + \dfrac{5}{(-1)^2}$ or 3

The tangent passes through the point $(-1, 6)$ and has a gradient $= 3$

Using $y - y_1 = m(x - x_1)$:

$y - 6 = 3(x - -1)$

$\quad y = 3x + 9$

2 **a** $y = 3x^3 + x^2 - 4x + 1$

Differentiating gives:

$\dfrac{dy}{dx} = 9x^2 + 2x - 4$

When $x = 0$, $\dfrac{dy}{dx} = 9 \times 0^2 + 2 \times 0 - 4$ or -4

The tangent has the gradient $m = -4$ and passes through the point $(0, 1)$

Using $y - y_1 = -\dfrac{1}{m}(x - x_1)$:

$y - 1 = \dfrac{1}{4}(x - 0)$

$y - 1 = \dfrac{1}{4}x$ or $y = \dfrac{1}{4}x + 1$ or $4y = x + 4$

c Given $y = (5 - 2x)^3$ use the chain rule to differentiate:

Let $u = 5 - 2x$ so $y = u^3$

$\dfrac{du}{dx} = -2$ and $\dfrac{dy}{du} = 3u^2$

$\dfrac{dy}{dx} = \dfrac{dy}{du} \times \dfrac{du}{dx}$

$\qquad = 3u^2 \times -2$

$\qquad = 3(5 - 2x)^2 \times -2$

$\qquad = -6(5 - 2x)^2$

When $x = 3$, $\dfrac{dy}{dx} = -6(5 - 2 \times 3)^2$ or -6

The tangent has the gradient $m = -6$ so the normal passes through the point $(3, -1)$ and has a gradient $\dfrac{1}{6}$.

Using $y - y_1 = -\dfrac{1}{m}(x - x_1)$:

$y - (-1) = \dfrac{1}{6}(x - 3)$

$y + 1 = \dfrac{1}{6}(x - 3)$

$6y + 6 = x - 3$

$x - 6y = 9$

3 a $y = \dfrac{8}{(x + 2)^2}$.

Rewrite as: $y = 8(x + 2)^{-2}$

Use the chain rule to differentiate:

Let $u = x + 2$ so $y = 8u^{-2}$

$\dfrac{du}{dx} = 1$ and $\dfrac{dy}{du} = -16u^{-3}$

$\dfrac{dy}{dx} = \dfrac{dy}{du} \times \dfrac{du}{dx}$

$\qquad = -16u^{-3} \times 1$

$\qquad = -16u^{-3}$

$\qquad = -\dfrac{16}{(x + 2)^3}$

When $x = 2$, $\dfrac{dy}{dx} = -\dfrac{16}{(2 + 2)^3}$ or $-\dfrac{1}{4}$

The tangent passes through the point $\left(2, \dfrac{1}{2}\right)$ and has a gradient

$m = -\dfrac{1}{4}$

Using $y - y_1 = m(x - x_1)$:

$y - \dfrac{1}{2} = -\dfrac{1}{4}(x - 2)$

$4y - 2 = -x + 2$

$x + 4y = 4$

b The normal passes through the point $\left(2, \dfrac{1}{2}\right)$ and has a gradient $-\dfrac{1}{-\frac{1}{4}} = 4$.

Using $y - y_1 = -\dfrac{1}{m}(x - x_1)$:

$y - \dfrac{1}{2} = 4(x - 2)$

$2y - 1 = 8(x - 2)$

$2y - 1 = 8x - 16$

$2y = 8x - 15$

$y = 4x - 7.5$

4 a $y = 5 - 3x - 2x^2$

$\dfrac{dy}{dx} = -3 - 4x$

At $x = -2$ the gradient of the curve is

$= -3 - 4(-2)$ or 5

The gradient of the tangent $m = 5$

The normal passes through the point $(-2, 3)$ and has a gradient

$-\dfrac{1}{m} = -\dfrac{1}{5}$

Using $y - y_1 = -\dfrac{1}{m}(x - x_1)$:

$y - 3 = -\dfrac{1}{5}[x - (-2)]$

$y - 3 = -\dfrac{1}{5}x - \dfrac{2}{5}$

$5y - 15 = -x - 2$

$x + 5y = 13$ shown

b The equation of the normal is $y = -\dfrac{1}{5}x + \dfrac{13}{5}$

Solving this equation with the curve equation $y = 5 - 3x - 2x^2$ gives:

$-\dfrac{1}{5}x + \dfrac{13}{5} = 5 - 3x - 2x^2$

$-x + 13 = 25 - 15x - 10x^2$

$10x^2 + 14x - 12 = 0$

$5x^2 + 7x - 6 = 0$

Don't spend too much time trying to factorise. Using the formula is perfectly acceptable.

This does not factorise so use the quadratic formula: $x = \dfrac{-b \pm \sqrt{b^2 - 4ac}}{2a}$

where $a = 5$, $b = 7$, $c = -6$

$x = \dfrac{-7 \pm \sqrt{7^2 - 4(5)(-6)}}{2(5)}$

$x = \dfrac{-7 \pm \sqrt{169}}{10}$

$x = 0.6$ or $x = -2$ (already used)

Substituting $x = 0.6$ into the linear equation $y = -\dfrac{1}{5}x + \dfrac{13}{5}$ gives:

$y = -\dfrac{1}{5}(0.6) + \dfrac{13}{5}$

$y = 2.48$

The new coordinates are at $(0.6, 2.48)$

5 $y = x^3 - 5x + 3$

Differentiating gives:

$\dfrac{dy}{dx} = 3x^2 - 5$

At $x = -1$ the gradient of the curve is

$= 3(-1)^2 - 5$ or -2

The gradient of the tangent is $m = -2$.

Then the normal passes through the point $(-1, 7)$ and has a gradient $-\dfrac{1}{m} = -\dfrac{1}{-2}$ or $\dfrac{1}{2}$

Using $y - y_1 = -\dfrac{1}{m}(x - x_1)$:

$y - 7 = \dfrac{1}{2}[x - (-1)]$

$y - 7 = \dfrac{1}{2}x + \dfrac{1}{2}$

$2y - 14 = x + 1$

$2y = x + 15$

The normal intersects the y-axis at P (where $x = 0$)

So, $2y = 0 + 15$

$y = 7.5$

P is at $(0, 7.5)$

6 $y = 5 - 3x - x^2$

$\dfrac{dy}{dx} = -3 - 2x$

At $x = -1$ the gradient of the curve is

$= -3 - 2(-1)$ or -1

The equation of the tangent is found using:

$y - y_1 = m(x - x_1)$

$y - 7 = -1[x - (-1)]$

$y - 7 = -x - 1$

$y = 6 - x$ ....[1]

At $x = -4$ the gradient of the curve is

$= -3 - 2(-4)$ or 5

The equation of the tangent is found using:

$y - y_1 = m(x - x_1)$

$y - 1 = 5[x - (-4)]$

$y - 1 = 5x + 20$

$y = 5x + 21$ ....[2]

Solving [1] and [2] simultaneously:

$6 - x = 5x + 21$

$6x = -15$

$x = -2.5$

Substituting $x = -2.5$ into [1] gives:

$y = 6 - (-2.5)$

$y = 8.5$

The coordinates of Q are $(-2.5, 8.5)$

7 a $y = 4 - 2\sqrt{x}$

Rewrite this as $y = 4 - 2x^{\frac{1}{2}}$

Differentiating gives:

$\dfrac{dy}{dx} = -x^{-\frac{1}{2}}$

At $x = 16$ the gradient of the curve is

$m = -16^{-\frac{1}{2}}$ or $-\dfrac{1}{4}$

The normal passes through the point $(16, -4)$ and has a gradient $-\dfrac{1}{m} = -\dfrac{1}{-\frac{1}{4}} = 4$

Using $y - y_1 = -\dfrac{1}{m}(x - x_1)$:

$y - (-4) = 4(x - 16)$

$\quad y + 4 = 4x - 64$

$\qquad y = 4x - 68$

At the x-axis, $y = 0$ so the normal crosses this axis at:

$4x - 68 = 0$

$x = 17$ i.e. the point Q has coordinates $(17, 0)$

The equation of the line PQ is found using:

$P(16, -4)$ and $Q(17, 0)$

Gradient $= \dfrac{y_2 - y_1}{x_2 - x_1}$ or $\dfrac{0 - -4}{17 - 16}$ or 4

Using $y - y_1 = m(x - x_1)$:

$y - (-4) = 4(x - 16)$

$\quad y + 4 = 4x - 64$

The equation of the normal PQ is $y = 4x - 68$

b The coordinates of Q are $(17, 0)$

8 a The equation of a curve is $y = 2x - \dfrac{10}{x^2} + 8$

Rewrite the equation as: $y = 2x - 10x^{-2} + 8$

Differentiating gives:

$\dfrac{dy}{dx} = 2 + 20x^{-3}$ or $\dfrac{dy}{dx} = 2 + \dfrac{20}{x^3}$

b The tangent to the curve at the point $x = -4$ has a gradient

$2 + \dfrac{20}{(-4)^3}$ or $\dfrac{27}{16}$. So $m = \dfrac{27}{16}$.

The normal to the curve at the point $\left(-4, -\dfrac{5}{8}\right)$ has a gradient $-\dfrac{1}{m} = -\dfrac{1}{\frac{27}{16}} = -\dfrac{16}{27}$

Using $y - y_1 = -\dfrac{1}{m}(x - x_1)$:

$y - -\dfrac{5}{8} = -\dfrac{16}{27}[x - (-4)]$

$y + \dfrac{5}{8} = -\dfrac{16}{27}(x + 4)$

This normal line meets the y-axis where $x = 0$.

So substituting gives:

$y + \dfrac{5}{8} = -\dfrac{16}{27}(0 + 4)$

$y = -\dfrac{64}{27} - \dfrac{5}{8}$

$y = -\dfrac{647}{216}$

Therefore the normal meets the y-axis at $\left(0, -\dfrac{647}{216}\right)$

9 $y = \dfrac{6}{\sqrt{x - 2}}$

Rewrite $y = 6(x - 2)^{-\frac{1}{2}}$

Use the chain rule to differentiate:

Let $u = x - 2$ so $y = 6u^{-\frac{1}{2}}$

$\dfrac{du}{dx} = 1$ and $\dfrac{dy}{du} = -3u^{-\frac{3}{2}}$

$\dfrac{dy}{dx} = \dfrac{dy}{du} \times \dfrac{du}{dx}$

$\dfrac{dy}{dx} = -3u^{-\frac{3}{2}} \times 1$

$\dfrac{dy}{dx} = -\dfrac{3}{(x - 2)^{\frac{3}{2}}}$

At the point where $x = 3$, the gradient of the tangent is:

$= -\dfrac{3}{(3 - 2)^{\frac{3}{2}}}$

$m = -3$

The gradient of the normal at the point $(3, 6)$ is $-\dfrac{1}{m} = -\dfrac{1}{-3}$ or $\dfrac{1}{3}$.

The equation of the normal at this point is found by using:

$y - y_1 = -\dfrac{1}{m}(x - x_1)$

$y - 6 = \dfrac{1}{3}(x - 3)$

$3y - 18 = x - 3$

$\quad 3y = x + 15$

The normal meets the x-axis (at P) where $y = 0$

So, $0 = x + 15$

$x = -15$

P is at $(-15, 0)$

The normal meets the y-axis (at Q) where $x = 0$

So, $3y = 0 + 15$

$y = 5$

Q is at $(0, 5)$

The midpoint of PQ is found by using:

$\left(\dfrac{x_1 + x_2}{2}, \dfrac{y_1 + y_2}{2}\right)$ so:

The midpoint of PQ is $\left(\dfrac{-15 + 0}{2}, \dfrac{0 + 5}{2}\right)$ or $(-7.5, 2.5)$.

10 $y = x^5 - 8x^3 + 16x$

Differentiating gives:

$\dfrac{dy}{dx} = 5x^4 - 24x^2 + 16$

At $x = 1$ the gradient of the curve is

$= 5(1)^4 - 24(1)^2 + 16$ or -3

The normal passes through the point $(1, 9)$

The gradient of the normal is $-\dfrac{1}{m} = -\dfrac{1}{-3} = \dfrac{1}{3}$

The equation of the normal at $P(1, 9)$ is found using:

$y - y_1 = -\dfrac{1}{m}(x - x_1)$

$y - 9 = \dfrac{1}{3}(x - 1)$

$y - 9 = \dfrac{1}{3}x - \dfrac{1}{3}$

$y = \dfrac{1}{3}x + \dfrac{26}{3}$ ....[1]

At $x = -1$ the gradient of the curve is

$= 5(-1)^4 - 24(-1)^2 + 16$ or -3

The equation of the tangent at $Q(-1, -9)$ is found using:

$y - y_1 = m(x - x_1)$

$y - (-9) = -3[x - (-1)]$

$y + 9 = -3x - 3$

$y = -3x - 12$ ....[2]

Solving [1] and [2] simultaneously gives the coordinates of R:

$\dfrac{1}{3}x + \dfrac{26}{3} = -3x - 12$

$x + 26 = -9x - 36$

$10x = -62$

$x = -6.2$

Substituting $x = -6.2$ into [2] gives:

$y = -3 \times -6.2 - 12$

$y = 6.6$

The coordinates of R are $(-6.2, 6.6)$

11 a $y = 2(\sqrt{x} - 1)^3 + 2$

Rewrite as: $y = 2\left(x^{\frac{1}{2}} - 1\right)^3 + 2$

Use the chain rule to differentiate:

Let $u = x^{\frac{1}{2}} - 1$ so $y = 2u^3 + 2$

$\dfrac{du}{dx} = \dfrac{1}{2}x^{-\frac{1}{2}}$ and $\dfrac{dy}{du} = 6u^2$

Use the chain rule

$\dfrac{dy}{dx} = \dfrac{dy}{du} \times \dfrac{du}{dx}$

$= 6u^2 \times \dfrac{1}{2}x^{-\frac{1}{2}}$

$= \dfrac{3(x^{\frac{1}{2}} - 1)^2}{x^{\frac{1}{2}}}$

At $x = 4$ the gradient of the curve is

$= \dfrac{3(4^{\frac{1}{2}} - 1)^2}{4^{\frac{1}{2}}}$ or $\dfrac{3}{2}$

So, $m = \dfrac{3}{2}$

The normal passes through the point $(4, 4)$

and has a gradient $= -\dfrac{1}{m} = -\dfrac{1}{\dfrac{3}{2}}$ or $-\dfrac{2}{3}$

The equation of the normal at $P(4, 4)$ is found using:

$$y - y_1 = -\frac{1}{m}(x - x_1)$$

$$y - 4 = -\frac{2}{3}(x - 4),$$

$$y - 4 = -\frac{2}{3}x + \frac{8}{3}$$

$$y = -\frac{2}{3}x + \frac{20}{3} \ldots\ldots\ldots[1]$$

At $x = 9$ the gradient of the curve is:

$$= \frac{3(9^{\frac{1}{2}} - 1)^2}{9^{\frac{1}{2}}} \text{ or } 4$$

So $m = 4$

The normal passes through the point $(9, 18)$

and has a gradient $= -\frac{1}{m} = -\frac{1}{4}$

The equation of the normal at $P(9, 18)$ is found using:

$$y - y_1 = -\frac{1}{4}(x - x_1)$$

$$y - 18 = -\frac{1}{4}(x - 9),$$

$$y - 18 = -\frac{1}{4}x + \frac{9}{4}$$

$$y = -\frac{1}{4}x + \frac{81}{4} \ldots\ldots\ldots[2]$$

Solving [1] and [2] simultaneously gives the coordinates of R:

$$-\frac{2}{3}x + \frac{20}{3} = -\frac{1}{4}x + \frac{81}{4}$$

$$-8x + 80 = -3x + 243$$

$$5x = -163$$

$$x = -32.6$$

Substituting $x = -32.6$ into [2] gives:

$$y = -\frac{1}{4} \times -32.6 + \frac{81}{4}$$

$$y = 28.4$$

The coordinates of R are $(-32.6, 28.4)$

b See sketch:

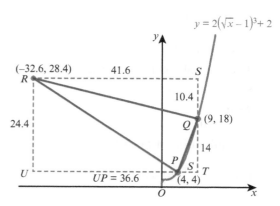

Area of the complete rectangle $RSTU$
$= 41.6 \times 24.4$ or 1015.04

Using area of a triangle

$= \frac{1}{2} \times \text{base} \times \text{perpendicular height}$

Area of $\triangle RSQ = \frac{1}{2} \times 10.4 \times 41.6$ or 216.32

Area of $\triangle QTP = \frac{1}{2} \times 14 \times 5$ or 35

Area of $\triangle RPU = \frac{1}{2} \times 24.4 \times 36.6$ or 446.52

Area of $\triangle PQR = 1015.04 - 216.32$
$\qquad\qquad\qquad - 35 - 446.52$
$\qquad\qquad = 317.2 \text{ units}^2$

12 a Gradient $= \frac{y_2 - y_1}{x_2 - x_1}$, $A(2, 12)$ and $B(6, 20)$

$$= \frac{20 - 12}{6 - 2} \text{ or } 2$$

Given the curve equation $y = 3x + \frac{12}{x}$,

Rewrite as: $y = 3x + 12x^{-1}$

Differentiating gives:

$$\frac{dy}{dx} = 3 - 12x^{-2} \text{ or } 3 - \frac{12}{x^2}$$

So, $3 - \frac{12}{x^2} = 2$

$$1 = \frac{12}{x^2}$$

$$x = \pm 2\sqrt{3}$$

If $x = 2\sqrt{3}$ then substituting into $y = 3x + \dfrac{12}{x}$ gives:

$y = 3 \times 2\sqrt{3} + \dfrac{12}{2\sqrt{3}}$

$y = 6\sqrt{3} + 2\sqrt{3}$ or $8\sqrt{3}$

If $x = -2\sqrt{3}$ then substituting into $y = 3x + \dfrac{12}{x}$ gives:

$y = 3 \times -2\sqrt{3} + \dfrac{12}{-2\sqrt{3}}$

$y = -6\sqrt{3} - 2\sqrt{3}$ or $-8\sqrt{3}$

C and D have coordinates $\left(2\sqrt{3}, 8\sqrt{3}\right)$ and $\left(-2\sqrt{3}, -8\sqrt{3}\right)$.

b The midpoint of CD is found by using:

$\left(\dfrac{x_1 + x_2}{2}, \dfrac{y_1 + y_2}{2}\right)$

$= \left(\dfrac{2\sqrt{3} + (-2\sqrt{3})}{2}, \dfrac{8\sqrt{3} + (-8\sqrt{3})}{2}\right)$

Midpoint is at $(0, 0)$

The gradient of CD is found by using:

Gradient $= \dfrac{y_2 - y_1}{x_2 - x_1}$

$= \dfrac{8\sqrt{3} - (-8\sqrt{3})}{2\sqrt{3} - (-2\sqrt{3})}$ or 4

The perpendicular bisector to CD has a gradient $-\dfrac{1}{4}$ and passes through $(0, 0)$.

Its equation is $y = -\dfrac{1}{4}x$ or $x + 4y = 0$

13 Given $y = x(x - 1)(x + 2)$

Expanding gives: $y = (x^2 - x)(x + 2)$

$y = x^3 + 2x^2 - x^2 - 2x$

$y = x^3 + x^2 - 2x$

Differentiating gives:

$\dfrac{dy}{dx} = 3x^2 + 2x - 2$

At $x = 1$ the gradient of the curve is

$= 3 \times 1^2 + 2 \times 1 - 2$ or 3

So $m = 3$

The normal passes through the point $(1, 0)$ and has a gradient $= -\dfrac{1}{m} = -\dfrac{1}{3}$

The equation of the normal at $P(1, 0)$ is found using:

$y - y_1 = -\dfrac{1}{m}(x - x_1), \; m \neq 0$

$y - 0 = -\dfrac{1}{3}(x - 1)$

$y - 0 = -\dfrac{1}{3}x + \dfrac{1}{3}$

$y = -\dfrac{1}{3}x + \dfrac{1}{3}$ ....[1]

At $x = -2$ the gradient of the curve is:

$= 3 \times (-2)^2 + 2 \times -2 - 2$ or 6

$m = 6$

The normal passes through point $(-2, 0)$ and has a gradient $= -\dfrac{1}{m} = -\dfrac{1}{6}$

The equation of the normal at $P(-2, 0)$ is found using:

$y - y_1 = -\dfrac{1}{6}(x - x_1)$

$y - 0 = -\dfrac{1}{6}[x - (-2)]$

$y - 0 = -\dfrac{1}{6}x - \dfrac{1}{3}$

$y = -\dfrac{1}{6}x - \dfrac{1}{3}$ ....[2]

Solving [1] and [2] simultaneously gives the coordinates of C:

$-\dfrac{1}{3}x + \dfrac{1}{3} = -\dfrac{1}{6}x - \dfrac{1}{3}$

$-2x + 2 = -x - 2$

$x = 4$

Substituting $x = 4$ into [1] gives:

$y = -\dfrac{1}{3} \times 4 + \dfrac{1}{3}$

$y = -1$

C is at $(4, -1)$.

14 Given $y = \dfrac{5}{2-3x}$

Rewrite as: $y = 5(2-3x)^{-1}$

Use the chain rule to differentiate:

Let $u = 2 - 3x$ so $y = 5u^{-1}$

$\dfrac{du}{dx} = -3$ and $\dfrac{dy}{du} = -5u^{-2}$

$\dfrac{dy}{dx} = \dfrac{dy}{du} \times \dfrac{du}{dx}$

$= -5u^{-2} \times -3$

$= \dfrac{15}{(2-3x)^2}$

At the point where $x = -1$ the gradient of the tangent is:

$= \dfrac{15}{(2 - 3 \times -1)^2}$

$= \dfrac{15}{25}$ or 0.6

Using $y - y_1 = m(x - x_1)$,
the equation of the tangent which passes through $(-1, 1)$ and has a gradient 0.6 is:

$y - 1 = 0.6(x - -1)$

$y - 1 = 0.6x + 0.6$

$y = 0.6x + 1.6$

This tangent line meets the x-axis where $y = 0$
i.e. $0 = 0.6x + 1.6$

$x = -\dfrac{8}{3}$

It also meets the y-axis where $x = 0$
i.e. $y = 0.6(0) + 1.6$

$y = 1.6$

See sketch:

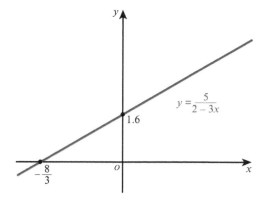

Tangent of the angle which this line makes with the x-axis

$= 1.6 \div \dfrac{8}{3}$ or 0.6

$\tan^{-1} 0.6 = 30.96°$

15 Given $y = \dfrac{12}{2x-3} - 4$

This curve intersects the x-axis where $y = 0$

i.e. $0 = \dfrac{12}{2x-3} - 4$

$\dfrac{12}{2x-3} = 4$

$12 = 4(2x - 3)$

$12 = 8x - 12$

$x = 3$

P is at $(3, 0)$

Rewrite as $y = 12(2x-3)^{-1} - 4$

Use the chain rule to differentiate:

Let $u = 2x - 3$ so $y = 12u^{-1} - 4$

$\dfrac{du}{dx} = 2$ and $\dfrac{dy}{du} = -12u^{-2}$

$\dfrac{dy}{dx} = \dfrac{dy}{du} \times \dfrac{du}{dx}$

$= -12u^{-2} \times 2$

$= -\dfrac{24}{(2x-3)^2}$

At the point where $x = 3$, the gradient of the tangent is:

$= \dfrac{24}{(2 \times 3 - 3)^2}$

$= \dfrac{24}{9}$ or $\dfrac{8}{3}$

Using $y - y_1 = m(x - x_1)$, $m = \dfrac{8}{3}$, $P = (3, 0)$

The tangent to the curve at P has equation:

$y - 0 = \dfrac{8}{3}(x - 3)$

$y = \dfrac{8}{3}x - 8$

This tangent intersects the y-axis where $x = 0$

$$y = \frac{8}{3}(0) - 8$$

$$y = -8$$

$$Q = (0, -8)$$

Using the distance formula:

$$PQ = \sqrt{(x_2 - x_1)^2 + (y_2 - y_1)^2}$$

and $P(3, 0)$, $Q(0, -8)$

$$PQ = \sqrt{(0 - 3)^2 + (-8 - 0)^2}$$

$$PQ = \sqrt{73}$$

16 a Given $y = 2x^2 + kx - 3$

Differentiating gives:

$$\frac{dy}{dx} = 4x + k$$

At $x = 3$ the gradient of the curve is

$$= 4 \times 3 + k$$

$$= 12 + k$$

The normal passes through the point $(3, -6)$ and has a gradient

$$= -\frac{1}{m} = -\frac{1}{12 + k}$$

The gradient of the line $x + 5y = 10$ is found by rearranging this equation and comparing it with $y = mx + c$:

$$5y = -x + 10$$

$$y = -\frac{1}{5}x + 2$$

Gradient $= -\frac{1}{5}$

So, $-\frac{1}{5} = -\frac{1}{12 + k}$

Comparing denominators:

$$12 + k = 5$$

$$k = -7$$

b The gradient of the normal can be found by substituting $k = -7$ into:

$$-\frac{1}{12 + k}$$

So $-\frac{1}{12 + -7}$ or $-\frac{1}{5}$

The equation of the normal at $P(3, -6)$ is found using:

$$y - y_1 = m(x - x_1)$$

$$y - (-6) = -\frac{1}{5}(x - 3)$$

$$y + 6 = -\frac{1}{5}x + \frac{3}{5}$$

$$y = -\frac{1}{5}x - \frac{27}{5}$$

The equation of the curve is

$y = 2x^2 + kx - 3$ but as $k = -7$, the equation of the curve is $y = 2x^2 - 7x - 3$

Solving $y = 2x^2 - 7x - 3$ and $y = -\frac{1}{5}x - \frac{27}{5}$ simultaneously gives the intersections of the normal and the curve.

So, $2x^2 - 7x - 3 = -\frac{1}{5}x - \frac{27}{5}$

$$10x^2 - 35x - 15 = -x - 27$$

$$10x^2 - 34x + 12 = 0$$

This does not factorise so use the quadratic formula: $x = \frac{-b \pm \sqrt{b^2 - 4ac}}{2a}$

where $a = 10$, $b = -34$, $c = 12$

$$x = \frac{-(-34) \pm \sqrt{(-34)^2 - 4(10)(12)}}{2(10)}$$

$$x = \frac{34 \pm \sqrt{676}}{20}$$

$x = 0.4$ or $x = 3$ (already used)

Substituting $x = 0.4$ into the linear equation gives:

$$y = -\frac{1}{5}x - \frac{27}{5}$$

Or $y = -\frac{1}{5}(0.4) - \frac{27}{5}$

$$y = -5.48$$

The coordinates of the point where the normal meets the curve again are $(0.4, -5.48)$.

1 d $y = (2x - 3)^4$

Using the chain rule twice:

$$\frac{dy}{dx} = 4(2x - 3)^3 \times 2$$

$$= 8(2x - 3)^3$$

$$\frac{d^2y}{dx^2} = 24(2x - 3)^2 \times 2$$

$$= 48(2x - 3)^2$$

f $y = \dfrac{2}{\sqrt{3x + 1}}$

Rewrite as: $y = 2(3x + 1)^{-\frac{1}{2}}$

Using the chain rule twice:

$$\frac{dy}{dx} = -1(3x + 1)^{-\frac{3}{2}} \times 3$$

$$= -3(3x + 1)^{-\frac{3}{2}}$$

$$\frac{d^2y}{dx^2} = \frac{9}{2}(3x + 1)^{-\frac{5}{2}} \times 3$$

$$= \frac{27}{2}(3x + 1)^{-\frac{5}{2}}$$

$$= \frac{27}{2(3x + 1)^{\frac{5}{2}}}$$

$$= \frac{27}{2\sqrt{(3x + 1)^5}}$$

2 c $f(x) = \dfrac{2x - 3\sqrt{x}}{x^2}$

Rewrite as: $f(x) = \dfrac{2x}{x^2} - \dfrac{3\sqrt{x}}{x^2}$

or $f(x) = 2x^{-1} - 3x^{-\frac{3}{2}}$

Differentiating twice gives:

$$f'(x) = -2x^{-2} + \frac{9}{2}x^{-\frac{5}{2}}$$

$$f''(x) = 4x^{-3} - \frac{45}{4}x^{-\frac{7}{2}}$$

$$= \frac{4}{x^3} - \frac{45}{4x^{\frac{7}{2}}}$$

$$= \frac{4}{x^3} - \frac{45}{4\sqrt{x^7}}$$

3 $y = 4x - (2x - 1)^4$

Using the chain rule twice for the bracketed term:

$$\frac{dy}{dx} = 4 - 4(2x - 1)^3 \times 2$$

$$= 4 - 8(2x - 1)^3$$

$$\frac{d^2y}{dx^2} = -24(2x - 1)^2 \times 2$$

$$= -48(2x - 1)^2$$

4 a $f(x) = x^3 + 2x^2 - 3x - 1$

$f(1) = 1^3 + 2 \times 1^2 - 3 \times 1 - 1$

$= -1$

b $f'(x) = 3x^2 + 4x - 3$

$f'(1) = 3 \times 1^2 + 4 \times 1 - 3$

$= 4$

c $f''(x) = 6x + 4$

$f''(1) = 6 \times 1 + 4$

$= 10$

5 $f'(x) = \dfrac{3}{(2x - 1)^8}$

Rewrite as: $f'(x) = 3(2x - 1)^{-8}$

Using the chain rule:

$$f''(x) = -24(2x - 1)^{-9} \times 2$$

$$f''(x) = -\frac{48}{(2x - 1)^9}$$

6 $f(x) = \dfrac{2}{\sqrt{1 - 2x}}$

Rewrite as: $f(x) = 2(1 - 2x)^{-\frac{1}{2}}$

Using the chain rule twice:

$$f'(x) = -1(1 - 2x)^{-\frac{3}{2}} \times -2$$

$$= 2(1 - 2x)^{-\frac{3}{2}}$$

$$f''(x) = -3(1 - 2x)^{-\frac{5}{2}} \times -2$$

$$= 6(1 - 2x)^{-\frac{5}{2}}$$

$$f''(-4) = 6(1 - 2 \times -4)^{-\frac{5}{2}}$$

$$= 6 \times 9^{-\frac{5}{2}}$$

$$= \frac{6}{\sqrt{9^5}} \text{ or } \frac{2}{81}$$

7 $y = 2x^3 - 21x^2 + 60x + 5$

Differentiating gives:

$$\frac{dy}{dx} = 6x^2 - 42x + 60$$

If $6x^2 - 42x + 60 = 0$

$$x^2 - 7x + 10 = 0$$

$$(x - 5)(x - 2) = 0$$

$x = 5$ or $x = 2$ give zero gradients if substituted into $\frac{dy}{dx}$

Substitutions of $x = 3$ or $x = 4$ give negative gradients and substitutions of $x < 2$ and $x > 5$ give positive gradients.

$$\frac{d^2y}{dx^2} = 12x - 42$$

If $12x = 42$

$$x = 3.5$$

In the table, substituting $x < 4$ gives a negative gradient and substituting $x \geqslant 4$ gives a positive gradient.

x	0	1	2	3	4	5	6	7
$\dfrac{dy}{dx}$	+	+	0	−	−	0	+	+
$\dfrac{d^2y}{dx^2}$	−	−	−	−	+	+	+	+

8 $y = x^3 - 6x^2 - 15x - 7$

Differentiating gives:

$$\frac{dy}{dx} = 3x^2 - 12x - 15$$

We want $3x^2 - 12x - 15 > 0$

i.e. $x^2 - 4x - 5 > 0$

$$(x - 5)(x + 1) > 0$$

The graph of $y = (x - 5)(x + 1)$ is a $\cup$ shaped parabola (see sketch).

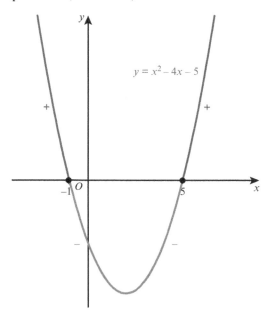

The x-intercepts are at $x = 5$ and $x = -1$

For $(x - 5)(x + 1) > 0$ we need to find the range of values of x for which the curve is positive (above the x-axis).

The solution is $x < -1$ and $x > 5$

$$\frac{d^2y}{dx^2} = 6x - 12$$

We want $6x - 12 > 0$

i.e. $x > 2$

Looking at the sketch:

For both $\dfrac{dy}{dx}$ and $\dfrac{d^2y}{dx^2}$ to be positive, $x > 5$

9 $y = x^2 - 2x + 5$

Differentiating gives:

$$\frac{dy}{dx} = 2x - 2$$

$$\frac{d^2y}{dx^2} = 2$$

Substituting into $4\dfrac{d^2y}{dx^2} + (x-1)\dfrac{dy}{dx}$ gives:

$4 \times 2 + (x-1)(2x-2)$

$8 + 2x^2 - 4x + 2$

$2x^2 - 4x + 10$

As $2y = 2(x^2 - 2x + 5)$ or $2x^2 - 4x + 10$,

$4\dfrac{d^2y}{dx^2} + (x-1)\dfrac{dy}{dx} = 2y$ shown

10 $y = 4\sqrt{x}$

Rewrite as $y = 4x^{\frac{1}{2}}$

Differentiating gives:

$\dfrac{dy}{dx} = 2x^{-\frac{1}{2}}$

$\dfrac{d^2y}{dx^2} = -x^{-\frac{3}{2}}$

Substituting into $4x^2\dfrac{d^2y}{dx^2} + 4x\dfrac{dy}{dx}$:

$y = 4x^2(-x^{-\frac{3}{2}}) + 4x(2x^{-\frac{1}{2}})$

$y = -4x^{2-\frac{3}{2}} + 8x^{1-\frac{1}{2}}$

$y = -4x^{\frac{1}{2}} + 8x^{\frac{1}{2}}$

$y = 4x^{\frac{1}{2}}$

$y = 4\sqrt{x}$ shown

11 a $y = x^3 + 2x^2 - 4x + 6$

Differentiating gives:

$\dfrac{dy}{dx} = 3x^2 + 4x - 4$

Substituting $x = -2$ gives:

$\dfrac{dy}{dx} = 3(-2)^2 + 4(-2) - 4$

$\dfrac{dy}{dx} = 12 - 8 - 4$ or 0 shown

Substituting $x = \dfrac{2}{3}$ gives:

$\dfrac{dy}{dx} = 3\left(\dfrac{2}{3}\right)^2 + 4\left(\dfrac{2}{3}\right) - 4$

$= 3 \times \dfrac{4}{9} + \dfrac{8}{3} - 4$

$= \dfrac{4}{3} + \dfrac{8}{3} - 4$

$= \dfrac{12}{3} - 4$

$= 4 - 4$ or 0 shown

b $\dfrac{d^2y}{dx^2} = 6x + 4$

Substituting $x = -2$ gives:

$\dfrac{d^2y}{dx^2} = 6 \times -2 + 4$ or -8

Substituting $x = \dfrac{2}{3}$ gives:

$\dfrac{d^2y}{dx^2} = 6 \times \dfrac{2}{3} + 4$ or 8

12 $y = \dfrac{ax + b}{x^2}$

Rewrite as:

$y = \dfrac{ax}{x^2} + \dfrac{b}{x^2}$ or $y = ax^{-1} + bx^{-2}$

Differentiating gives:

$\dfrac{dy}{dx} = -ax^{-2} - 2bx^{-3}$

Substituting $x = 2$:

$= -a \times 2^{-2} - 2b \times 2^{-3}$

$= \dfrac{-a}{4} - \dfrac{2b}{8}$

$= \dfrac{-b - a}{4}$

Given that $\dfrac{dy}{dx} = 0$

$\dfrac{-b - a}{4} = 0$

$-b - a = 0$

$b = -a$ ....[1]

Differentiating $\dfrac{dy}{dx}$ gives:

$\dfrac{d^2y}{dx^2} = 2ax^{-3} + 6bx^{-4}$

Substituting $x = 2$:

$\dfrac{d^2y}{dx^2} = 2a \times 2^{-3} + 6b \times 2^{-4}$

$= \dfrac{2a}{8} + \dfrac{6b}{16}$

$= \dfrac{2a + 3b}{8}$

Given that $\dfrac{d^2y}{dx^2} = \dfrac{1}{2}$

$\dfrac{2a + 3b}{8} = \dfrac{1}{2}$

$2a + 3b = 4$ ....[2]

From [1] $a = -b$, so substituting for a in [2] gives:

So, $-2b + 3b = 4$

$b = 4$ and $a = -4$

1 **d** $f(x) = x^3 - 12x^2 + 2$

For $f(x)$ to be an increasing function, the $f(x)$ values should increase as the x-values increase.

These regions can be identified from the sketch shown.

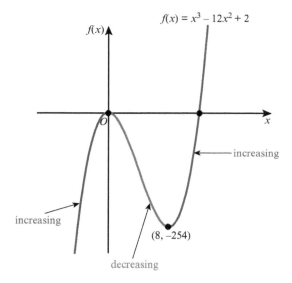

$$f(x) = x^3 - 12x^2 + 2$$

(8, −254)

increasing

increasing

decreasing

If the gradient of a function is positive at any particular point then the function is increasing there.

i.e. $f'(x) > 0$

So, for the parts of the function $f(x) = x^3 - 12x^2 + 2$ where $f(x)$ is increasing, we need to differentiate to find $f'(x)$, then solve $f'(x) > 0$.

$$f'(x) = 3x^2 - 24x$$

So, $3x^2 - 24x > 0$

Or $3x(x - 8) > 0$

Critical values [values of x which solve $3x(x - 8) = 0$] are represented on the diagram:

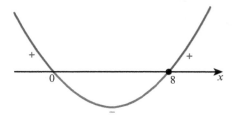

We want $3x^2 - 24x > 0$ which is the part of the graph where $f'(x) > 0$ i.e. above the x-axis.

So, $x < 0$ and $x > 8$

f Given: $f(x) = 16 + 16x - x^2 - x^3$

For $f(x)$ to be an increasing function, the $f(x)$ values should increase as the x values increase.

These regions can be identified from the sketch.

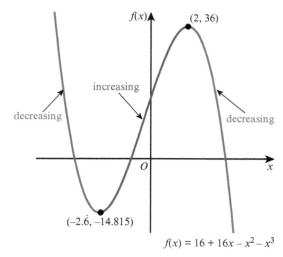

(2, 36)

increasing

decreasing

decreasing

(−2.6̇, −14.815)

$$f(x) = 16 + 16x - x^2 - x^3$$

If the gradient of a function is positive at any particular point then the function is increasing there.

i.e. $f'(x) > 0$

So, for the parts of the function
f(x) = 16 + 16x − x² − x³ where f(x) is
increasing, we need to differentiate to find
f′(x), then solve f′(x) > 0.

$$f'(x) = 16 - 2x - 3x^2$$

So, $16 - 2x - 3x^2 > 0$

Or $(2 - x)(3x + 8) > 0$

Critical values [values of x which solve
$(2 - x)(3x + 8) = 0$] $x = 2$ and $x = -2\frac{2}{3}$ are
represented on the diagram:

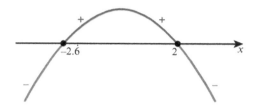

We want $16 - 2x - 3x^2 > 0$ which is the part of
the graph where f′(x) > 0 i.e above the x-axis.

So, $-2\frac{2}{3} < x < 2$

2 b $f(x) = 10 + 9x - x^2$

For f(x) to be an decreasing function, the
f(x) values should decrease as the x values
increase.

If the gradient of a function is negative at
any particular point then the function is
decreasing there.

i.e. f′(x) < 0

So, for the parts of the function
f(x) = 10 + 9x − x² where f(x) is decreasing,
we need to differentiate to find f′(x), then
solve f′(x) < 0.

$$f'(x) = 9 - 2x$$

So, $9 - 2x < 0$

Or $-2x < -9$

> Remember: dividing or multiplying by a
> negative number, reverses the inequality sign.

$x > 4.5$

For f(x) to be a decreasing function, f′(x) < 0.

∴ $x > 4.5$

d $f(x) = x^3 - 3x^2 - 9x + 5$

For f(x) to be an decreasing function, the
f(x) values should decrease as the x values
increase.

These regions can be identified from the
sketch.

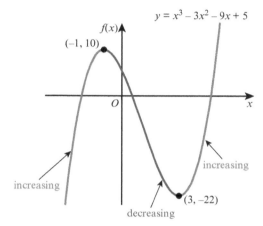

If the gradient of a function is negative at
any particular point then the function is
decreasing there.

i.e. f′(x) < 0

So, for the parts of the function
f(x) = x³ − 3x² − 9x + 5 where f(x) is
decreasing, we need to differentiate to find
f′(x), then solve f′(x) < 0.

$$f'(x) = 3x^2 - 6x - 9$$
$$3x^2 - 6x - 9 < 0$$
$$x^2 - 2x - 3 < 0$$
$$(x - 3)(x + 1) < 0$$

Critical values [values of x which solve
$(x - 3)(x + 1) = 0$] $x = 1$ and $x = 3$ are
represented on the diagram:

We want $3x^2 - 6x - 9 < 0$ which is the part of the graph where $f'(x) < 0$ i.e. below the x-axis.

So, $1 < x < 3$

3 $f(x) = \dfrac{1}{6}(5 - 2x)^3 + 4x$

Now find $f'(x)$

[Use the chain rule to differentiate the first term].

$f'(x) = \dfrac{1}{2}(5 - 2x)^2 \times -2 + 4$

$= -(5 - 2x)^2 + 4$

$= 4 - (5 - 2x)^2$

For an increasing function, $f'(x) > 0$

i.e. $4 - (5 - 2x)^2 > 0$

Critical values are found by considering:

$4 - (5 - 2x)^2 = 0$

$(5 - 2x)^2 = 4$

$5 - 2x = \pm 2$

If $5 - 2x = 2$ then $x = 1.5$

If $5 - 2x = -2$ then $x = 3.5$

Critical values are $x = 1.5$ and $x = 3.5$

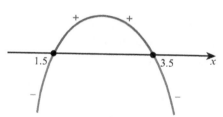

We want $4 - (5 - 2x)^2 > 0$ which is the part of the graph where $f'(x) > 0$ i.e. above the x-axis.

So, $1.5 < x < 3.5$

4 $f(x) = \dfrac{4}{1 - 2x}$ for $x \geqslant 1$

$= 4(1 - 2x)^{-1}$

$f'(x) = -4(1 - 2x)^{-2} \times -2$

$= 8(1 - 2x)^{-2}$

$f'(x) = \dfrac{8}{(1 - 2x)^2}$

As the domain is $x \geqslant 1$ then $(1 - 2x)^2 > 0$ for all values of x in this domain.

So $f'(x) > 0$ for all values of x in the domain of f

$\therefore$ f is an increasing function.

5 $f(x) = \dfrac{5}{(x + 2)^2} - \dfrac{2}{x + 2}$ for $x \geqslant 0$

$f(x) = 5(x + 2)^{-2} - 2(x + 2)^{-1}$

$f'(x) = -10(x + 2)^{-3} \times 1 + 2(x + 2)^{-2} \times 1$

$f'(x) = \dfrac{-10}{(x + 2)^3} + \dfrac{2}{(x + 2)^2}$

Adding the fractions gives:

$f'(x) = \dfrac{-10}{(x + 2)^3} + \dfrac{2(x + 2)}{(x + 2)^3}$

$f'(x) = \dfrac{2x - 6}{(x + 2)^3}$

The critical values of x are found by solving $2x - 6 = 0$

$x = 3$ (is the only critical value)

Substitute one value each side of $x = 3$.

Substituting $x = 2$ into

$f'(x) = \dfrac{2x - 6}{(x + 2)^3}$ gives:

$f'(x) = \dfrac{2(2) - 6}{(2 + 2)^3}$ or $-\dfrac{1}{32}$

The function is decreasing here.

Substituting $x = 4$ into

$f'(x) = \dfrac{2x - 6}{(x + 2)^3}$ gives:

$f'(x) = \dfrac{2(4) - 6}{(4 + 2)^3}$ or $\dfrac{1}{108}$

The function is increasing here.

Considering the domain $x \geqslant 0$, the function is decreasing and increasing so asking, 'Is it increasing for all values of $x \geqslant 0$?', the answer would be no, and asking, 'Is it decreasing for all values of $x \geqslant 0$?', the answer would be no.

Therefore, the function is neither.

6 Given $f(x) = \dfrac{x^2 - 4}{x}$

Rewrite as $f(x) = x - 4x^{-1}$

$f'(x) = 1 + 4x^{-2}$

Or $f'(x) = 1 + \dfrac{4}{x^2}$

Whatever value of x we choose (apart from $x = 0$), x^2 is always positive.

The graph has an asymptote at $x = 0$. This is because $f(0) = \dfrac{0^2 - 4}{0}$ is undefined.

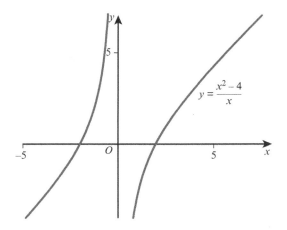

$$y = \frac{x^2 - 4}{x}$$

The sketch shows that f is an increasing function.

7 $f(x) = (2x+5)^2 - 3$ for $x \geq 0$

$f'(x) = 2(2x+5) \times 2$

$f'(x) = 8x + 20$

For all values of the domain $x \geq 0$,

$f'(x) > 0$.

∴ f is an increasing function.

8 $f(x) = \frac{2}{x^4} - x^2$ for $x > 0$

$f(x) = 2x^{-4} - x^2$

$f'(x) = -8x^{-5} - 2x$

$f'(x) = -\frac{8}{x^5} - 2x$

$f'(x) = -\frac{8}{x^5} - \frac{2x^6}{x^5}$

$f'(x) = \frac{-8 - 2x^6}{x^5}$

$f'(x) = -\frac{(8 + 2x^6)}{x^5}$

As $x > 0$ i.e. positive,

$f'(x) = -\frac{\text{positive}}{\text{positive}}$ i.e. negative.

∴ This is a decreasing function for values of $x > 0$.

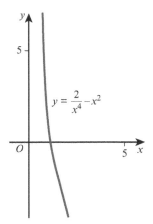

$$y = \frac{2}{x^4} - x^2$$

9 $P(x) = 2x^3 - 81x^2 + 840x$

So, for the parts of the function $P(x) = 2x^3 - 81x^2 + 840x$ where f(x) is decreasing, we need to solve $P'(x) < 0$.

$P'(x) = 6x^2 - 162x + 840$

$6x^2 - 162x + 840 < 0$

$x^2 - 27x + 140 < 0$

$(x - 20)(x - 7) < 0$

Critical values [values of x which solve $(x - 20)(x - 7) = 0$] $x = 20$ and $x = 7$ are represented on the diagram:

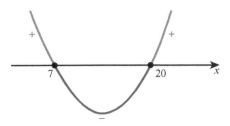

The range of values of x for which the profit is decreasing is $7 < x < 20$.

1 c $y = x^3 - 12x + 6$

Method 1

$$\frac{dy}{dx} = 3x^2 - 12$$

For stationary points: $\frac{dy}{dx} = 0$

$$3x^2 - 12 = 0$$
$$x^2 - 4 = 0$$
$$(x + 2)(x - 2) = 0$$
$$x = -2 \text{ or } x = 2$$

When $x = -2$, $y = (-2)^3 - 12(-2) + 6 = 22$

When $x = 2$, $y = (2)^3 - 12(2) + 6 = -10$

The stationary points are $(-2, 22)$ and $(2, -10)$.

Now consider the gradient on either side of the points $(-2, 22)$ and $(2, -10)$:

x	−2.1	−2	−1.9
$\dfrac{dy}{dx}$	$3(-2.1)^2 - 12 =$ positive	0	$3(-1.9)^2 - 12 =$ negative
direction of tangent	╱	─	╲
shape of curve	⌢		

x	1.9	2	2.1
$\dfrac{dy}{dx}$	$3(1.9)^2 - 12 =$ negative	0	$3(2.1)^2 - 12 =$ Positive
direction of tangent	╲	─	╱
shape of curve	⌣		

So $(-2, 22)$ is a maximum point and $(2, -10)$ is a minimum point.

The sketch graph of $y = x^3 - 12x + 5$ is:

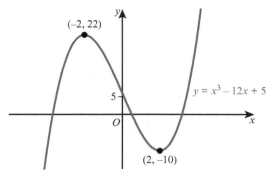

Method 2

$$\frac{dy}{dx} = 3x^2 - 12$$

For stationary points: $\frac{dy}{dx} = 0$

$$3x^2 - 12 = 0$$
$$x^2 - 4 = 0$$
$$(x + 2)(x - 2) = 0$$
$$x = -2 \text{ or } x = 2$$

When $x = -2$, $y = (-2)^3 - 12(-2) + 6 = 22$

When $x = 2$, $y = (2)^3 - 12(2) + 6 = -10$

The stationary points are $(-2, 22)$ and $(2, -10)$.

Find the second derivative: $\frac{d^2y}{dx^2}$

$$\frac{d^2y}{dx^2} = 6x$$

When $x = -2$, $\frac{d^2y}{dx^2} = 6 \times -2 = -12$

So $\frac{d^2y}{dx^2} < 0$

When $x = 2$, $y = 6 \times 2 = 12$

So $\frac{d^2y}{dx^2} > 0$

$\therefore$ $(-2, 22)$ is a maximum point and $(2, -10)$ is a minimum point.

e $y = x^4 + 4x - 1$

$$\frac{dy}{dx} = 4x^3 + 4$$

For stationary points: $\frac{dy}{dx} = 0$

$4x^3 + 4 = 0$

$\quad 4x^3 = -4$

$\quad\; x^3 = -1$

$x = -1 \quad y = (-1)^4 + 4 \times -1 - 1 \text{ or } -4$

The stationary point is at $(-1, -4)$

To determine the nature of the stationary point:

Method 1

Find the second derivative: $\frac{d^2y}{dx^2}$

$$\frac{d^2y}{dx^2} = 12x^2$$

When $x = -1$, $\frac{d^2y}{dx^2} = 12 \times (-1)^2$ or 12

So $\frac{d^2y}{dx^2} > 0$

∴ $(-1, -4)$ is a minimum point.

Method 2

Now consider the gradient on either side of the point $(-1, -4)$. Substitute one value each side of $x = -1$

Substituting $x = -2$ into $\frac{dy}{dx} = 4x^3 + 4$ gives:

$$\frac{dy}{dx} = 4(-2)^3 + 4 \text{ or } -28 \text{ which is negative}$$

Substituting $x = 0$ into $\frac{dy}{dx} = 4x^3 + 4$ gives:

$$\frac{dy}{dx} = 4(0)^3 + 4 \text{ or } 4 \text{ which is positive}$$

Since the gradient changes sign from negative to positive as the values of x move along the curve from left to right, and pass through the critical value, $(-1, -4)$ is a minimum point.

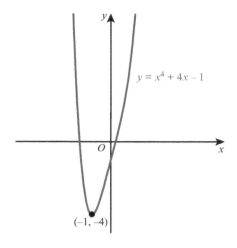

$y = x^4 + 4x - 1$

$(-1, -4)$

Be careful when substituting x-values either side of a stationary point into the first derivative in order to determine its nature. In general choose integer values which are as close as possible to the stationary point being aware of:

- the close proximity of other stationary points and

- the presence of asymptotes which give rise to undefined values when substituted into the first derivative.

2 a $y = \sqrt{x} + \dfrac{9}{\sqrt{x}}$

Rewrite as: $y = x^{\frac{1}{2}} + 9x^{-\frac{1}{2}}$

$$\frac{dy}{dx} = \frac{1}{2}x^{-\frac{1}{2}} - \frac{9}{2}x^{-\frac{3}{2}}$$

$$= \frac{1}{2x^{\frac{1}{2}}} - \frac{9}{2x^{\frac{3}{2}}}$$

For stationary points: $\frac{dy}{dx} = 0$

$$\frac{1}{2x^{\frac{1}{2}}} - \frac{9}{2x^{\frac{3}{2}}} = 0$$

Multiply both sides by $2x^{\frac{3}{2}}$:

$$\frac{2x^{\frac{3}{2}}}{2x^{\frac{1}{2}}} - \frac{18x^{\frac{3}{2}}}{2x^{\frac{3}{2}}} = 0 \times x^{\frac{3}{2}}$$

$$x - 9 = 0$$

$$x = 9 \quad y = \sqrt{9} + \frac{9}{\sqrt{9}} \text{ or } 6$$

The stationary point is at (9, 6).
To determine the nature of the stationary point:

Method 1

Find the second derivative: $\dfrac{d^2y}{dx^2}$

$$\frac{d^2y}{dx^2} = -\frac{1}{4}x^{-\frac{3}{2}} + \frac{27}{4}x^{-\frac{5}{2}}$$

When $x = 9$,

$$\frac{d^2y}{dx^2} = -\frac{1}{4}(9)^{-\frac{3}{2}} + \frac{27}{4}(9)^{-\frac{5}{2}}$$

$$= -\frac{1}{108} + \frac{27}{972}$$

$$= \frac{1}{54}$$

So $\dfrac{d^2y}{dx^2} > 0$

$\therefore$ (9, 6) is a minimum point.

Method 2

Now consider the gradient on either side of the point (9, 6): substitute one value each side of $x = 9$.

Substituting $x = 8$ into $\dfrac{dy}{dx} = \dfrac{1}{2x^{\frac{1}{2}}} - \dfrac{9}{2x^{\frac{3}{2}}}$ gives:

$$\frac{dy}{dx} = \frac{1}{2(8)^{\frac{1}{2}}} - \frac{9}{2(8)^{\frac{3}{2}}}$$

or $-0.0220\ldots$ which is negative.

Substituting $x = 10$ into $\dfrac{dy}{dx} = \dfrac{1}{2x^{\frac{1}{2}}} - \dfrac{9}{2x^{\frac{3}{2}}}$ gives:

$$\frac{dy}{dx} = \frac{1}{2(10)^{\frac{1}{2}}} - \frac{9}{2(10)^{\frac{3}{2}}}$$

or $0.0158\ldots$ which is positive.

Since the gradient changes sign from negative to positive as the values of x move along the curve from left to right, and pass through the critical value, (9, 6) is a minimum point.

c $y = \dfrac{(x-3)^2}{x}$

Rewrite as: $y = \dfrac{x^2 - 6x + 9}{x}$

$$y = x - 6 + 9x^{-1}$$

$$\frac{dy}{dx} = 1 - 9x^{-2}$$

$$= 1 - \frac{9}{x^2}$$

For stationary points: $\dfrac{dy}{dx} = 0$

$$1 - \frac{9}{x^2} = 0$$

Multiply both sides by x^2:

$$x^2 - 9 = 0$$
$$x^2 = 9$$
$$x = \pm 3$$

If $x = 3$, $y = \dfrac{(3-3)^2}{3}$ or 0

If $x = -3$, $y = \dfrac{(-3-3)^2}{-3}$ or -12

The stationary points are at (3, 0) and (-3, -12)

To determine the nature of the stationary points:

Method 1

Find the second derivative: $\dfrac{d^2y}{dx^2}$

$$\frac{d^2y}{dx^2} = 18x^{-3}$$

$$= \frac{18}{x^3}$$

When $x = 3$, $\dfrac{d^2y}{dx^2} = \dfrac{18}{3^3}$ or $\dfrac{2}{3}$

So $\dfrac{d^2y}{dx^2} > 0$

$\therefore$ (3, 0) is a minimum point.

When $x = -3$, $\dfrac{d^2y}{dx^2} = \dfrac{18}{(-3)^3}$ or $-\dfrac{2}{3}$

So $\dfrac{d^2y}{dx^2} < 0$

$\therefore$ (-3, -12) is a maximum point.

Method 2

Now consider the gradient on either side of the point $(3, 0)$. Substitute one value each side of $x = 3$.

Substituting $x = 2$ into $\dfrac{dy}{dx} = 1 - \dfrac{9}{x^2}$ gives:

$$\dfrac{dy}{dx} = 1 - \dfrac{9}{2^2}$$

or $-\dfrac{5}{4}$ which is negative.

Substituting $x = 4$ into $\dfrac{dy}{dx} = 1 - \dfrac{9}{x^2}$ gives:

$\dfrac{dy}{dx} = 1 - \dfrac{9}{4^2}$ or $\dfrac{7}{16}$ which is positive.

Since the gradient changes sign from negative to positive as the values of x move along the curve from left to right, and pass through the critical value, $(3, 0)$ is a minimum point.

Now consider the gradient on either side of the point $(-3, -12)$. Substitute one value each side of $x = -3$.

Substituting $x = -4$ into $\dfrac{dy}{dx} = 1 - \dfrac{9}{x^2}$ gives:

$\dfrac{dy}{dx} = 1 - \dfrac{9}{(-4)^2}$ or $\dfrac{7}{16}$ which is positive.

Substituting $x = -2$ into $\dfrac{dy}{dx} = 1 - \dfrac{9}{x^2}$ gives:

$\dfrac{dy}{dx} = 1 - \dfrac{9}{(-2)^2}$ or $\dfrac{-5}{4}$ which is negative.

Since the gradient changes sign from positive to negative as the values of x move along the curve from left to right, and pass through the critical value, $(-3, -12)$ is a maximum point.

3 Given $y = \dfrac{x^2 - 9}{x^2}$

Rewrite as: $y = 1 - 9x^{-2}$

$\dfrac{dy}{dx} = 18x^{-3}$

Or $\dfrac{dy}{dx} = \dfrac{18}{x^3}$

For stationary points: $\dfrac{dy}{dx} = 0$

$\dfrac{18}{x^3} = 0$

There are no solutions to this equation.

So there are no stationary points.

4 a Given $y = 2x^3 - 3x^2 - 36x + k$

$\dfrac{dy}{dx} = 6x^2 - 6x - 36$

For stationary points: $\dfrac{dy}{dx} = 0$

$6x^2 - 6x - 36 = 0$
$x^2 - x - 6 = 0$
$(x - 3)(x + 2) = 0$

The x-coordinates of the stationary points on the curve are $x = -2$ or $x = 3$.

b If $x = -2$, $y = 2(-2)^3 - 3(-2)^2 - 36(-2) + k$
$= k + 44$

There is a stationary point at $(-2, k + 44)$
If $x = 3$, $y = 2(3)^3 - 3(3)^2 - 36(3) + k$
$= k - 81$

There is a stationary point at $(3, k - 81)$
If the stationary points are on the x-axis then:

$k + 44 = 0$ so $k = -44$

and $k - 81 = 0$ so $k = 81$

The two values of k are -44 and 81.

5 a Given $y = x^3 + ax^2 - 9x + 2$

$\dfrac{dy}{dx} = 3x^2 + 2ax - 9$

For stationary points: $\dfrac{dy}{dx} = 0$

$3x^2 + 2ax - 9 = 0$

Substituting $x = -3$ into this equation gives:
$3(-3)^2 + 2a(-3) - 9 = 0$
$27 - 6a - 9 = 0$
$-6a = -18$
$a = 3$

b $y = x^3 + 3x^2 - 9x + 2$

So, for the parts of the function $y = x^3 + 3x^2 - 9x + 2$ where y is decreasing, we need to differentiate to find $\dfrac{dy}{dx}$ then solve $\dfrac{dy}{dx} < 0$.

$\dfrac{dy}{dx} < 3x^2 + 6x - 9$

$3x^2 + 6x - 9 < 0$

$x^2 + 2x - 3 < 0$

$(x + 3)(x - 1) < 0$

Critical values [values of x which solve $(x + 3)(x - 1) = 0$] $x = 1$ and $x = -3$ are represented on the diagram:

We want $3x^2 + 6x - 9 < 0$ which is the part of the graph where $\dfrac{dy}{dx} < 0$ i.e. below the x-axis.

So, $-3 < x < 1$

6 a Given $y = 2x^3 + ax^2 + bx - 30$

$\dfrac{dy}{dx} = 6x^2 + 2ax + b$

For stationary points: $\dfrac{dy}{dx} = 0$

$6x^2 + 2ax + b = 0$

Substituting $x = 3$ into this equation gives:

$6(3)^2 + 2a(3) + b = 0$

$54 + 6a + b = 0$

$6a + b = -54$ ....[1]

As the curve $y = 2x^3 + ax^2 + bx - 30$ passes through $(4, 2)$, then substituting $x = 4$ and $y = 2$ into this equation gives:

$2 = 2(4)^3 + a(4)^2 + b(4) - 30$

$2 = 128 + 16a + 4b - 30$

$16a + 4b = -96$

$4a + b = -24$ ....[2]

Subtracting [2] from [1] gives:

$2a = -30$

$a = -15$

Substituting $a = -15$ into [2] gives:

$4(-15) + b = -24$

$b = 36$

b $y = 2x^3 - 15x^2 + 36x - 30$

$\dfrac{dy}{dx} = 6x^2 - 30x + 36$

For stationary points: $\dfrac{dy}{dx} = 0$

$6x^2 - 30x + 36 = 0$

$x^2 - 5x + 6 = 0$

$(x - 3)(x - 2) = 0$

$x = 3$ (already known), or $x = 2$

If $x = 2$, $y = 2(2)^3 - 15(2)^2 + 36(2) - 30 = -2$

There is another stationary point at $(2, -2)$. To determine the nature of the stationary point:

Method 1

Find the second derivative $\dfrac{d^2y}{dx^2}$

$\dfrac{d^2y}{dx^2} = 12x - 30$

When $x = 2$, $\dfrac{d^2y}{dx^2} = 12(2) - 30 = -6$

So $\dfrac{d^2y}{dx^2} < 0$

$\therefore$ $(2, -2)$ is a maximum point.

Method 2

Now consider the gradient on either side of the point $(2, -2)$.

Substituting $x = 1$ into $\dfrac{dy}{dx} = 6x^2 - 30x + 36$ gives:

$\dfrac{dy}{dx} = 6(1)^2 - 30(1) + 36 = 12$ which is positive.

Substituting $x = 3$ will not help since $x = 3$ is a stationary point.

Substituting $x = 2.5$ into $\dfrac{dy}{dx} = 6x^2 - 30x + 36$ gives:

$\dfrac{dy}{dx} = 6(2.5)^2 - 30(2.5) + 36$ or $-\dfrac{3}{2}$ which is negative.

Since the gradient changes sign from positive to negative as the values of x move along the curve from left to right, and pass through the critical value, $(2, -2)$ is a maximum point.

7   Given $y = 2x^3 + ax^2 + bx - 30$

$\dfrac{dy}{dx} = 6x^2 + 2ax + b$

For stationary points: $\dfrac{dy}{dx} = 0$

$6x^2 + 2ax + b = 0$

Comparing this equation with $ax^2 + bx + c = 0$ and using the quadratic formula:

$x = \dfrac{-b \pm \sqrt{b^2 - 4ac}}{2a}$ where $a = 6$, $b = 2a$, $c = b$

$x = \dfrac{-2a \pm \sqrt{(2a)^2 - 4(6)(b)}}{2(6)}$

There are no real solutions if $(2a)^2 - 4(6)(b) < 0$

So, $4a^2 - 24b < 0$

$a^2 - 6b < 0$

$a^2 < 6b$ shown

8   Given $y = 1 + 2x + \dfrac{k^2}{2x - 3}$

Rewrite as: $y = 1 + 2x + k^2(2x - 3)^{-1}$

$\dfrac{dy}{dx} = 2 + k^2 \times -1(2x-3)^{-2} \times 2$

$= 2 - 2k^2(2x-3)^{-2}$

$= 2 - \dfrac{2k^2}{(2x-3)^2}$

For stationary points: $\dfrac{dy}{dx} = 0$

$2 - \dfrac{2k^2}{(2x-3)^2} = 0$

$2 = \dfrac{2k^2}{(2x-3)^2}$

$1 = \dfrac{k^2}{(2x-3)^2}$

$(2x-3)^2 = k^2$

$2x - 3 = \pm k$

$x = \dfrac{\pm k + 3}{2}$

The stationary points occur where:

$x = \dfrac{k+3}{2}$ or $x = \dfrac{-k+3}{2}$

> Be careful when reading instructions; this question only asks for the x-values not both coordinates so don't waste time finding the y-values.

To determine their natures find $\dfrac{d^2y}{dx^2}$:

As $\dfrac{dy}{dx} = 2 - 2k^2(2x-3)^{-2}$

$\dfrac{d^2y}{dx^2} = -2 \times -2k^2(2x-3)^{-3} \times 2$

$= 8k^2(2x-3)^{-3}$

$= \dfrac{8k^2}{(2x-3)^3}$

Substituting $x = \dfrac{k+3}{2}$

$\dfrac{d^2y}{dx^2} = \dfrac{8k^2}{\left(2 \times \dfrac{k+3}{2} - 3\right)^3}$

$= \dfrac{8k^2}{k^3}$

$= \dfrac{8}{k}$ which is positive because k is positive.

So, $x = \dfrac{k+3}{2}$ is a minimum point

Substituting $x = \dfrac{-k+3}{2}$

$\dfrac{d^2y}{dx^2} = \dfrac{8k^2}{\left(2 \times \dfrac{-k+3}{2} - 3\right)^3}$

$= \dfrac{8k^2}{-k^3}$

$= \dfrac{8}{-k}$ which is negative because k is positive.

So, $x = \dfrac{-k+3}{2}$ is a maximum point.

The method of determining the nature of the stationary points by finding the gradients either side of the stationary points requires much more work than the method above and is more prone to errors.

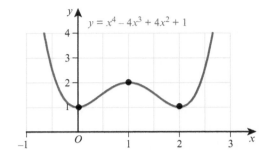

$y = x^4 - 4x^3 + 4x^2 + 1$

9 Given $y = x^4 - 4x^3 + 4x^2 + 1$

$$\frac{dy}{dx} = 4x^3 - 12x^2 + 8x$$

For stationary points: $\frac{dy}{dx} = 0$

$4x^3 - 12x^2 + 8x = 0$

(Do not 'divide through' by x as this will lose one of the solutions.)

$4x(x^2 - 3x + 2) = 0$
$4x(x - 1)(x - 2) = 0$
$x = 0$, or $x = 2$, or $x = 1$

If $x = 0$, $y = 0^4 - 4(0)^3 + 4(0)^2 + 1$ or 1

If $x = 1$, $y = 1^4 - 4(1)^3 + 4(1)^2 + 1$ or 2

If $x = 2$, $y = 2^4 - 4(2)^3 + 4(2)^2 + 1$ or 1

The stationary points are at: $(0, 1)$, $(1, 2)$ and $(2, 1)$

To determine the nature of these stationary points which are so close together, it is much easier to use the second derivative.

Now find $\frac{d^2y}{dx^2}$:

$$\frac{d^2y}{dx^2} = 12x^2 - 24x + 8$$

Substituting

$x = 0$ gives $12(0)^2 - 24(0) + 8 = 8$ which is positive so $(0, 1)$ is a minimum point.

$x = 1$ gives $12(1)^2 - 24(1) + 8 = -4$ which is negative so $(1, 2)$ is a maximum point.

$x = 2$ gives $12(2)^2 - 24(2) + 8 = 8$ which is positive so $(2, 1)$ is a minimum point.

10 a Given $y = x^3 + ax^2 + b$

$$\frac{dy}{dx} = 3x^2 + 2ax$$

For stationary points: $\frac{dy}{dx} = 0$

$3x^2 + 2ax = 0$

As $x = 4$, substituting into $3x^2 + 2ax = 0$ gives:

$3(4)^2 + 2 \times a \times 4 = 0$

$8a = -48$

$a = -6$

Substituting $x = 4$, $y = -27$ and $a = -6$ into $y = x^3 + ax^2 + b$ gives:

$-27 = 4^3 + (-6) \times 4^2 + b$

$b = 5$

b The curve equation is $y = x^3 - 6x^2 + 5$

So, $\frac{dy}{dx} = 3x^2 - 12x$

To determine the nature of the stationary point:

Method 1

$$\frac{d^2y}{dx^2} = 6x - 12$$

At $x = 4$, $\frac{d^2y}{dx^2} = 6 \times 4 - 12$ or 12 which is positive.

So $(4, -27)$ is a minimum point.

Method 2

Now consider the gradient on either side of the point $(4, -27)$. Substitute one value each side of $x = 4$.

Substituting $x = 3$ into $\dfrac{dy}{dx} = 3x^2 - 12x$ gives:

$\dfrac{dy}{dx} = 3(3)^2 - 12(3)$ or -9 which is negative.

Substituting $x = 5$ into $\dfrac{dy}{dx} = 3x^2 - 12x$ gives:

$\dfrac{dy}{dx} = 3(5)^2 - 12(5)$ or 15 which is positive.

Since the gradient changes sign from negative to positive as the values of x move along the curve from left to right, and pass through the critical value, $(4, -27)$ is a minimum point.

c   As $\dfrac{dy}{dx} = 3x^2 - 12x$ and for stationary points:

$\dfrac{dy}{dx} = 0$,

$3x^2 - 12x = 0$

> Do not 'divide through' by x as it will lose a solution.

$3x(x - 4) = 0$

$x = 4$ already known, or $x = 0$

If $x = 0$ then find the y-coordinate by substituting into the curve equation
i.e. $y = x^3 - 6x^2 + 5$:

So, $y = 0^3 - 6(0)^2 + 5$ or 5

So $(0, 5)$ is the other stationary point.

To determine the nature of the stationary point:

Method 1

To determine its nature substitute $x = 0$ into
$\dfrac{d^2y}{dx^2} = 6x - 12$:

So, $\dfrac{d^2y}{dx^2} = 6 \times 0 - 12$ or -12 which is negative.

$(0, 5)$ is a maximum point.

Method 2

Now consider the gradient on either side of the point $(0, 5)$. Substitute one value each side of $x = 0$.

Substituting $x = -1$ into $\dfrac{dy}{dx} = 3x^2 - 12x$ gives:

$\dfrac{dy}{dx} = 3(-1)^2 - 12(-1)$ or 15 which is positive.

Substituting $x = 1$ into $\dfrac{dy}{dx} = 3x^2 - 12x$ gives:

$\dfrac{dy}{dx} = 3(1)^2 - 12(1)$ or -9 which is negative.

Since the gradient changes sign from positive to negative as the values of x move along the curve from left to right, $(0, 5)$ is a maximum point.

d   We need to find the point on the curve where $\dfrac{dy}{dx}$ is a minimum, i.e. $3x^2 - 12x$ is a minimum.

Completing the square of $3x^2 - 12x$:

$= 3[x^2 - 4x]$

$= 3[(x - 2)^2 - 2^2]$

$= 3[(x - 2)^2 - 4]$

$= 3(x - 2)^2 - 12$

The minimum value of $3(x - 2)^2 - 12$ is -12

This occurs when $x = 2$ since $3(x - 2)^2 \geqslant 0$

Substituting $x = 2$ into the curve equation gives the y-coordinate.

i.e. $y = x^3 - 6x^2 + 5$ becomes

$y = 2^3 - 6(2)^2 + 5$ or -11

The minimum value of the gradient is -12 at the point $(2, -11)$.

11 a   Given $y = ax + \dfrac{b}{x^2}$

Substituting $x = 2$, $y = 12$ gives:

$12 = 2a + \dfrac{b}{2^2}$

$48 = 8a + b$ ....[1]

Rewriting $y = ax + \dfrac{b}{x^2}$ as $y = ax + bx^{-2}$, then differentiating gives:

$\dfrac{dy}{dx} = a - 2bx^{-3}$

Or $\dfrac{dy}{dx} = a - \dfrac{2b}{x^3}$

For stationary points: $\frac{dy}{dx} = 0$

$a - \frac{2b}{x^3} = 0$

As there is a stationary point at $x = 2$,

$a - \frac{2b}{2^3} = 0$

$a = \frac{2b}{8}$ so $b = 4a$ ....[2]

Using [2] and substituting for b in [1] gives:

$48 = 8a + 4a$

$a = 4$

Substituting $a = 4$ into [2] gives $b = 16$

b The curve has equation $y = 4x + \frac{16}{x^2}$ and

$\frac{dy}{dx} = 4 - \frac{32}{x^3}$ or $\frac{dy}{dx} = 4 - 32x^{-3}$

To determine the nature of the stationary point at $x = 2$:

Method 1

Find $\frac{d^2y}{dx^2}$

$\frac{d^2y}{dx^2} = 96x^{-4}$ or $\frac{96}{x^4}$

Substituting $x = 2$ into $\frac{d^2y}{dx^2} = \frac{96}{x^4}$ gives:

$\frac{d^2y}{dx^2} = \frac{96}{2^4}$ or 6 which is positive so, $x = 2$ is a minimum point.

Method 2

Now consider the gradient on either side of the point $x = 2$.

Substituting $x = 1$ into $\frac{dy}{dx} = 4 - \frac{32}{x^3}$ gives:

$\frac{dy}{dx} = 4 - \frac{32}{1^3}$ or -28 which is negative.

Substituting $x = 3$ into $\frac{dy}{dx} = 4 - \frac{32}{x^3}$ gives:

$\frac{dy}{dx} = 4 - \frac{32}{3^3}$ or $\frac{76}{27}$ which is positive.

Since the gradient changes sign from negative to positive as the values of x move along the curve from left to right, and pass through the critical value, $x = 2$ is a minimum point.

c

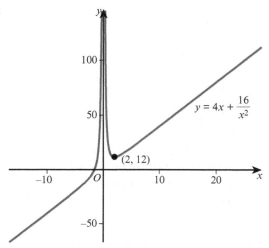

For values of $x > 2$, the curve is increasing.
For values of x which satisfy $0 < x < 2$ the curve is decreasing.
This curve is undefined when $x = 0$
(an asymptote) because $y = 4(0) + \frac{16}{0^2}$

From the sketch, the curve is increasing for values of x which satisfy $-\infty < x < 0$.

Solution: $x < 0$ and $x > 2$

12 a Given $y = x^2 + \frac{a}{x} + b$

Substituting $x = 3$ and $y = 5$ gives:

$5 = 3^2 + \frac{a}{3} + b$

$15 = 27 + a + 3b$

$a + 3b = -12$ ....[1]

Rewrite $y = x^2 + \frac{a}{x} + b$ as $y = x^2 + ax^{-1} + b$

Then $\frac{dy}{dx} = 2x - ax^{-2}$

Or $\frac{dy}{dx} = 2x - \frac{a}{x^2}$

For stationary points: $\frac{dy}{dx} = 0$

So $2x - \frac{a}{x^2} = 0$

At $x = 3$, $2(3) - \dfrac{a}{3^2} = 0$

$6 - \dfrac{a}{9} = 0$

$a = 54$

Substituting $a = 54$ into [1] gives:

$a + 3b = -12$ so:

$54 + 3b = -12$

$b = -22$

The equation of the curve is:

$y = x^2 + \dfrac{54}{x} - 22$

$a = 54, b = -22$

b To determine the nature of the stationary point at $(3, 5)$:

Method 1

Find $\dfrac{\mathrm{d}^2 y}{\mathrm{d}x^2}$

$\dfrac{\mathrm{d}y}{\mathrm{d}x} = 2x - ax^{-2}$ or $\dfrac{\mathrm{d}y}{\mathrm{d}x} = 2x - 54x^{-2}$

$\dfrac{\mathrm{d}^2 y}{\mathrm{d}x^2} = 2 + 108x^{-3}$ or $\dfrac{\mathrm{d}^2 y}{\mathrm{d}x^2} = 2 + \dfrac{108}{x^3}$

Substituting $x = 3$ gives:

$2 + \dfrac{108}{3^3}$ or 6 which is positive.

The point $(3, 5)$ is a minimum point.

Method 2

Now consider the gradient on either side of the point $(3, 5)$.

Substituting $x = 2$ into $\dfrac{\mathrm{d}y}{\mathrm{d}x} = 2x - \dfrac{54}{x^2}$ gives:

$\dfrac{\mathrm{d}y}{\mathrm{d}x} = 2(2) - \dfrac{54}{2^2} = -\dfrac{19}{2}$ which is negative.

Substituting $x = 4$ into $\dfrac{\mathrm{d}y}{\mathrm{d}x} = 2x - \dfrac{54}{x^2}$ gives:

$\dfrac{\mathrm{d}y}{\mathrm{d}x} = 2(4) - \dfrac{54}{4^2}$ or $\dfrac{37}{8}$ which is positive.

Since the gradient changes sign from negative to positive as the values of x move along the curve from left to right, and pass through the critical value, $(3, 5)$ is a minimum point.

c This curve has the equation:

$y = x^2 + \dfrac{54}{x} - 22$

For $x > 3$ the curve is increasing.

For values of x which satisfy $0 < x < 3$ the curve is decreasing.

The curve is undefined when $x = 0$ (since $y = 0^2 + \dfrac{a}{0} + b$ is undefined).

The curve is decreasing for values of x which satisfy $-\infty < x < 0$.

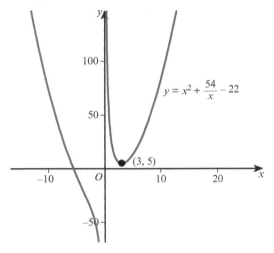

The range of values of x for which the curve is a decreasing function is $x < 0$ and $0 < x < 3$.

13 a Given $y = 2x^3 + ax^2 + bx + 7$

$x = 2$ and $y = -13$ gives:

$-13 = 2 \times 2^3 + a \times 2^2 + b \times 2 + 7$

$-13 = 23 + 4a + 2b$

$4a + 2b = -36$ ....[1]

As $y = 2x^3 + ax^2 + bx + 7$

$\dfrac{\mathrm{d}y}{\mathrm{d}x} = 6x^2 + 2ax + b$

For stationary points: $\dfrac{\mathrm{d}y}{\mathrm{d}x} = 0$

So $6x^2 + 2ax + b = 0$

Substituting $x = 2$ gives:

$6 \times 2^2 + 2 \times a \times 2 + b = 0$

$4a + b = -24$ ....[2]

Subtracting [2] from [1] gives:

$b = -12$

Substituting into [2] gives:

$4a + (-12) = -24$

$a = -3$

b Solving $\dfrac{dy}{dx} = 0$ gives all the stationary points on the curve.

From previous part: $\dfrac{dy}{dx} = 6x^2 + 2ax + b$

As $a = -3$ and $b = -12$,

$\dfrac{dy}{dx} = 6x^2 - 6x - 12$

So, $6x^2 - 6x - 12 = 0$

Or $x^2 - x - 2 = 0$

$(x - 2)(x + 1) = 0$

$x = 2$, already known, or $x = -1$

When $x = -1$, substituting into the curve equation gives the y-coordinate

$y = 2x^3 + ax^2 + bx + 7$

$y = 2x^3 - 3x^2 - 12x + 7$

$y = 2(-1)^3 - 3(-1)^2 - 12(-1) + 7$

$y = 14$

The other stationary point is at $(-1, 14)$.

c To determine the nature of the stationary points:

Method 1

Find $\dfrac{d^2y}{dx^2}$.

$\dfrac{dy}{dx} = 6x^2 - 6x - 12$

$\dfrac{d^2y}{dx^2} = 12x - 6$

Substituting $x = 2$ gives $12 \times 2 - 6$ or 18 which is positive so $(2, -13)$ is a minimum point.

$x = -1$ gives $12 \times -1 - 6$ or -18 which is negative so $(-1, 14)$ is a maximum point.

Method 2

Now consider the gradient on either side of the point $(2, -13)$.

Substituting $x = 1$ into $\dfrac{dy}{dx} = 6x^2 - 6x - 12$ gives:

$\dfrac{dy}{dx} = 6(1)^2 - 6(1) - 12$ or -12 which is negative.

Substituting $x = 3$ into $\dfrac{dy}{dx} = 6x^2 - 6x - 12$ gives:

$\dfrac{dy}{dx} = 6(3)^2 - 6(3) - 12$ or 24 which is positive.

Since the gradient changes sign from negative to positive as the values of x move along the curve from left to right, and pass through the critical value, $(2, -13)$ is a minimum point.

Now consider the gradient on either side of the point $(-1, 14)$.

Substituting $x = -2$ into $\dfrac{dy}{dx} = 6x^2 - 6x - 12$ gives:

$\dfrac{dy}{dx} = 6(-2)^2 - 6(-2) - 12$ or 24 which is positive

Substituting $x = 0$ into $\dfrac{dy}{dx} = 6x^2 - 6x - 12$ gives:

$\dfrac{dy}{dx} = 6(0)^2 - 6(0) - 12$ or -12 which is negative.

Since the gradient changes sign from positive to negative as the values of x move along the curve from left to right, and pass through the critical value, $(-1, 14)$ is a maximum point.

d We need to find where $\dfrac{dy}{dx} = 6x^2 - 6x - 12$ is a minimum.

Completing the square gives:

$= 6[x^2 - x] - 12$

$= 6\left[\left(x - \dfrac{1}{2}\right)^2 - \left(\dfrac{1}{2}\right)^2\right] - 12$

$= 6\left[\left(x - \dfrac{1}{2}\right)^2 - \dfrac{1}{4}\right] - 12$

$= 6\left(x - \dfrac{1}{2}\right)^2 - 13.5$

The minimum value of $6\left(x-\dfrac{1}{2}\right)^2 - 13.5$ is -13.5

This occurs when $x=\dfrac{1}{2}$ since $6\left(x-\dfrac{1}{2}\right)^2 \geqslant 0$

Substituting $x=\dfrac{1}{2}$ into the curve equation gives the y-coordinate.

$y = 2x^3 - 3x^2 - 12x + 7$

$y = 2\left(\dfrac{1}{2}\right)^3 - 3\left(\dfrac{1}{2}\right)^2 - 12\left(\dfrac{1}{2}\right) + 7$

$y = \dfrac{1}{2}$

The point on the curve where the gradient is minimum is $\left(\dfrac{1}{2}, \dfrac{1}{2}\right)$ and the value of the minimum gradient is -13.5.

EXERCISE 8C

1 a $x + y = 9$
$y = 9 - x$

b i Given $P = x^2 y$,
$P = x^2(9 - x)$
$P = 9x^2 - x^3$

ii $\dfrac{dP}{dx} = 18x - 3x^2$

The maximum value of P is found by solving $\dfrac{dP}{dx} = 0$

$18x - 3x^2 = 0$

Do not 'divide through' by x as this will destroy one solution.

$3x(6 - x) = 0$
$x = 0$ and $x = 6$

There are stationary points at $x = 0$ and $x = 6$.

Substituting $x = 0$ into $P = 9x^2 - x^3$ gives:
$P = 0$

Substituting $x = 6$ into $P = 9x^2 - x^3$ gives:
$P = 9 \times 6^2 - 6^3$ or 108

The maximum value of P is 108.

c i Given $Q = 3x^2 + 2y^2$

As $y = 9 - x$

Substituting for y in $Q = 3x^2 + 2y^2$

$Q = 3x^2 + 2(9 - x)^2$
$Q = 3x^2 + 2(9 - x)(9 - x)$
$Q = 3x^2 + 162 - 36x + 2x^2$
$Q = 5x^2 - 36x + 162$

ii The minimum value of Q can be found by completing the square.

$Q = 5\left[x^2 - \dfrac{36}{5}x\right] + 162$

$= 5\left[\left(x - \dfrac{36}{10}\right)^2 - \left(\dfrac{36}{10}\right)^2\right] + 162$

$= 5\left[\left(x - \dfrac{18}{5}\right)^2 - \dfrac{324}{25}\right] + 162$

$= 5\left(x - \dfrac{18}{5}\right)^2 + \dfrac{486}{5}$

The minimum value of

$Q = 5\left(x - \dfrac{18}{5}\right)^2 + 97.2$ is 97.2 (this occurs when $x = \dfrac{18}{5}$).

2 a Arc length $s = r\theta$ (θ in radians)

Perimeter of wire $= r\theta + 2r$ cm

$40 = r\theta + 2r$
$r\theta = 40 - 2r$
$\theta = \dfrac{40 - 2r}{r}$

b Area of sector $= \frac{1}{2}r^2\theta$

$$A = \frac{1}{2}r^2\left(\frac{40-2r}{r}\right)$$

$$= \frac{r^2(40-2r)}{2r}$$

$$= \frac{40r^2 - 2r^3}{2r}$$

$A = 20r - r^2$ shown

c There is a stationary value of A when $\dfrac{dA}{dr} = 0$

$$\frac{dA}{dr} = 20 - 2r$$

$$20 - 2r = 0$$

$$r = 10$$

d The magnitude of this stationary value is the value of A at $r = 10$

$$A = 20r - r^2$$
$$A = 20 \times 10 - 10^2$$
$$A = 100 \text{ cm}^2$$

The nature of the stationary value is found by:

Method 1

Finding $\dfrac{d^2A}{dr^2}$

$\dfrac{d^2A}{dr^2} = -2$ which is negative so this stationary value is a maximum.

Method 2

Now consider the gradient on either side of the point $r = 10$

Substituting $r = 9$ into $\dfrac{dA}{dr} = 20 - 2r$ gives:

$$\frac{dA}{dr} = 20 - 2(9) \text{ or } 2 \text{ which is positive}$$

Substituting $r = 11$ into $\dfrac{dA}{dr} = 20 - 2r$ gives:

$$\frac{dA}{dr} = 20 - 2(11) \text{ or } -2 \text{ which is negative.}$$

Since the gradient changes sign from positive to negative as the values of r move along the curve from left to right, and pass through the critical value, $r = 10$ is a maximum value.

3 a $2y + x = 50$

$$y = \frac{50 - x}{2}$$

b $A = x \times y$

$$A = x \times \frac{(50 - x)}{2}$$

$$A = \frac{1}{2}x(50 - x) \text{ shown.}$$

c The maximum area enclosed is found by solving $\dfrac{dA}{dx} = 0$

$$A = 25x - \frac{1}{2}x^2$$

$$\frac{dA}{dx} = 25 - x$$

$$\frac{dA}{dx} = 0 \text{ when } 25 - x = 0$$

$$x = 25$$

To show that this is a maximum point, find $\dfrac{d^2A}{dx^2} = -1$ as this is negative, $x = 25$ must represent a maximum value for the area.

> The question does not ask you to show that this is a maximum point. If in doubt, it is best to do so. Compare with End-of-chapter review exercise 8 Question 6 ii.

If $x = 25$ then the area is

$$A = \frac{1}{2} \times 25 \times (50 - 25)$$

Maximum area is 312.5 cm² when $x = 25$ m

4 a Completing the diagram with all lengths:

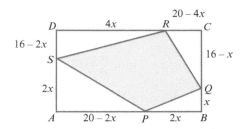

Area of $ABCD = 20 \times 16$
$$= 320 \text{ cm}^2$$

Area of a triangle $= \frac{1}{2} \times$ base $\times$ perpendicular height

Area of $\triangle SDR = \frac{1}{2} \times 4x \times (16 - 2x)$ or $32x - 4x^2$

Area of $\triangle RCQ = \frac{1}{2} \times (20 - 4x) \times (16 - x)$
$$= (10 - 2x)(16 - x)$$
$$= 160 - 42x + 2x^2$$

Area of $\triangle QBP = \frac{1}{2} \times 2x \times x$ or x^2

Area of $\triangle PAS = \frac{1}{2} \times 2x \times (20 - 2x)$
$$= 20x - 2x^2$$

Shaded area $PQRS$

$= 320 - [(32x - 4x^2) + (160 - 42x + 2x^2) + x^2 + (20x - 2x^2)]$
$= 320 - [32x - 4x^2 + 160 - 42x + 2x^2 + x^2 + 20x - 2x^2]$
$= 320 - 32x + 4x^2 - 160 + 42x - 2x^2 - x^2 - 20x + 2x^2$
$= 3x^2 - 10x + 160 \text{ cm}^2$

---

b A stationary value occurs when $\frac{dA}{dx} = 0$
(where A is the area of $PQRS$)

$$\frac{dA}{dx} = 6x - 10$$

$\frac{dA}{dx} = 0$ when $6x - 10 = 0$

i.e. $x = \frac{5}{3}$

To show that this area is a minimum:

Method 1

Find $\frac{d^2A}{dx^2}$

$\frac{d^2A}{dx^2} = 6$ which is positive, so the area is a minimum.

Method 2

Now consider the gradient on either side of the point $x = \frac{5}{3}$

Substituting $x = 1$ into $\frac{dA}{dx} = 6x - 10$ gives:

$$\frac{dA}{dx} = 6(1) - 10 \text{ or } -4 \text{ which is negative}$$

Substituting $x = 2$ into $\frac{dA}{dx} = 6x - 10$ gives:

$$\frac{dA}{dx} = 6(2) - 10 \text{ or } 2 \text{ which is positive}$$

Since the gradient changes sign from negative to positive as the values of x move along the curve from left to right, and pass through the critical value, $x = \frac{5}{3}$ represents a minimum area.

To find the minimum area, substitute $x = \frac{5}{3}$ into $3x^2 - 10x + 160$.

i.e. $3\left(\frac{5}{3}\right)^2 - 10\left(\frac{5}{3}\right) + 160$ or $151\frac{2}{3}$ cm²

The area has a minimum value $151\frac{2}{3}$ cm² when $x = \frac{5}{3}$ cm.

5 a Given $3x + 2y = 30$,

$2y = 30 - 3x$

$y = \frac{30 - 3x}{2}$ or $15 - \frac{3}{2}x$

Area $OPQR = x \times y$

$A = x \times \left(15 - \frac{3}{2}x\right)$

$A = 15x - \frac{3}{2}x^2$

b Find $\frac{dA}{dx} = 15 - 3x$

At a stationary point, $\frac{dA}{dx} = 0$

So, $15 - 3x = 0$

$x = 5$

The stationary value of A is found by substituting $x = 5$ into $A = 15x - \frac{3}{2}x^2$

i.e. $A = 15 \times 5 - \frac{3}{2} \times 5^2$

$A = 37.5$ cm²

To determine its nature:

Method 1

Find $\frac{d^2A}{dx^2}$

$\frac{d^2A}{dx^2} = -3$ which is negative so the point is a maximum value.

Method 2

Now consider the gradient on either side of the point $x = 5$

Substituting $x = 4$ into $\frac{dA}{dx} = 15 - 3x$ gives:

$\frac{dA}{dx} = 15 - 3(4)$ or 3 which is positive

Substituting $x = 6$ into $\frac{dA}{dx} = 15 - 3x$ gives:

$\frac{dA}{dx} = 15 - 3(6)$ or -3 which is negative.

Since the gradient changes sign from positive to negative as the values of x move along the curve from left to right, and pass through the critical value, the point is a maximum value.

6 a Substituting $x = p$ into $y = 9 - x^2$ gives the y-coordinate of Q

$QR = 9 - p^2$

b Area of PQRS = length × width

$= 2p \times (9 - p^2)$

$A = 2p(9 - p^2)$ shown

c $A = 18p - 2p^3$

To determine a stationary value, find $\frac{dA}{dP}$

$\frac{dA}{dP} = 18 - 6p^2$

At a stationary point $\frac{dA}{dP} = 0$

$18 - 6p^2 = 0$

$18 = 6p^2$

$p = \pm\sqrt{3}$ reject $-\sqrt{3}$ as length is not negative

$p = \sqrt{3}$

d If $p = \sqrt{3}$ then $A = 2 \times \sqrt{3} \times (9 - (\sqrt{3})^2)$

$A = 12\sqrt{3}$

To determine the nature of the stationary point:

Method 1

Find $\frac{d^2A}{dp^2} = -12p$ and then substitute $p = \sqrt{3}$.

This gives $\frac{d^2A}{dp^2} = -12 \times \sqrt{3}$

As $-12\sqrt{3}$ is negative, $p = \sqrt{3}$ is a maximum point.

At $p = \sqrt{3}$, A has a maximum value which is $12\sqrt{3}$ cm².

Method 2

Now consider the gradient on either side of the point $p = \sqrt{3}$

Substituting $x = 1$ into $\dfrac{\mathrm{d}A}{\mathrm{d}P} = 18 - 6p^2$ gives:

$\dfrac{\mathrm{d}A}{\mathrm{d}P} = 18 - 6(1)^2$ or 12 which is positive

Substituting $x = 2$ into $\dfrac{\mathrm{d}A}{\mathrm{d}P} = 18 - 6p^2$ gives:

$\dfrac{\mathrm{d}A}{\mathrm{d}P} = 18 - 6(2)^2$ or –6 which is negative

Since the gradient changes sign from positive to negative as the values of p move along the curve from left to right, and pass through the critical value, the point $p = \sqrt{3}$ is a maximum value.

At $p = \sqrt{3}$, A has a maximum value which is $12\sqrt{3}$ cm².

7 **a** The dimensions of the base of the box when folded are:

Length $(24 - 2x)$ cm

Width $(15 - 2x)$ cm

Volume of the folded box (V)
$$= \text{area of the base} \times \text{height of the box}$$
$V = (24 - 2x) \times (15 - 2x) \times x$
$V = (24 - 2x)(15x - 2x^2)$
$V = 360x - 48x^2 - 30x^2 + 4x^3$
$V = 4x^3 - 78x^2 + 360x$ shown

b Stationary values of V are found by solving

$\dfrac{\mathrm{d}V}{\mathrm{d}x} = 0$

$\dfrac{\mathrm{d}V}{\mathrm{d}x} = 12x^2 - 156x + 360$

So $12x^2 - 156x + 360 = 0$

Or $x^2 - 13x + 30 = 0$

$(x - 10)(x - 3) = 0$

$x = 10$ (reject as width $= 15 - 2x$ and width $= 15 - 2 \times 10$ would be negative)

$x = 3$

The stationary value for the volume is found by substituting $x = 3$ into
$V = 4x^3 - 78x^2 + 360x$
$V = 4 \times 3^3 - 78 \times 3^2 + 360 \times 3$
$V = 486$

c To determine the nature of the stationary point:

Method 1

Find $\dfrac{\mathrm{d}^2V}{\mathrm{d}x^2} = 24x - 156$ and then substitute $x = 3$

This gives $\dfrac{\mathrm{d}^2V}{\mathrm{d}x^2} = 24 \times 3 - 156$ or –84 which is negative.

∴ $x = 3$ is a maximum point.

At $x = 3$, V has a maximum value which is 486 cm³.

Method 2

Now consider the gradient on either side of the point $x = 3$

Substituting $x = 2$ into

$\dfrac{\mathrm{d}V}{\mathrm{d}x} = 12x^2 - 156x + 360$ gives:

$\dfrac{\mathrm{d}V}{\mathrm{d}x} = 12(2)^2 - 156(2) + 360$ or 96 which is positive.

Substituting $x = 4$ into

$\dfrac{\mathrm{d}V}{\mathrm{d}x} = 12x^2 - 156x + 360$ gives:

$\dfrac{\mathrm{d}V}{\mathrm{d}x} = 12(4)^2 - 156(4) + 360$ or –72 which is negative.

Since the gradient changes sign from positive to negative as the values of x move along the curve from left to right, and pass through the critical value, the point is a maximum value.

At $x = 3$, V has a maximum value which is 486 cm³.

8 a Volume of cuboid = length × width × height

$$= 2x \times x \times y$$
$$= 2x^2 y$$

So, $2x^2 y = 576$

$$x^2 y = 288$$
$$y = \frac{288}{x^2}$$

b Area $A = 2 \times 2x \times x + 2 \times x \times y + 2 \times 2x \times y$

$$= 4x^2 + 2xy + 4xy$$
$$= 4x^2 + 6xy$$

Substituting $y = \frac{288}{x^2}$

$$A = 4x^2 + 6x \times \frac{288}{x^2}$$

$$A = 4x^2 + \frac{1728}{x} \text{ shown}$$

c Rewrite $A = 4x^2 + \frac{1728}{x}$ as:

$$A = 4x^2 + 1728x^{-1}$$

$$\frac{dA}{dx} = 8x - 1728x^{-2}$$

or $\frac{dA}{dx} = 8x - \frac{1728}{x^2}$

At a stationary point, $\frac{dA}{dx} = 0$

$$8x - \frac{1728}{x^2} = 0$$

$$8x^3 - 1728 = 0$$

$$x^3 = 216$$

$$x = 6$$

To show that this is a minimum value,

Method 1

Find $\frac{d^2 A}{dx^2}$

$$\frac{d^2 A}{dx^2} = 8 + 3456x^{-3} \text{ or}$$

$$\frac{d^2 A}{dx^2} = 8 + \frac{3456}{x^3}$$

Substituting $x = 6$ into $\frac{d^2 A}{dx^2}$ gives:

$$\frac{d^2 A}{dx^2} = 8 + \frac{3456}{6^3} \text{ or } 24$$

As this is positive, this is a minimum value.

Method 2

Now consider the gradient on either side of the point $x = 6$

Substituting $x = 5$ into $\frac{dA}{dx} = 8x - \frac{1728}{x^2}$ gives:

$\frac{dA}{dx} = 8(5) - \frac{1728}{5^2}$ or $-\frac{728}{25}$ which is negative.

Substituting $x = 7$ into $\frac{dA}{dx} = 8x - \frac{1728}{x^2}$ gives:

$\frac{dA}{dx} = 8(7) - \frac{1728}{7^2}$ or $\frac{1016}{49}$ which is positive.

Since the gradient changes sign from negative to positive as the values of x move along the curve from left to right, and pass through the critical value, the point $x = 6$ is a minimum value.

Substituting $x = 6$ into $A = 4x^2 + \frac{1728}{x}$ gives:

$$A = 4(6)^2 + \frac{1728}{6}$$

$$A = 432$$

Substituting $x = 6$ into $y = \frac{288}{x^2}$ gives the height of the cuboid

So, $y = 8$

The minimum value of A is 432 cm² which occurs when the dimensions are 12 cm by 6 cm by 8 cm.

9 a Arc length = $r\theta$

Arc $SRQ = \frac{x}{2} \times \pi$ or $\frac{\pi x}{2}$

Perimeter $PQRST = x + 2y + \frac{\pi x}{2}$

$$x + 2y + \frac{\pi x}{2} = 2$$

$$2x + 4y + \pi x = 4$$

$$4y = 4 - 2x - \pi x$$

$$y = 1 - \frac{1}{2}x - \frac{1}{4}\pi x$$

b Area of a sector $= \frac{1}{2}r^2\theta$

Area of sector $= \frac{1}{2}\left(\frac{1}{2}x\right)^2 \pi$ or $\frac{1}{8}\pi x^2$

Total area $A = xy + \frac{1}{8}\pi x^2$

Using $y = 1 - \frac{1}{2}x - \frac{1}{4}\pi x$,

Substituting for y gives:

$A = x\left(1 - \frac{1}{2}x - \frac{1}{4}\pi x\right) + \frac{1}{8}\pi x^2$

$A = x - \frac{1}{2}x^2 - \frac{1}{4}\pi x^2 + \frac{1}{8}\pi x^2$

$A = x - \frac{1}{2}x^2 - \frac{1}{8}\pi x^2$

c $\frac{dA}{dx} = 1 - x - \frac{1}{4}\pi x$

$\frac{d^2A}{dx^2} = -1 - \frac{1}{4}\pi$

d At a stationary point, $\frac{dA}{dx} = 0$

$1 - x - \frac{1}{4}\pi x = 0$

$4 - 4x - \pi x = 0$

$4x + \pi x = 4$

$x(4 + \pi) = 4$

$x = \frac{4}{4 + \pi}$

e Substituting $x = \frac{4}{4 + \pi}$ into $A = x - \frac{1}{2}x^2 - \frac{1}{8}\pi x^2$ gives:

$A = \frac{4}{4 + \pi} - \frac{1}{2}\left(\frac{4}{4 + \pi}\right)^2 - \frac{1}{8}\pi\left(\frac{4}{4 + \pi}\right)^2$

$A = \frac{4}{4 + \pi} - \frac{8}{(4 + \pi)^2} - \frac{2\pi}{(4 + \pi)^2}$

$A = \frac{4(4 + \pi)}{(4 + \pi)^2} - \frac{8}{(4 + \pi)^2} - \frac{2\pi}{(4 + \pi)^2}$

$A = \frac{4(4 + \pi) - 8 - 2\pi}{(4 + \pi)^2}$

$A = \frac{16 + 4\pi - 8 - 2\pi}{(4 + \pi)^2}$

$A = \frac{8 + 2\pi}{(4 + \pi)^2}$

$A = \frac{2(4 + \pi)}{(4 + \pi)^2}$

$A = \frac{2}{4 + \pi}$

To determine the nature of the stationary point:

Method 1

Looking at $\frac{d^2A}{dx^2} = -1 - \frac{1}{4}\pi$ which is negative shows that $x = \frac{4}{4 + \pi}$ is a maximum point.

The maximum value of A is $\frac{2}{4 + \pi}$ m^2

Method 2

Now consider the gradient on either side of the point $x = \frac{4}{4 + \pi}$ (which is approximately 0.560)

Substituting $x = 0$ into $\frac{dA}{dx} = 1 - x - \frac{1}{4}\pi x$ gives:

$\frac{dA}{dx} = 1 - 0 - \frac{1}{4}\pi(0)$ or 1 which is positive.

Substituting $x = 1$ into $\frac{dA}{dx} = 1 - x - \frac{1}{4}\pi x$ gives:

$\frac{dA}{dx} = 1 - 1 - \frac{1}{4}\pi(1)$ or $-\frac{1}{4}\pi$ which is negative.

Since the gradient changes sign from positive to negative as the values of x move along the curve from left to right, and pass through the critical value, the point $x = \frac{4}{4 + \pi}$ is a maximum value.

The maximum value of A is $\frac{2}{4 + \pi}$ m^2

10 a Arc length $= \pi r$

Perimeter of the window $= 2r + 2h + \pi r$

$5 = 2r + 2h + \pi r$

$2h = 5 - 2r - \pi r$

$h = \frac{5 - 2r - \pi r}{2}$

b Area of a sector $= \frac{1}{2}\pi r^2$

Area of the window $= 2r \times h + \frac{1}{2}\pi r^2$

$A = 2rh + \frac{1}{2}\pi r^2$

Subtituting for h gives:

$$A = 2r\left(\frac{5 - 2r - \pi r}{2}\right) + \frac{1}{2}\pi r^2$$

$$A = 5r - 2r^2 - \pi r^2 + \frac{1}{2}\pi r^2$$

$$A = 5r - 2r^2 - \frac{1}{2}\pi r^2$$

c $\dfrac{\mathrm{d}A}{\mathrm{d}r} = 5 - 4r - \pi r$

$$\frac{\mathrm{d}^2 A}{\mathrm{d}r^2} = -4 - \pi$$

d At a stationary value, $\dfrac{\mathrm{d}A}{\mathrm{d}r} = 0$

$$5 - 4r - \pi r = 0$$
$$4r + \pi r = 5$$
$$r(4 + \pi) = 5$$
$$r = \frac{5}{4 + \pi}$$

e Substituting $r = \dfrac{5}{4 + \pi}$ into $A = 5r - 2r^2 - \dfrac{1}{2}\pi r^2$ gives:

$$A = 5\left(\frac{5}{4 + \pi}\right) - 2\left(\frac{5}{4 + \pi}\right)^2 - \frac{1}{2}\pi\left(\frac{5}{4 + \pi}\right)^2$$

$$A = \frac{25}{4 + \pi} - \frac{50}{(4 + \pi)^2} - \frac{12.5\pi}{(4 + \pi)^2}$$

$$A = \frac{25(4 + \pi)}{(4 + \pi)^2} - \frac{50}{(4 + \pi)^2} - \frac{12.5\pi}{(4 + \pi)^2}$$

$$A = \frac{100 + 25\pi - 50 - 12.5\pi}{(4 + \pi)^2}$$

$$A = \frac{50 + 12.5\pi}{(4 + \pi)^2}$$

$$A = \frac{12.5(4 + \pi)}{(4 + \pi)^2}$$

$$A = \frac{12.5}{4 + \pi}$$

$$A = \frac{25}{8 + 2\pi}$$

To determine the nature of this stationary value:

Method 1

As $\dfrac{\mathrm{d}^2 A}{\mathrm{d}r^2} = -4 - \pi$ is a negative value, the stationary point is a maximum.

Method 2

Now consider the gradient on either side of the point $r = \dfrac{5}{4 + \pi}$ which is $0.700\ldots$

Substituting $r = 0.5$ into $\dfrac{\mathrm{d}A}{\mathrm{d}r} = 5 - 4r - \pi r$ gives:

$$\frac{\mathrm{d}A}{\mathrm{d}r} = 5 - 4(0.5) - \pi(0.5) \text{ or } 1.42\ldots \text{ which is positive.}$$

Substituting $r = 1$ into $\dfrac{\mathrm{d}A}{\mathrm{d}r} = 5 - 4r - \pi r$ gives:

$$\frac{\mathrm{d}A}{\mathrm{d}r} = 5 - 4(1) - \pi(1) \text{ or } -2.14\ldots \text{ which is negative.}$$

Since the gradient changes sign from positive to negative as the values of r move along the curve from left to right, and pass through the critical value, the stationary point is a maximum value.

So the maximum value of the area of the window is $\dfrac{25}{8 + 2\pi}$ m².

11 a Square perimeter $4x$ and area x^2

Circle circumference $2\pi \times r$ and area πr^2

$$4x + 2\pi r = 100 \ldots\ldots\ldots\ldots\ldots[1]$$

Total area $A = x^2 + \pi r^2 \ldots\ldots[2]$

From $[1]$, $2\pi r = 100 - 4x$

$$\pi r = 50 - 2x$$
$$r = \frac{50 - 2x}{\pi}$$

b Using $[2]$: $A = x^2 + \pi r^2$

Substituting for r gives:

$$A = x^2 + \pi\left(\frac{50 - 2x}{\pi}\right)^2$$

$$A = x^2 + \frac{\pi(50 - 2x)(50 - 2x)}{\pi^2}$$

$$A = \frac{\pi x^2}{\pi} + \frac{2500 - 200x + 4x^2}{\pi}$$

$$A = \frac{\pi x^2 + 2500 - 200x + 4x^2}{\pi}$$

$$A = \frac{(\pi + 4)x^2 - 200x + 2500}{\pi} \text{ shown}$$

c At a stationary value, $\dfrac{\mathrm{d}A}{\mathrm{d}x} = 0$

$$A = \frac{1}{\pi}[(\pi + 4)x^2 - 200x + 2500]$$

$$\frac{\mathrm{d}A}{\mathrm{d}x} = \frac{1}{\pi}[2(\pi + 4)x - 200]$$

$$\frac{1}{\pi}[2(\pi + 4)x - 200] = 0$$

$\dfrac{1}{\pi}$ cannot be 0 so $2(\pi + 4)x - 200 = 0$

$$\therefore\ 2(\pi + 4)x = 200$$
$$(\pi + 4)x = 100$$

$$x = \frac{100}{\pi + 4} \text{ or } 14.002....$$

> If the answer does not ask for exact values, then you can work with decimal value approximations to at least 4 significant figures.

There is a stationary point at $x = 14.002$

Substituting $x = 14.002$ into A gives:

$$A = \frac{(\pi + 4)x^2 - 200x + 2500}{\pi}$$

$$A = \frac{(\pi + 4) \times 14.002^2 - 200 \times 14.002 + 2500}{\pi}$$

$$A = 350.061...$$

To determine the nature of this stationary value:

Method 1

Substitute $x = 14.002$ into $\dfrac{\mathrm{d}^2A}{\mathrm{d}x^2}$:

$$\frac{\mathrm{d}A}{\mathrm{d}x} = \frac{1}{\pi}[2(\pi + 4)x - 200]$$

$$\frac{\mathrm{d}A}{\mathrm{d}x} = \frac{2(\pi + 4)x}{\pi} - \frac{200}{\pi}$$

$$\frac{\mathrm{d}^2A}{\mathrm{d}x^2} = \frac{2(\pi + 4)}{\pi} \text{ which is positive.}$$

So $x = 14.0$ cm and $A = 350$ cm^2 (to 3 significant figures) is a minimum point.

Method 2

Now consider the gradient on either side of the point $x = 14.002$.

Substituting $x = 14$ into

$\dfrac{\mathrm{d}A}{\mathrm{d}x} = \dfrac{2(\pi + 4)x}{\pi} - \dfrac{200}{\pi}$ gives:

$$\frac{\mathrm{d}A}{\mathrm{d}x} = \frac{2(\pi + 4) \times 14}{\pi} - \frac{200}{\pi}$$

or $-0.0112...$ which is negative.

Substituting $x = 15$ into

$\dfrac{\mathrm{d}A}{\mathrm{d}x} = \dfrac{2(\pi + 4)x}{\pi} - \dfrac{200}{\pi}$ gives:

$$\frac{\mathrm{d}A}{\mathrm{d}x} = \frac{2(\pi + 4) \times 15}{\pi} - \frac{200}{\pi}$$

or $4.535...$ which is positive.

Since the gradient changes sign from negative to positive as the values of x move along the curve from left to right, and pass through the critical value, $x = 14.002$ is a minimum point.

So $x = 14.0$ cm and $A = 350$ cm^2 (to 3 significant figures) is a minimum point.

12 a Volume of a cylinder $= \pi r^2 h$

$$\pi r^2 h = 432\pi$$

$$h = \frac{432\pi}{\pi r^2}$$

$$h = \frac{432}{r^2}$$

b Surface area of a solid cylinder $A = 2\pi r^2 + 2\pi rh$

Substituting for h gives:

$$A = 2\pi r^2 + 2\pi r \times \left(\frac{432}{r^2}\right)$$

$$A = 2\pi r^2 + \frac{864\pi}{r} \text{ shown}$$

c There is a stationary value of A when $\dfrac{\mathrm{d}A}{\mathrm{d}r} = 0$

$$A = 2\pi r^2 + \frac{864\pi}{r} \text{ or } A = 2\pi r^2 + 864\pi r^{-1}$$

$$\frac{\mathrm{d}A}{\mathrm{d}r} = 4\pi r - 864\pi r^{-2}$$

$$\frac{\mathrm{d}A}{\mathrm{d}r} = 4\pi r - \frac{864\pi}{r^2}$$

So,

$$4\pi r - \frac{864\pi}{r^2} = 0$$

$$4\pi r = \frac{864\pi}{r^2}$$

$$4\pi r^3 = 864\pi$$

$$r^3 = \frac{864}{4} \text{ or } r^3 = 216$$

$$r = 6$$

There is a stationary value of A when $r = 6$.

d Substituting $r = 6$ into $A = 2\pi r^2 + \frac{864\pi}{r}$ gives:

$$A = 2\pi \times 6^2 + \frac{864\pi}{6} \text{ or } 216\pi \text{ cm}^2$$

The nature of this stationary point is found by:

Method 1

Substituting $x = 6$ into $\frac{d^2A}{dr^2}$:

$$\frac{dA}{dr} = 4\pi r - 864\pi r^{-2}$$

$$\frac{d^2A}{dr^2} = 4\pi + 1728\pi r^{-3}$$

$$\frac{d^2A}{dr^2} = 4\pi + \frac{1728}{r^3}$$

Substituting for r gives:

$$\frac{d^2A}{dr^2} = 4\pi + \frac{1728}{216} \text{ or } 20.566\ldots$$

As this is a positive value, the stationary point is a minimum point.

So, there is a minimum value for A which is 216π cm^2 when $r = 6$ cm.

Method 2

Now consider the gradient on either side of the point $r = 6$.

Substituting $r = 5$ into $\frac{dA}{dr} = 4\pi r - \frac{864\pi}{r^2}$ gives:

$$\frac{dA}{dr} = 4\pi(5) - \frac{864\pi}{5^2} \text{ or } -\frac{364\pi}{25} \text{ which is}$$
negative.

Substituting $r = 7$ into $\frac{dA}{dr} = 4\pi r - \frac{864\pi}{r^2}$ gives:

$$\frac{dA}{dr} = 4\pi(7) - \frac{864\pi}{7^2} \text{ or } \frac{508\pi}{49} \text{ which is}$$
positive.

Since the gradient changes sign from negative to positive as the values of r move along the curve from left to right, and pass through the critical value, so, there is a minimum value for A which is 216π cm^2 when $r = 6$ cm.

13 a Volume of a prism = area of cross-section × length

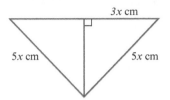

The height of this isosceles triangle can be found using Pythagoras or by considering a 3, 4, 5 triangle.

$$\text{Height} = \sqrt{(5x)^2 - (3x)^2}$$

$$= \pm\sqrt{16x^2} \text{ (reject negative value as length cannot be negative).}$$

$$\text{Height} = 4x$$

Area of cross-section = area of the $\triangle$

$$= \frac{1}{2} \times \text{base} \times \text{perpendicular height}$$

$$= \frac{1}{2} \times 6x \times 4x \text{ or } 12x^2$$

Volume of prism $V = 12x^2 \times y$

Note the prism is open.

Total surface area $= 2 \times 12x^2 + 5x \times y + 5x \times y$

$$= 24x^2 + 10xy$$

$$\therefore 500 = 24x^2 + 10xy$$

$$10xy = 500 - 24x^2$$

$$y = \frac{500 - 24x^2}{10x}$$

b Volume of prism $V = 12x^2 \times y$

$$V = 12x^2 \times \left(\frac{500 - 24x^2}{10x}\right)$$

$$V = \frac{6000x^2}{10x} - \frac{288x^4}{10x}$$

$$V = 600x - \frac{144}{5}x^3 \text{ shown}$$

c There is a stationary value of V when $\dfrac{\mathrm{d}V}{\mathrm{d}x} = 0$

$$V = 600x - \frac{144}{5}x^3$$

$$\frac{\mathrm{d}V}{\mathrm{d}x} = 600 - 86.4x^2$$

$$0 = 600 - 86.4x^2$$

$$86.4x^2 = 600$$

$$x^2 = \frac{600}{86.4}$$

$$x = \frac{5\sqrt{10}}{6}$$

There is a stationary point at $x = \dfrac{5\sqrt{10}}{6}$

d To determine the nature of this stationary point, substitute $x = \dfrac{5\sqrt{10}}{6}$ into $\dfrac{\mathrm{d}^2V}{\mathrm{d}x^2}$:

$$\frac{\mathrm{d}^2V}{\mathrm{d}x^2} = -172.8x$$

$$\frac{\mathrm{d}^2V}{\mathrm{d}x^2} = -172.8 \times \frac{5\sqrt{10}}{6} \text{ or } -455.367\ldots$$

As this is a negative value, this a maximum point.

14 a Total surface area = surface area of half the sphere + curved surface area of the cylinder + circular end of the cylinder

$$\text{Total surface area} = \frac{1}{2} \times 4\pi \times r^2 + 2\pi rh + \pi r^2$$

$$320\pi = 3\pi r^2 + 2\pi rh$$

$$320 = 3r^2 + 2rh$$

$$2rh = 320 - 3r^2$$

$$h = \frac{160}{r} - \frac{3}{2}r$$

b Volume required = $\dfrac{1}{2}$ volume of a sphere + volume of a cylinder

$$\text{Volume } V = \frac{1}{2} \times \frac{4}{3}\pi r^3 + \pi r^2 h$$

$$V = \frac{2\pi r^3}{3} + \pi r^2 \times \left(\frac{160}{r} - \frac{3}{2}r\right)$$

$$V = \frac{2\pi r^3}{3} + 160\pi r - \frac{3\pi r^3}{2}$$

$$V = \frac{4\pi r^3}{6} + 160\pi r - \frac{9\pi r^3}{6}$$

$$V = 160\pi r - \frac{5}{6}\pi r^3 \text{ shown}$$

c There is a stationary value of V when $\dfrac{\mathrm{d}V}{\mathrm{d}r} = 0$

$$\frac{\mathrm{d}V}{\mathrm{d}r} = 160\pi - \frac{5}{2}\pi r^2$$

$$160\pi - \frac{5}{2}\pi r^2 = 0$$

$$160\pi = \frac{5}{2}\pi r^2$$

$$r^2 = 64$$

$r = \pm 8$ (reject negative as length cannot be negative).

$$r = 8$$

> Read the question carefully, as in this case you are not asked to find the maximum volume.

To determine the nature of the stationary point at $r = 8$, substitute $r = 8$ into $\dfrac{\mathrm{d}^2V}{\mathrm{d}r^2}$:

$$\frac{\mathrm{d}V}{\mathrm{d}r} = 160\pi - \frac{5}{2}\pi r^2$$

$$\frac{\mathrm{d}^2V}{\mathrm{d}r^2} = -5\pi r$$

When $r = 8$, $\dfrac{\mathrm{d}^2V}{\mathrm{d}r^2} = -40\pi$ which is negative.

So the stationary point gives the maximum volume.

15 a

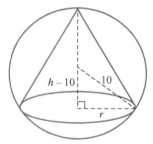

Looking at the diagram, and using Pythagoras:

$$(h - 10)^2 + r^2 = 10^2$$

$$h^2 - 20h + 100 + r^2 = 100$$

$$h^2 - 20h + r^2 = 0$$

$$r^2 = 20h - h^2$$

$$r = \sqrt{20h - h^2}$$

b Volume of a cone $= \frac{1}{3}\pi r^2 h$

$$V = \frac{1}{3}\pi \times \left(\sqrt{20h - h^2}\right)^2 \times h$$

$$V = \frac{1}{3}\pi h(20h - h^2)$$

$$V = \frac{1}{3}\pi h^2(20 - h) \text{ shown.}$$

c There is a stationary value for V
when $\frac{dV}{dh} = 0$

$$V = \frac{1}{3}\pi h^2(20 - h)$$

$$V = \frac{20\pi h^2}{3} - \frac{1}{3}\pi h^3$$

$$\frac{dV}{dh} = \frac{40\pi h}{3} - \pi h^2$$

So,

$$\frac{40\pi h}{3} - \pi h^2 = 0$$

$$h\left(\frac{40\pi}{3} - \pi h\right) = 0$$

Either $h = 0$ reject or $\frac{40\pi}{3} - \pi h = 0$

$$\frac{40\pi}{3} = \pi h$$

$$h = \frac{40}{3} \text{ or } 13\frac{1}{3}$$

There is a stationary value at $h = 13\frac{1}{3}$

Substitute into $V = \frac{1}{3}\pi h^2(20 - h)$ to find the value of V at this stationary point.

$$V = \frac{1}{3}\pi\left(\frac{40}{3}\right)^2\left(20 - \frac{40}{3}\right)$$

$$V = 1241.12\ldots$$

d To determine the nature of this stationary value,

Method 1

Substitute $h = 13\frac{1}{3}$ into $\frac{d^2V}{dh^2}$:

$$\frac{dV}{dh} = \frac{40\pi h}{3} - \pi h^2$$

$$\frac{d^2V}{dh^2} = \frac{40\pi}{3} - 2\pi h$$

Substituting $h = \frac{40}{3}$ into $\frac{d^2V}{dh^2}$ gives:

$$\frac{40\pi}{3} - 2\pi \times \frac{40}{3} \text{ or } -\frac{40\pi}{3} \text{ which is negative.}$$

So this suggests V is a maximum value.

Method 2

Now consider the gradient on either side of the point $h = \frac{40}{3}$

Substituting $x = 13$ into $\frac{dV}{dh} = \frac{40\pi h}{3} - \pi h^2$ gives:

$$\frac{dV}{dh} = \frac{40\pi(13)}{3} - \pi(13)^2$$

or $\frac{13\pi}{3}$ which is positive.

Substituting $x = 14$ into $\frac{dV}{dh} = \frac{40\pi h}{3} - \pi h^2$ gives:

$$\frac{dV}{dh} = \frac{40\pi(14)}{3} - \pi(14)^2$$

or $-\frac{28\pi}{3}$ which is negative.

Since the gradient changes sign from positive to negative as the values of h move along the curve from left to right, and pass through the critical value, the point is a maximum value.

The maximum value for V is 1241 cm^3 (to 4 significant figures) when $h = 13\frac{1}{3}$ cm.

EXERCISE 8D

1 $y = 3x - 2x^3$

$\dfrac{dy}{dx} = 3 - 6x^2$ and $\dfrac{dx}{dt} = 0.015$

When $x = 2$, $\dfrac{dy}{dx} = 3 - 6(2)^2$ or -21

You are required to find $\dfrac{dy}{dt}$

Using the chain rule:

$\dfrac{dy}{dt} = \dfrac{dy}{dx} \times \dfrac{dx}{dt}$

$\dfrac{dy}{dt} = -21 \times 0.015$

$\quad\ = -0.315$

Solution: -0.315 units per second.

The y-coordinate is decreasing since $\dfrac{dy}{dt}$ is a negative value.

2 $y = \sqrt{1 + 2x}$

Rewrite as: $y = (1 + 2x)^{\frac{1}{2}}$

$\dfrac{dy}{dx} = \dfrac{1}{2} \times (1 + 2x)^{-\frac{1}{2}} \times 2$ or $(1 + 2x)^{-\frac{1}{2}}$

and $\dfrac{dx}{dt} = 0.01$

When $x = 4$, $\dfrac{dy}{dx} = (1 + 2 \times 4)^{-\frac{1}{2}}$ or $\dfrac{1}{3}$

You are required to find $\dfrac{dy}{dt}$

Using the chain rule:

$\dfrac{dy}{dt} = \dfrac{dy}{dx} \times \dfrac{dx}{dt}$

$\dfrac{dy}{dt} = \dfrac{1}{3} \times 0.01$

Solution: $\dfrac{1}{300}$ units per second

3 $y = \dfrac{8}{x^2 - 2}$

Rewrite as: $y = 8(x^2 - 2)^{-1}$

$\dfrac{dy}{dx} = -1 \times 8(x^2 - 2)^{-2} \times 2x$ or $16x(x^2 - 2)^{-2}$

and $\dfrac{dx}{dt} = 0.005$

When $x = 2$, $\dfrac{dy}{dx} = -16 \times 2(2^2 - 2)^{-2}$ or -8

You are required to find $\dfrac{dy}{dt}$

Using the chain rule:

$\dfrac{dy}{dt} = \dfrac{dy}{dx} \times \dfrac{dx}{dt}$

$\dfrac{dy}{dt} = -8 \times 0.005$

Solution: -0.04 units per second

4 $y = 3\sqrt{x} - \dfrac{5}{\sqrt{x}}$

Rewrite as: $y = 3x^{\frac{1}{2}} - 5x^{-\frac{1}{2}}$

$\dfrac{dy}{dx} = \dfrac{3}{2}x^{-\frac{1}{2}} + \dfrac{5}{2}x^{-\frac{3}{2}}$ or $\dfrac{3}{2\sqrt{x}} + \dfrac{5}{2\sqrt{x^3}}$

and $\dfrac{dx}{dt} = 0.02$

When $x = 1$, $\dfrac{dy}{dx} = \dfrac{3}{2\sqrt{1}} + \dfrac{5}{2\sqrt{1^3}}$ or 4

You are required to find $\dfrac{dy}{dt}$

Using the chain rule:

$\dfrac{dy}{dt} = \dfrac{dy}{dx} \times \dfrac{dx}{dt}$

$\dfrac{dy}{dt} = 4 \times 0.02$

Solution: 0.08 units per second

5 $y = 3x + \dfrac{1}{\sqrt{x}}$

Rewrite as: $y = 3x + x^{-\frac{1}{2}}$

$\dfrac{dy}{dx} = 3 - \dfrac{1}{2}x^{-\frac{3}{2}}$ or $3 - \dfrac{1}{2\sqrt{x^3}}$

and $\dfrac{dx}{dt} = 0.5$

When $x = 1$, $\dfrac{dy}{dx} = 3 - \dfrac{1}{2\sqrt{1^3}}$ or $\dfrac{5}{2}$

You are required to find $\dfrac{dy}{dt}$

Using the chain rule:

$$\frac{dy}{dt} = \frac{dy}{dx} \times \frac{dx}{dt}$$

$$\frac{dy}{dt} = \frac{5}{2} \times 0.5$$

Sloution: 1.25 units per second

6 $y = \frac{2}{x} + 5x$

Rewrite as: $y = 2x^{-1} + 5x$

$$\frac{dy}{dx} = -2x^{-2} + 5 \text{ or } -\frac{2}{x^2} + 5$$

and $\frac{dx}{dt} = 0.02$

When $x = 2$, $\frac{dy}{dx} = -\frac{2}{2^2} + 5$ or $\frac{9}{2}$

You are required to find $\frac{dy}{dt}$

Using the chain rule:

$$\frac{dy}{dt} = \frac{dy}{dx} \times \frac{dx}{dt}$$

$$\frac{dy}{dt} = \frac{9}{2} \times 0.02$$

Solution: 0.09 units per second. The y-coordinate is increasing since $\frac{dy}{dt}$ is a positive value.

7 $y = \frac{8}{7 - 2x}$

Rewrite as: $y = 8(7 - 2x)^{-1}$

$$\frac{dy}{dx} = -1 \times 8(7 - 2x)^{-2} \times -2 \text{ or } 16\,(7 - 2x)^{-2}$$

and $\frac{dx}{dt} = 0.125$ $\frac{dy}{dt} = 0.08$

Using the chain rule:

$$\frac{dy}{dt} = \frac{dy}{dx} \times \frac{dx}{dt}$$

$$0.08 = \frac{dy}{dx} \times 0.125$$

$$\frac{dy}{dx} = 0.08 \div 0.125 \text{ or } 0.64$$

$16(7 - 2x)^{-2} = 0.64$

$$\frac{16}{(7 - 2x)^2} = 0.64$$

$$16 = 0.64(7 - 2x)^2$$

$$(7 - 2x)^2 = 25$$

$$7 - 2x = \pm 5$$

If $7 - 2x = 5$ then $x = 1$

If $7 - 2x = -5$ then $x = 6$

The possible x-coordinates of P are $x = 1$ and $x = 6$

8 $y = \sqrt[3]{2x^2 - 3}$

Rewrite as: $(2x^2 - 3)^{\frac{1}{3}}$

$$\frac{dy}{dx} = \frac{1}{3} \times (2x^2 - 3)^{-\frac{2}{3}} \times 4x \text{ or } \frac{4x}{3(2x^2 - 3)^{\frac{2}{3}}}$$

and $\frac{dx}{dt} = 0.012$

When $x = 1$, $\frac{dy}{dx} = \frac{4 \times 1}{3(2 \times 1^2 - 3)^{\frac{2}{3}}}$ or $\frac{4}{3}$

You are required to find $\frac{dy}{dt}$

Using the chain rule:

$$\frac{dy}{dt} = \frac{dy}{dx} \times \frac{dx}{dt}$$

$$\frac{dy}{dt} = \frac{4}{3} \times 0.012$$

Solution: 0.016 units per second

9 $y = x^3 - 5x^2 + 5x$

$\dfrac{dy}{dx} = 3x^2 - 10x + 5$

Let $\dfrac{dx}{dt} = k$ so $\dfrac{dy}{dt} = 2k$

Using the chain rule:

$\dfrac{dy}{dt} = \dfrac{dy}{dx} \times \dfrac{dx}{dt}$

$2k = \dfrac{dy}{dx} \times k$

$\dfrac{dy}{dx} = 2$

$3x^2 - 10x + 5 = 2$

$3x^2 - 10x + 3 = 0$

$(3x - 1)(x - 3) = 0$

Either $3x - 1 = 0$ $\quad \therefore\ x = \dfrac{1}{3}$

Or $x - 3 = 0$ $\quad \therefore\ x = 3$

Solution: $x = \dfrac{1}{3}$ and $x = 3$

EXERCISE 8E

1 Area of a circle $A = \pi r^2$

$\dfrac{dA}{dr} = 2\pi r$

when $r = 4$, $\dfrac{dA}{dr} = 2\pi \times 4$ or 8π

$\dfrac{dr}{dt} = 0.1$

We need to find $\dfrac{dA}{dt}$

Using the chain rule:

$\dfrac{dA}{dt} = \dfrac{dA}{dr} \times \dfrac{dr}{dt}$

$\dfrac{dA}{dt} = 8\pi \times 0.1$

The rate of increase of A when $r = 4$ is $\dfrac{4}{5}\pi$ cm² s⁻¹

2 Volume of a sphere $V = \dfrac{4}{3}\pi r^3$

$V = 36\pi$ so:

$\dfrac{4}{3}\pi r^3 = 36\pi$

$r^3 = 27$

$r = 3$

$\dfrac{dV}{dr} = 4\pi r^2$

As $r = 3$, $\dfrac{dV}{dr} = 4\pi(3)^2$ or 36π

$\dfrac{dr}{dt} = \dfrac{1}{2\pi}$

We need to find $\dfrac{dV}{dt}$

Using the chain rule:

$\dfrac{dV}{dt} = \dfrac{dV}{dr} \times \dfrac{dr}{dt}$

$\dfrac{dV}{dt} = 36\pi \times \dfrac{1}{2\pi}$

The rate of increase of the volume when $V = 36\pi$ is 18 cm³ s⁻¹

3 Volume of a cone $= \dfrac{1}{3}\pi r^2 h$

As the height is fixed at 30 cm

$V = \dfrac{1}{3}\pi r^2 \times 30$ or $V = 10\pi r^2$

$\dfrac{dV}{dr} = 20\pi r$

And as $r = 5$, $\dfrac{dV}{dr} = 20\pi \times 5$ or 100π

$\dfrac{dr}{dt} = 0.01$

We need to find $\dfrac{dV}{dt}$

Using the chain rule:

$$\frac{\mathrm{d}V}{\mathrm{d}t} = \frac{\mathrm{d}V}{\mathrm{d}r} \times \frac{\mathrm{d}r}{\mathrm{d}t}$$

$$\frac{\mathrm{d}V}{\mathrm{d}t} = 100\pi \times 0.01$$

The rate of change of the volume when $r = 5$ is π cm^3 s^{-1}

4 Area of a square $= x^2$

If $A = 25$, then $x^2 = 25$ so $x = 5$

$$\frac{\mathrm{d}A}{\mathrm{d}x} = 2x \text{ or } 2 \times 5 = 10$$

$$\frac{\mathrm{d}A}{\mathrm{d}t} = 0.03$$

We need to find $\dfrac{\mathrm{d}x}{\mathrm{d}t}$

Using the chain rule:

$$\frac{\mathrm{d}A}{\mathrm{d}t} = \frac{\mathrm{d}A}{\mathrm{d}x} \times \frac{\mathrm{d}x}{\mathrm{d}t}$$

$$0.03 = 10 \times \frac{\mathrm{d}x}{\mathrm{d}t}$$

$$\frac{\mathrm{d}x}{\mathrm{d}t} = 0.03 \div 10$$

The rate of increase of x when $A = 25$ is 0.003 cm s^{-1}

5 Volume of a cube $= x^3$

If $V = 8$ then $x^3 = 8$ so $x = 2$

$$\frac{\mathrm{d}V}{\mathrm{d}x} = 3x^2$$

When $x = 2$, $\dfrac{\mathrm{d}V}{\mathrm{d}x} = 3 \times 2^2$ or 12

$$\frac{\mathrm{d}V}{\mathrm{d}t} = 1.5$$

We need to find $\dfrac{\mathrm{d}x}{\mathrm{d}t}$

Using the chain rule:

$$\frac{\mathrm{d}V}{\mathrm{d}t} = \frac{\mathrm{d}V}{\mathrm{d}x} \times \frac{\mathrm{d}x}{\mathrm{d}t}$$

$$1.5 = 12 \times \frac{\mathrm{d}x}{\mathrm{d}t}$$

$$\frac{\mathrm{d}x}{\mathrm{d}t} = 1.5 \div 12 \text{ or } 0.125$$

The rate of increase of x when $V = 8$ is 0.125 cm s^{-1}

6 Volume of a cuboid $= x \times x \times 4x$ or $4x^3$

$$\frac{\mathrm{d}V}{\mathrm{d}x} = 12x^2$$

As $x = 2$, $\dfrac{\mathrm{d}V}{\mathrm{d}x} = 12 \times 2^2$ or 48

$$\frac{\mathrm{d}V}{\mathrm{d}t} = 0.15$$

We need to find $\dfrac{\mathrm{d}x}{\mathrm{d}t}$

Using the chain rule:

$$\frac{\mathrm{d}V}{\mathrm{d}t} = \frac{\mathrm{d}V}{\mathrm{d}x} \times \frac{\mathrm{d}x}{\mathrm{d}t}$$

$$0.15 = 48 \times \frac{\mathrm{d}x}{\mathrm{d}t}$$

$$\frac{\mathrm{d}x}{\mathrm{d}t} = 0.15 \div 48$$

$$= \frac{1}{320}$$

The rate of increase of x when $x = 2$ is $\dfrac{1}{320}$ cm s^{-1}

7 $A = 2\pi r^2 + \dfrac{400\pi}{r}$

Rewrite as $A = 2\pi r^2 + 400\pi r^{-1}$

$$\frac{\mathrm{d}A}{\mathrm{d}r} = 4\pi r - 400\pi r^{-2} \text{ or } 4\pi r - \frac{400\pi}{r^2}$$

$$\frac{\mathrm{d}A}{\mathrm{d}r} = 4\pi \times 10 - \frac{400\pi}{10^2} \text{ or } 36\pi$$

$$\frac{\mathrm{d}r}{\mathrm{d}t} = 0.25$$

We need to find $\dfrac{\mathrm{d}A}{\mathrm{d}t}$

Using the chain rule

$$\frac{\mathrm{d}A}{\mathrm{d}t} = \frac{\mathrm{d}A}{\mathrm{d}r} \times \frac{\mathrm{d}r}{\mathrm{d}t}$$

$$\frac{\mathrm{d}A}{\mathrm{d}t} = 36\pi \times 0.25$$

$$= 9\pi$$

The rate of change of A when $r = 10$ is 9π cm^2 s^{-1}

8 a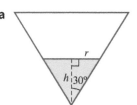

Volume of prism = cross-sectional area × length

The cross-sectional area is found using trigonometry.

$$\tan 30° = \frac{r}{h}$$

$$r = h \times \tan 30°$$

$$r = \frac{h\sqrt{3}}{3}$$

The cross-sectional area is a triangle.

The area of a triangle

$$= \frac{1}{2} \times \text{base} \times \text{perpendicular height}$$

Cross-sectional area $= \frac{1}{2} \times 2r \times h$

Substituting for r gives:

Cross-sectional area $= \frac{1}{2} \times 2 \times \frac{h\sqrt{3}}{3} \times h$

Volume of water $V = \frac{1}{2} \times 2 \times \frac{h\sqrt{3}}{3} \times h \times 120$

$$V = 40\sqrt{3}\ h^2 \text{ shown}$$

b $\dfrac{\mathrm{d}V}{\mathrm{d}t} = 24$

$$V = 40\sqrt{3}\ h^2$$

$$\frac{\mathrm{d}V}{\mathrm{d}h} = 80\sqrt{3}h$$

As $h = 12$, $\dfrac{\mathrm{d}V}{\mathrm{d}h} = 80\sqrt{3} \times 12$ or $960\sqrt{3}$

We need to find $\dfrac{\mathrm{d}h}{\mathrm{d}t}$

Using the chain rule:

$$\frac{\mathrm{d}V}{\mathrm{d}t} = \frac{\mathrm{d}V}{\mathrm{d}h} \times \frac{\mathrm{d}h}{\mathrm{d}t}$$

$$24 = 960\sqrt{3} \times \frac{\mathrm{d}h}{\mathrm{d}t}$$

$$\frac{\mathrm{d}h}{\mathrm{d}t} = 24 \div 960\sqrt{3} \text{ or } \frac{1}{40\sqrt{3}} \text{ or } \frac{\sqrt{3}}{120}$$

The rate of change of h when $h = 12$

is $\dfrac{\sqrt{3}}{120}$ cm s^{-1}

9 a $V = 5\pi h^2 - \dfrac{1}{3}\pi h^3$

$$\frac{\mathrm{d}V}{\mathrm{d}h} = 10\pi h - \pi h^2$$

When $h = 1$, $\dfrac{\mathrm{d}V}{\mathrm{d}h} = 10\pi \times 1 - \pi \times 1^2$ or 9π

$$\frac{\mathrm{d}V}{\mathrm{d}t} = 3\pi$$

We need to find $\dfrac{\mathrm{d}h}{\mathrm{d}t}$

Using the chain rule:

$$\frac{\mathrm{d}V}{\mathrm{d}t} = \frac{\mathrm{d}V}{\mathrm{d}h} \times \frac{\mathrm{d}h}{\mathrm{d}t}$$

$$3\pi = 9\pi \times \frac{\mathrm{d}h}{\mathrm{d}t}$$

$$\frac{\mathrm{d}h}{\mathrm{d}t} = 3\pi \div 9\pi \text{ or } \frac{1}{3}$$

The rate of change of h when $h = 1$ is $\dfrac{1}{3}$ cm s^{-1}

b When $h = 3$, $\dfrac{\mathrm{d}V}{\mathrm{d}h} = 10\pi h - \pi h^2$ is:

$$\frac{\mathrm{d}V}{\mathrm{d}h} = 10\pi \times 3 - \pi \times 3^2 \text{ or } 21\pi$$

$$\frac{\mathrm{d}V}{\mathrm{d}t} = \frac{\mathrm{d}V}{\mathrm{d}h} \times \frac{\mathrm{d}h}{\mathrm{d}t}$$

$$3\pi = 21\pi \times \frac{\mathrm{d}h}{\mathrm{d}t}$$

$$\frac{\mathrm{d}h}{\mathrm{d}t} = 3\pi \div 21\pi \text{ or } \frac{1}{7}$$

The rate of change of h when $h = 3$ is $\dfrac{1}{7}$ cm s^{-1}

10 a

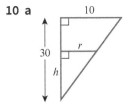

From the diagram, it can be seen that there are two similar triangles.

So, $\dfrac{r}{h} = \dfrac{10}{30}$

$$r = \frac{h}{3}$$

As the volume of a cone $(V) = \frac{1}{3}\pi r^2 h$

Substituting for r gives:

$$V = \frac{1}{3}\pi \left(\frac{h}{3}\right)^2 \times h$$

$$V = \frac{1}{27}\pi h^3 \text{ shown}$$

b $\quad V = \frac{1}{27}\pi h^3$

$$\frac{dV}{dh} = \frac{1}{9}\pi h^2$$

When $h = 20$,

$$\frac{dV}{dh} = \frac{1}{9}\pi \times 20^2 \text{ or } \frac{400\pi}{9}$$

We are told that the rate that water leaks out of the cone $= 4 \text{ cm}^3 \text{ s}^{-1}$

So, $\dfrac{dV}{dt} = -4$

We need to find $\dfrac{dh}{dt}$

Using the chain rule:

$$\frac{dV}{dt} = \frac{dV}{dh} \times \frac{dh}{dt}$$

$$-4 = \frac{400\pi}{9} \times \frac{dh}{dt}$$

$$\frac{dh}{dt} = -4 \div \frac{400\pi}{9} \text{ or } -\frac{9}{100\pi} \text{ cm s}^{-1}$$

The rate of change of h when $h = 20$ is

$-\dfrac{9}{100\pi}$ cm s^{-1}

11 Circumference of a circle $C = 2\pi r$

$C = 8\pi$ so $2\pi r = 8$

$\therefore r = 4$

$\dfrac{dr}{dt} = 2\sqrt{r}$ At $r = 4$, $\dfrac{dr}{dt} = 2\sqrt{4}$ or 4

Area of a circle is $A = \pi r^2$

$$\frac{dA}{dr} = 2\pi r$$

At $r = 4$, $\dfrac{dA}{dr} = 2\pi \times 4$ or 8π

We need to find $\dfrac{dA}{dt}$

Using the chain rule:

$$\frac{dA}{dt} = \frac{dA}{dr} \times \frac{dr}{dt}$$

$$\frac{dA}{dt} = 8\pi \times 4 \text{ or } 32\pi$$

The rate at which the area is increasing when the circumference is 8π cm is 32π cm^2 s^{-1}

12 a After 8 seconds the area of the patch is

$8 \times 5 = 40 \text{ cm}^2$

Area of a circle is $A = \pi r^2$

$$r = \sqrt{\frac{A}{\pi}}$$

So, $r = \sqrt{\dfrac{40}{\pi}}$ or $2\sqrt{\dfrac{10}{\pi}}$ cm

Radius after 8 seconds is $2\sqrt{\dfrac{10}{\pi}}$ cm

b $\dfrac{dA}{dr} = 2\pi r$ at 8 seconds

$$\frac{dA}{dr} = 2\pi \times 2\sqrt{\frac{10}{\pi}} \text{ or } 4\pi\sqrt{\frac{10}{\pi}}$$

$$\frac{dA}{dt} = 5$$

We need to find $\dfrac{dr}{dt}$

Using the chain rule:

$$\frac{dA}{dt} = \frac{dA}{dr} \times \frac{dr}{dt}$$

$$5 = 4\pi\sqrt{\frac{10}{\pi}} \times \frac{dr}{dt}$$

$$\frac{dr}{dt} = 5 \div 4\pi\sqrt{\frac{10}{\pi}}$$

$$= \frac{5}{4\pi\sqrt{\dfrac{10}{\pi}}}$$

$$= \frac{5\sqrt{\dfrac{\pi}{10}}}{4\pi\sqrt{\dfrac{10}{\pi}} \times \sqrt{\dfrac{\pi}{10}}}$$

$$= \frac{5\sqrt{\dfrac{\pi}{10}}}{4\pi}$$

The rate of increase of the radius after 8 seconds is $\dfrac{5}{4\pi}\sqrt{\dfrac{\pi}{10}}$ cm s^{-1}

13 a Volume of a cylinder $= \pi r^2 h$

Volume of the cylinder $= \pi \times 8^2 \times 25$

$= 1600\pi$ cm^3

If 1600π cm^3 is transferred in 40 seconds, the rate of transfer is:

$1600\pi \div 40$ or 40π cm^3 s^{-1}

Rate of transfer $\dfrac{\mathrm{d}V}{\mathrm{d}t} = 40\pi$ cm^3 s^{-1}

b i We need to find $\dfrac{\mathrm{d}h}{\mathrm{d}t}$

The diagram shows the cross-section of the cone, it is made of two similar triangles: one with the cone completely full and the other when the cone has a water height 10 cm.

We need to find the relationship between the radius and the height at any instant in time, since both are changing.

Using:

radius / height $= \dfrac{15}{24}$

radius $= \dfrac{15h}{24}$ or $\dfrac{5h}{8}$ .....[1]

As the volume of a cone $= \dfrac{1}{3}\pi r^2 h$

substituting for r gives:

Volume $V = \dfrac{1}{3}\pi\left(\dfrac{5h}{8}\right)^2 \times h$

$V = \dfrac{25\pi h^3}{192}$

Now find $\dfrac{\mathrm{d}V}{\mathrm{d}h} = \dfrac{75\pi h^2}{192}$

As $h = 10$, substituting into $\dfrac{\mathrm{d}V}{\mathrm{d}h}$ gives:

$\dfrac{\mathrm{d}V}{\mathrm{d}h} = \dfrac{75\pi \times 100}{192}$

$= \dfrac{625\pi}{16}$

You are required to find $\dfrac{\mathrm{d}h}{\mathrm{d}t}$

Using the chain rule:

$\dfrac{\mathrm{d}V}{\mathrm{d}t} = \dfrac{\mathrm{d}V}{\mathrm{d}h} \times \dfrac{\mathrm{d}h}{\mathrm{d}t}$

$40\pi = \dfrac{625\pi}{16} \times \dfrac{\mathrm{d}h}{\mathrm{d}t}$

$\dfrac{\mathrm{d}h}{\mathrm{d}t} = 40\pi \div \dfrac{625\pi}{16}$

$\dfrac{\mathrm{d}h}{\mathrm{d}t} = 1.024$

The rate of change of the height of the water in the cone is 1.024 cm s^{-1}

ii The horizontal surface area of the water in the cone is a circle.

Area of a circle $A = \pi r^2$

From [1] in part **a**, radius $= \dfrac{5h}{8}$

So substituting into $A = \pi r^2$,

$A = \pi \times \left(\dfrac{5h}{8}\right)^2$

$A = \dfrac{25\pi h^2}{64}$

$\dfrac{\mathrm{d}A}{\mathrm{d}h} = \dfrac{50\pi h}{64}$

At $h = 10$, $\dfrac{\mathrm{d}A}{\mathrm{d}h} = \dfrac{50\pi \times 10}{64}$

$\dfrac{\mathrm{d}A}{\mathrm{d}h} = \dfrac{500\pi}{64}$

You are required to find $\dfrac{\mathrm{d}A}{\mathrm{d}t}$

Using the chain rule:

$\dfrac{\mathrm{d}A}{\mathrm{d}t} = \dfrac{\mathrm{d}A}{\mathrm{d}h} \times \dfrac{\mathrm{d}h}{\mathrm{d}t}$

$\dfrac{\mathrm{d}A}{\mathrm{d}t} = \dfrac{500\pi}{64} \times 1.024$

$\dfrac{\mathrm{d}A}{\mathrm{d}t} = 8\pi$

The rate of change of the horizontal surface area of the water in the cone is 8π cm^2 s^{-1}

1 e $\dfrac{dy}{dx} = \dfrac{1}{2x^3}$

Rewrite in index form: $\dfrac{dy}{dx} = \dfrac{1}{2}x^{-3}$

Using if $\dfrac{dy}{dx} = x^n$ then $y = \dfrac{1}{n+1}x^{n+1} + c$,

$y = \dfrac{1}{-3+1} \times \dfrac{1}{2}x^{-3+1} + c$

$y = -\dfrac{1}{4}x^{-2} + c$

$y = -\dfrac{1}{4x^2} + c$

f $\dfrac{dy}{dx} = \dfrac{4}{\sqrt{x}}$

Rewrite in index form: $\dfrac{dy}{dx} = 4x^{-\frac{1}{2}}$

Using if $\dfrac{dy}{dx} = x^n$ then $y = \dfrac{1}{n+1}x^{n+1} + c$,

$y = \dfrac{1}{-\frac{1}{2}+1} \times 4x^{-\frac{1}{2}+1} + c$

$y = \dfrac{1}{\frac{1}{2}} \times 4x^{\frac{1}{2}} + c$

$y = 2 \times 4x^{\frac{1}{2}} + c$

$y = 8x^{\frac{1}{2}} + c$

$y = 8\sqrt{x} + c$

2 d $f'(x) = \dfrac{9}{x^7} - \dfrac{3}{x^2} - 4$

Rewrite in index form: $f'(x) = 9x^{-7} - 3x^{-2} - 4x^0$

Using if $f'(x) = x^n$ then $f(x) = \dfrac{1}{n+1}x^{n+1} + c$

$f(x) = \dfrac{1}{-7+1} \times 9x^{-7+1} - \left(\dfrac{1}{-2+1} \times 3x^{-2+1}\right)$

$- \dfrac{1}{0+1} \times 4x^{0+1} + c$

Be careful with '−' signs.

$f(x) = -\dfrac{1}{6} \times 9x^{-6} - (-1 \times 3x^{-1}) - 1 \times 4x^1 + c$

$f(x) = -\dfrac{3}{2x^6} + \dfrac{3}{x} - 4x + c$

3 e $\dfrac{dy}{dx} = \sqrt{x}(x-3)^2$

Expand brackets:

$\dfrac{dy}{dx} = \sqrt{x}(x-3)(x-3)$

Rewrite in index form:

$\dfrac{dy}{dx} = \left(x^{\frac{3}{2}} - 3x^{\frac{1}{2}}\right)(x-3)$

$\dfrac{dy}{dx} = x^{\frac{5}{2}} - 3x^{\frac{3}{2}} - 3x^{\frac{3}{2}} + 9x^{\frac{1}{2}}$

$\dfrac{dy}{dx} = x^{\frac{5}{2}} - 6x^{\frac{3}{2}} + 9x^{\frac{1}{2}}$

Using if $\dfrac{dy}{dx} = x^n$ then $y = \dfrac{1}{n+1}x^{n+1} + c$,

$y = \dfrac{1}{\frac{5}{2}+1}x^{\frac{5}{2}+1} - \dfrac{1}{\frac{3}{2}+1} \times 6x^{\frac{3}{2}+1}$

$+ \dfrac{1}{\frac{1}{2}+1} \times 9x^{\frac{1}{2}+1} + c$

$y = \dfrac{1}{\frac{7}{2}}x^{\frac{7}{2}} - \dfrac{1}{\frac{5}{2}} \times 6x^{\frac{5}{2}} + \dfrac{1}{\frac{3}{2}} \times 9x^{\frac{3}{2}} + c$

$y = \dfrac{2}{7}x^{\frac{7}{2}} - \dfrac{12}{5}x^{\frac{5}{2}} + 6x^{\frac{3}{2}} + c$

f $\dfrac{dy}{dx} = \dfrac{5x^2 + 3x + 1}{\sqrt{x}}$

Rewrite in index form:

$\dfrac{dy}{dx} = \left(\dfrac{5x^2}{x^{\frac{1}{2}}} + \dfrac{3x}{x^{\frac{1}{2}}} + \dfrac{1}{x^{\frac{1}{2}}}\right)$

Or $\dfrac{dy}{dx} = 5x^{\frac{3}{2}} + 3x^{\frac{1}{2}} + x^{-\frac{1}{2}}$

If $\dfrac{dy}{dx} = x^n$ then $y = \dfrac{1}{n+1}x^{n+1} + c$,

So:

$y = \dfrac{1}{\frac{3}{2}+1} \times 5x^{\frac{3}{2}+1} + \dfrac{1}{\frac{1}{2}+1} \times 3x^{\frac{1}{2}+1}$

$\qquad + \dfrac{1}{-\frac{1}{2}+1}x^{-\frac{1}{2}+1} + c$

$y = \dfrac{1}{\frac{5}{2}} \times 5x^{\frac{5}{2}} + \dfrac{1}{\frac{3}{2}} \times 3x^{\frac{3}{2}} + \dfrac{1}{\frac{1}{2}}x^{\frac{1}{2}} + c$

$y = 2x^{\frac{5}{2}} + 2x^{\frac{3}{2}} + 2x^{\frac{1}{2}} + c$

$y = 2x^{\frac{5}{2}} + 2x^{\frac{3}{2}} + 2\sqrt{x} + c$

4 e $\displaystyle\int \dfrac{2}{3\sqrt{x}}\,dx$

Rewrite in index form: $\displaystyle\int \dfrac{2}{3}x^{-\frac{1}{2}}\,dx$

$\displaystyle\int k\mathrm{f}(x)\,dx = k\int \mathrm{f}(x)\,dx$, where k is a constant

$= \dfrac{2}{3}\displaystyle\int x^{-\frac{1}{2}}\,dx$

$= \dfrac{2}{3} \times \dfrac{1}{-\frac{1}{2}+1}x^{-\frac{1}{2}+1} + c$

$= \dfrac{2}{3} \times \dfrac{1}{\frac{1}{2}}x^{\frac{1}{2}} + c$

$= \dfrac{4}{3}x^{\frac{1}{2}} + c$

$= \dfrac{4}{3}\sqrt{x} + c$ or $\dfrac{4\sqrt{x}}{3} + c$

f $\displaystyle\int \dfrac{5}{x\sqrt{x}}\,dx$

Rewrite in index form: $\displaystyle\int \dfrac{5}{x \times x^{\frac{1}{2}}}\,dx$ or

$\displaystyle\int \dfrac{5}{x^{\frac{3}{2}}}\,dx$ or $\displaystyle\int 5x^{-\frac{3}{2}}\,dx$

Using $\displaystyle\int k\mathrm{f}(x)\,dx = k\int \mathrm{f}(x)\,dx$, where k is a constant:

$= 5 \times \dfrac{1}{-\frac{3}{2}+1}x^{-\frac{3}{2}+1} + c$

$= 5 \times \dfrac{1}{-\frac{1}{2}}x^{-\frac{1}{2}} + c$

$= -10x^{-\frac{1}{2}} + c$

$= -\dfrac{10}{x^{\frac{1}{2}}} + c$

$= -\dfrac{10}{\sqrt{x}} + c$

5 e $\displaystyle\int \dfrac{x^2-1}{2x^2}\,dx$

Rewrite in index form: $\displaystyle\int \dfrac{x^2}{2x^2} - \dfrac{1}{2x^2}\,dx$

Or $\displaystyle\int \dfrac{1}{2}x^0 - \dfrac{1}{2}x^{-2}\,dx$

Using $\displaystyle\int k\mathrm{f}(x)\,dx = k\int \mathrm{f}(x)\,dx$, where k is a constant:

$= \dfrac{1}{0+1} \times \dfrac{1}{2}x^{0+1} - \left(\dfrac{1}{-2+1} \times \dfrac{1}{2}x^{-2+1}\right) + c$

$= \dfrac{1}{2}x + \dfrac{1}{2}x^{-1} + c$

$= \dfrac{1}{2}x + \dfrac{1}{2x} + c$ or $\dfrac{x}{2} + \dfrac{1}{2x} + c$

i $\displaystyle\int \left(2\sqrt{x} - \dfrac{3}{x^2\sqrt{x}}\right)^2\,dx$

Rewrite in index form:

$\displaystyle\int \left(2\sqrt{x} - \dfrac{3}{x^2\sqrt{x}}\right)\left(2\sqrt{x} - \dfrac{3}{x^2\sqrt{x}}\right)\,dx$

$\displaystyle\int \left(2x^{\frac{1}{2}} - \dfrac{3}{x^{\frac{5}{2}}}\right)\left(2x^{\frac{1}{2}} - \dfrac{3}{x^{\frac{5}{2}}}\right)\,dx$

$\displaystyle\int 4x - \dfrac{6x^{\frac{1}{2}}}{x^{\frac{5}{2}}} - \dfrac{6x^{\frac{1}{2}}}{x^{\frac{5}{2}}} + \dfrac{9}{x^5}\,dx$

$\displaystyle\int 4x - 6x^{-2} - 6x^{-2} + 9x^{-5}\,dx$

$\displaystyle\int 4x - 12x^{-2} + 9x^{-5}\,dx$

Using $\int k\mathrm{f}(x)\mathrm{d}x = k\int \mathrm{f}(x)\mathrm{d}x,$ where k is a constant:

$$\frac{1}{1+1} \times 4x^{1+1} - \left(\frac{1}{-2+1} \times 12x^{-2+1}\right) + \left(\frac{1}{-5+1} \times 9x^{-5+1}\right) + c$$

$$= 2x^2 + 12x^{-1} - \frac{9}{4}x^{-4} + c$$

$$= 2x^2 + \frac{12}{x} - \frac{9}{4x^4} + c$$

EXERCISE 9B

1 d $\dfrac{\mathrm{d}y}{\mathrm{d}x} = \dfrac{2x^3 - 6}{x^2}$

Rewrite in index form:

$$\frac{\mathrm{d}y}{\mathrm{d}x} = 2x - 6x^{-2}$$

Integrating gives:

$$y = x^2 + 6x^{-1} + c$$

$$= x^2 + \frac{6}{x^1} + c$$

When $x = 3$, $y = 7$

$$7 = 3^2 + \frac{6}{3} + c$$

$$7 = 9 + 2 + c$$

$$c = -4$$

The equation of the curve is $y = x^2 + \dfrac{6}{x} - 4$.

f $\dfrac{\mathrm{d}y}{\mathrm{d}x} = \dfrac{\left(1 - \sqrt{x}\right)^2}{\sqrt{x}}$

Rewrite in index form:

$$\frac{\mathrm{d}y}{\mathrm{d}x} = \frac{\left(1 - x^{\frac{1}{2}}\right)\left(1 - x^{\frac{1}{2}}\right)}{x^{\frac{1}{2}}}$$

$$\frac{\mathrm{d}y}{\mathrm{d}x} = \frac{1 - 2x^{\frac{1}{2}} + x}{x^{\frac{1}{2}}}$$

$$\frac{\mathrm{d}y}{\mathrm{d}x} = \frac{1}{x^{\frac{1}{2}}} - 2 + x^{\frac{1}{2}}$$

$$\frac{\mathrm{d}y}{\mathrm{d}x} = x^{-\frac{1}{2}} - 2 + x^{\frac{1}{2}}$$

Integrating gives:

$$y = 2x^{\frac{1}{2}} - 2x + \frac{2}{3}x^{\frac{3}{2}} + c$$

When $x = 9$, $y = 5$

$$5 = 2 \times 9^{\frac{1}{2}} - 2 \times 9 + \frac{2}{3} \times 9^{\frac{3}{2}} + c$$

$$5 = 6 - 18 + 18 + c$$

$$c = -1$$

$$y = 2x^{\frac{1}{2}} - 2x + \frac{2}{3}x^{\frac{3}{2}} - 1 \text{ or}$$

$$y = 2\sqrt{x} - 2x + \frac{2}{3}x^{\frac{3}{2}} - 1$$

2 $\dfrac{\mathrm{d}y}{\mathrm{d}x} = -\dfrac{k}{x^2}$

Rewrite in index form:

$$\frac{\mathrm{d}y}{\mathrm{d}x} = -kx^{-2}$$

Integrating gives:

$$y = kx^{-1} + c$$

$$y = \frac{k}{x} + c$$

When $x = 6$, $y = 2.5$

$$2.5 = \frac{k}{6} + c$$

$$15 = k + 6c \quad\ldots\ldots\ldots\ldots\ldots\ldots[1]$$

When $x = -3$, $y = 1$

$$1 = \frac{k}{-3} + c$$

$$-3 = k - 3c \quad\ldots\ldots\ldots\ldots\ldots\ldots[2]$$

Subtracting [2] from [1] gives:

$18 = 9c$

$c = 2$

Substituting $c = 2$ into [1]:

$15 = k + 6(2)$

$k = 3$

The equation of the curve is $y = \dfrac{3}{x} + 2$

3 $\dfrac{dy}{dx} = kx^2 - 12x + 5$

Integrating gives:

$y = \dfrac{k}{3}x^3 - 6x^2 + 5x + c$

When $x = 1, y = -3$

$-3 = \dfrac{k}{3}(1)^3 - 6(1)^2 + 5(1) + c$

$-9 = k - 18 + 15 + 3c$

$-6 = k + 3c$ ....[1]

When $x = 3, y = 11$

$11 = \dfrac{k}{3}(3)^3 - 6(3)^2 + 5(3) + c$

$11 = 9k - 54 + 15 + c$

$50 = 9k + c$ ....[2]

Using [1], multiply by 9 and subtract [2]:

$-104 = 26c$

$c = -4$

Substituting $c = -4$ into [1] gives:

$-6 = k - 12$

$k = 6$

The equation of the curve is $y = 2x^3 - 6x^2 + 5x - 4$

4 $\dfrac{dy}{dx} = kx^2 - \dfrac{6}{x^3}$

Rewrite in index form:

$\dfrac{dy}{dx} = kx^2 - 6x^{-3}$

Integrating gives:

$y = \dfrac{k}{3}x^3 + 3x^{-2} + c$

$y = \dfrac{k}{3}x^3 + \dfrac{3}{x^2} + c$

When $x = 1, y = 6$

$6 = \dfrac{k}{3}(1)^3 + \dfrac{3}{1^2} + c$

$18 = k + 9 + 3c$

$9 = k + 3c$ ....[1]

At $x = 1, \dfrac{dy}{dx} = 9$

$9 = k(1)^2 - \dfrac{6}{(1)^3}$

$k = 15$

Substituting $k = 15$ into [1] gives:

$9 = 15 + 3c$

$c = -2$

Substituting $k = 15$ and $c = -2$ into

$y = \dfrac{k}{3}x^3 + 3x^{-2} + c$ gives:

$y = \dfrac{15}{3}x^3 + \dfrac{3}{x^2} - 2$

$y = 5x^3 + \dfrac{3}{x^2} - 2$

5 a $\dfrac{dy}{dx} = 5x\sqrt{x} + 2$

Rewrite in index form:

$\dfrac{dy}{dx} = 5x^{\frac{3}{2}} + 2$

Integrating gives:

$y = \dfrac{5}{\frac{5}{2}}x^{\frac{5}{2}} + 2x + c$

$y = 2x^{\frac{5}{2}} + 2x + c$

When $x = 1, y = 3$

$3 = 2 \times 1^{\frac{5}{2}} + 2 \times 1 + c$

$c = -1$

The equation of the curve is $y = 2x^{\frac{5}{2}} + 2x - 1$ or $y = 2x^2\sqrt{x} + 2x - 1$

There is no single 'correct' form in which to give your answers to questions like this. In general, simplify fractions, write terms with positive indices rather than negative ones (especially fractional indices) and replace simple fractional indices such as $x^{\frac{1}{2}}$ with $\sqrt{x}$.

b $\dfrac{dy}{dx} = 5x\sqrt{x} + 2$

Substitute $x = 4$ to find the gradient of the curve at that point (i.e. the gradient of the tangent).

> As a tangent is a straight line, express its equation as $y = mx + c$ (or equivalent), preferably in a form without fractions or decimals. Use $y - y_1 = m(x - x_1)$ in your working.

$\dfrac{dy}{dx} = 5 \times 4 \times \sqrt{4} + 2$ (always take the positive root here)

$\dfrac{dy}{dx} = 42$

As the equation of the curve is $y = 2x^{\frac{5}{2}} + 2x - 1$, the y-coordinate when $x = 4$ is:

$y = 2 \times 4^{\frac{5}{2}} + 2 \times 4 - 1$

$y = 71$

Using $y - y_1 = m(x - x_1)$

$m = 42$, $x_1 = 4$, $y_1 = 71$

$y - 71 = 42(x - 4)$

$y - 71 = 42x - 168$

$\qquad y = 42x - 97$

6 $\dfrac{dy}{dx} = kx + 3$

If the gradient of the normal at $x = 1$ is $-\dfrac{1}{7}$, then the gradient of the tangent at that point is 7

[since $m_1 \times m_2 = -1$ (Chapter 3)]

So as $\dfrac{dy}{dx} = kx + 3$ and $\dfrac{dy}{dx} = 7$, $x = 1$

$7 = k \times 1 + 3$

$k = 4$

$\dfrac{dy}{dx} = 4x + 3$

Integrating gives:

$y = 2x^2 + 3x + c$

As $(1, -2)$ lies on the curve, substituting $x = 1$, $y = -2$ gives the value of c.

$-2 = 2 \times 1^2 + 3 \times 1 + c$

$\quad c = -7$

The equation of the curve is: $y = 2x^2 + 3x - 7$

7 $f'(x) = 8 - 2x$

Integrating this gives:

$f(x) = 8x - x^2 + c$

Completing the square:

$f(x) = -[x^2 - 8x] + c$

$f(x) = -[(x - 4)^2 - 4^2] + c$

$f(x) = -[(x - 4)^2 - 16] + c$

$f(x) = -(x - 4)^2 + 16 + c$

$f(x) = c + 16 - (x - 4)^2$

The maximum value of the function (20), occurs when $x = 4$, so:

$20 = c + 16 - (4 - 4)^2$

$\quad c = 4$

The equation of the curve is: $y = 4 + 8x - x^2$

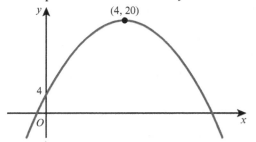

8 a Given $\dfrac{dy}{dx} = 3x^2 + x - 10$

Integrating gives:

$y = x^3 + \dfrac{1}{2}x^2 - 10x + c$

Substituting $x = 2$ and $y = -7$ gives:

$-7 = 2^3 + \dfrac{1}{2} \times 2^2 - 10 \times 2 + c$

$-7 = 8 + 2 - 20 + c$

$\quad c = 3$

The equation of the curve is

$y = x^3 + \dfrac{1}{2}x^2 - 10x + 3$

b The stationary points on the curve are found by solving $\dfrac{dy}{dx} = 0$

$$3x^2 + x - 10 = 0$$
$$(3x - 5)(x + 2) = 0$$

Either $3x - 5 = 0$

$$x = \frac{5}{3}$$

Or $x = -2$

The curve is a positive cubic so a sketch would look like:

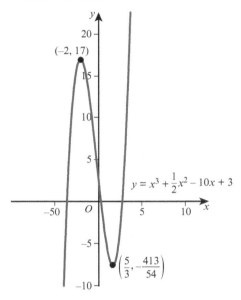

The set of values of x for which the gradient of the curve is positive is:

$$x < -2 \text{ and } x > 1\frac{2}{3}$$

9 a $\dfrac{d^2y}{dx^2} = 12x + 12$

Integrating gives:

$$\frac{dy}{dx} = 6x^2 + 12x + c$$

As the gradient of the curve at the point $(0, 4)$ is 10:

$$10 = 6 \times 0^2 + 12 \times 0 + c$$
$$c = 10$$

$$\frac{dy}{dx} = 6x^2 + 12x + 10$$

Integrating gives:

$$y = 2x^3 + 6x^2 + 10x + c$$

As $(0, 4)$ lies on the curve then substituting $x = 0, y = 4$ gives:

$$4 = 2 \times 0^3 + 6 \times 0^2 + 10 \times 0 + c$$
$$c = 4$$
$$y = 2x^3 + 6x^2 + 10x + 4$$

b $\dfrac{dy}{dx} = 6x^2 + 12x + 10$

Completing the square gives:

$$\frac{dy}{dx} = 6[\, x^2 + 2x] + 10$$

$$\frac{dy}{dx} = 6[\, (x + 1)^2 - 1^2] + 10$$

$$\frac{dy}{dx} = 6(x + 1)^2 - 6 + 10$$

$$\frac{dy}{dx} = 6(x + 1)^2 + 4$$

The minimum value of the gradient is 4. This occurs when $x = -1$ since the minimum value of $6(x + 1)^2$ is zero.

∴ The gradient is never less than 4.

10 $\dfrac{d^2y}{dx^2} = -6x - 4$

Integrating gives:

$$\frac{dy}{dx} = -3x^2 - 4x + c$$

At $x = -2$ $\dfrac{dy}{dx} = 0$ so substituting gives:

$$0 = -3 \times (-2)^2 - 4 \times -2 + c$$
$$c = 4$$

$$\frac{dy}{dx} = -3x^2 - 4x + 4$$

Integrating gives:

$$y = -x^3 - 2x^2 + 4x + c$$

As $(-2, -6)$ lies on the curve then substituting $x = -2, y = -6$ gives:

$$-6 = -(-2)^3 - 2(-2)^2 + 4 \times -2 + c$$
$$c = 2$$

The equation of the curve is: $y = 2 + 4x - 2x^2 - x^3$

11 a $f'(x) = 2x^2 + 3x - k$

At the stationary point $x = 2$, $f'(x) = 0$

So, $0 = 2 \times 2^2 + 3 \times 2 - k$

$\quad k = 14$

$f'(x) = 2x^2 + 3x - 14$

To find the other stationary point, solve:

$0 = 2x^2 + 3x - 14$

$(x - 2)(2x + 7) = 0$

$x = 2$ (already known) or as $2x + 7 = 0$,

$x = -3.5$

Q is at $x = -3.5$

b To determine the nature of the stationary points P and Q, find $f''(x)$

$f''(x) = 4x + 3$

Substituting $x = 2$ into $f''(x)$ gives:

$f''(2) = 4 \times 2 + 3$ or 11 which is positive.
So P is a minimum point.

Substituting $x = -3.5$ into $f''(x)$ gives:

$f''(-3.5) = 4 \times -3.5 + 3$ or -11 which is negative.
So, Q is a maximum point.

12 a $\dfrac{dy}{dx} = k + x$

At $x = 5$, $\dfrac{dy}{dx} = k + 5$

At $x = 7$, $\dfrac{dy}{dx} = k + 7$

If the tangents are perpendicular then:

$(k + 5) \times \dfrac{1}{(k + 7)} = -1$ (since $m_1 \times m_2 = -1$)

$\quad\quad\quad k + 5 = -(k + 7)$

$\quad\quad\quad\quad 2k = -12$

$\quad\quad\quad\quad\, k = -6$

b $\dfrac{dy}{dx} = x - 6$

Integrating gives:

$y = \dfrac{1}{2}x^2 - 6x + c$

As the curve passes through $(10, -8)$, substituting $x = 10$, $y = -8$ gives:

$-8 = \dfrac{1}{2} \times 10^2 - 6 \times 10 + c$

$c = 2$

The equation of the curve is $y = \dfrac{1}{2}x^2 - 6x + 2$

13 $f''(x) = 2 + \dfrac{4}{x^3}$

Rewrite in index form:

$f''(x) = 2 + 4x^{-3}$

Integrating gives:

$f'(x) = 2x - 2x^{-2} + c$

At the stationary point $x = 1$, $f''(x) = 0$

$0 = 2 \times 1 - 2 \times 1^{-2} + c$

$c = 0$

$f'(x) = 2x - \dfrac{2}{x^2}$

Integrating $f''(x) = 2x - 2x^{-2}$ gives:

$f(x) = x^2 + 2x^{-1} + c$ or $f(x) = x^2 + \dfrac{2}{x} + c$

As $(1, -1)$ lies on the curve, substituting $x = 1$, $y = -1$ gives:

$-1 = 1^2 + \dfrac{2}{1} + c$

$c = -4$

The equation of the curve is $f(x) = x^2 + \dfrac{2}{x} - 4$

14 $\dfrac{d^2y}{dx^2} = 2x + 8$

Integrating gives:

$\dfrac{dy}{dx} = x^2 + 8x + c$

At any stationary point $\dfrac{dy}{dx} = 0$

Substituting $x = 3$ and $\dfrac{dy}{dx} = 0$ gives:

$0 = 3^2 + 8 \times 3 + c$

$c = -33$

So, $\dfrac{dy}{dx} = x^2 + 8x - 33$

At the maximum point, $\dfrac{dy}{dx} = 0$

So, $x^2 + 8x - 33 = 0$

$(x - 3)(x + 11) = 0$

$x = 3$ (minimum point) or $x = -11$ (maximum point)

To find the equation of the curve, integrate $\dfrac{dy}{dx}$

This gives $y = \dfrac{1}{3}x^3 + 4x^2 - 33x + c$

As $(3, -49)$ lies on the curve, substituting $x = 3$, $y = -49$ gives:

$-49 = \dfrac{1}{3} \times 3^3 + 4 \times 3^2 - 33 \times 3 + c$

$-49 = 9 + 36 - 99 + c$

$c = 5$

So the equation of the curve is

$y = \dfrac{1}{3}x^3 + 4x^2 - 33x + 5$

To find the y-coordinate of the maximum point, substitute $x = -11$:

$y = \dfrac{1}{3}x^3 + 4x^2 - 33x + 5$

$y = \dfrac{1}{3} \times (-11)^3 + 4 \times (-11)^2 - 33 \times (-11) + 5$

$y = 408\dfrac{1}{3}$

The coordinates of the maximum point are $\left(-11, 408\dfrac{1}{3}\right)$

16 a $\dfrac{dy}{dx} = 3\sqrt{x} - 6$

Rewrite in index form:

$\dfrac{dy}{dx} = 3x^{\frac{1}{2}} - 6$

Integrating gives:

$y = 2x^{\frac{3}{2}} - 6x + c$ or $y = 2x\sqrt{x} - 6x + c$

Substituting $x = 1$, $y = 6$ gives:

$6 = 2 \times (1)^{\frac{3}{2}} - 6 \times 1 + c$

$c = 10$

The equation of the curve is

$y = 2x\sqrt{x} - 6x + 10$

b At a stationary point, $\dfrac{dy}{dx} = 0$

$3\sqrt{x} - 6 = 0$

$\sqrt{x} = 2$

$x = 4$

Substituting $x = 4$ into $y = 2x\sqrt{x} - 6x + 10$ gives:

$y = 2 \times 4 \times \sqrt{4} - 6 \times 4 + 10$

$y = 2$

So $(4, 2)$ is the stationary point.

As $\dfrac{dy}{dx} = 3x^{\frac{1}{2}} - 6$

$\dfrac{d^2y}{dx^2} = \dfrac{3}{2}x^{-\frac{1}{2}}$

Substituting $x = 4$ into $\dfrac{d^2y}{dx^2}$ gives:

$\dfrac{d^2y}{dx^2} = \dfrac{3}{2}(4)^{-\frac{1}{2}}$ or $\dfrac{3}{4}$ which is positive

So, $(4, 2)$ is a minimum.

17 $\dfrac{d^2y}{dx^2} = 2 - \dfrac{12}{x^3}$

Substituting $x = 1$ into $\dfrac{d^2y}{dx^2}$ gives:

$\dfrac{d^2y}{dx^2} = 2 - \dfrac{12}{1^3}$ or -10

So the stationary point is a maximum.

Now find the equation of the curve in order to find the y-coordinate of the stationary point:

Rewrite in index form:

$\dfrac{d^2y}{dx^2} = 2 - 12x^{-3}$

Integrating gives:

$\dfrac{dy}{dx} = 2x + 6x^{-2} + c$ or $\dfrac{dy}{dx} = 2x + \dfrac{6}{x^2} + c$

At the stationary point where $x = 1$, $\dfrac{dy}{dx} = 0$

$0 = 2 \times 1 + \dfrac{6}{1^2} + c$

$c = -8$

$\dfrac{dy}{dx} = 2x + \dfrac{6}{x^2} - 8$ or $\dfrac{dy}{dx} = 2x + 6x^{-2} - 8$

Integrating gives:

$y = x^2 - 6x^{-1} - 8x + c$

Or $y = x^2 - \dfrac{6}{x} - 8x + c$

As $(2, 5)$ lies on the curve:

$5 = 2^2 - \dfrac{6}{2} - 8 \times 2 + c$

$c = 20$

The equation of the curve is $y = x^2 - \dfrac{6}{x} - 8x + 20$

When $x = 1$, the y-coordinate is:

$$y = 1^2 - \frac{6}{1} - 8 \times 1 + 20$$

$$y = 7$$

So, $(1, 7)$ is a maximum point.

18 a $\dfrac{dy}{dx} = 2x - 5$

Integrating gives:

$$y = x^2 - 5x + c$$

Substituting $x = 3$, $y = -4$ gives:

$$-4 = 3^2 - 5 \times 3 + c$$

$$c = 2$$

The equation of the curve is

$$y = x^2 - 5x + 2 \quad ....[1]$$

b Gradient of the tangent at $x = 3$ is:

$$\frac{dy}{dx} = 2 \times 3 - 5 \text{ or } 1$$

Gradient of the normal at $x = 3$ is -1 (since $m_1 \times m_2 = -1$)

Using $-y_1 = -\dfrac{1}{m}(x - x_1)$, $m = 1$, $x_1 = 3$, $y_1 = -4$:

$$y - (-4) = -1(x - 3)$$

$$y + 4 = -x + 3$$

$$x + y = -1 \quad ....[2]$$

c To find the coordinates of Q, solve [1] and [2] simultaneously.

Making y the subject of [2] gives:

$$y = -1 - x$$

Substituting for y in [1] gives:

$$-1 - x = x^2 - 5x + 2$$

$$x^2 - 4x + 3 = 0$$

$$(x - 3)(x - 1) = 0$$

$$x = 3 \text{ (already known) or } x = 1$$

Substituting $x = 1$ into [2] gives:

$$1 + y = -1$$

$$y = -2$$

The coordinates of Q are $(1, -2)$.

EXERCISE 9C

1 d $\displaystyle\int 3(1 - 2x)^5 \, dx$

$$= 3\int (1 - 2x)^5 \, dx$$

$$= 3\left[\frac{1}{-2(5 + 1)}(1 - 2x)^{5+1} \right] + c$$

$$= -\frac{1}{4}(1 - 2x)^6 + c$$

g $\displaystyle\int \frac{2}{\sqrt{3x - 2}} \, dx$

$$= 2\int \frac{1}{\sqrt{3x - 2}} \, dx$$

$$= 2\int (3x - 2)^{-\frac{1}{2}} \, dx$$

$$= \frac{2}{3\left(-\dfrac{1}{2} + 1\right)}(3x - 2)^{-\frac{1}{2}+1} + c$$

$$= \frac{4}{3}\sqrt{3x - 2} + c$$

2 b $\dfrac{dy}{dx} = \sqrt{2x + 5}$, $P = (2, 2)$

$$\frac{dy}{dx} = (2x + 5)^{\frac{1}{2}}$$

$$y = \frac{1}{2\left(\dfrac{1}{2} + 1\right)}(2x + 5)^{\frac{1}{2}+1} + c$$

$$y = \frac{1}{3}(2x + 5)^{\frac{3}{2}} + c$$

Substituting $x = 2$, $y = 2$,

$$2 = \frac{1}{3}(2 \times 2 + 5)^{\frac{3}{2}} + c$$

$$2 = 9 + c$$

$$c = -7$$

$$y = \frac{1}{3}(2x + 5)^{\frac{3}{2}} - 7$$

3 $\dfrac{dy}{dx} = k(x-5)^3$

At $x = 4$, $\dfrac{dy}{dx} = k(4-5)^3$

$\dfrac{dy}{dx} = -k$

The gradient of the tangent is $-k$

So the gradient of the normal at $x = 4$ is $\dfrac{1}{k}$
(since $m_1 \times m_2 = -1$)

$\dfrac{1}{k} = \dfrac{1}{12}$

$k = 12$

So, $\dfrac{dy}{dx} = 12(x-5)^3$

Integrating gives:

$y = \dfrac{12}{4}(x-5)^4 + c$

$y = 3(x-5)^4 + c$
Substituting $x = 4$, $y = 2$,

$2 = 3(4-5)^4 + c$

$c = -1$
The equation of the curve is $y = 3(x-5)^4 - 1$

4 a $\dfrac{dy}{dx} = \dfrac{5}{\sqrt{2x-3}}$.

At $x = 2$,

$\dfrac{dy}{dx} = \dfrac{5}{\sqrt{2 \times 2 - 3}}$.

$\dfrac{dy}{dx} = 5$

Gradient of the tangent is 5

So the gradient of the normal is $-\dfrac{1}{5}$
(since $m_1 \times m_2 = -1$)

The equation of the normal using

$y - y_1 = -\dfrac{1}{m}(x - x_1)$, $x_1 = 2$, $y_1 = 1$, $m = -\dfrac{1}{5}$ is:

$y - 1 = -\dfrac{1}{5}(x-2)$

$5y - 5 = -x + 2$

$x + 5y = 7$

b $\dfrac{dy}{dx} = \dfrac{5}{\sqrt{2x-3}}$.

Rewriting in index form:

$\dfrac{dy}{dx} = 5(2x-3)^{-\frac{1}{2}}$

Integrating gives:

$y = \dfrac{5}{2\left(-\dfrac{1}{2}+1\right)}(2x-3)^{-\frac{1}{2}+1} + c$

$y = 5(2x-3)^{\frac{1}{2}} + c$
As the curve passes through $P(2, 1)$
substituting $x = 2$, $y = 1$ gives:

$1 = 5(2 \times 2 - 3)^{\frac{1}{2}} + c$

$c = -4$

$y = 5\sqrt{2x-3} - 4$

5 a $\dfrac{dy}{dx} = \dfrac{12}{\sqrt{3x+1}} - 4x - 2$

If there is a stationary point at $x = 1$ then
substitution into $\dfrac{dy}{dx}$ should give 0.

$\dfrac{dy}{dx} = \dfrac{12}{\sqrt{3 \times 1 + 1}} - 4 \times 1 - 2$

$\dfrac{dy}{dx} = \dfrac{12}{2} - 4 - 2$

$= 6 - 4 - 2$ or 0

So, $x = 1$ is a stationary point.

To determine its nature find $\dfrac{d^2y}{dx^2}$

Rewrite $\dfrac{dy}{dx} = \dfrac{12}{\sqrt{3x+1}} - 4x - 2$ in index form:

$\dfrac{dy}{dx} = 12(3x+1)^{-\frac{1}{2}} - 4x - 2$

Differentiate using the chain rule:

$\dfrac{d^2y}{dx^2} = -\dfrac{1}{2} \times 12(3x+1)^{-\frac{3}{2}} \times 3 - 4$

$\dfrac{d^2y}{dx^2} = -18(3x+1)^{-\frac{3}{2}} - 4$

Substitute $x = 1$:

$\dfrac{d^2y}{dx^2} = -18(3 \times 1 + 1)^{-\frac{3}{2}} - 4$

$= -\dfrac{18}{8} - 4$

$= -\dfrac{25}{4}$ which is negative.

Therefore $x = 1$ is a maximum point.

b Integrating $\dfrac{dy}{dx} = 12(3x+1)^{-\frac{1}{2}} - 4x - 2$

$y = \dfrac{12}{3\left(-\dfrac{1}{2}+1\right)}(3x+1)^{\frac{1}{2}} - 2x^2 - 2x + c$

$y = 8(3x+1)^{\frac{1}{2}} - 2x^2 - 2x + c$

Substitute $x = 0$, $y = 13$ to find c:

$13 = 8(3 \times 0 + 1)^{\frac{1}{2}} - 2 \times 0^2 - 2 \times 0 + c$

$13 = 8 + c$

$c = 5$

The equation of the curve is

$y = 8\sqrt{3x+1} - 2x^2 - 2x + 5$

6 $\dfrac{dy}{dx} = \dfrac{4}{\sqrt{2x+k}}$

As the normal at P has the equation $x + 4y = 11$ rearranging gives:

$4y = -x + 11$

$y = -\dfrac{1}{4}x + \dfrac{11}{4}$

Gradient of the normal at P is $-\dfrac{1}{4}$

Gradient of the tangent at $P = 4$

(since $m_1 \times m_2 = -1$)

So, $\dfrac{dy}{dx} = 4$ at $P(3, 2)$

$4 = \dfrac{4}{\sqrt{2 \times 3 + k}}$

$4\sqrt{6 + k} = 4$

$\sqrt{6 + k} = 1$

$6 + k = 1$

$k = -5$

$\dfrac{dy}{dx} = \dfrac{4}{\sqrt{2x-5}}$

Rewrite in index form:

$\dfrac{dy}{dx} = 4(2x-5)^{-\frac{1}{2}}$

Integrating:

$y = \dfrac{4}{2\left(-\dfrac{1}{2}+1\right)}(2x-5)^{\frac{1}{2}} + c$

$y = 4(2x-5)^{\frac{1}{2}} + c$

To find c, substitute $x = 3$, $y = 2$:

$2 = 4(2 \times 3 - 5)^{\frac{1}{2}} + c$

$c = -2$

The equation of the curve is $y = 4\sqrt{2x-5} - 2$

EXERCISE 9D

1 a Let $y = (x^2 + 2)^4$

Using the chain rule:

$\dfrac{dy}{dx} = (2x)(4)(x^2+2)^{4-1}$

$= 8x(x^2+2)^3$

b $\displaystyle\int x(x^2+2)^3 \, dx = \dfrac{1}{8}\int 8x(x^2+2)^3 \, dx$

$= \dfrac{1}{8}(x^2+2)^4 + c$

3 a Let $y = \dfrac{1}{x^2 - 5}$

Rewrite in index form:

$y = (x^2 - 5)^{-1}$

Using the chain rule:

$\dfrac{dy}{dx} = -1(x^2-5)^{-2} \times 2x$

$\dfrac{dy}{dx} = \dfrac{-2x}{(x^2-5)^2}$

Comparing this with $\dfrac{dy}{dx} = \dfrac{kx}{(x^2-5)^2}$

$k = -2$

b $\displaystyle\int \dfrac{4x}{(x^2-5)^2} \, dx = -2\int \dfrac{-2x}{(x^2-5)^2} \, dx$

$= -2 \times \dfrac{1}{x^2-5} + c$

$= -\dfrac{2}{x^2-5} + c$

4 a Let $y = \dfrac{1}{4-3x^2}$

Rewrite in index form:

$y = (4-3x^2)^{-1}$

Using the chain rule:

$\dfrac{dy}{dx} = -1(4-3x^2)^{-2} \times -6x$

$\dfrac{dy}{dx} = \dfrac{6x}{(4-3x^2)^2}$

b $\displaystyle\int \dfrac{3x}{(4-3x^2)^2}\,dx = \dfrac{1}{2}\int \dfrac{6x}{(4-3x^2)^2}\,dx$

$= \dfrac{1}{2} \times \dfrac{1}{4-3x^2} + c$

$= \dfrac{1}{8-6x^2} + c$

6 a Let $y = (\sqrt{x}+3)^8$

Rewrite in index form:

$y = \left(x^{\frac{1}{2}}+3\right)^8$

Using the chain rule:

$\dfrac{dy}{dx} = 8\left(x^{\frac{1}{2}}+3\right)^7 \times \dfrac{1}{2}x^{-\frac{1}{2}}$

$\dfrac{dy}{dx} = 4x^{-\frac{1}{2}}\left(x^{\frac{1}{2}}+3\right)^7$

$= \dfrac{4(\sqrt{x}+3)^7}{\sqrt{x}}$

b $\displaystyle\int \dfrac{(\sqrt{x}+3)^7}{\sqrt{x}}\,dx = \dfrac{1}{4}\int \dfrac{4(\sqrt{x}+3)^7}{\sqrt{x}}\,dx$

$= \dfrac{1}{4}(\sqrt{x}+3)^8 + c$

7 a Let $y = \left(2x\sqrt{x}-1\right)^5$

Rewrite in index form:

$y = \left(2x^{\frac{3}{2}}-1\right)^5$

Using the chain rule:

$\dfrac{dy}{dx} = 5\left(2x^{\frac{3}{2}}-1\right)^4 \times 3x^{\frac{1}{2}}$

$\dfrac{dy}{dx} = 15x^{\frac{1}{2}}\left(2x^{\frac{3}{2}}-1\right)^4$

$= 15\sqrt{x}\left(2x\sqrt{x}-1\right)^4$

b $\displaystyle\int 3\sqrt{x}\left(2x\sqrt{x}-1\right)^4 dx$

$= \dfrac{1}{5}\int 15\sqrt{x}\left(2x\sqrt{x}-1\right)^4 dx$

$= \dfrac{1}{5}\left(2x\sqrt{x}-1\right)^5 + c$

1 c $\displaystyle\int_{-1}^{1}(2x-3)\,dx = [x^2-3x]_{-1}^{1}$

$= (1^2-3(1)) - ((-1)^2-3(-1))$

$= -2-4$

$= -6$

e $\displaystyle\int_{-1}^{2}(4x^2-2x)\,dx = \left[\dfrac{4}{3}x^3-x^2\right]_{-1}^{2}$

$= \left(\dfrac{4}{3}\times 2^3 - 2^2\right)$

$- \left(\dfrac{4}{3}\times(-1)^3 - (-1)^2\right)$

$= \dfrac{20}{3} - \left(-\dfrac{7}{3}\right)$

$= \dfrac{20}{3} + \dfrac{7}{3}$

$= 9$

2 b $\displaystyle\int_{-2}^{-1}\left(\dfrac{8-x^2}{x^2}\right)dx$

$= \displaystyle\int_{-2}^{-1}(8x^{-2}-1)\,dx$

$= \left[\dfrac{8}{-1}x^{-1}-x\right]_{-2}^{-1}$

$= \left[-8x^{-1}-x\right]_{-2}^{-1}$

$= (-8(-1)^{-1}-(-1)) - (-8(-2)^{-1}-(-2))$

$= (8+1) - (4+2)$

$= 3$

e $\displaystyle\int_1^2 \frac{(3-x)(8+x)}{x^4}\,dx$

$\displaystyle = \int_1^2 \left[\frac{24+3x-8x-x^2}{x^4}\right]dx$

$\displaystyle = \int_1^2 \left[\frac{24-5x-x^2}{x^4}\right]dx$

$\displaystyle = \int_1^2 \left[\frac{24}{x^4} - \frac{5x}{x^4} - \frac{x^2}{x^4}\right]dx$

$\displaystyle = \int_1^2 \left[24x^{-4} - 5x^{-3} - x^{-2}\right]dx$

$\displaystyle = \left[\frac{24}{-3}x^{-3} - \frac{5}{-2}x^{-2} - \frac{1}{-1}x^{-1}\right]_1^2$

$\displaystyle = \left[-8x^{-3} + \frac{5}{2}x^{-2} + x^{-1}\right]_1^2$

$\displaystyle = \left(-8(2)^{-3} + \frac{5}{2}(2)^{-2} + (2)^{-1}\right)$
$\displaystyle \quad - \left(-8(1)^{-3} + \frac{5}{2}(1)^{-2} + (1)^{-1}\right)$

$\displaystyle = \left(-1 + \frac{5}{8} + \frac{1}{2}\right) - \left(-8 + \frac{5}{2} + 1\right)$

$\displaystyle = \frac{1}{8} - \left(-\frac{9}{2}\right)$

$\displaystyle = \frac{37}{8}$

3 b $\displaystyle\int_0^4 \sqrt{2x+1}\,dx$

$\displaystyle = \int_0^4 (2x+1)^{\frac{1}{2}}\,dx$

$\displaystyle = \left[\frac{1}{(2)^{\frac{3}{2}}}(2x+1)^{\frac{3}{2}}\right]_0^4$

$\displaystyle = \left[\frac{1}{3}(2x+1)^{\frac{3}{2}}\right]_0^4$

$\displaystyle = \left(\frac{1}{3}(2(4)+1)^{\frac{3}{2}}\right) - \left(\frac{1}{3}(2(0)+1)^{\frac{3}{2}}\right)$

$\displaystyle = 9 - \frac{1}{3}$

$\displaystyle = \frac{26}{3}$

f $\displaystyle\int_{-2}^2 \frac{4}{\sqrt{5-2x}}\,dx$

$\displaystyle = \int_{-2}^2 4(5-2x)^{-\frac{1}{2}}\,dx$

$\displaystyle = \left[\frac{4}{(-2)^{\frac{1}{2}}}(5-2x)^{\frac{1}{2}}\right]_{-2}^2$

$\displaystyle = \left[-4(5-2x)^{\frac{1}{2}}\right]_{-2}^2$

$\displaystyle = \left(-4(5-2(2))^{\frac{1}{2}}\right) - \left(-4(5-2(-2))^{\frac{1}{2}}\right)$

$\displaystyle = (-4) - (-12)$

$\displaystyle = 8$

4 a $\displaystyle y = \frac{2}{x^2+5}$

> Remember, the rule:
> $$\int (ax+b)^n\,dx = \frac{1}{a(n+1)}(ax+b)^{n+1} + c,$$
> $n \neq -1$ and $a \neq 0$
> **only** works for powers of **linear** functions.

Write in index form:

$y = 2(x^2+5)^{-1}$

$\displaystyle \frac{dy}{dx} = -1 \times 2(x^2+5)^{-2} \times 2x$

$\displaystyle \frac{dy}{dx} = -4x(x^2+5)^{-2}$

$\displaystyle \frac{dy}{dx} = -\frac{4x}{(x^2+5)^2}$

b $\displaystyle\int_0^2 \frac{2x}{(x^2+5)^2}\,dx = -\frac{1}{2}\int_0^2 \frac{4x}{(x^2+5)^2}$

$\displaystyle = -\frac{1}{2}\left[\frac{2}{x^2+5}\right]_0^2$

$\displaystyle = -\frac{1}{2}\left(\frac{2}{2^2+5}\right) - -\frac{1}{2}\left(\frac{2}{0^2+5}\right)$

$\displaystyle = -\frac{1}{9} + \frac{1}{5}$

$\displaystyle = \frac{4}{45}$

5 a $\displaystyle y = (x^3-2)^5$

$\displaystyle \frac{dy}{dx} = 5(x^3-2)^4 \times 3x^2$

$\displaystyle \frac{dy}{dx} = 15x^2(x^3-2)^4$

b $\int_0^1 x^2(x^3-2)^4\,dx = \frac{1}{15}\int_0^1 x^2(x^3-2)^4$

$$= \frac{1}{15}\Big[(x^3-2)^5\Big]_0^1$$

$$= \frac{1}{15}(1^3-2)^5 - \frac{1}{15}(0^3-2)^5$$

$$= -\frac{1}{15} + \frac{32}{15}$$

$$= 2\frac{1}{15}$$

6 a Given that $y = \dfrac{(\sqrt{x}+1)^5}{10}$

Write in index form:

$$y = \frac{1}{10}\left(x^{\frac{1}{2}}+1\right)^5$$

$$\frac{dy}{dx} = 5 \times \frac{1}{10}\left(x^{\frac{1}{2}}+1\right)^4 \times \frac{1}{2}x^{-\frac{1}{2}}$$

$$\frac{dy}{dx} = \frac{1}{4}x^{-\frac{1}{2}}\left(x^{\frac{1}{2}}+1\right)^4 \text{ or } \frac{(\sqrt{x}+1)^4}{4\sqrt{x}}$$

b $\int_1^4 \dfrac{(\sqrt{x}+1)^4}{\sqrt{x}}\,dx = 4\int_1^4 \dfrac{(\sqrt{x}+1)^4}{4\sqrt{x}}$

$$= \left[4 \times \frac{1}{10}\left(x^{\frac{1}{2}}+1\right)^5\right]_1^4$$

$$= \left(\frac{4}{10}\left(4^{\frac{1}{2}}+1\right)^5\right)$$

$$\quad - \left(\frac{4}{10}\left(1^{\frac{1}{2}}+1\right)^5\right)$$

$$= \frac{486}{5} - \frac{64}{5}$$

$$= 84\frac{2}{5}$$

1 a $\text{Area} = \int_a^b y\,dx$

$$\text{Area} = \int_0^4 (x^3 - 8x^2 + 16x)\,dx$$

$$= \left[\frac{1}{4}x^4 - \frac{8}{3}x^3 + 8x^2\right]_0^4$$

$$= \left(\frac{1}{4}(4)^4 - \frac{8}{3}(4)^3 + 8(4)^2\right)$$

$$\quad - \left(\frac{1}{4}(0)^4 - \frac{8}{3}(0)^3 + 8(0)^2\right)$$

$$= \left(64 - \frac{512}{3} + 128\right) - (0)$$

$\text{Area} = 21\frac{1}{3}$ units².

c $\text{Area} = \int_a^b y\,dx$

$$\text{Area} = \int_0^5 x(x-5)\,dx$$

$$= \int_0^5 (x^2 - 5x)\,dx$$

$$= \left[\frac{1}{3}x^3 - \frac{5}{2}x^2\right]_0^5$$

$$= \left(\frac{1}{3}(5)^3 - \frac{5}{2}(5)^2\right) - \left(\frac{1}{3}(0)^3 - \frac{5}{2}(0)^2\right)$$

$$= -\frac{125}{6}$$

> We obtain a negative value because the required area is below the x-axis. Give your answer as the positive value.

$\text{Area} = 20\dfrac{5}{6}$ units².

2 $\text{Area} = \int_a^b y\,dx$

$$= \int_0^2 x(x-2)(x-4)\,dx$$

$$= \int_0^2 (x^3 - 6x^2 + 8x)\,dx$$

$$= \left[\frac{1}{4}x^4 - 2x^3 + 4x^2\right]_0^2$$

$$= \left(\frac{1}{4}(2)^4 - 2(2)^3 + 4(2)^2\right)$$

$$\quad - \left(\frac{1}{4}(0)^4 - 2(0)^3 + 4(0)^2\right)$$

$$= 4 - 0$$
$$= 4$$

Area = 4 units².

$$\int_2^4 x(x-2)(x-4)\,dx$$

$$= \int_2^4 (x^3 - 6x^2 + 8x)\,dx$$

$$= \left[\frac{1}{4}x^4 - 2x^3 + 4x^2\right]_2^4$$

$$= \left(\frac{1}{4}(4)^4 - 2(4)^3 + 4(4)^2\right) - \left(\frac{1}{4}(2)^4 - 2(2)^3 + 4(2)^2\right)$$

$$= 0 - 4$$

$$= -4 \text{ (This is negative because the area is below the } x\text{-axis).}$$

Area = 4 units².

The areas of the shaded regions are both the same.

3 c Area $= \int_a^b y\,dx$

$$y = x(2x-1)(x+2)$$

The coefficient of x^3 is positive (if the brackets are expanded), so the shape of the curve is:

The x-intercepts are found by solving
$$x(2x-1)(x+2) = 0$$

$$x = 0 \text{ and } x = \frac{1}{2} \text{ and } x = -2$$

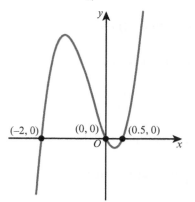

$$\int_{-2}^0 x(2x-1)(x+2)\,dx$$

$$= \int_{-2}^0 (2x^3 + 3x^2 - 2x)\,dx$$

$$= \left[\frac{1}{2}x^4 + x^3 - x^2\right]_{-2}^0$$

$$= \left(\frac{1}{2}(0)^4 + (0)^3 - (0)^2\right)$$

$$\quad - \left(\frac{1}{2}(-2)^4 + (-2)^3 - (-2)^2\right)$$

$$= 0 - -4$$

$$= 4$$

Area = 4 units².

$$\int_0^{0.5} x(2x-1)(x+2)\,dx$$

$$= \int_0^{0.5} (2x^3 + 3x^2 - 2x)\,dx$$

$$= \left[\frac{1}{2}x^4 + x^3 - x^2\right]_0^{0.5}$$

$$= \left(\frac{1}{2}(0.5)^4 + (0.5)^3 - (0.5)^2\right)$$

$$\quad - \left(\frac{1}{2}(0)^4 + (0)^3 - (0)^2\right)$$

$$= -\frac{3}{32} - 0$$

$$= -\frac{3}{32}$$

Area $= \frac{3}{32}$ units².

Total area $= 4\frac{3}{32}$ units².

4 a Area $= \int_a^b y\,dx$

$$y = x^4 - 6x^2 + 9$$

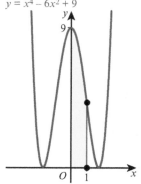

$$\text{Area} = \int_0^1 (x^4 - 6x^2 + 9)\ dx$$

$$= \left[\frac{1}{5}x^5 - 2x^3 + 9x\right]_0^1$$

$$= \left(\frac{1}{5}(1)^5 - 2(1)^3 + 9(1)\right)$$

$$- \left(\frac{1}{5}(0)^5 - 2(0)^3 + 9(0)\right)$$

$$= 7\frac{1}{5}\ \text{units}^2$$

4 e $\text{Area} = \int_a^b y\ dx$

$$y = \frac{4}{\sqrt{x}}$$

Write in index form:

$$y = 4x^{-\frac{1}{2}}$$

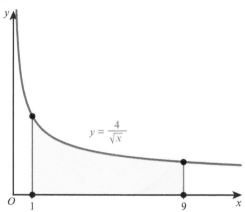

$$\text{Area} = \int_a^b y\ dx$$

$$\text{Area} = \int_1^9 4x^{-\frac{1}{2}}\ dx$$

$$= \left[\frac{4}{\frac{1}{2}}x^{\frac{1}{2}}\right]_1^9$$

$$= \left[8x^{\frac{1}{2}}\right]_1^9$$

$$= \left(8(9)^{\frac{1}{2}}\right) - \left(8(1)^{\frac{1}{2}}\right)$$

$$= 16\ \text{units}^2$$

5 a $\text{Area} = \int_a^b x\ dy$

$$y = x^3$$

$$x = y^{\frac{1}{3}}$$

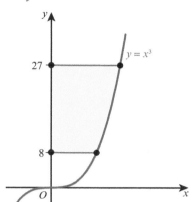

$$\text{Area} = \int_8^{27} y^{\frac{1}{3}}\ dy$$

$$= \left[\frac{3}{4}y^{\frac{4}{3}}\right]_8^{27}$$

$$= \left(\frac{3}{4}(27)^{\frac{4}{3}} - \frac{3}{4}(8)^{\frac{4}{3}}\right)$$

$$= \frac{243}{4} - 12$$

$$= 48\frac{3}{4}\ \text{units}^2$$

b $x = y^2 + 1$

$$\text{Area} = \int_a^b x\ dy$$

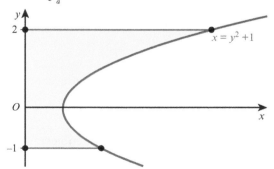

$$\text{Area} = \int_{-1}^{2} (y^2 + 1)\, dy$$

$$= \left[\frac{1}{3}y^3 + y\right]_{-1}^{2}$$

$$= \left(\frac{1}{3}(2)^3 + 2\right) - \left(\frac{1}{3}(-1)^3 + (-1)\right)$$

$$= \frac{14}{3} - \left(-\frac{4}{3}\right)$$

$$= 6 \text{ units}^2$$

6 $y = \sqrt{2x+1}$

Write in index form:

$y = (2x+1)^{\frac{1}{2}}$

Make x the subject:

$y^2 = 2x + 1$

$2x = y^2 - 1$

$x = \frac{1}{2}y^2 - \frac{1}{2}$

$$\text{Area} = \int_{a}^{b} x\, dy$$

$$\text{Area} = \int_{1}^{3} \left(\frac{1}{2}y^2 - \frac{1}{2}\right) dy$$

$$= \left[\frac{1}{6}y^3 - \frac{1}{2}y\right]_{1}^{3}$$

$$= \left(\frac{1}{6}(3)^3 - \frac{1}{2}(3)\right) - \left(\frac{1}{6}(1)^3 - \frac{1}{2}(1)\right)$$

$$= 3 - \left(-\frac{1}{3}\right)$$

$$= 3\frac{1}{3} \text{ units}^2$$

7 $y = 2x^2 + 1$

Substitute $x = 0$ to find the y-intercept:

$y = 2(0)^2 + 1$

$y = 1$

Given $= 2x^2 + 1$, make x the subject:

$y - 1 = 2x^2$

$x^2 = \frac{1}{2}y - \frac{1}{2}$

$x = \pm\left(\frac{1}{2}y - \frac{1}{2}\right)^{\frac{1}{2}}$

Take the positive value for this graph.

$$\text{Area} = \int_{a}^{b} x\, dy$$

$$\text{Area} = \int_{1}^{9} \left(\frac{1}{2}y - \frac{1}{2}\right)^{\frac{1}{2}} dy$$

$$= \left[\frac{1}{\left(\frac{3}{2}\right)\left(\frac{1}{2}\right)}\left(\frac{1}{2}y - \frac{1}{2}\right)^{\frac{3}{2}}\right]_{1}^{9}$$

$$= \left[\left(\frac{4}{3}\left(\frac{1}{2}(9) - \frac{1}{2}\right)^{\frac{3}{2}}\right) - \left(\frac{4}{3}\left(\frac{1}{2}(1) - \frac{1}{2}\right)^{\frac{3}{2}}\right)\right]_{1}^{9}$$

$$= \frac{32}{3} - 0$$

$$= 10\frac{2}{3} \text{ units}^2$$

8 a $y = \dfrac{12}{x^2}$

Write in index form:

$y = 12x^{-2}$

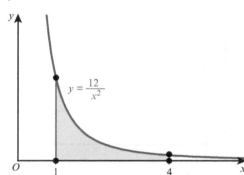

$$\text{Area} = \int_{a}^{b} y\, dx$$

$$\text{Area} = \int_{1}^{4} 12x^{-2}\, dx$$

$$= \left[\frac{12}{-1}x^{-1}\right]_{1}^{4}$$

$$= [-12x^{-1}]_{1}^{4}$$

$$= (-12(4)^{-1}) - (-12(1)^{-1})$$

$$= -3 - (-12)$$

$$= 9 \text{ units}^2$$

b

$$\int_1^p 12x^{-2}\,dx = \int_p^4 12x^{-2}\,dx$$

$$[-12x^{-1}]_1^p = [\_12x^{-1}]_p^4$$

$$(-12(p)^{-1}) - (-12(1)^{-1}) = (-12(4)^{-1}) - (-12(p)^{-1})$$

$$-\frac{12}{p} - (-12) = -\frac{12}{4} + \frac{12}{p}$$

$$-\frac{12}{p} + 12 = -3 + \frac{12}{p}$$

$$12 + 3 = \frac{12}{p} + \frac{12}{p}$$

$$15 = \frac{24}{p}$$

$$p = 1.6$$

9 a Let $y = \sqrt{x^2 + 5}$

Write in index form:

$$y = (x^2 + 5)^{\frac{1}{2}}$$

Using the chain rule:

$$\frac{dy}{dx} = \frac{1}{2}(x^2 + 5)^{-\frac{1}{2}} \times 2x$$

$$\frac{dy}{dx} = x(x^2 + 5)^{-\frac{1}{2}}$$

$$\frac{dy}{dx} = \frac{x}{\sqrt{x^2 + 5}}$$

$$\frac{d}{dx}\left(\sqrt{x^2 + 5}\right) = \frac{x}{\sqrt{x^2 + 5}}\quad \text{shown}$$

b Area $= \int_a^b y\,dx$

$$\text{Area} = \int_0^2 \frac{x}{\sqrt{x^2 + 5}}\,dx$$

$$= \left[\sqrt{x^2 + 5}\right]_0^2$$

$$= \left(\sqrt{2^2 + 5}\right) - \left(\sqrt{0^2 + 5}\right)$$

$$= 3 - \sqrt{5}\ \text{units}^2$$

10 y

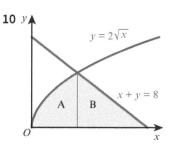

The line $x + y = 8$ (or $y = 8 - x$), crosses the x-axis at $x = 8$.

Find the intersection of the curve and line:

$$2\sqrt{x} = 8 - x$$

$$x + 2\sqrt{x} - 8 = 0$$

Let $a = \sqrt{x}$ then:

$$a^2 + 2a - 8 = 0$$

$$(a + 4)(a - 2) = 0$$

$$a = -4 \text{ and } a = 2$$

If $\sqrt{x} = -4$ (no solutions)

If $\sqrt{x} = 2$ then $x = 4$

If $x = 4$, the y-coordinate is found by substituting into $x + y = 8$

i.e. $4 + y = 8$ or $y = 4$

The curve and the line intersect at $(4, 4)$.

Required area $= A + B$

Using area of a $\triangle = \frac{1}{2} \times$ base $\times$ perpendicular height

Area B $= \frac{1}{2} \times 4 \times 4$ or 8

Use area $= \int_a^b y\,dx$

Area A $= \int_0^4 2x^{\frac{1}{2}}\,dx$

$$A = \left[\frac{2}{\frac{3}{2}}x^{\frac{3}{2}}\right]_0^4$$

$$A = \left[\frac{4}{3}x^{\frac{3}{2}}\right]_0^4$$

$$A = \left(\frac{4}{3}(4)^{\frac{3}{2}}\right) - \left(\frac{4}{3}(0)^{\frac{3}{2}}\right)$$

$$A = \frac{32}{3}$$

Area A + B $= 8 + \frac{32}{3}$

Shaded area $= 18\frac{2}{3}\ \text{units}^2$

11 a

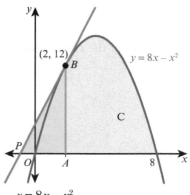

$y = 8x - x^2$

$\dfrac{dy}{dx} = 8 - 2x$

At $x = 2$, the gradient of the tangent is:

$8 - 2(2) = 4$

Using $y - y_1 = m(x - x_1)$, $m = 4$, $x = 2$, $y = 12$:

$y - 12 = 4(x - 2)$

$y - 12 = 4x - 8$

$y = 4x + 4$

Equation of the tangent is $y = 4x + 4$

To find where this tangent crosses the x-axis, substitute $y = 0$

$y = 4x + 4$

$0 = 4x + 4$

$x = -1$

P is at $(-1, 0)$

b Shaded region = area $\triangle PAB$ + area C

Using area of a $\triangle = \dfrac{1}{2} \times$ base $\times$ perpendicular height:

Area $\triangle PAB = \dfrac{1}{2} \times 3 \times 12$ or 18

Area $C = \displaystyle\int_a^b y\, dx$

Area $C = \displaystyle\int_2^8 8x - x^2\, dx$

$= \left[4x^2 - \dfrac{1}{3}x^3 \right]_2^8$

$= \left(4(8)^2 - \dfrac{1}{3}(8)^3 \right) - \left(4(2)^2 - \dfrac{1}{3}(2)^3 \right)$

$= \dfrac{256}{3} - \dfrac{40}{3}$

$= 72$

Total area $= 18 + 72$

$= 90$ units^2

12 $y = \sqrt{2x + 1}$

To find the coordinates of A, substitute $y = 0$:

$0 = \sqrt{2x + 1}$

$2x + 1 = 0$

$x = -\dfrac{1}{2}$

$A = \left(-\dfrac{1}{2}, 0 \right)$

$y = \sqrt{2x + 1}$

Write in index form:

$y = (2x + 1)^{\frac{1}{2}}$

To find the equation of the normal at B:

Using the chain rule:

$\dfrac{dy}{dx} = \dfrac{1}{2}(2x + 1)^{-\frac{1}{2}} \times 2$

$\dfrac{dy}{dx} = (2x + 1)^{-\frac{1}{2}}$

At $x = 4$,

$\dfrac{dy}{dx} = (2 \times 4 + 1)^{-\frac{1}{2}}$

Gradient of the tangent $= \dfrac{1}{3} = m$

Gradient of the normal $= -3$

The equation of the normal is found by using

$y - y_1 = -\dfrac{1}{m}(x - x_1)$ and $x_1 = 4$, $y_1 = 3$

$y - 3 = -3(x - 4)$

$y - 3 = -3x + 12$

$y + 3x = 15$

To find where the normal meets the x-axis, substitute $y = 0$

$0 + 3x = 15$

$x = 5$

$C = (5, 0)$

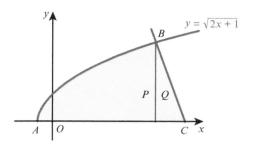

Shaded area = area P + area of the triangle Q

Using area of a $\Delta = \frac{1}{2} \times$ base $\times$ perpendicular height

Area Q $= \frac{1}{2} \times 1 \times 3$ or $\frac{3}{2}$

Area of P $= \displaystyle\int_a^b y\,dx$

$= \displaystyle\int_{-\frac{1}{2}}^{4} (2x+1)^{\frac{1}{2}}\,dy$

$= \left[\dfrac{1}{\left(\dfrac{3}{2}\right)(2)}(2x+1)^{\frac{3}{2}} \right]_{-\frac{1}{2}}^{4}$

$= \left[\dfrac{1}{3}(2x+1)^{\frac{3}{2}} \right]_{-\frac{1}{2}}^{4}$

$= \left(\dfrac{1}{3}(2 \times 4 + 1)^{\frac{3}{2}} \right) - \left(\dfrac{1}{3}\left(2 \times \left(-\dfrac{1}{2}\right) + 1\right)^{\frac{3}{2}} \right)$

$= 9$

Total shaded area $= \dfrac{3}{2} + 9$

$= 10\dfrac{1}{2}$ units^2

13

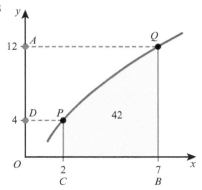

Looking at the diagram:

$\displaystyle\int_4^{12} x\,dy =$ area $AQBO -$ area $DPCO - 42$

$= 12 \times 7 - 4 \times 2 - 42$

$= 34$ units^2

14 Looking at the diagrams:

The value of $\displaystyle\int_1^8 x\,dy = 12 + 14 = 26$

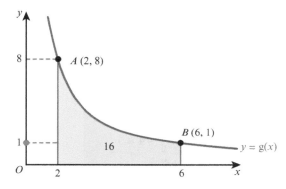

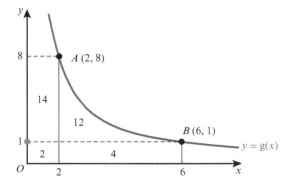

1 Use area $= \displaystyle\int_a^b y \, dx$

$$\text{Area} = \int_0^4 (5 + 6x - x^2) \, dx$$

$$= \left[5x + 3x^2 - \frac{1}{3}x^3 \right]_0^4$$

$$= \left(5(4) + 3(4)^2 - \frac{1}{3}(4)^3 \right)$$

$$- \left(5(0) + 3(0)^2 - \frac{1}{3}(0)^3 \right)$$

$$= \left(\frac{140}{3} \right) - (0)$$

$$\text{Area} = 46\frac{2}{3}$$

Shaded area $= 46\dfrac{2}{3} - 4 \times 5$

Shaded area $= 26\dfrac{2}{3}$ units^2

2 Find the coordinates of A and B by solving $y = (x-3)^2$ and $y = 2x - 3$ simultaneously.

$$(x-3)^2 = 2x - 3$$
$$x^2 - 6x + 9 = 2x - 3$$
$$x^2 - 8x + 12 = 0$$
$$(x-6)(x-2) = 0$$
$$x = 6 \text{ and } x = 2$$

A is at $x = 2$, B is at $x = 6$

$$A = \int_a^b f(x) \, dx - \int_a^b g(x) \, dx$$

Using $f(x) = 2x - 3$ and $g(x) = (x-3)^2$

$$\text{Area} = \int_2^6 f(x) \, dx - \int_2^6 g(x) \, dx$$

$$= \int_2^6 (2x - 3) \, dx - \int_2^6 (x^2 - 6x + 9) \, dx$$

$$= \int_2^6 (-x^2 + 8x - 12) \, dx$$

$$= \left[-\frac{1}{3}x^3 + 4x^2 - 12x \right]_2^6$$

$$= \left(-\frac{1}{3}(6)^3 + 4(6)^2 - 12(6) \right)$$

$$- \left(-\frac{1}{3}(2)^3 + 4(2)^2 - 12(2) \right)$$

$$= 10\frac{2}{3} \text{ units}^2$$

3 Find the coordinates of A and B by solving simultaneously:

$y = -x^2 + 11x - 18$ and $2x + y = 12$

$2x + y = 12$ rearranged gives $y = 12 - 2x$

So,

$$-x^2 + 11x - 18 = 12 - 2x$$
$$x^2 - 13x + 30 = 0$$
$$(x-10)(x-3) = 0$$
$$x = 10 \text{ and } x = 3$$

A is at $x = 3$, B is at $x = 10$

$$\text{Area} = \int_a^b f(x) \, dx - \int_a^b g(x) \, dx$$

Using $f(x) = -x^2 + 11x - 18$ and $g(x) = 12 - 2x$

$$\text{Area} = \int_3^{10} f(x) \, dx - \int_3^{10} g(x) \, dx$$

$$= \int_3^{10} (-x^2 + 11x - 18) \, dx - \int_3^{10} (12 - 2x) \, dx$$

$$= \int_3^{10} (-x^2 + 13x - 30) \, dx$$

$$= \left[-\frac{1}{3}x^3 + \frac{13}{2}x^2 - 30x \right]_3^{10}$$

$$= \left(-\frac{1}{3}(10)^3 + \frac{13}{2}(10)^2 - 30(10) \right)$$

$$- \left(-\frac{1}{3}(3)^3 + \frac{13}{2}(3)^2 - 30(3) \right)$$

$$= 57\frac{1}{6} \text{ units}^2$$

4 c $y = x^2 - 4x + 4$ ....[1]

and $2x + y = 12$ ....[2]

From [1],

$y = (x-2)^2$

To find the x-intercept, substitute $y = 0$:

$$(x-2)^2 = 0$$
$$x - 2 = 0$$
$$x = 2$$

The curve is a $\cup$ shaped parabola which just touches the x-axis at $x = 2$

From [2],

$2x + y = 12$

To find the x-intercept, substitute $y = 0$:

$2x = 12$

$x = 6$

To find the y-intercept, substitute $x = 0$:

$2(0) + y = 12$

$y = 12$

The intersection points of the two graphs can be found by solving [1] and [2] simultaneously.

The sketch looks like:

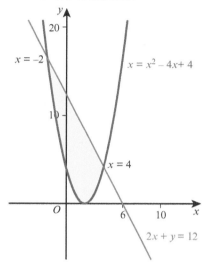

From [2],

$2x + y = 12$

$y = 12 - 2x$

Now using [1]:

$x^2 - 4x + 4 = 12 - 2x$

$x^2 - 2x - 8 = 0$

$(x + 2)(x - 4) = 0$

$x = -2$ and $x = 4$

The curve and the straight line intersect at $x = -2$ and $x = 4$.

Using $f(x) = 12 - 2x$ and $g(x) = x^2 - 4x + 4$,

$$\text{Area} = \int_{-2}^{4} f(x)\ dx - \int_{-2}^{4} g(x)\ dx$$

$$= \int_{-2}^{4} (12 - 2x)\ dx - \int_{-2}^{4} (x^2 - 4x + 4)\ dx$$

$$= \int_{-2}^{4} (8 + 2x - x^2)\ dx$$

$$= \left[8x + x^2 - \frac{1}{3}x^3 \right]_{-2}^{4}$$

$$= \left(8(4) + 4^2 - \frac{1}{3}(4)^3 \right)$$

$$- \left(8(-2) + (-2)^2 - \frac{1}{3}(-2)^3 \right)$$

$$= 36 \text{ units}^2$$

6   Using $f(x) = \sqrt{x + 4} \ldots [1]$

and $g(x) = \frac{1}{2}x + 2 \ldots [2]$

Rewrite [1] in index form:

$f(x) = (x + 4)^{\frac{1}{2}}$

Integrating $f(x) = (x + 4)^{\frac{1}{2}}$ gives:

$$\frac{1}{\left(\frac{3}{2}\right)(1)}(x + 4)^{\frac{3}{2}} \text{ or } \frac{2}{3}(x + 4)^{\frac{3}{2}} + c$$

Using:

$$\text{Area} = \int_{-4}^{0} f(x)dx - \int_{-4}^{0} g(x)dx$$

$$= \int_{-4}^{0} (x + 4)^{\frac{1}{2}}dx - \int_{-4}^{0} \left(\frac{1}{2}x + 2 \right)dx$$

$$= \int_{-4}^{0} \left[(x + 4)^{\frac{1}{2}} - \frac{1}{2}x - 2 \right]dx$$

$$= \left[\frac{2}{3}(x + 4)^{\frac{3}{2}} - \frac{1}{4}x^2 - 2x \right]_{-4}^{0}$$

$$= \left(\frac{2}{3}(0 + 4)^{\frac{3}{2}} - \frac{1}{4}(0)^2 - 2(0) \right)$$

$$- \left(\frac{2}{3}(-4 + 4)^{\frac{3}{2}} - \frac{1}{4}(-4)^2 - 2(-4) \right)$$

$$= 1\frac{1}{3} \text{ units}^2$$

7 a Given $y = \sqrt{2x+3}$

Write in index form:

$y = (2x+3)^{\frac{1}{2}}$

Differentiate using the chain rule:

$\dfrac{dy}{dx} = \dfrac{1}{2}(2x+3)^{-\frac{1}{2}} \times 2$

$\qquad = (2x+3)^{-\frac{1}{2}}$

The gradient of the curve at $x = 3$ is:

$= (2 \times 3 + 3)^{-\frac{1}{2}}$ or $\dfrac{1}{3}$

The equation of the tangent is found using:

$y - y_1 = m(x - x_1)$, where $m = \dfrac{1}{3}$ and $x_1 = 3, y_1 = 3$

$y - 3 = \dfrac{1}{3}(x - 3)$

$y - 3 = \dfrac{1}{3}x - 1$

$y = \dfrac{1}{3}x + 2$

b Using $f(x) = \dfrac{1}{3}x + 2$ and $g(x) = \sqrt{2x+3}$

$\text{Area} = \displaystyle\int_0^3 f(x)\,dx - \int_0^3 g(x)\,dx$

$\qquad = \displaystyle\int_0^3 \left(\dfrac{1}{3}x + 2\right) dx - \int_0^3 (2x+3)^{\frac{1}{2}}\,dx$

Integrating $(2x+3)^{\frac{1}{2}}$:

$= \dfrac{1}{\left(\dfrac{3}{2}\right)(2)}(2x+3)^{\frac{3}{2}} + c$

$= \dfrac{1}{3}(2x+3)^{\frac{3}{2}} + c$

$\displaystyle\int_0^3 \left(\dfrac{1}{3}x + 2 - (2x+3)^{\frac{1}{2}}\right) dx$

$= \left[\dfrac{1}{6}x^2 + 2x - \dfrac{1}{3}(2x+3)^{\frac{3}{2}}\right]_0^3$

$= \left(\dfrac{1}{6}(3)^2 + 2(3) - \dfrac{1}{3}(2(3)+3)^{\frac{3}{2}}\right)$

$\quad - \left(\dfrac{1}{6}(0)^2 + 2(0) - \dfrac{1}{3}(2(0)+3)^{\frac{3}{2}}\right)$

$= \dfrac{15}{2} - 9 + \dfrac{1}{3}(3)^{\frac{3}{2}}$

$= \dfrac{15}{2} - 9 + (3^{-1})\left(3^{\frac{3}{2}}\right)$

$= \dfrac{15}{2} - 9 + 3^{\frac{1}{2}}$

$= -\dfrac{3}{2} + \sqrt{3}$

$= \dfrac{1}{2}\left(2\sqrt{3} - 3\right)$

8 a Given $y = 10 + 9x - x^2$

$\dfrac{dy}{dx} = 9 - 2x$

The gradient of the curve at $x = 6$ is:

$= 9 - 2(6)$ or -3

The equation of the tangent is found using:

$y - y_1 = m(x - x_1)$, where $m = -3$ and $x_1 = 6, y_1 = 28$

$y - 28 = -3(x - 6)$

$y - 28 = -3x + 18$

$\qquad y = -3x + 46$

The equation of the tangent at P is:

$y = -3x + 46$

b To find where this tangent intersects the x-axis, substitute $y = 0$:

$-3x + 46 = 0$

$x = \dfrac{46}{3}$

R is at $\left(\dfrac{46}{3}, 0\right)$

Using $f(x) = -3x + 46$ and $g(x) = 10 + 9x - x^2$,

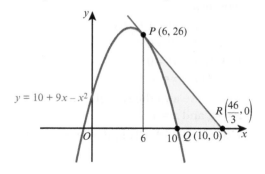

Area $=$ area of $\Delta - \displaystyle\int_{6}^{10} g(x)\,\mathrm{d}x$

Area $= \dfrac{1}{2} \times \left(\dfrac{46}{3} - 6\right) \times 28 - \displaystyle\int_{6}^{10} g(x)\,\mathrm{d}x$

$= \dfrac{1}{2} \times \dfrac{28}{3} \times 28 - \displaystyle\int_{6}^{10}(10 + 9x - x^2)\,\mathrm{d}x$

$= \dfrac{392}{3} - \displaystyle\int_{6}^{10}(10 + 9x - x^2)\,\mathrm{d}x$

$= \dfrac{392}{3} - \left[10x + \dfrac{9}{2}x^2 - \dfrac{1}{3}x^3\right]_{6}^{10}$

$= \dfrac{392}{3} - \left[10(10) + \dfrac{9}{2}(10)^2 - \dfrac{1}{3}(10)^3\right]$

$\quad - \left[10(6) + \dfrac{9}{2}(6)^2 - \dfrac{1}{3}(6)^3\right]$

> Be careful with brackets!

$= \dfrac{392}{3} - \left\{\left[100 + 450 - \dfrac{1000}{3}\right]\right.$

$\quad \left. - [60 + 162 - 72]\right\}$

$= \dfrac{392}{3} - \dfrac{200}{3}$

$= 64$

9 a Given $y = 4x - x^3$

$\dfrac{\mathrm{d}y}{\mathrm{d}x} = 4 - 3x^2$

The gradient of the curve at $x = 2$ is:

$= 4 - 3(2)^2$ or -8

The equation of the tangent is found using:

$y - y_1 = m(x - x_1)$, where $m = -8$ and
$x_1 = 2,\ y_1 = 0$

$y - 0 = -8(x - 2)$

$y = -8x + 16$

The equation of the tangent at P is:
$y = 16 - 8x$

b To find the shaded area use:

$f(x) = 16 - 8x$ and $g(x) = 4x - x^3$

Area $= \displaystyle\int_{-4}^{2} f(x)\,\mathrm{d}x - \int_{-4}^{2} g(x)\,\mathrm{d}x$

$= \displaystyle\int_{-4}^{2}(16 - 8x)\,\mathrm{d}x - \int_{-4}^{2}(4x - x^3)\,\mathrm{d}x$

$= \displaystyle\int_{-4}^{2}(16 - 12x + x^3)\,\mathrm{d}x$

$= \left[16x - 6x^2 - \dfrac{1}{4}x^4\right]_{-4}^{2}$

$= \left(16(2) - 6(2)^2 + \dfrac{1}{4}(2)^4\right)$

$\quad - \left(16(-4) - 6(-4)^2 + \dfrac{1}{4}(-4)^4\right)$

$= 108$ units^2

10 a Given $y = 5 - \sqrt{10 - x}$

Write in index form:

$y = 5 - (10 - x)^{\frac{1}{2}}$

Differentiate using the chain rule:

$\dfrac{\mathrm{d}y}{\mathrm{d}x} = -\dfrac{1}{2}(10 - x)^{-\frac{1}{2}} \times -1$

$= \dfrac{1}{2}(10 - x)^{-\frac{1}{2}}$

The gradient of the curve at $x = 9$ is:

$= \dfrac{1}{2}(10 - 9)^{-\frac{1}{2}}$ or $\dfrac{1}{2}$

The equation of the tangent is found using:

$y - y_1 = m(x - x_1)$, where $m = \dfrac{1}{2}$ and
$x_1 = 9,\ y_1 = 4$

$y - 4 = \dfrac{1}{2}(x - 9)$

$2y - 8 = x - 9$

The equation of the tangent at P is:

$2y = x - 1$

Or $y = \dfrac{1}{2}x - \dfrac{1}{2}$

b To find the shaded area use:

$f(x) = 5 - (10 - x)^{\frac{1}{2}}$

and $g(x) = \dfrac{1}{2}x - \dfrac{1}{2}$

$$\text{Area} = \int_0^9 f(x)\, dx - \int_0^9 g(x)\, dx$$

$$= \int_0^9 5 - (10-x)^{\frac{1}{2}}\, dx - \int_0^9 \left(\frac{1}{2}x - \frac{1}{2}\right) dx$$

$$= \int_0^9 \left(\frac{11}{2} - \frac{1}{2}x - (10-x)^{\frac{1}{2}}\right) dx$$

$$= \left[\frac{11}{2}x - \frac{1}{4}x^2 - \frac{1}{\left(\frac{3}{2}\right)(-1)}(10-x)^{\frac{3}{2}}\right]_0^9$$

$$= \left[\frac{11}{2}x - \frac{1}{4}x^2 + \frac{2}{3}(10-x)^{\frac{3}{2}}\right]_0^9$$

$$= \left(\frac{11}{2}(9) - \frac{1}{4}(9)^2 + \frac{2}{3}(10-9)^{\frac{3}{2}}\right) - \left(\frac{11}{2}(0) - \frac{1}{4}(0)^2 + \frac{2}{3}(10-0)^{\frac{3}{2}}\right)$$

$$= 8.834$$

$$= 8.83 \text{ units}^2 \text{(to 3 significant figures)}$$

EXERCISE 9H

1 a $\displaystyle\int_1^\infty \frac{2}{x^2}\, dx$

Write the integral with an upper limit X

$$\int_1^X \frac{2}{x^2}\, dx = \int_1^X 2x^{-2}\, dx$$

$$= [-2x^{-1}]_1^X$$

$$= \left(-\frac{2}{X}\right) - \left(-\frac{2}{1}\right)$$

$$= 2 - \frac{2}{X}$$

As $X \to \infty$, $\dfrac{2}{X} \to 0$

$$\therefore \int_1^\infty \frac{2}{x^2}\, dx = 2 - 0 = 2$$

Hence, the improper integral $\displaystyle\int_1^\infty \frac{2}{x^2}\, dx$ has a finite value of 2.

c $\displaystyle\int_{-\infty}^{-2} \frac{10}{x^3}\, dx$

Write the integral with an lower limit X

$$\int_X^{-2} \frac{10}{x^3}\, dx = \int_X^{-2} 10x^{-3}\, dx$$

$$= [-5x^{-2}]_X^{-2}$$

$$= \frac{-5}{(-2)^2} - \frac{-5}{(X)^2}$$

$$= -\frac{5}{4} + \frac{5}{X^2}$$

As $X \to -\infty$, $\dfrac{5}{X^2} \to 0$

Hence, as $X \to -\infty$ the integral has a finite value of $-\dfrac{5}{4}$.

If the question **1 c** referred to a **graph** and asked for the finite value of the **area,** the answer would have been $\dfrac{5}{4}$.

2 $\displaystyle\int_0^p \frac{20}{(2x+5)^2}\, dx$

Write in index form:

$$\int_0^p 20(2x+5)^{-2}\, dx$$

Integrate:

$$= \left[\frac{20}{(-1)(2)}(2x+5)^{-1} \right]_0^p$$

$$= \left[\frac{-10}{2x+5} \right]_0^p$$

$$= \left(-\frac{10}{2p+5} \right) - \left(-\frac{10}{5} \right)$$

$$= 2 - \frac{10}{2p+5}$$

As $p \to \infty$, $\dfrac{10}{2p+5} \to 0$

$\therefore$ The shaded area tends to the value 2.

3 b $\displaystyle\int_0^\infty \frac{4}{x\sqrt{x}}\,dx$

Write in index form:

$$\int_0^\infty \frac{4}{x^{\frac{3}{2}}}\,dx = \int_0^\infty 4x^{-\frac{3}{2}}\,dx$$

Write the integral with an upper limit X and lower limit Y.

$$\int_Y^X 4x^{-\frac{3}{2}}\,dx$$

Integrating:

$$= \left[-8x^{-\frac{1}{2}} \right]_Y^X$$

$$= \left[-\frac{8}{\sqrt{x}} \right]_Y^X$$

$$= -\frac{8}{\sqrt{X}} - \left(-\frac{8}{\sqrt{Y}} \right)$$

As $X \to \infty$, $\dfrac{8}{\sqrt{X}} \to 0$

As $Y \to 0$, $\dfrac{8}{\sqrt{Y}}$ tends to infinity.

$\therefore$ The integral does not exist.

e $\displaystyle\int_{\frac{1}{2}}^2 \frac{5}{(2x-1)^2}\,dx$

Write in index form:

$$= \int_{\frac{1}{2}}^2 5(2x-1)^{-2}\,dx$$

$$= \left[\frac{5}{(-1)(2)}(2x-1)^{-1} \right]_{\frac{1}{2}}^2$$

$$= \left[-\frac{5}{2(2x-1)} \right]_{\frac{1}{2}}^2$$

$$= \left[-\frac{5}{4x-2} \right]_{\frac{1}{2}}^2$$

$$= -\frac{5}{6} - \left(-\frac{5}{2-2} \right)$$

As $-\dfrac{5}{2-2}$ is undefined, the integral does not exist.

1 a $y = x^2 + \dfrac{2}{x}$

$$\text{Volume} = \pi \int_1^2 y^2\,dx = \pi \int_1^2 \left(x^2 + \frac{2}{x} \right)^2 dx$$

$$= \pi \int_1^2 \left(x^4 + 4x + \frac{4}{x^2} \right) dx$$

Write in index form:

$$= \pi \int_1^2 (x^4 + 4x + 4x^{-2})\, dx$$

$$= \pi \left[\frac{1}{5}x^5 + 2x^2 - 4x^{-1} \right]_1^2$$

$$= \pi \left[\left(\frac{1}{5}(2)^5 + 2(2)^2 - 4(2)^{-1} \right) \right.$$

$$\left. - \left(\frac{1}{5}(1)^5 + 2(1)^2 - 4(1)^{-1} \right) \right]$$

$$= \frac{71\pi}{5} \text{ units}^3$$

d $y = \dfrac{5}{3-x}$

$$\text{Volume} = \pi \int_{-1}^1 y^2\, dx = \pi \int_{-1}^1 \left(\frac{5}{3-x} \right)^2 dx$$

$$= \pi \int_{-1}^1 25(3-x)^{-2}\, dx$$

$$= \pi \left[\frac{25}{(-1)(-1)}(3-x)^{-1} \right]_{-1}^1$$

$$= \pi \left[25(3-x)^{-1} \right]_{-1}^1$$

$$= \pi [\, (25(3-1)^{-1}) - (25(3-(-1))^{-1}) \,]$$

$$= \pi \left[\left(\frac{25}{2} \right) - \left(\frac{25}{4} \right) \right]$$

$$= \frac{25\pi}{4} \text{ units}^3$$

2 a Given $y = x^2 + 2$

$$x^2 = y - 2$$

$$\text{Volume} = \pi \int_2^{11} x^2\, dy = \pi \int_2^{11} (y-2)\, dy$$

$$= \pi \left[\frac{1}{2}y^2 - 2y \right]_2^{11}$$

$$= \pi \left[\left(\frac{121}{2} - 22 \right) - (2-4) \right]$$

$$= \frac{81\pi}{2} \text{ units}^3$$

b Given $y = \sqrt{2x+1}$

$$y^2 = 2x + 1$$

$$2x = y^2 - 1$$

$$x = \frac{1}{2}y^2 - \frac{1}{2}$$

$$x^2 = \left(\frac{1}{2}y^2 - \frac{1}{2} \right)^2 \text{ or } \left(\frac{1}{2}y^2 - \frac{1}{2} \right)\left(\frac{1}{2}y^2 - \frac{1}{2} \right)$$

$$x^2 = \frac{1}{4}y^4 - \frac{1}{2}y^2 + \frac{1}{4}$$

$$\text{Volume} = \pi \int_1^3 x^2\, dy = \pi \int_1^3 \left(\frac{1}{4}y^4 - \frac{1}{2}y^2 + \frac{1}{4} \right) dy$$

$$= \pi \left[\frac{1}{20}y^5 - \frac{1}{6}y^3 + \frac{1}{4}y \right]_1^3$$

$$= \pi \left[\left(\frac{1}{20}(3)^5 - \frac{1}{6}(3)^3 + \frac{1}{4}(3) \right) \right.$$

$$\left. - \left(\frac{1}{20}(1)^5 - \frac{1}{6}(1)^3 + \frac{1}{4}(1) \right) \right]$$

$$= \frac{124\pi}{15} \text{ units}^3$$

3 Given: $y = \dfrac{a}{x}$

$$\text{Volume} = \pi \int_1^2 y^2\, dx = \pi \int_1^2 \left(\frac{a}{x} \right)^2 dx$$

$$= \pi \int_1^2 \left(\frac{a^2}{x^2} \right) dx$$

Write in index form:

$$= \pi \int_1^2 (a^2 x^{-2})\, dx$$

$$= \pi [-a^2 x^{-1}]_1^2$$

$$= \pi [\, (-a^2(2)^{-1}) - (-a^2(1)^{-1}) \,]$$

$$18\pi = \frac{a^2 \pi}{2}$$

$$a = \pm 6$$

a has to be positive for the graph to be in the first quadrant.

$$a = 6$$

4 $y = \sqrt{x^3 + 4x^2 + 3x + 2}$

$$y^2 = x^3 + 4x^2 + 3x + 2$$

$$\text{Volume} = \pi \int_{-2}^1 y^2\, dx$$

$$= \pi \int_{-2}^1 (x^3 + 4x^2 + 3x + 2)\, dx$$

$$= \pi \left[\frac{1}{4}x^4 + \frac{4}{3}x^3 + \frac{3}{2}x^2 + 2x \right]_{-2}^1$$

$$= \pi\left[\left(\frac{1}{4}(1)^4 + \frac{4}{3}(1)^3 + \frac{3}{2}(1) + 2(1)\right)\right.$$

$$\left. - \left(\frac{1}{4}(-2)^4 + \frac{4}{3}(-2)^3 + \frac{3}{2}(-2)^2 + 2(-2)\right)\right]$$

$$= \frac{39\pi}{4} \text{ units}^3$$

5 a Given $3x + 8y = 24$

Rearrange: $8y = 24 - 3x$

$$y = 3 - \frac{3}{8}x$$

$$y^2 = 9 - \frac{9}{4}x + \frac{9}{64}x^2$$

$$\text{Volume} = \pi\int_0^8 y^2\,\mathrm{d}x = \pi\int_0^8\left(9 - \frac{9}{4}x + \frac{9}{64}x^2\right)\mathrm{d}x$$

$$= \pi\left[9x - \frac{9}{8}x^2 + \frac{9}{192}x^3\right]_0^8$$

$$= \pi\left[\left(9(8) - \frac{9}{8}(8)^2 + \frac{9}{192}(8)^3\right)\right.$$

$$\left. - \left(9(0) - \frac{9}{8}(0)^2 + \frac{9}{192}(0)^3\right)\right]$$

$$= 24\pi \text{ units}^3$$

b Volume of a cone $= \frac{1}{3}\pi r^2 h$

$$= \frac{1}{3}\pi(3)^2(8)$$

$$= 24\pi \text{ units}^3$$

6 a

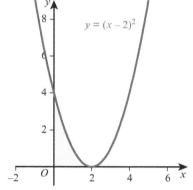

b $y = (x - 2)^2$

$y^2 = (x - 2)^4$

$$\text{Volume} = \pi\int_0^2 y^2\,\mathrm{d}x = \pi\int_0^2 (x - 2)^4\,\mathrm{d}x$$

$$= \pi\left[\frac{1}{5}(x - 2)^5\right]_0^2$$

$$= \pi\left[\left(\frac{1}{5}(2 - 2)^5\right) - \left(\frac{1}{5}(0 - 2)^5\right)\right]$$

$$= \frac{32\pi}{5} \text{ units}^3$$

7 a Given $y = 5\sqrt{x} - x$

To find the x-intercept at P, substitute $y = 0$

$5\sqrt{x} - x = 0$

> Do not be tempted to divide by $\sqrt{x}$ as this will lose a solution.

Factorise: $\sqrt{x}\left(5 - \sqrt{x}\right) = 0$

Either $\sqrt{x} = 0$ so $x = 0$

or $5 - \sqrt{x} = 0$ so $\sqrt{x} = 5$

So, $x = 25$

P is at $(25, 0)$

b $y = 5\sqrt{x} - x$

$y^2 = \left(5\sqrt{x} - x\right)\left(5\sqrt{x} - x\right)$

$y^2 = \left(5x^{\frac{1}{2}} - x\right)\left(5x^{\frac{1}{2}} - x\right)$

$y^2 = 25x - 10x^{\frac{3}{2}} + x^2$

$$\text{Volume} = \pi\int_0^{25} y^2\,\mathrm{d}x = \pi\int_0^{25}\left(25x - 10x^{\frac{3}{2}} + x^2\right)\mathrm{d}x$$

$$= \pi\left[\frac{25}{2}x^2 - 4x^{\frac{5}{2}} + \frac{1}{3}x^3\right]_0^{25}$$

$$= \pi\left[\left(\frac{25}{2}(25)^2 - 4(25)^{\frac{5}{2}} + \frac{1}{3}(25)^3\right)\right.$$

$$\left. - \left(\frac{25}{2}(0)^2 - 4(0)^{\frac{5}{2}} + \frac{1}{3}(0)^3\right)\right]$$

$$= \frac{3125\pi}{6} \text{ units}^3$$

8 a Given $x = \dfrac{9}{y^2} - 1$

Substitute $x = 0$ to find the y-intercept:

$$0 = \frac{9}{y^2} - 1$$

$$9 - y^2 = 0$$

$$y^2 = 9$$

$\qquad y = \pm 3$ (reject -3 as P is above the x-axis).

P is at $(0, 3)$.

b $\quad x = \dfrac{9}{y^2} - 1$

$$x^2 = \left(\frac{9}{y^2} - 1\right)^2$$

$$x^2 = (9y^{-2} - 1)(9y^{-2} - 1)$$

$$x^2 = 81y^{-4} - 18y^{-2} + 1$$

$$\text{Volume} = \pi \int_1^3 x^2 \, dy = \pi \int_1^3 (81y^{-4} - 18y^{-2} + 1) \, dy$$

$$= \pi[-27y^{-3} + 18y^{-1} + y]_1^3$$

$$= \pi[(-27(3)^{-3} + 18(3)^{-1} + (3))$$

$$\quad - (-27(1)^{-3} + 18(1)^3 + (1))]$$

$$= 16\pi \text{ units}^3$$

9 a Given $y = 3x + \dfrac{2}{x}$ ....[1]

$$y = 7 \; ....[2]$$

To find the intersection of P and Q, solve [1] and [2] simultaneously.

$$7 = 3x + \frac{2}{x}$$

$$7x = 3x^2 + 2$$

$$3x^2 - 7x + 2 = 0$$

$$(3x - 1)(x - 2) = 0$$

$$x = \frac{1}{3} \text{ and } x = 2$$

P is at $\left(\dfrac{1}{3}, 7\right)$ and Q is at $(2, 7)$

b $\quad y = 3x + \dfrac{2}{x}$ or $y = 3x + 2x^{-1}$

$$y^2 = (3x + 2x^{-1})(3x + 2x^{-1})$$

$$y^2 = 9x^2 + 12 + 4x^{-2}$$

$$\text{Volume} = \pi \int_{\frac{1}{3}}^2 y^2 \, dx$$

Using $\displaystyle\int_a^b [f(x) - g(x)] \, dx$

$$\text{Volume} = \pi \int_{\frac{1}{3}}^2 (7^2 - (9x^2 + 12 + 4x^{-2})) \, dx$$

$$= \pi \int_{\frac{1}{3}}^2 (7^2 - 9x^2 - 12 - 4x^{-2}) \, dx$$

$$= \pi \int_{\frac{1}{3}}^2 (37 - 9x^2 - 4x^{-2}) \, dx$$

$$= \pi \left[37x - 3x^3 + 4x^{-1}\right]_{\frac{1}{3}}^2$$

$$= \pi \left[(37(2) - 3(2)^3 + 4(2)^{-1})\right.$$

$$\left. - \left(37\left(\frac{1}{3}\right) - 3\left(\frac{1}{3}\right)^3 + 4\left(\frac{1}{3}\right)^{-1}\right)\right]$$

$$= \frac{250\pi}{9} \text{ units}^3$$

10 Given $y = \dfrac{2}{2x + 1}$

$$y^2 = \frac{4}{(2x + 1)^2}$$

$$y^2 = 4(2x + 1)^{-2}$$

$$\text{Volume} = \pi \int_0^p y^2 \, dx = \pi \int_0^p (4(2x + 1)^{-2}) \, dx$$

$$= \pi \left[\frac{4}{(-1)(2)}(2x + 1)^{-1}\right]_0^p$$

$$= \pi[-2(2x + 1)^{-1}]_0^p$$

$$= \pi[(-2(2p + 1)^{-1}) - (-2(2(0) + 1)^{-1})]$$

$$= \pi\left(\frac{-2}{2p + 1} + 2\right)$$

$$= \pi\left(2 - \frac{2}{2p + 1}\right)$$

As $p \to \infty$, $\dfrac{2}{2p + 1} \to 0$

$\therefore$ The volume approaches 2π (units^3).

11 a Given $y = \sqrt{25 - x^2}$

Substitute $x = 0$ to find the y-intercept:

$$y = \sqrt{25 - 0^2}$$

$y = \pm 5$ (reject -5 as the curve intersects the y-axis above $y = 0$)

As $y = \sqrt{25 - x^2}$

$$y^2 = 25 - x^2$$

$$x^2 = 25 - y^2$$

$$\text{Volume} = \pi \int_3^5 x^2 \, dy$$

$$= \pi \int_3^5 (25 - y^2) \, dy$$

$$= \pi \left[25y - \frac{1}{3} y^3 \right]_3^5$$

$$= \pi \left[\left(25(5) - \frac{1}{3}(5)^3 \right) - \left(25(3) - \frac{1}{3}(3)^3 \right) \right]$$

$$= \frac{52}{3} \pi \text{ units}^3$$

b $\text{Volume} = \pi \int_0^4 y^2 \, dx - \text{volume of cylinder}$

$$= \pi \int_0^4 \left(\sqrt{25 - x^2} \right)^2 dx - \pi r^2 h$$

$$= \pi \int_0^4 (25 - x^2) \, dx - \pi \times 3^2 \times 4$$

$$= \pi \left[25x - \frac{1}{3} x^3 \right]_0^4 - 36\pi$$

$$= \pi \left[\left(25(4) - \frac{1}{3}(4)^3 \right) - \left(25(0) - \frac{1}{3}(0)^3 \right) - 36\pi \right]$$

$$= \frac{128\pi}{3} \text{ units}^3$$

12 a Given $y = \sqrt{4 - x}$ .....[1]

and $x + 2y = 4$ ....[2]

Using [1], $y^2 = 4 - x$

Using [2], $2y = 4 - x$

$$y = 2 - \frac{1}{2} x$$

$$y^2 = \left(2 - \frac{1}{2}x \right)\left(2 - \frac{1}{2}x \right)$$

$$y^2 = 4 - 2x + \frac{1}{4} x^2$$

$$\text{Volume} = \pi \int_0^4 y^2 \, dx$$

Using $\int_a^b [f(x) - g(x)] \, dx$

$$\text{Volume} = \pi \int_0^4 \left(4 - x - \left(4 - 2x + \frac{1}{4}x^2 \right) \right) dx$$

$$= \pi \int_0^4 \left(4 - x - 4 + 2x - \frac{1}{4}x^2 \right) dx$$

$$= \pi \int_0^4 \left(x - \frac{1}{4}x^2 \right) dx$$

$$= \pi \left[\frac{1}{2}x^2 - \frac{1}{12}x^3 \right]_0^4$$

$$= \pi \left[\left(\frac{1}{2}(4)^2 - \frac{1}{12}(4)^3 \right) - \left(\frac{1}{2}(0)^2 - \frac{1}{12}(0)^3 \right) \right]$$

$$= \frac{8\pi}{3} \text{ units}^3$$

b Using $y = \sqrt{4 - x}$

$$y^2 = 4 - x$$

$$x = 4 - y^2$$

$$x^2 = (4 - y^2)(4 - y^2)$$

$$x^2 = 16 - 8y^2 + y^4$$

Using $x + 2y = 4$

$$x = 4 - 2y$$

$$x^2 = (4 - 2y)(4 - 2y)$$

$$x^2 = 16 - 16y + 4y^2$$

$$\text{Volume} = \pi \int_0^2 x^2 \, dx$$

Using $\int_a^b [f(x) - g(x)] \, dx$

$$\text{Volume} = \pi \int_0^2 [(16 - 8y^2 + y^4) - (16 - 16y + 4y^2)] \, dy$$

$$= \pi \int_0^2 (16y - 12y^2 + y^4) \, dy$$

$$= \pi \left[8y^2 - 4y^3 + \frac{1}{5}y^5 \right]_0^2$$

$$= \pi \left[8(2)^2 - 4(2)^3 + \frac{1}{5}(2)^5 - \left(8(0)^2 - 4(0)^3 + \frac{1}{5}(0)^5 \right) \right]$$

$$= \frac{32\pi}{5} \text{ units}^3$$

13 a Given $x^2 + y^2 = 100$

$$x^2 = 100 - y^2$$

$$\text{Volume} = \pi \int_{-8}^{0} x^2 \, dy$$

$$= \pi \int_{-8}^{0} (100 - y^2) \, dy$$

$$= \pi \left[100y - \frac{1}{3}y^3 \right]_{-8}^{0}$$

$$= \pi \left[\left(100(0) - \frac{1}{3}(0)^3 \right) - \left(100(-8) - \frac{1}{3}(-8)^3 \right) \right]$$

$$= \frac{1888\pi}{3} \text{ cm}^3$$

b $x^2 + y^2 = 100$

Since the water depth is 3 cm, the water level has the coordinates $(0, -5)$ on the y-axis.

Volume of water in the

$$\text{bowl} = \pi \left[100y - \frac{1}{3}y^3 \right]_{-8}^{-5}$$

$$= \pi \left[\left(100(-5) - \frac{1}{3}(-5)^3 \right) - \left(100(-8) - \frac{1}{3}(-8)^3 \right) \right]$$

$$= 171\pi \text{ cm}^3$$

14 Given a sphere with radius r

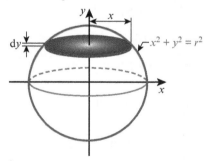

Consider this hemisphere. When the cylinder of height dy and radius x is rotated about the y-axis, the volume of the cylinder is given by $dV = \pi x^2 \, dy$.

The sum of all the cylindrical elements from 0 to r is a hemisphere. Twice the volume of the hemisphere will give the volume of the sphere.

So, $V = 2\pi \int_{0}^{r} x^2 \, dy$

From the equation of a circle $x^2 + y^2 = r^2$

So, $x^2 = r^2 - y^2$

$$V = 2\pi \int_{0}^{r} (r^2 - y^2) \, dy$$

$$V = 2\pi \left[r^2 y - \frac{1}{3}y^3 \right]_{0}^{r}$$

$$V = 2\pi \left[\left(r^3 - \frac{1}{3}r^3 \right) - \left(0^3 - \frac{1}{3}(0)^3 \right) \right]$$

$$V = 2\pi \left[\frac{2}{3}r^3 \right]$$

$$V = \frac{4}{3}\pi r^3 \text{ shown}$$